Dependent Communities
Aid and Politics in
Cambodia and East Timor

Cornell University

Caroline Hughes

Dependent Communities
Aid and Politics in
Cambodia and East Timor

SOUTHEAST ASIA PROGRAM PUBLICATIONS
Southeast Asia Program
Cornell University
Ithaca, New York
2009

Cornell Southeast Asia Program Publications
640 Stewart Avenue, Ithaca, NY 14850-3857

Studies on Southeast Asia No. 48

Printed in the United States of America

ISBN: hc 978-0-87727-778-1
ISBN: pb 978-0-87727-748-4

Cover Design: Kat Dalton; photograph by Binsar Bakkara, reprinted with permission
Index: Paula Douglass
Maps: 1) Cambodia, no. 3860, Rev. 4, January 2004. 2) Regions of Timor-Leste, no. 4117, Rev. 6, March 2007. Reprinted with permission from the UN Cartographic Section.

TABLE OF CONTENTS

ACKNOWLEDGMENTS

Many agencies and individuals generously provided assistance with this project. Fieldwork in Cambodia, in 1995–96, and in Australia and East Timor in 2004–05, was funded by the UK government's Economic and Social Research Council; I am grateful to ESRC staff for their flexibility and efficiency. Fieldwork in Cambodia in 1998–99 and in 2000–01 was funded by the Leverhulme Trust, and in 2003 by the British Academy Committee for South-East Asian Studies. Thanks, also, to the wonderful Department of Political Science and International Studies at the University of Birmingham for generosity regarding my research leave. I would like to thank the Royal University of Phnom Penh for their hospitality in 1998. During subsequent fieldwork in Cambodia, I have been privileged to engage with the brilliant Governance Research Team at the Cambodia Development Resource Institute, and many thanks are due to them for sharing their vast knowledge of Cambodia. During fieldwork in Australia I was hosted as a visiting fellow by the Melbourne Institute of Asian Languages and Societies, at the University of Melbourne and by the Centre for Humanities Research, at the Australian National University, and I am grateful to the staff of these institutions for facilitating my stay. Many thanks also to George Quinn and Adelaide Lopez for allowing me to audit the Tetum language course at ANU.

I owe a great deal to those who helped me in the course of fieldwork, most notably my indefatigable research assistants, Sok Ty in Cambodia and Marco Artur Neves de Sousa in East Timor, without whom I would have had great difficulty understanding what was meant by the people whom we interviewed, as well as what was said. Thanks very much to the staff and patients of Klibur Domin for hosting such a fun stay in Tibar; to Lucas De Sousa for my visit to Laleia; and to the members of Ratelauk for their assistance in Liquiça. Many other people put me up or helped me out along the way, notably Juanita Rice, Shirley Williamson, and the Ryder Cheshire Foundation in Australia, Patricia McDonnell, Patricia Woodcroft-Lee, the Canberra Friends of Dili, Madelena Alvez, Filomeno da Cruz, Reinaldo Soares, May Sam Oeun, Oeur Hunly, and Nouv Phearit.

During the composition of this book, I was greatly assisted by the opportunity to present sections of my work at the Universities of Birmingham, Oxford, and Bristol. I would like to thank, in particular, Eva-Lotta Hedman, Graham Brown, Andrew Wyatt, and Thomas Diez for extending those invitations, and to thank the various audiences for their valuable comments. I would also like to thank Doug Porter and Oliver Richmond for their encouragement, and John Marston for his timely criticisms. I am very grateful to the two anonymous reviewers appointed by Cornell Southeast Asia Program Publications, who went through the manuscript line by line and made very insightful comments with respect to the content; and thanks to Deborah Homsher and Fred Conner, who did the same with respect to the writing style.

This research was possible due to the support of my family. My fieldwork in East Timor happened thanks to the kindness of my relatives in Australia, particularly Mary Brown, Nicole, Derek, and Tom Scott, Andrew, Kestin and Angus Brown, Ingrid Wijeyewardene, and Pam and Sarah Jane Ploughman, who took in and took care of my family while I was away. My parents, Tom and Dawn Hughes, as always, facilitated all of our moves backwards and forwards with their usual generosity, and I am very grateful to them. Finally, thanks to my husband, Richard Brown, and my children, Alice and Hephzibah, for putting up with it.

NOTE ON TERMS AND NAMES

Both of the case-study countries in this book have been assigned a variety of names over the past fifty years. Cambodia's first official name, following independence in 1953, was the "Kingdom of Cambodia." The Lon Nol regime of 1970–75 replaced this with a "Khmer Republic"; the Pol Pot regime of 1975–79 took the name "Democratic Kampuchea" (DK); while the Vietnamese-backed Heng Samrin regime in Phnom Penh, from 1979–89, took the name "People's Republic of Kampuchea" (PRK), changing this in 1989 to the "State of Cambodia" (SoC). To make things more complicated, exiled representatives of the 1960s Kingdom of Cambodia regime, and from the Khmer Republic and DK regimes, grouped together in the 1980s to form a government-in-exile called the "Coalition Government of Democratic Kampuchea" (CGDK). This coalition continued to represent Cambodia at the United Nations until peace agreements between the CGDK members, the SoC, and various external parties were signed in 1991.

In this volume, I generally use the names of these various regimes to refer to the regimes themselves, the historical periods of their rule, and the administrative structures they built, while sticking to "Cambodia," the official short form of the current name (once again, the "Kingdom of Cambodia"), to refer to the country more generally. I occasionally use the term *srok khmae* (Khmer land) to refer to the country's territory in circumstances where I am paraphrasing nationalist rhetoric, in which this phrase frequently appears. The Cambodian people often refer to themselves as the Khmer, but, strictly speaking, this is the name of the majority ethnic group and of the national language, rather than the name of the modern nation. Consequently, I generally refer to citizens of the country as Cambodians.

With respect to the Cambodian communist movement led by Pol Pot, which took the name "Communist Party of Kampuchea" in the 1960s and early 1970s, "Democratic Kampuchea" when it came to power from 1975–79, and "Partie of Democratic Kampuchea" when it participated in the UN-sponsored peace process from 1991–93, I tend to use the term "Democratic Kampuchea" when referring to the 1975–79 regime and the name "Khmer Rouge" at other times. This is in line with common usage in Cambodia and internationally.

"Timor-Leste" is the Portuguese term for East Timor, and the latter is the name that has commonly been used in English for the eastern half of the island of Timor, at the southern tip of the Indonesian archipelago. Until 1975, this region was often called Portuguese Timor in acknowledgement of the fact that, unlike the western half of the island and the rest of the archipelago, it was colonized by the Portuguese rather than the Dutch. On November 28, 1975, a unilateral declaration of independence on the part of the Frente Revolucionária de Timor-Leste Independente (FRETILIN) proclaimed the formation of a Democratic Republic of East Timor. Subsequently, the Indonesian army invaded and annexed the territory, renaming it the twenty-seventh Indonesian province of East Timor, or "Timor Timur" (sometimes "Timtim") in Bahasa.

The United Nations never officially accepted either FRETILIN's declaration of independence or the Indonesian annexation, continuing to regard the country as a "non-self-governing territory under Portuguese administration" throughout the period of Indonesian occupation from 1975 to 1999. During the Indonesian era, and throughout the period of UN administration from 1999 to 2002, the UN referred to the country as East Timor. Once independence was restored in May 2002, the new FRETILIN government readopted the name "Democratic Republic of East Timor," which was rendered in the country's two official languages—in the colonial language of Portuguese (República Democrática de Timor-Leste, or RDTL) and in the local lingua franca, Tetum (Repúblika Demokrátika Timor Lorosa'e). The government requested that the short form "Timor-Leste" be used internationally, and this term is now listed by the UN as the official short form of the country's name in English.

Clearly, this request presents a dilemma for writers in English, since "East Timor" is the name by which the country is better known in that language. Consequently, and with slightly embarrassed apologies to the government of Timor-Leste, I have used "East Timor" in the title of this book, in order that English-speakers will recognize the subject matter more easily. In the pages that follow, I tend to use "East Timor" or simply "Timor" generally to refer to the country in various historical eras, when use of that term in English was uncontroversial. I use "Timor-Leste" to refer to the state since restoration of independence in 2002. I comply with common practice in referring to the people of Timor-Leste as "Timorese," a translation of the Portuguese term *"timorense"* used in Article 3 of the 2002 Constitution. I occasionally use "East Timorese" in circumstances where "Timorese" could be understood as including the inhabitants of West Timor also. There are no ethnic connotations to the term "Timorese": the Timorese people (of the East and West) enjoy a diverse set of ethnic identities, but "Timorese" is not one of them.

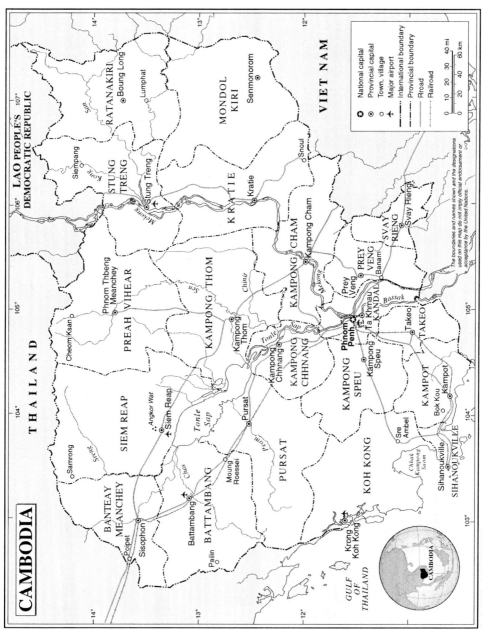

CAMBODIA

THAILAND

LAO PEOPLE'S DEMOCRATIC REPUBLIC

VIET NAM

BANTEAY MEANCHEY

SIEM REAP

BATTAMBANG

PAILIN

PURSAT

KOH KONG

KAMPONG CHHNANG

KAMPONG THOM

PREAH VIHEAR

STUNG TRENG

RATANAKIRI

MONDOL KIRI

KRATIE

KAMPONG CHAM

KAMPONG SPEU

KANDAL

PREY VENG

SVAY RIENG

KAMPOT

TAKEO

SIHANOUKVILLE

Poipet
Sisophon
Samrong
Cheom Ksan
Siempang
Stung Treng
Boung Long
Lumphat
Battambang
Moung Roessei
Pailin
Angkor Wat
Siem Reap
Phnom Thbeng Meanchey
Kampong Thom
Kratie
Snoul
Senmonorom
Kampong Cham
Kampong Chhnang
Pursat
Phnom Penh
Ta Khmau
Prey Veng
Banam
Svay Rieng
Takeo
Takeo
Kampong Speu
Sre Ambel
Bok Kou
Kampot
Kampot
Krong Koh Kong
Sihanoukville

Mekong
Sre Pok
Kong
Sen
Chinit
Tonlé Sap
Sap
Mekong
Bassak
Tonle Sap
Pursat
Chus
Sreng
Stung
Chhuk Kampong Saom

GULF OF THAILAND

14°
13°
12°

103° 104° 105° 106° 107°

Legend:
⊗ National capital
◉ Provincial capital
○ Town, village
✈ Major airport
–·–·– International boundary
– – – Provincial boundary
——— Rroad
········· Railroad

0 10 20 30 40 mi
0 20 40 60 km

The boundaries and names shown and the designations used on this map do not imply official endorsement or acceptance by the United Nations.

CAMBODIA

Department of Peacekeeping Operations
Cartographic Section

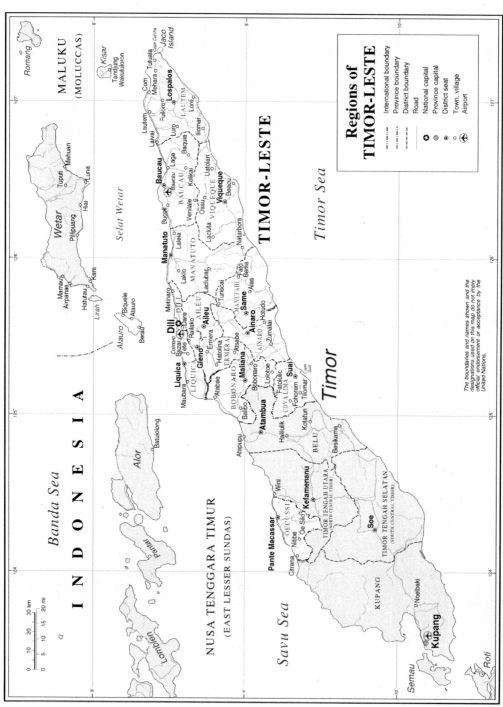

Regions of
TIMOR-LESTE

International boundary
Province boundary
District boundary
Road
National capital
Province capital
District seat
Town, village
Airport

The boundaries and names shown and the
designations used on this map do not imply
official endorsement or acceptance by the
United Nations.

TIMOR-LESTE

Timor Sea

Timor

INDONESIA

Banda Sea

MALUKU
(MOLUCCAS)

Wetar

Selat Wetar

NUSA TENGGARA TIMUR
(EAST LESSER SUNDAS)

Savu Sea

Alor

Pantar

Lomblen

Semau

Roti

KUPANG

TIMOR TENGAH UTARA
(NORTH CENTRAL TIMOR)

TIMOR TENGAH SELATAN
(SOUTH CENTRAL TIMOR)

BELU

Kupang
Noelbaki
Soe
Kefamenanu
Pante Macassar
OECUSSI
Citrana
Nitibe
Oe Silo
Wini
Besikama
Batuolong

Atapupu
Balibo
Atabae
Maubara
Liquica
LIQUICA
Comoro
Bazar Tete
Dili
Dare
Metinaro
DILI
Tibar
Hatolia
Ermera
Gleno
ERMERA
Railako
AILEU
Aileu
Atsabe
Maliana
BOBONARO
Bobonaro
Lolotoe
Fatolulic
Atambua
Hatudo
Ainaro
AINARO
Zumalai
Same
MANUFAHI
Turiscai
Lakio
Laleia
MANATUTO
Manatuto
Bucoli
Baucau
BAUCAU
Laga
Luro
LAUTEM
Com Tutuala
Mehara
Lospalos
Jaco Island
Cabe Cutcha
Laivai
Lautem
Laclo
Laclubar
Barique
Natarbora
FatoBerlia
Alas
COVALINA
Suai
Kota Fohorem
Tilomar
Cape Suai
Hialulik
Kotafun
Beaco
Uatolari
Laluta
Ossu
Venilale
Kelikai
Baguia
Iliomar
Loré
Vemasse
VIQUEQUE
Viqueque
Ossu

Lirah

Atauro

Biquele
Atauro
Berau

Hatutau
Mamauo
Airpanas
Pilipuang
Hiai
Kara
Luna
Tuputi
Mahuan

Romang

Kisar
Tandjung Wakuluboron

Map No. 4117 Rev. 6   UNITED NATIONS
March 2007

Department of Peacekeeping Operations
Cartographic Section

CHAPTER I

"WELCOME TO DILI, FUCKEN AUSTRALIEN": AMBIVALENT RESPONSES TO INTERVENTION

"Welcome to Dili, fucken Australien."
—Graffiti, near Australian Embassy, Dili, 2005

In the 1990s, Cambodia and Timor-Leste were on the receiving end of unprecedented forms of international intervention in the name of peace. Cambodia, from 1992 to 1993, was one of the subjects of a first wave of post-Cold War "complex peacebuilding operations," which defined peace in new, expanded ways and which authorized interveners to undertake tasks that had previously been regarded as sacred to sovereign governments, such as organizing elections and conducting security sector reform. East Timor was one of the first subjects of "peace enforcement"—the use of peacekeeping forces to restore order by force in a situation of armed conflict.

While much has been written about these unprecedented peace operations, particularly from perspectives of international relations and international ethics, much less has been written about the subsequent development experience in these countries. In particular, the link between the politics of intervention, as this plays out in national and local political arenas on the ground, and the subsequent politics of aid-dependent development, has not attracted much analytic attention.

This volume is intended as a contribution to filling this gap. To that end, it will examine some of the internal political struggles ongoing in Cambodia and Timor-Leste since each was subjected to international intervention in the 1990s. It uses these struggles as a window into the business of reconstruction of power relations in aid-dependent, post-conflict states. A central concern will be the business of examining the way that international interveners—a term I use to encompass peacekeepers, international multilateral organizations such as the United Nations and World Bank, and bilateral or non-governmental aid agencies—interact with local political actors. In particular, I address the question of how, in post-conflict conditions of aid dependence, in which sovereignty is observably held hostage by a veritable army of international experts, advisors, donors, and peacekeepers, different groups visualize their own status as citizens of a community and develop political strategies accordingly.

Within development studies and development policy, the question of international–local relations in the politics of aid has largely been tackled in the form of debates over "partnership" and the promotion of "ownership." Yet, the question of the relationship between "inside" and "outside" in the context of polities that have been invaded by foreign armies, fragmented by civil conflict, and subject to influxes of foreign peacekeeping and humanitarian personnel, has wider ramifications than these debates generally allow, focused as the latter are on the "effectiveness" of aid in generating "development." This study starts from the contention that the relationship between inside and outside is fundamental to the ability to envision, theoretically, the workings of modern politics in post-conflict, aid-dependent countries, since some of the most highly and universally valued political innovations of modernity are bound up with the question of citizenship and sovereignty.

Democracy represents one example of such an innovation. It is inextricably connected to the idea of the "nation"—a sovereign community that asserts moral authority over government and policy. The forging of "nations," although a highly contested, never fulfilled, over-romanticized, and appallingly bloody process, has been a mechanism second to none for mobilizing populations and legitimating institutions and policies in times of hardship and uncertainty in the modern world. Both democracy and nationalism rely upon ideals of sovereignty in bounded, territorial, and autonomous political communities. Sovereign communities are identified by the scope they enjoy to create mechanisms for extracting and redistributing resources; to formulate rhetorics of identity and commitment that support this process; and to mobilize participation in a manner that can finesse context-specific political disputes and manage local constellations of political coalition.[1] Sovereign communities, in short, employ local knowledge and deploy locally generated legitimacy to give them the flexibility to manage conflict-specific resources and problems.

United Nations Special Representatives are fond of pronouncing, on arrival in one war zone or another, their intention to "build a new country,"[2] using international expertise and resources and "lessons learned" from experience in other trouble spots. However, this ambition is one that has historically never been realized by outsiders; the emergence of the sovereign nation-state was historically achieved by domestic political mobilization, often as a means to fight foreign wars. The historical significance of domestic political struggles in nation-building raises important questions as to the role of external actors and their ability to achieve this on behalf of nations emerging from conflict. Is nation-building something that outsiders can do, or does the intrusive presence and obvious power of such outsiders, and their tendency to focus on "international best practice" rather than local imperative, damage the concept of the sovereign community beyond repair? This study focuses on the politics of Cambodia and Timor in the post-intervention setting to address this question.

Of course, the inexorable progress of globalization makes too sharp a distinction between modern sovereign states and war zones undergoing extensive intervention misleading. As Stephen Krasner points out, sovereignty in any circumstance is little

---

[1] See John Gerard Ruggie, "Territoriality and Beyond: Problematizing Modernity in International Relations," *International Organization* 47 (Winter 1993): 108; and David S. Stern, "State Sovereignty: The Politics of Identity and the Place of the Political," in *Perspectives on Third World Sovereignty: The Postmodern Paradox*, ed. Mark Denham and Mark Owen Lombardi (London: Macmillan, 1996), p. 28.

[2] Yasushi Akashi, "To Build a New Country: The Task of the UN Transitional Authority in Cambodia," *Harvard International Review* (1992–93): 34–35, 68–69.

more than "organised hypocrisy."[3] Yet democracy and nationalism—in short, modern mass politics—both rely, for their legitimating force, on the power of this fiction. This study will show that in the absence of the founding conceit of a national community with either actual or potential sovereign status, politics starts to look very different indeed.

Furthermore, despite the best of intentions on the part of interveners, and a preoccupation with the ethics of justifying violations of sovereignty, polities that have been the subject of intensive recent intervention do not appear to have found the experience particularly emancipatory—quite the reverse. This close-grained investigation of two such experiences—those of Cambodia and Timor-Leste—suggests that the fact that interventions are fraught with global relations of power is clearly perceived and acutely felt by those on the receiving end. The result, from the perspective of the village, is twofold. On the one hand, the post-conflict citizen perceives the dramatic widening of fields of possibility, and the influx of ideational and material resources that can transform, modernize, and empower the local sphere, significantly shifting terms of political engagement among domestic groups. On the other hand, the post-conflict citizen experiences the devaluation of the national community as the appropriate stage upon which human dramas of power, right, and obligation are enacted; and, at the same time, these citizens experience their own confinement within this particular theater, such that, if they manage to escape into the outside world, they do so under either criminalized or heavily policed conditions that disempower them further.

The impact of these kinds of processes on different social groups is varied. Some groups in the post-conflict situation are adept at capturing resources and using them to promote their own position. For others, the international sphere appears remote and unapproachable, even when its representatives are observably in town, and feelings of marginalization and disempowerment are intensified as a result of the micro-exercise of power by global actors. But broadly speaking, the response to intervention, as the pithy comment of the graffiti artist quoted at the top of this chapter reflects, is highly ambivalent. The promotion of the neoliberal peace offers an array of opportunities to different local actors, but it can also function as a political straitjacket that limits the potential for the emergence of a genuinely empowered national public sphere that can provide a setting for deliberation and accommodation. These problems and limitations obtain both at the level of intra-elite politics and at the level of elite–mass relations.

Ultimately, this study argues, the award of international resources occurs in return for the subordination of the national public to international surveillance and regimentation. The most successful actors in dependent communities are those who can coopt international power in public while maintaining discretionary room to maneuver politically out of the glare of international supervision, thus avoiding rentier status and awarding themselves local power. The strategies attempted by elites in Cambodia and Timor-Leste, in this respect, and the joint impact of international tutelage and elite maneuvering on conceptions of political power, political status, and political space are the subjects of this study.

---

[3] Stephen Krasner, *Sovereignty: Organised Hypocrisy* (Princeton, NJ: Princeton University Press, 1999).

MODERNITY AND NATIONALISM

The rise of the modern nation in Asia is described by Benedict Anderson as emerging from the coincidence of economic imperative and political contingency.[4] The economic imperative underlying modern nationalism results from changes in the production process, which ushered in the era of print capitalism—an era in which larger swathes of the population than ever before were required to be socialized into a literate culture. This pressing need prompted the spread of literacy in vernacular languages and the proliferation of reading materials in the same, providing the basis for the emergence of an "imagined community" composed of reading citizens. The nature and shape of those "imagined communities," in particular in the last wave of nationalism, were a matter of political contingency. The extent of colonial state institutions and the geography of transport connections was frequently a matter as much of colonial caprice as of perennialist loyalties. The line across Timor distinguishing Timorese from Indonesians, like the intensely problematic borders of Cambodia, where thousands have died in struggles to shift boundary lines just a few miles east or west, are contingent, colonial constructions. Yet, Anderson argues, the status such boundaries attained reflects the pressing logic of nationalism, and the potential for states, through the rise of modern educational, military, industrial, and governmental institutions, to both instill a national identity into an unruly population, and to be, in turn, legitimized and empowered by it. The combination of the astonishing promise of economic modernization and the regimenting power of modern institutions transformed multitudes into imagined communities of juridical citizens.

Both Anderson and Thongchai Winichakul describe the amount of power that was required to achieve this feat.[5] The range of national institutions that sprang up in modernizing Southeast Asia, as elsewhere in the colonized world, reflected the need constantly to work and rework the national imagination through the production of maps, museums, school curricula, the national census, and so forth. Colonial and postcolonial status produced a dense web of cross-cutting knowledges and status ascriptions within which individuals were entangled in every sphere of their lives. The "ethnosymbolic" content of these varied from one nation to another, in each case building upon historical incidents, folklore, and invented tradition associated with a particular "ethnie," in Anthony Smith's term, to create a picture of the national character that was both unique in content and standard in form.[6]

By the end of the twentieth century, the appalling scope for violence engendered by the nationalism and the state-making projects nationalists set in train was well-documented. Cambodia and East Timor, part of Benedict Anderson's "last wave," suffered particularly acutely, as nationalist movements were sucked into the ideological conflicts of the Cold War in Southeast Asia. In fact, Cambodians and East Timorese were among the last of the last populations to conceive mass projects of nation-building. Nationalism was confined to an unusually narrow elite in Cambodia until efforts were made to propagate it as official history after independence. In East Timor, national consciousness made few inroads beyond a

[4] Benedict Anderson, *Imagined Communities: Reflections on the Origin and Spread of Nationalism* (London: Verso, 1991).

[5] Thongchai Winichakul, *Siam Mapped: A History of a Geobody of a Nation* (Honolulu, HI: University of Hawai'i Press, 1994).

[6] Anthony Smith, *The Ethnic Revival* (Cambridge: Cambridge University Press, 1981).

small circle of ex-seminarians in Dili until the opportunities offered by the Carnation Revolution, in Portugal, in 1974, and the imminent end of Portuguese colonialism it portended, ignited nationalist enthusiasm more broadly. In both cases, the violence associated with nationalism at home was exacerbated by the competitive processes of state-making initiated by larger neighbors along Cold War fault lines. In both Cambodia and East Timor, nationalist and irredentist aspirations harbored by larger neighbors, and the way these fed into Cold War geopolitical struggles, caused the deaths of up to a quarter of the population, the devastation of the land, and the emergence of mutually incompatible nationalist imaginings, espoused by different groups of Timorese and Khmer, influenced by the extended occupation and government of the country by foreign powers.

Since the end of the Cold War, both these countries emerged from warfare in a context dominated by international actors, who remained important in the post-conflict setting in a context of post-conflict aid dependence. Both have seen, to some extent, the emergence of new explanations of the war in each country that focus attention upon flaws in the national character—on the content of the specific nationalism bred domestically, rather than on the pressures exerted upon them by the competing nationalist ambitions of neighbors and competing ideological ambitions of superpowers in the Cold War world—although this has been less evident in Timor than in Cambodia. Both have been inundated by a postwar rhetoric in which claims that the post-conflict polity constitutes a "terra nullus," characterized above all by "lack of capacity," have been used to justify the erection of a post-nationalist order of international supervision and assistance, in accordance with international standards, and enacted by international experts.[7]

In these latter respects, Timor and Cambodia are merely extreme examples of a phenomenon that was widespread in the 1990s—the international pursuit of projects of "state–building" and "good governance" as a means to facilitate the spread of neoliberal economics across the globe in the aftermath of the Cold War. Increasing activism in support of the good governance agenda has been accompanied by the assertion that corruption and state failure are the key security threats in the contemporary world. Institutions have been granted higher priority vis-à-vis economics in the agenda of development organizations; yet the key question of how the construction of institutions by external agencies correlates with the conduct of either national or local politics has been rarely addressed in the expanding literature on the subject. Core values that animate liberal institutions in the ideal-world of peacebuilding policy—values such as democracy and citizenship—are intimately connected to the notion of an autonomous national sphere. Without conceiving of the nation as the salient political sphere to which the state owes allegiance, it is difficult to conceive of modern politics at all; and international agencies have been at pains to promote and celebrate particular forms of patriotism, as this study will show. But how are these values to be promoted in a sphere that is thoroughly penetrated by international agencies? What might a post-nationalist, internationally penetrated polity look like, not only from the perspective of political analysts and policy makers, but from the perspective of its own people?

---

[7] Astrid Suhrke, "Peacekeepers as Nation-Builders: Dilemmas of the UN in East Timor," *International Peacekeeping* 8,4 (2001): 1–20.

AID AND DEPENDENCE

My interest in this subject was sparked back in 1998, when, in the course of fieldwork on the question of electoral accountability in Cambodia, I found myself discussing the significance of the election with a local NGO election monitor in a provincial town shortly before polling day. The local NGO observer commented, as many informants had done during the course of the election campaign, that given the military superiority of the de facto incumbent party, the Cambodian People's Party (CPP), over its recently ousted opponents, the question of a transfer of power following the election was problematic. Indeed, the CPP had shown its willingness to use military power against its elected rivals in a battle in Phnom Penh the previous year. That military battle had ousted the leaders of the CPP's erstwhile senior coalition partner from power and from the country, to the consternation of international donors, some of whom had cut aid programs in response.

In my reply, I mentioned some of the (admittedly very limited) avenues the CPP's opponents might use to challenge the CPP should it refuse to hand over power in the event of an opposition victory, or in the event of evidence of large-scale fraud. The observer then asked, "But my biggest concern is, if the election is free and fair, and the CPP wins, how would we organize a transfer of power to the opposition then?" Rather confused, I said that presumably, if the CPP won in a fair election, a transfer of power would not be necessary, to which the observer replied, "But if there is no transfer of power away from the CPP, will the United States restore aid?"

This analysis of the implications and stakes of the election campaign was initially startling in its stark violation of the central principle of electoralism—that whichever party gains the most votes must take power, regardless of international reaction, and that this outcome should be desired, above all, by those who volunteered to scrutinize elections. However, I later came to understand this comment as indicative of the ways in which the power relations implicit in the international promotion of democracy serve to hollow out practices of democracy themselves. From the perspective of individuals, like the election observer, who work and act on a day-to-day basis in a context framed by international prescriptions of appropriate conduct and fair play, the international promotion of democracy is less a matter of discreet technical support by professionals remaining modestly in the wings, while democratic actors perform for the crowds, than a puppet show in which the strings, and the fingers pulling them, are all too clearly observed. The democratic process emerges less as the demonstration of the supreme sovereignty of the people's will than as an attempt by members of a fragmented and nervous electorate to use their vote strategically as a bargaining chip to negotiate international assistance for their country.

This is not to suggest that all voters viewed the election in this way. But this scenario offers just one example of the ways in which the ideal of democracy suffered a certain degree of "slippage" in the process of transposition into contexts in which the notion of a bounded community, comprising governments and citizens, is problematized by international intervention.

The concerns of the local election observer cited above are not, in my view, attributable to any cultural dispositions or "lack of capacity" that might pertain in provincial Cambodia; instead, they reflect a fairly accurate view of the rather flexible way in which concepts of "democracy" were used to justify inconsistent policy stances by donors in the 1990s. It was by no means obvious that the US would restore aid to a government they considered to be corrupt and tainted by "communism," even if that government won a "free and fair election." Indeed, one of the murkier aspects of the 1998 election in Cambodia was the operation of the various international observer groups deployed to determine the status of the elections on behalf of the "international community." These bodies, and in particular the largest Joint International Observer Group, comprising representatives from the major donor nations, were characterized by their extreme secrecy and bizarre recruitment procedures and were plagued by defections and rumors of would-be whistleblowers subjected to gag orders.[8] The concerns of donors, and their deployment of power in pursuit of those concerns, clashed with their own lip service to democratic ideals in a variety of ways, raising the question as to whether the presence of donors, their influence over government policy, and their orientation towards goals and pressures that were international in nature—and, in consequence, were only problematically connected with any expressed preference of "the Cambodian people"—in effect made democracy, understood broadly and intuitively rather than narrowly and legalistically, extremely difficult to achieve.

This story indicates the key condition of aid dependence, as the term is used in this study—the pressing and continuous orientation of local political practices towards a monitoring, evaluating, and decision-making international audience. This is a view of dependence that differs from those already existing in the literature.

The literature on international aid and political economy offers two distinct definitions of dependence. The first is the dependence of the dependency theorists.[9] In this formulation, dependence represents a subordinate position in the global economy, which locks particular populations of particular countries into primary commodity production. According to dependency theorists, this subordination is coerced by the structural violence inherent in a world system they characterize as oppressive. A second, and sharply different, perspective on dependence is linked to the rise of neoliberal economics in the 1970s. For neoliberal economists, dependence is a condition in which overreliance on aid produces economic distortions that affect local decision-making and reduce efficiency. In particular, this kind of dependence is associated with welfarism, regarded as stifling individual enterprise and innovation. This is a view of dependence that has been much discussed in the literature on aid and development, and proponents of this approach generally regard such dependence as something that should be avoided at all costs.[10]

This study investigates the political, rather than economic, effects of dependence. It concurs with dependency theory in its starting point: that aid dependence is a condition arising from global structures rather than from local inadequacies. It is critical of the view that, while aid itself is well-meant, aid dependence encourages social, economic, and even moral flabbiness in recipient communities. Rather, I regard aid dependence as a condition that is promoted by both donors and national elites as a means to exercise power. Part of the way in which donors exert power is by their use of resources for ideological purposes—in particular, they tend to project

---

[8] Matthew Grainger, "International Observers' Report 'Too Political,'" *Phnom Penh Post*, July 17–23, 1998.

[9] Andre Gunder Frank, *Capitalism and Underdevelopment in Latin America* (New York, NY: Monthly Review Press, 1967); Immanuel Wallerstein, *The Origins of the Modern World System* (New York, NY: Academic Press, 1974); Samir Amin, *Unequal Development* (New York, NY: Monthly Review Press, 1976).

[10] For a fascinating review of the literature, see Paul Harvey and Jeremy Lind, *Dependency and Humanitarian Relief: A Critical Analysis* (London: Overseas Develoment Institute, 2005).

failings onto internal actors and exculpate external actors from blame in a manner that ensures that donors always retain the moral upper hand. Furthermore, the resources available to donors often overwhelm local resources, in a manner that is highly disempowering to local elites and communities, and that actively militates against the emergence of a local politics within which local relationships of obligation and accountability can be worked out. This elicits an ambivalent response from recipients, who devote large amounts of time to maneuvering to capture aid resources and external backing while deeply resenting the hierarchies of power and obligation within which they are required to participate as a result.

This study will argue further that the essential problem is not addiction on the part of recipients, but ideological attachment on the part of donors to rigid and doctrinaire templates that *cannot* work in a post-conflict state on the periphery of the global economy. I will show in later chapters, through analysis of policy areas ranging from refugee return and demobilization to democratization, funding for services, and budgets for local government, that the intrusions of donors take place within a neoliberal framework that works against the prospects for popular participation in a public sphere of political engagement and debate. Rather, current aid orthodoxy is framed within a neoliberal belief in the transformative power of imposed institutions and a global market—a belief that runs directly counter to the experience of post-conflict developing countries like Cambodia and Timor-Leste. Current aid and "peacebuilding" orthodoxy works with a model that prioritizes the breaking up of collective allegiances and support structures in favor of individual engagement with state agencies and the market.

These models prioritize economic activity over political activity and promote individualism, competitiveness, and a particular liberal rationality, even in contexts where preexisting forms of collective identification and action might offer considerable political resources for nation-building. Furthermore, to the extent that donor prescriptions are rigid and doctrinaire, rather than flexible and locally negotiated, they place great pressure upon elite aid recipients to conform to donor demands. As such, elites find themselves stretched in two different directions—attempting to comply with donor demands for the kind of individualizing, market-oriented governance that neoliberal orthodoxy expects, while at the same time attempting to develop support among domestic political constituencies by appealing to—and being seen to support—the aspirations of key local groups. This study examines the ways in which elites attempt to gain control over inflows of aid while at the same time trying to develop realms of discretionary action that can be used to award the political community with the necessary autonomy to imbue *de jure* sovereignty with local meaning.

This study is not, however, a normatively charged effort to pit an innocent local sphere against a rapacious "international community." Rather, the aim is to examine how different strategies, exercised by two sharply different local elites—those of Cambodia and Timor-Leste—have worked out politically. To answer this question, I examine the broad issue of who, within the domestic polity, got what, when, and how, in the context of post-conflict reconstruction activities. Particular concerns are: what kinds of opportunities were perceived by local actors; how different elites tried to mobilize support in an aid-dependent context; and how the strategies they espoused were perceived by those whose support was elicited. In the chapters that follow, I explore the dimensions of aid dependence, thus defined, from three perspectives: those of international actors engaged in intervention, of national elites, and of householders in village settings. In each case, I examine the ways in which these groups perceive the problems of post-conflict reconstruction and the ways in which they attempt to gain access to resources in order to promote particular solutions. Ultimately, the concern is to examine the construction of the imagined community that emerges from these conceptions and strategies. Do local perceptions of the dependent community resemble or differ sharply from nationalist ideals? If they differ sharply from ideals of modern nationhood, what does that mean for the condition of citizenship in such aid-dependent communities?

DEPENDENCE AND GLOBAL GOVERNANCE

These questions are significant in calling attention to the ways in which emerging practices and institutions of "global governance" affect the prospects for modern politics in peripheral states. "Global governance" is a term that has gained in popularity over the past twenty years as it has been used to describe the ways in which the international realm is increasingly organized around powerful international organizations and other global non-state actors. The term "governance" is used analytically to refer to the activities of a wide variety of actors, with different purposes and objectives, that serve to sustain coordination and coherence in response to societal problems. The rise of the term "governance" in both political science and public policy debates over recent decades reflects a rethinking of the significance of formal and centralized authorities in the work of government. The deregulation of capital and the "roll-back of the state" in the 1980s produced new forms of social and transnational action that reflected processes of globalization and the erosion of state capacity, both in domestic and international politics. Awareness of the impact of these trends led to increased focus in political science on the ways in which the state operates as merely one actor—and not always the most important one—of a variety of actors that engage in problem solving in society.

While theories of government had placed more emphasis upon authority and coercion in securing compliance with policy goals, theories of governance emerged that emphasized the role of influence and negotiation among a variety of networks of actors. An important contribution of the concept of "governance" is its ability to explain unintended outcomes and the "messiness" of implementation, both conditions that tend to result from the looseness of coordination between key governance actors, some of whom have explicitly conflicting goals. Yet at the same time, analyses of "governance" permit scholars to trace powerful patterns emerging from the stochastic noise of implementation—patterns that reflect underlying and highly unequal distributions of power and influence among a range of social actors. Although "governance" appears less purposive, more plural, and more flexible than "government," its effects, particularly on the weakest members of society, can be just as profound.[11]

"Global governance," likewise, emerged as a key term in both political science and international policy during the 1990s, in response to perceptions of declining state power, increased interdependence, and the rise of global problems that

---

[11] For a more detailed discussion of the rise of "governance" theory, see Jon Pierre, "Introduction: Understanding Governance," in *Debating Governance: Authority, Steering and Democracy*, ed. Jon Pierre (Oxford: Oxford University Press, 2000), pp. 1–12; see also the collection of classic essays presented in R. A. W. Rhodes, *Understanding Governance: Policy Networks, Governance, Reflexivity, and Accountability* (Maidenhead: Open University Press, 1997).

required multilateral solutions. In 1995, the Commission on Global Governance, endorsed by the United Nations, produced a report, entitled *Our Global Neighbourhood*, that made recommendations on issues to be considered by a World Conference on Global Governance scheduled for 1998.[12] On the first page of the report, the commission defined governance as follows:

> Governance is the sum of the many ways individuals and institutions, public and private, manage their common affairs. It is a continuing process through which conflicting or diverse interests may be accommodated and cooperative action may be taken. It includes formal institutions and regimes empowered to enforce compliance, as well as informal arrangements that people and institutions either have agreed to or perceive to be in their interest.[13]

At the global level, the report went on to state:

> ... governance has been viewed primarily as intergovernmental relationships, but it must now be understood as also involving nongovernmental organizations (NGOs), citizens' movements, multinational corporations, and the global capital market. Interacting with these are global mass media of dramatically enlarged influence.[14]

To an extent, this was regarded as an empirical statement of fact; in part, it was regarded as an aspiration for the future.

With these definitions in mind, the commission outlined a system of governance based upon the recognition of interdependence among states and the emergence of a framework of "global ethics" that would prompt states increasingly to coordinate action—through ad hoc measures, but also by establishing binding treaties and institutions—to govern international behavior. Among the suggestions included in the report were recommendations for verdicts of the International Court of Justice to become binding; for the institution of a UN standing army and global taxation; and for the abolition of veto powers in the UN Security Council. While these recommendations have not been realized, there has been a significant shift towards supra-national and multilateral action mediated through international institutions such as the United Nations and treaty organizations such as the North Atlantic Treaty Organization (NATO) since the end of the Cold War. New institutions such as the World Trade Organization and the International Criminal Court reflect some of the commission's aspirations, as do efforts to promote uniform practices among a range of international institutions and actors concerning the key tenets of sound post-conflict reconstruction and development policies.

In political science, the term "global governance" has increasingly been used to analyze these shifts, inheriting from international regime theory the task of showing how institutions, and the norms and codes they promote, operate internationally to mediate political outcomes, and how they both reflect and constrain the power and

---

[12] Commission on Global Governance, *Our Global Neighbourhood* (Oxford: Oxford University Press, 1995), online at www-old.itcilo.org/actrav/actrav-english/telearn/global/ilo/globe/gove.htm, accessed May 10, 2008.

[13] Ibid.

[14] Ibid.

influence traditionally assumed to reside in sovereign states.[15] There has been a particular focus in the literature on the relative decline of states and the growth of the power of international organizations such as the United Nations, the World Trade Organization, and the World Bank.[16] Within the extensive literature that has developed on the subject, a central question is where the fault lines between elites and non-elites lie, and how effectively non-elites are able to resist elite power in a global political sphere.[17]

Large numbers of studies have subsequently emerged, examining networks of governance in the context of different issue areas such as control of weapons of mass destruction; regulation of trade; governance of the commons; and so on. In each issue area, analysts identified a specific web of treaties, norms, procedures, and protocols in the process of being promoted, upheld, interpreted or challenged by networks of international agencies, nongovernmental organizations, transnational communities of experts, and transnational corporations. Although far from forming a global government, these networks of actors, responding to rules, agreements, and emerging norms of conduct, are highly influential in determining trajectories of response in transnational social, economic, and political spheres.[18] In the sphere of development policy, in particular, there is a clear emergence of strong norms and assumptions regarding "best practice" that are associated with institutions, such as the United Nations and the World Bank, that wield immense power in relation to underdeveloped states. The terms "Washington Consensus" and "Post-Washington Consensus" used to describe the stated policies of key international development organizations since the 1980s reflect the significant extent to which international organizations' attitudes towards poor countries, although emerging from a diverse set of actors, are uniform in their assumptions. The power of this consensus and the uniform picture it proffers of the dilemmas of poor countries, and their possible solutions, will be discussed in detail in Chapter Three as a precursor to discussing policies implemented in Cambodia and Timor-Leste.

A critical school within the governance literature discusses the difficulties of establishing representative practices as government gives way to governance,[19] and as key governance actors are increasingly found in the international rather than the

---

[15] James Rosenau, "Governance in the Twenty-First Century," *Global Governance* 1,1 (1995): 25–50; Robert Nye and John D. Donahue, eds., *Governance in a Globalizing World* (Washington, DC: Brookings Institute, 2000).

[16] Martin Hewson and Timothy Sinclair, "The Emergence of Global Governance Theory," in *Approaches to Global Governance Theory,* ed. Martin Hewson and Timothy Sinclair (New York, NY: State University of New York Press, 1999), pp. 3–22.

[17] See for example, Margaret Keck and Kathryn Sikkink, *Activists Beyond Borders: Advocacy Networks in International Politics* (Ithaca, NY: Cornell University Press, 1998); Robert O'Brien, Anne Marie Goetz, Jan Aart Scholte, and Marc Williams, *Contesting Global Governance: Multilateral Economic Institutions and Global Social Movements* (Cambridge: Cambridge University Press, 2000); Mary Kaldor, *Global Civil Society: An Answer to War* (Cambridge: Polity, 2003); Sidney Tarrow, *The New Transnational Activism* (Cambridge: Cambridge University Press, 2005).

[18] Many such studies have appeared in the journal *Global Governance,* published by Lynne Rienner since 1995.

[19] R. A. W. Rhodes, "Governing without Government: Order and Change in British Politics," in Rhodes, *Understanding Governance,* p. 5.

domestic sphere.[20] This accountability deficit applies not only to global elites, multinational corporations, and intergovernmental structures, such as the UN Security Council and the boards of the World Bank and International Monetary Fund, which are dominated by powerful Northern governments, but also to the "global civil society" charged with resisting these elites in the name of the poor. As with most civil societies, global civil-society activism tends to be the preserve of those with quite substantial reserves of money and skills. At best, poor people's interests are interpreted by international activists, but routes of downward accountability, offering the poor the opportunity to exercise some kind of control over the activities conducted in their name, are frequently unclear.

Accountability and representation are important for discussions of intervention, the ethics of which are frequently couched in a rhetoric of concern for and responsibility towards "victims" and "the poor." Although the poor and victims of violence in countries in conflict are the targets of assistance, the extent to which they have any kind of say over the assistance they receive is questionable. This is a key question that is addressed in this book. My discussion of the relationship between global governance actors, national elites, and ordinary people in post-conflict Cambodia and Timor-Leste takes place within a framework informed by the work of Mark Duffield and Robert Cox, who are highly critical of the impact of global governance, and the power relations inherent within it, on states and peoples on the periphery of a globalizing international economy.

Duffield sees the rise of global governance as comprising a shift in North–South relations, where the North is conceptualized as the industrialized core of the global economy, in dependency models, and the South is the underdeveloped periphery. Shifts in North-South relations attendant upon the end of the Cold War promoted the emerging power of "strategic complexes" of global governance—shifting concatenations of international organizations, bilateral donors, aid agencies, international NGOs, and multinational corporations—headquartered in states of the North but intruding with increasing assuredness in the politics and economics of the subordinate South. These complexes, Duffield argues, are "the operational basis of the liberal peace."[21]

Duffield describes these strategic complexes as arising from the impact of globalization on the role and functioning of the nation-state. Under conditions of globalization, the function of the nation-state is changing everywhere, but globalization has particular implications for countries of the global South for which the state was envisaged, in previous decades, as the solution to problems of conflict and underdevelopment. In the heyday of modernization theory from the 1940s to the 1960s, as Ashis Nandy has pointed out, postcolonial elites saw the state as "*the* clue to the West's economic success and political dominance," an entity that through its secular, scientific, and managerial interventions could usher populations along the long, integrating march to Progress.[22] Belief in the ability of the state to deliver

---

[20] Joseph Nye, "Globalization's Democratic Deficit: How to Make International Institutions More Accountable," *Foreign Affairs* 80,4 (2001): 2–6; see also various essays in Christopher J. Bickerton, Philip Cunliffe, and Alexander Gourevitch, *Politics without Sovereignty: A Critique of Contemporary International Relations* (London: University College London Press, 2007).

[21] Mark Duffield, *Global Governance and the New Wars: The Merging of Development and Security* (London: Zed Books, 2001), pp. 44–45.

[22] Ashis Nandy, "State," in *The Development Dictionary: A Guide to Knowledge as Power*, ed. Wolfgang Sachs (London: Zed Books, 1992), pp. 265–66.

change was a key, although not always determining, factor in the trajectory of Southern states following independence from colonial rule.

However, just as the state is no longer regarded as necessarily preeminent in the global North in an era of globalization, so the idea that the state could be transformative in the South, offering the hope of development and modernity to millions of poverty-stricken people, has been questioned in the contemporary era. Ideas about the ability of states to deliver development have been largely discarded; as explained in detail in Chapter Three, development is now conceptualized exclusively in terms of economic growth and is regarded as the province of the market. Yet at the same time, international agencies continue to emphasize "statist" solutions—solutions that feature the rebuilding or reform of collapsed or failed states as their centerpiece. This apparent contradiction, as Robert Cox has argued, reflects the transformation of the role of the state in a globalizing world. The nature of the state in the South in the global system has changed radically since the heyday of anticolonial nationalism and modernization theory. Rather than operating as the heroic repository of sovereignty and context for political and economic action, the state is reformulated as an agent for transmitting and implementing global policies for "welfare and riot control"[23] designed to facilitate the unfettered spread of the market.

The state's importance in the contemporary policies of a variety of international agencies, including both inter-governmental organizations, such as the World Bank and the United Nations, *and* international nongovernmental organizations, is not as the driver of modernity but as the handmaiden of the market. Philip Cerny describes this as a "residual state" that comprises "a potentially unstable mix of civil association and enterprise association ... with state actors, no longer so autonomous, feeling their way uneasily in an unfamiliar world."[24] Although this phenomenon is apparent throughout the contemporary world, it bears most heavily on the state in the South. It has far-reaching implications for solutions to civil war that rely on the state—a state increasingly shorn of its vaulting ambition and heroic aspects—to maintain significant local support during difficult post-conflict periods.

The changing role of the state requires transformed state-making processes, and these are what networks of global governance operate to impose. The response to this within the field of development studies has been the rise of "good governance"—a term that attributes normative value to particular forms of state operation and state-society relation, and that justifies these primarily with respect to the needs of the global market, rather than the needs of local populations. The understanding of statehood, as expressed in this literature, differs sharply from the bloody, messy process of deal-making, cooptation, and repression associated with scholarship on state-making in the field of Southeast Asian studies. Rather, it seeks to delineate a clinical, by-prescription version of the state that can be implemented expeditiously by technical personnel armed with the conceptual instruments to swiftly diagnose any simmering cease-fire situation that might arise. Formulated, most strikingly, in the context of the World Bank's 1997 World Development

---

[23] Robert Cox, "Critical Political Economy," in *International Political Economy: Understanding Global Disorder,* ed. Bjorn Hettne (London: Zed Books, 1995), pp. 31–45.

[24] Philip Cerny, "Globalisation and the Changing Logic of Collective Action," *International Organisation* 49,4 (1995): 619.

Report,[25] the concept of "good governance" presaged increasingly intrusive attention to the workings of state institutions; this new level of scrutiny was brought to bear on these states, not just by political scientists, but also by powerful and interventionist global institutions.

Conceptualizations of state-building in the context of the post-conflict reconstruction policy literature pay minimal attention to the role of attitudes in constructing a national politics. The World Bank acknowledges in passing that "getting societies to accept a redefinition of the state's responsibilities" is "one part" of this endeavor.[26] However, the bank's prescriptions leave little room for this sort of negotiation as a political endeavor; it suggests that "states with weaker institutions may need to err on the side of less flexibility and more restraint,"[27] permitting the private sector to prevail, or subordinating its own policy-making mechanisms to regional or international arrangements. This prescription suggests a powerful prioritization of the regimenting power of institutions and markets over the art of politics as a means to award individuals and groups in the South power over their own futures.

This view of the state-building process as ideally an instrumental rather than an explicitly political process is reflected further in the increasingly carefully drawn distinction between "state-building" and "nation-building" and the comparative reluctance, on the part of those who intervene, to get involved with unruly and unpredictable "nations" as compared with their growing enthusiasm for the aspiration of building legal-rational and supervisable "states."[28] State-building policy thus tends to at least downplay, if not jettison, much concern for the link between the functioning of institutions and the ways in which those institutions impinge upon the construction of a social imaginary that entails particular constellations of political identification. In so doing, it removes state policy from the purview of nations and subordinates it to the twin imperatives of international notions of governability and competitiveness with respect to a globalizing market. This study focuses on the ways in which this approach to post-conflict reconstruction affects visions of national identity produced during the war, and it questions the impact of the rise of technocratic liberal governance on people in the periphery.

SOVEREIGNTY AND EMPOWERMENT

A particular preoccupation of this study is with the implications of aid dependence for some local sense of empowerment. Empowerment has been largely associated in the thinking of aid and development agencies, as in the thinking of international peacekeepers, with procedural democracy and some form of local participatory development. Democracy, in particular, has been promoted internationally since the end of the Cold War as part of a broader agenda of "good governance" for underdeveloped and post-conflict countries. However, the type of

---

[25] World Bank, *World Development Report 1997: The State in a Changing World* (Washington DC: World Bank, 1997).

[26] Ibid., p. 3.

[27] Ibid., p. 6.

[28] See Jochen Hippler, "Violent Conflicts, Conflict Prevention, and Nation Building—Terminology and Political Concepts," in *Nation-Building: A Key Concept for Peaceful Conflict Transformation?*, ed. Jochen Hippler (London: Pluto, 2005), pp. 3–14.

democracy that has been advanced has, arguably, represented a rather tame and ineffectual liberal substitute for the earlier aspirations of modernization theory. Modernization theory advocated the rise of a state that effectively represented the progressive interests of a self-identifying and autonomous nation. This volume will argue that the new type of democracy advanced as a matter of policy in post-conflict states reflects a desire on the part of international actors to detach democracy from nationalism, to minimize dangers of demagoguery, aggression, and mass action, and to replace these with a polite set of procedures for aggregating individual interests.

It is important to note that this view of democracy is not inherent in the concept itself—indeed, democracy is, and has been for two thousand years, an "essentially contested concept"[29] that attracts perpetual dispute over how it should be realized. There has been much debate in political science over the degree of weight that should be accorded, for example, to individual choice as opposed to community deliberation in producing democracy. Such disputes cannot be settled by empirical investigation or logical reasoning since the different claims appeal to different and incommensurate value systems.[30]

Given this contested status within Western political science, it is all the more significant that "democracy" as promoted in post-conflict countries by liberal interveners since the 1990s is an extremely monochrome affair. Approaches to democracy promotion conspire to render "democracy" an objective concept with positive attributes, rather than an essentially contested concept raising fundamental questions about the nature of power. More complex discussions of the meaning of democracy were dismissed in the mainstream democratization literature in the 1990s as redundant and unhelpful in an era when radical change demanded clear-cut principles as a basis for resolute international action.[31] Such a dismissal reflects the recasting of democracy as it applies to underdeveloped countries in the global South, in a manner that serves the interests of interveners and Northern policy-makers. Following from this clear-cut agenda are both implicit and explicit attempts to detach democracy from wider social goals. Theoreticians advocated tying the normative power of democracy to a single alleged quality—the efficiency of democratic institutions in managing conflict. Adam Przeworski, for example, demonstrates that democracy, procedurally defined, is not representative of voters' interests, nor does it redistribute power, but he claims it is worth defending because it appears to reduce political violence.[32]

Within the democracy-promotion literature there is a strong predilection for highly procedural forms of democracy that limit participation to ritualized occasions on which individuals are asked, as individuals, to express constrained choices. Forms of democracy that emphasize community deliberation have been far less significant, particularly in post-conflict situations. Defining democracy as procedural democracy

---

[29] W. B. Gallie, "Essentially Contested Concepts," *Proceedings of the Aristotelian Society* 56 (1956): 167–98.

[30] Ibid.

[31] Giuseppe DiPalma, *To Craft Democracies: An Essay on Democratic Transitions* (Berkeley, CA: University of California Press, 1990), p. 15.

[32] Adam Przeworski, "Minimalist Conceptions of Democracy: A Defense," in *Democracy's Value*, ed. Ian Shapiro and Casiano Hacker-Cordon (Cambridge: Cambridge University Press, 1999), pp. 23–55.

achieves two things—it offers citizens the opportunity to engage in formal acts of sovereignty, while actually imposing narrow limits on its political content.

This form of democracy has been specifically promoted by a range of external actors intervening in post-conflict societies, where too much politics and too little citizenship are regarded as the central problem. The new wave of democratization studies that emerged in the 1980s offered potentially inclusive solutions to conflict in the form of the "elite pact" that could underpin transitions from authoritarian rule.[33] These studies described democracy as emerging from short-term policy implementation by specific elite actors recognizing interests in the stability that could be generated by limited liberalization, replacing the modernization theorists' account of democracy arising from the emergence of specific class interests, forged through long-term processes of social struggle, and prompting genuine redistributions of power. This view of democracy's genesis made it possible for international donors and policy makers to define a much more emphatic role for themselves in promoting democracy in various countries around the world. Thus, throughout the 1990s, a variety of former one-party states in the global South were pressured by donors and multilateral organizations to shift towards multiparty electoral systems. As it turned out, as North–South relations underwent a seismic shift at the end of the Cold War, getting aid-dependent elites to sign up to pacts came to be fairly easy, although it subsequently emerged that sustaining these agreements might be more difficult. The idea of the "elite pact," permitting a rewritten constitution, a founding election, and a new order, became a centerpiece of post-Cold War interventionary practice as practiced by multilateral organizations and by aid donors.

Two major criticisms have been leveled at this incorporation of a particular, ideologically inflected conception of democracy into international policy making concerned with underdeveloped countries since the end of the Cold War. The first problem is that the research agenda of mainstream democratization studies in the 1990s did not problematize or question specifically liberal assumptions regarding the importance of the individual and of choice—assumptions that underpin the accounts of elite-led democratization that prevailed in policy-oriented studies. In this, studies of consolidation of democracy in the South differ sharply from studies problematizing the quality of democracy in the North. In studies of "new" democracy in the South, analyses of the "depth" or quality of democracy are focused entirely upon the status of observable institutions and procedures offering fairly minimal opportunities for electoral choice, participation, and respect for civil and political rights. Unlike analyses of quality of democracy in the North, this literature focuses far less on messy issues of how choices were made, how participation was understood, how power was distributed, and how emancipation might be conceptualized in fragmented and possibly alienated societies.

Defining democracy in a purely procedural way served a practical policy agenda through simplifying diagnosis, justifying criticism of the nation receiving aid, and, consequently, enhancing Northern power over Southern governments in an era when levels of democracy were explicitly in rhetoric—if inconsistently in practice— tied to levels of aid.[34] The focus—in both academic studies and a range of policy

---

[33] Guillermo O'Donnell and Philippe Schmitter, *Transitions from Authoritarian Rule: Prospects for Democracy, Tentative Conclusions About Uncertain Democracies*, vol. 4 (Baltimore, MD: Johns Hopkins University Press, 1986).

[34] The Clinton administration's policy of "democratic enlargement" and Francois Mitterand's 1990 declaration at the World Investment Conference at La Baule exemplify this trend, along

speeches trumpeting democracy promotion in the 1990s—on a narrow form of procedural democracy, rather than on grassroots politics, served international policy agendas well. This was because this kind of focus allowed the international policy makers to equate democracy and security with the implementation, by problematic governments in the South, of a fairly simple checklist of institutional reforms, rather than bothering about contested issues of power and representation. This had the effect of subordinating the notion of democracy as an idea that has concrete but contradictory effects on the living of lives to the notion of democracy as a litmus test, thus tying the concept tightly to structures of Northern power and surveillance brought to bear on states in the South. Thus Barry Gills and Joel Rocamora in 1992 claimed that the "struggle to define 'democracy'" was a "major ideological battle" with profound effects for the emerging post-Cold War world.[35]

This leads to the second criticism of "Third Wave" accounts of democracy—that the diminished form of democracy promoted in these accounts represents little more than a means by which states better manage their populations in the interests of global capital. Thus critics suggest that detaching democracy from concerns with social justice is less a pragmatic approach to post-conflict instability than it is a rhetorical trick that harnesses democracy's brand appeal to a process of mystification aimed at limiting citizens' resistance to economic exploitation. Different versions of this critique include Gills and Rocamora's account of "low-intensity democracy"; Mkandawire's account of "choiceless democracy," in which the political repertoire of governments is severely constrained by the deployment of internationally supported "technocrats" in key government agencies; Abrahamsen's critique of "disciplined" democracy; and Ayers's critique of "(neo)liberal democracy."[36] "Low intensity democracy"—the term coined by Gills and Rocamora to describe the minimalist, election-focused procedures of democracy promoted internationally in the 1990s—is what remains when democracy is successfully sundered from wider social and economic issues. The failure to redistribute social and economic power results in a failure to infuse democratic institutions with any real connection to political struggles in society, thus prompting alienation and "mystification" among voters. According to the critiques cited here, the promotion of constrained forms of democracy not only fails to deliver real power over substantive issues to ordinary people, but serves to "preempt" more radical forms of democracy that might be capable of achieving full participation by the citizenry. As such, constrained democracy serves the hegemonic aims of global capital.

---

with the European Union's embrace of democracy promotion in the Maastricht Treaty. See Anthony Lake, "From Containment to Enlargement," lecture presented at the Johns Hopkins University School of Advanced International Studies, Washington, DC, published in *US Policy Information and Text* 97 (October 23, 1993): 6–12; and Gorm Rye Olsen, "Europe and the Promotion of Democracy in Post-Cold War Africa: How Serious is Europe and for What Reason?" *African Affairs* 97,388 (1998): 343–67.

[35] Barry Gills and Joel Rocamora, "Low Intensity Democracy," *Third World Quarterly* 13,3 (1997): 501; see also Alison Ayers, "Demystifying Democratisation: The Global Constitution of (Neo)liberal Polities in Africa," *Third World Quarterly* 27,2 (2006): 321.

[36] Barry Gills and Joel Rocamora, "Low Intensity Democracy," pp. 501–23; Thandika Mkandawire, "Crisis Management and the Making of 'Choiceless Democracies,'" in *State, Conflict, and Democracy in Africa*, ed. Richard Joseph (Boulder, CO: Lynne Rienner, 1999), pp. 119–36; Rita Abrahamsen, *Disciplining Democracy: Development Discourse and Good Governance in Africa* (London: Zed Books, 2000); Alison Ayers, "Demystifying Democratisation," pp. 321–38.

Critical theorists of democracy argue that any kind of democracy involves regimenting and disciplinary political processes, requiring the same degree of exclusionary violence as nationalism. Michael Hardt and Antonio Negri regard the process of citizen formation as a disciplinary process, distinguishing between a "multitude" of pre-citizens—"a multiplicity, a plane of singularities, an open set of relations, which is not homogeneous or identical with itself and bears an indistinct, inclusive relation to those outside of it," and a "people" of citizens, who "tend toward identity and homogeneity internally while posing its difference from and excluding what remains outside of it." They conclude that, to acquire modern sovereignty, "every nation must make its multitude into a people."[37] Similarly, Chantal Mouffe gives an account of the "democratic paradox"—the paradoxical tension between a liberal humanist commitment to inclusion, and the "logic of democracy" which "impl[ies] a moment of closure which is required by the very process of constituting 'the people.'"[38]

For Mouffe, "the identity of a democratic political community hinges on the possibility of drawing a frontier between 'us' and 'them'"[39]—it is inherently exclusionary, and devices for justifying such exclusion are therefore fraught with power relations. For Mouffe, the exclusionary impulse is an inherently violent one, and to the extent that exclusion is institutionalized, so too is violence. Democracy demands that a finite and autonomous political community is constituted to serve as the sovereign will. In the so-called "established democracies" of the industrialized North, the constitution of such a community engenders significant violence in, for example, policies designed to keep immigrants out.

According to Mouffe, the paradox of democracy lies in the inherent tension between the empowerment of insiders and the exclusion of outsiders. In response, she argues, the aim of democracy promotion should not be to reify or naturalize power relations, but to bring them to the surface and for advocates to remain self-consciously aware of the violence these policies engender. She develops a model of agonistic democracy in response to this challenge—a model of democracy that rejects ideas of consensus, agreement, or legitimation in favor of recognizing "the importance of leaving this space of contestation forever open, instead of trying to fill it through the establishment of a supposedly 'rational' consensus."[40] Mouffe advocates a form of democracy that is continually self-reflective and self-critical, particularly with respect to its own presuppositions and procedures, in a bid to avoid the descent into regimentation and to maintain the political—the "recognition of undecidability"—always in the foreground.[41]

Such a critique is useful in empirical studies of dependent post-conflict communities, since a diminuendo of violence on battlefields and in public spaces brought about by elite pacts under conditions of dependence may be accompanied by continuing violence on the periphery of the public stage, for example, in the

---

[37] Michael Hardt and Antonio Negri, *Empire* (Cambridge, MA: Harvard University Press, 2000), p. 103.

[38] Chantal Mouffe, *The Democratic Paradox* (London: Verso, 2000), p. 43.

[39] Ibid.

[40] Ibid., p. 56.

[41] Chantal Mouffe, "Democracy, Power, and the 'Political,'" in *Democracy and Difference: Contesting the Boundaries of the Political*, ed. Seyla Benhabib (New Haven, CT: Princeton University Press, 1996), p. 254.

home, in the brothel, and in the spheres of both organized and disorganized crime. Mouffe's critique of the exclusions of modern forms of democracy are highly pertinent to this study, since this volume is devoted to showing that the specific forms of democracy promoted by international interveners within the ideological parameters of the liberal peace emphasize the exclusionary, regimenting aspects of democracy while draining it specifically of the substantive deliberative content that Mouffe regards as worthy of preservation. Democracy promotion in a globalized sphere is focused on the demobilization of the collective, and the regimentation and atomization of political communities into agglomerations of isolated individuals, thus ritualizing, rather than unsettling, power relations left increasingly exposed by the emptiness of democratic deliberation in the context of global governance and liberal peace.

To challenge this ossifying form of democracy, one must reinvigorate democracy in a global setting. This requires reconceptualizing political identity in an emancipatory way. As Mouffe asks:

> How can the maximum of pluralism be defended—in order to respect the rights of the widest possible groups—without destroying the very framework of the political community as constituted by the institutions and practices that construe modern democracy and define our identity as citizens? ... What kind of political identity does it require? In other words, since ... the creation of a common political identity can no longer be conceived in terms of *class*, what kind of political identity can contribute to the constitution of the "we" of the radical democratic forces?[42]

This normative ambition is a large one, and this study is not sufficient in scope to meet it. However, in investigating the nature of political allegiance and political community in post-conflict states, this study orients itself within a conceptual framework that admits the challenge of an emancipatory alternative as a basis upon which to critique the regimenting and atomizing reality encountered in the field. As such, this study is not intended to provide policy solutions to would-be interveners; rather, it aims at showing the power relations inherent in the models of politics that interveners promote. The primary purpose of this volume, in terms of Robert Cox's seminal distinction, is thus critical rather than problem-solving. As Cox argues, problem-solving theory "takes the world as it finds it, with the prevailing social and power relationships and the institutions into which they are organised, as the given framework for action."[43] Much theorizing on intervention and post-conflict reconstruction falls into this pragmatic category, as it examines what should be done and how in order to maximize success, narrowly conceived.

Much less of this literature has been devoted to critical theorizing—theorizing that "stands apart from the prevailing order of the world and asks how that order came about."[44] For Cox, problem-solving theory is theory that seeks to smooth out

---

[42] Chantal Mouffe, "Preface: Democratic Politics Today," in *Dimensions of Radical Democracy: Pluralism, Citizenship, Community*, ed. Chantal Mouffe (London: Verso, 1992), p. 3.

[43] Robert W. Cox, "On Perspectives and Purposes," in *Approaches to World Order*, ed. Robert W. Cox and Timothy Sinclair (Cambridge: Cambridge University Press, 1996), p. 88.

[44] Ibid.

the functioning of a particular order, an order that always serves some specific set of national, sectional, or class interests. Critical theory seeks to uncover the interests served as a preliminary step in the process of conceiving of emancipatory alternatives.[45] This study aims at the latter. I will argue over subsequent chapters that models of intervention and post-conflict reconstruction, developed by policy makers in institutions that occupy key positions in Duffield's "strategic complexes," should not be regarded so much as plans that transcend politics in pursuit of universal goals, but instead as models that facilitate the gathering of political power into the hands of interveners. I will explore the impact of this for national politics and for local perceptions of the state in post-conflict Cambodia and Timor-Leste.

NEW WARS AND LIBERAL PEACE

Duffield points out the similarity between the "liberal peace" and the new or "post-modern" wars.[46] The latter are characterized by ethnic identifications, transnational connections, and prosaic local concerns, expressed in the form of disorganized looting and killing, rather than in the organized disposition of modern armies. The liberal peace, despite the fact that many of its constituent processes are derived from the familiar institutions of modern democratic politics, and despite its concerted policing of borders and building of states, represents a means by which to facilitate a transition between liberal subjectivities and post-modern ones. Post-conflict reconstruction in Cambodia and East Timor demonstrates this phenomenon—these conflicts were not primarily "new wars," but old ones, fought over modernist issues of nationalism, statehood, and mass ideology, given force by the Cold War context in which they were suspended. As they limped into the 1990s, these wars became anachronistic and began to take on post-modern aspects. In the context of Cambodia, this took the form of increasing integration into what Duffield describes as the "shadow economies of the borderlands," as both state military and anti-government insurgents stripped Cambodia's natural resources to replace superpower funding. In the case of East Timor, the transition into post-modern forms was reflected in attempts by Timorese in exile, a range of clandestine organizations and student groups, and leading community figures such as Bishop Belo in the 1990s to appeal to transnational solidarity groups. These efforts were made in an attempt to influence emerging and shifting single-issue alliances of non-governmental actors and to mobilize international media networks in their support. However, essentially, the wars were fought over the question of who rules over heroic national spheres, and how; the salience of that sphere as an arena of power in a globalizing world was less in question.

The forms of liberal governance hold out the promise of autonomous statehood while emptying it of content in a manner that attempts to bridge the transition between nationalist struggles and post-modern alienation. As Oliver Richmond notes, the liberal peace is an imposed disciplinary peace, designed to repress emancipatory struggles, alienating such struggles from any national level of collective action. The liberal peace favors the incorporation of splintered constituencies into an impersonal global sphere of governance in which actors from

---

[45] Robert Cox, "Social Forces, States, and World Orders: Beyond International Relations Theory," *Millennium: Journal of International Studies* 10,2 (1981): 128–30.

[46] Duffield, *Global Governance and the New Wars*, p. 189.

poor, post-conflict, peripheral economies can expect to gain little purchase. As such, the institutions of the liberal peace represent merely the veneer for a post-modern politics, policed by international intervention, fragmented by post-modern political procedures, and subordinated to global economic imperatives, on the borders of the global economy. Transition to peace is a transition to a new subjectivity, oriented towards the new vectors of power and territoriality in a globalizing world.

This study interrogates the experience of Cambodians and Timorese, caught between the disciplinary mechanisms of global governance and the threatening alienation of a post-modern peace. Cambodia and East Timor are interesting cases in that they form a bridge between the modernist devastation and aspiration of late nationalism, and the disciplinary power of the liberal interventions of the 1990s, in the context of a fragmenting and globalizing world. The account offered here is drawn from ten years of study of Cambodia and more limited but intensive fieldwork undertaken in East Timor in 2005. The concern is to represent Cambodians and East Timorese neither as traumatized victims of modernity, nor as more or less cooperative guinea pigs of global governance, but as living and breathing people attempting to make sense of their lives in the midst of extraordinary transformations, not only in the economic and political conditions in which they live, but in the very possibility of imagining economics and politics. In so doing, I attempt to depict them as they appeared to me when I met them: as people who make choices, foster hopes, and develop tactics for dealing with the situation they face, employing—always creatively, if not always successfully—whatever resources are to hand in an effort to gain purchase on a shifting, uncontrollable, and fundamentally unimaginable political world.

Ultimately, I draw three conclusions. First, I contend that international intervention, for all its claims to protect, reconstruct, and reconcile, appears from the perspective of people in war-torn and aid-dependent societies as remote, unfathomable, and coercive, and, as such, beyond the purview of any national public sphere that might conceivably be constructed. This has a highly disempowering effect upon local societies; as a result, politics—and, hence, participatory decision-making, democratic sovereignty, inter-group accommodation, and legitimation of institutions—becomes much more difficult. Elites sometimes try to counter this by pursuing strategies to manufacture discretionary spheres of influence beyond the purview of aid donors or international interveners. The most successful strategy, in the context of these case studies, was the Cambodian People's Party strategy of removing politics into the "back rooms" of power, out of sight of the public venues where formal negotiations took place. This rendered politics opaque not only to international interveners but also to the domestic public, including their own supporters. Politics survived international intervention by becoming secretive and elitist.

Second, international interveners and aid donors promote a politics that is confining, in that it attempts to resurrect borders that will contain potentially unruly populations, and atomizing, in the sense that it seeks specifically to break down non-state authority structures regarded as the source of such unruliness and focuses on the individual and individual action, rather than upon the public sphere and the fostering of collective action. The prioritization of the individual over the collective undermines relations of solidarity and drains the national sphere of heroism and import. It promotes decentralization of politics to micro-polities across the territory, each of which conducts elaborate rituals of participation, but which ultimately controls few resources, limiting its viability as a political entity. This pattern promotes increased dependence upon top-down resource allocations and reduces political participation to competition for these allocations. In this context, policy debate becomes redundant, and therefore legitimation becomes a pressing problem. Elites in both case studies retreat into a politics of cultural authenticity as a means to fill the legitimacy gap. In so doing they produce a politics that may intensify conflicts among identity-based groups within society, and thus cause further political and social instability. In these case studies, I argue, this is an effect not of the legacy of war, but of aid dependence and the neo-liberal politics of intervention.

Third, the state's legitimacy deficit leads to demands for more intimate relations of dependence with those who clearly control the power and the money—the donors themselves. Thus in East Timor, and in Cambodia in the 1990s, calls for international interveners to deal directly with villages, bypassing the middle-man of the state, were common, prompting interveners to decry the "mentality of dependence" that was frequently portrayed as culturally innate. This volume will suggest that dependence is an outcome of glaring disparities of power inherent in the liberal peace. This rejection of the state by the poor is particularly significant, at a time when proponents of a new, post-Washington consensus have declared, in the shift to focusing on "good governance" and the rise of a Polanyi-an counter-movement against the dominance of the global market.

The book proceeds to these conclusions as follows: Chapter Two investigates the place of the nation in the politics of war, paying particular attention to the ways in which economies and institutions deployed ethnosymbolic resources as a means to construct the nation as a heroic sphere of action, worthy of the ultimate sacrifice. I consider the success, or otherwise, of their efforts in order to depict national moods and institutional legacies that impinged upon the period of post-conflict reconstruction. Chapter Three then examines in more detail post-Cold War constructions of conflict and post-conflict reconstruction in key policy documents produced by international agencies, highlighting the clash of perspectives between interveners and locals experienced in the case study countries of Cambodia and East Timor, following intervention. Chapters Four and Five describe the ways in which interveners intruded into Cambodia and Timor, first in the context of peacekeeping operations and then in the context of longer term post-conflict reconstruction activities. Thus, Chapter Four examines the ways in which peacekeeping operations both violate and attempt to resurrect the importance of the territorial boundaries of the state in the context of refugee repatriation and transitional justice mechanisms, as well as in day-to-day interactions between "international" and "local" staff in interventionary organizations. Chapter Five goes on to examine the regimenting technologies of power imposed within these boundaries on populations at large, with particular reference to demobilization of armies, promotion of democracy, and participatory development.

Chapters Six to Eight shift focus, to foreground the ways in which local actors have responded to these international strategies. My intention in these chapters is to invoke the communities in which broadly similar international strategies have been pursued, through examining responses to intervention and dependence, and the ways in which actors draw upon the economies, identities, and institutions inherited from the war as resources with which to contest the power of international interveners. Chapter Six investigates relations between elites and interveners and the contrasting ways in which Cambodian and Timorese elites attempted to stake out spheres of discretionary action that they could use to facilitate political accommodation. I argue that the Cambodian government, building upon the experience of the preceding decade of state-building guided by Vietnamese "advice," proved highly adept at this and consequently was successful in attaining political stability. However, this is a stability that works to the distinct advantage of one violent and exploitative section of the elite, a group that was empowered during the war years. The Timorese government, by contrast, has failed to maintain security thus far, in part because it employed a strategy of branding itself as an outstanding performer with respect to international aid in the early years, thus drastically reducing its own room for maneuver. The Timorese government, under Mari Alkatiri, left itself with few discretionary powers and as a result was unable to cope with escalating social demands as the economy collapsed. The result was instability, reintervention by the Australian military, and the government's demise.

Chapter Seven looks at relations between the government and society, examining the ways in which elite political actors are able to use the art of politics to legitimize their strategies. In aid-dependent environments, I argue, a politics of gatekeeping and authenticity emerges in which a key strategy involves presenting oneself either as powerful by virtue of one's ability to attract and channel international resources, and to interact with the international sphere, or by virtue of one's capability to represent, in an international sphere, an authentically local voice. Once again, the politics of authenticity draws heavily upon the legacy of the war, while the politics of gatekeeping speaks to an ability to reorient to new international imperatives. Again, the success of the CPP in Cambodia in this regard is contrasted with the failures of the Cambodian opposition and of the Alkatiri government in Timor.

Chapter Eight, finally, examines the view from the village. Based primarily on fieldwork in two districts in East Timor in 2005, and from research in five communes in Cambodia during the 2003 elections, I present responses obtained through interviews and surveys with householders and local authorities to suggest that the combined impact of elite and international activity results in an acute sense of political disenfranchisement at the local level. The imagined community of the modern nation in both these cases has been significantly undermined, in contrast to the foregrounding of international and local-level action. Thinking globally and acting locally leaves little room for the nation as a heroic sphere. Paradoxically, the tendency of interveners to regard war zones as "empty shells" becomes a self-fulfilling prophecy, as the status of both nation and citizen is significantly reduced, and links between the face-to-face world of the village and the imagined community of the nation are undermined. In my conclusion, I reflect upon the implications of this development for Cambodians and Timorese, adrift in an atomizing liberal peace.

CHAPTER II

"EXTREMISTS" AND "HEROES": WAR-TORN CAMBODIA AND TIMOR

"I think that our people have a particular character. They are a little bit extremist."
Cambodian NGO worker, Phnom Penh, 1996

"Actually we have no idea who did what during the resistance. We only know we are a nation of heroes."
Timorese NGO worker, Dili, June 2005

From an international perspective, Cambodia and Timor-Leste emerged from decades of disastrous warfare into the pure light of international intervention under markedly similar circumstances. Both were wars that, from an international standpoint, made sense only in the logic of the Cold War. Once the Cold War was over, possibilities opened up for external intervention to bring both countries into the expanding circle of "post-conflict" states, subject to intrusive international attention in the interests of good governance. In Cambodia this happened quickly— the changed regional environment made ending the war a key interest of all major external protagonists, namely, the Soviet Union, China, and Vietnam. In East Timor, a relative backwater, the possibilities for ending the war were much more slender, requiring not only the emergence of an international movement determined to make the human rights atrocities in Timor into an international political issue, but also the significant weakening of the occupying Indonesian state. When these conditions fell into place, in both cases, United Nations peacekeeping operations were unrolled in what looked like very similar circumstances, involving small and impoverished Southeast Asian states suffering from twenty-five years of Cold War-fueled occupation, warfare, atrocity, and upheaval that had claimed the lives of up to a quarter of the population. In both cases, the end of the war was regarded as a new start—a year zero, in which not only a new state, but a new society, could be built on the ruins of the old.

However, this external view masks sharp differences between the two countries in terms of the nature of warfare in each case, the war's legacy, and the kinds of resources available to Cambodian and Timorese populations looking to an aid-dependent future. This chapter sketches out the ways in which the wars in Cambodia and Timor affected three key factors that were to prove significant in the unfolding peace: the production of the idea of the "nation"; the organization of nationalist movements that prescribed the substantive connection between the nation and the individual; and the ways in which these movements were able to harness economic resources that could be distributed as a means to cement such connections.

THE WAR IN CAMBODIA

In both Cambodia and Timor, nationalism was the major issue at stake during the wars. In Cambodia, nationalism was overlaid with communist ideological rhetoric, but ultimately, for the deposed head of state, former King Norodom Sihanouk, as for the mass murderers of the Pol Pot regime, and for Pol Pot's successors, the Vietnamese-backed People's Republic of Kampuchea, the war was about reclaiming, in the guise of the post-colonial state, a glorious era of Khmer domination over Southeast Asia: a future "more glorious than Angkor."[1]

The glories of Angkor, the ruined temples at the heart of a Khmer civilization that dominated mainland Southeast Asia between the eleventh and the fifteenth centuries, have provided the central motif of Cambodian nationalism and, also, in the words of historian David Chandler, its chief burden.[2] French colonial discourses describing Cambodian decline since the Angkorean era—a decline that allegedly would have ended in the submergence of the Khmer altogether beneath tides of encroaching Vietnamese and Thais had the French not imposed a "Protectorate"—were recirculated with increasing panic in post-colonial Cambodian politics. Both the myth of Angkor and the concern to resurrect Angkorean greatness were harnessed initially by contenders for power amongst the royal family and the urban elite; they were then swiftly monopolized by the king, Norodom Sihanouk, who dominated Cambodian politics in the 1950s and 60s with his state ideology of Buddhist Socialism and his Sangkum Reastr Niyum (Populist Society) movement, which was allegedly modeled on Angkorean state-society relations.[3] However, Angkorean dreams proved a slender foundation for managing a modern society, particularly as Indochina slipped into the bloody maw of the Cold War following American deployment of troops to Vietnam, and the commencement of carpet bombing of Cambodia in 1965.

Sihanouk was overthrown in 1970, but his visions of Oriental splendor lived on, notably in the ideals of the Khmer Rouge regime of Pol Pot. Although aided, albeit selectively, by North Vietnam during the early 1970s, the Khmer Rouge embraced the myth of Cambodia's decline at Vietnamese hands, and their regime reflected this legacy in two major ways: the ill-fated attempt to produce a "Super Great Leap Forward," based upon the belief that the builders of Angkor were at least capable of constructing, in short order, an irrigation scheme that could permit cultivation of five tonnes of rice per hectare; and the suicidal attacks on eastern Vietnam that took place when the failure to achieve this target was blamed upon Vietnamese infiltrators and saboteurs. These policies were not only ill-conceived, but were executed with such systematic brutality that up to two million Cambodians died as a direct result of them.[4]

---

[1] Kate Frieson, "The Political Nature of Democratic Kampuchea," *Pacific Affairs* 61,3 (1998): 405–29.

[2] David Chandler, "The Burden of Cambodia's Past," in *Cambodia and the International Community: The Quest for Peace, Development, and Democracy*, ed. Frederick Z. Brown and David G. Timberman (New York, NY: Asia Society, 1998), pp. 33–47.

[3] Penny Edwards, *Cambodge: The Cultivation of a Nation, 1860–1945*, (Honolulu, HI: University of Hawai'i Press, 2007).

[4] The most comprehensive account of this period is to be found in Ben Kiernan, *The Pol Pot Regime: Race, Power, and Genocide in Cambodia under the Khmer Rouge, 1975–1979* (Chiang Mai: Silkworm, 1997).

The Khmer Rouge regime ended when Vietnam invaded Cambodia in December 1978, reaching Phnom Penh on January 7, 1979. This invasion inaugurated a new civil war between the Vietnamese-supported regime installed in Phnom Penh and a coalition of resistance armies, including those of the Khmer Rouge, operating out of small enclaves and refugee camps on the Thai-Cambodian border. Regional and global interests entailed further international intervention in the conflict. A new proxy war resulted, in which China, Thailand, and, more distantly, the Western Cold War bloc supported the resistance while the Soviet bloc supported the Phnom Penh administration. The latter operated under the purview of Vietnamese government advisors and in the context of continued occupation of Cambodia by the Vietnamese army. The West imposed blanket trade and aid sanctions on the Phnom Penh administration; even Cambodia's seat at the United Nations was retained by the Khmer Rouge, while the UN Border Relief Operation fed, housed, and otherwise administered thousands of Cambodian refugees on the Thai border.

This situation continued throughout the 1980s and was important in creating deep divisions in Cambodian society that persisted well into the postwar era. The Phnom Penh administration was led by a group of former Khmer Rouge Eastern Zone commanders, who had fled to Vietnam ahead of a planned purge of Eastern Zone cadre. The group, including current Prime Minister Hun Sen and current Cambodian People's Party president, Chea Sim, called themselves the United Front for the National Salvation of Kampuchea, and subsequently formed the Politburo of a new People's Revolutionary Party of Kampuchea, the party that controlled the new People's Republic of Kampuchea (PRK) regime. The PRK was heavily dependent upon Vietnamese support, funding, protection, and advice throughout the 1980s. Evan Gottesman's study of the period indicates that the relationship was not an altogether happy one; however, it remained the *sine qua non* of the regime's existence, and the key challenge for the regime throughout the 1980s was promoting its own legitimacy in a context of extreme economic hardship, continued warfare, and the overt presence and dominance of the long-reviled Vietnamese at the center of government and across the rural heartland.[5]

Under the PRK, a new politics of "nation-building" emerged, inherited by its successor, the State of Cambodia (SoC) and the associated Cambodian People's Party (CPP). The latter dominates Cambodian politics today. This was a politics that eschewed flights of ideological fancy and delusions of ethnic grandeur for a practical concern with survival in the present. In the devastated aftermath of Democratic Kampuchea, and with the feared Vietnamese looking over their shoulders, the new regime embraced pragmatism as the only possible response. Gottesman describes the involved debates between Marxists and liberals, idealists and pragmatists, and between Vietnamese advisors and their Khmer counterparts, inside ministries such as those of Defense, Justice, and Interior, over questions of military and economic policy, citizens' rights, law, and policing. However, as revealing as these debates are with regard to the political orientations of individuals within the new regime, they were ultimately constrained in their import for the Cambodian people by the inability of the central government to achieve much in terms of policy

---

[5] Evan Gottesman, *Cambodia after the Khmer Rouge: Inside the Politics of Nation Building* (New Haven, CT: Yale University Press, 2002); see also Bunhaeng Ang and Martin Stuart Fox, *The Murderous Revolution: Bunhaeng Ang's Life with Deuch in Pol Pot's Kampuchea* (Bangkok: Orchid Press, 1998).

implementation. Military, police, and provincial authorities went their own way, and noncompliance with official directives was common. Within the PRK, the overriding preoccupation concerned how to extract resources and power from the provinces as a means to facilitate action by the central state.[6]

The solution to this problem was a de facto policy of delegation and deployment of patronage networks, which permitted provincial officials to reap personal financial rewards from taking on responsibility for state projects. Thus the "K5" project—the construction of an enormous barrier comprising earthworks and booby-trapped ditches along the Thai border, designed to prevent infiltration by resistance soldiers—was visualized initially as a centrally directed state project, mobilizing the masses in the spirited defense of the nation. However, it quickly degenerated into "an enormous network of self-supporting economic ventures involving provincial authorities and branches of the Ministries of Defense, Communications, and Commerce," supported by revenues raised by provincial authorities from logging and gem mining and by infusions of aid from the Soviet Union.[7] Goods intended for the border, including food and medical supplies for the workers, were siphoned off by provincial authorities and fed into patronage networks that supported local fiefdoms. Meanwhile, huge numbers of workers died in conditions explicitly compared to those under the DK.[8]

State-building in the 1980s comprised the establishment and cementing of clientelist networks running through the ministry, military, and provincial structures. These networks drew upon the cultural repertoires of clientelism that had characterized pre-war, and even pre-colonial, governance in Cambodia. In their new iteration, they were focused upon the eliciting of personal profits from state-led mobilizations prompted by Vietnamese ideals and supported by Soviet aid. Based on a solid foundation of self-interest guiding the actions of local authorities, whose early 1970s ideological zeal had been jaded by the appalling disaster of collectivization under Pol Pot, these structures proved highly durable, surviving the withdrawal of the Vietnamese, the collapse of the Soviet Union, the arrival of a peacekeeping operation, and the transition to a free market dependent on Western aid. The state as it emerged in the 1980s and persisted in the 1990s represented the business interests of a pragmatic Khmer elite, rather than either the ideological or cultural influence of Vietnam. It legitimized itself with respect to two basic claims: success in ousting Democratic Kampuchea and in restoring the food supply. The PRK and the SoC that succeeded it in 1989 reflected the extreme disillusionment with ideas touting Khmer greatness; however, it also provided a salutary lesson in the effective conduct of politics under conditions of dependence.

In the refugee camps on the border, quite a different narrative of contemporary history was emerging, which continues to reverberate in Cambodia today. For those exiled, Cambodia's position in the Cold War, particularly during the period of Vietnamese occupation in the 1980s, fostered long-standing anxieties, inherited at least from the French, regarding the possibility of Cambodia's imminent "disappearance" in the face of Vietnamese annexation. The harnessing of these anxieties to the international campaign—conducted by ASEAN, China, and Western

---

[6] Sorpong Peou, *Intervention and Change in Cambodia: Towards Democracy?* (New York, NY: St. Martin's Press, 2000).

[7] Gottesman, *Cambodia after the Khmer Rouge*, p. 233.

[8] Ibid., pp. 233–34.

powers—to contain supposed Vietnamese "expansionism" in Southeast Asia rendered them particularly troubling. The Vietnamese occupation of Cambodia was accompanied by rumors of a campaign of "Vietnamization"—a process characterized as comprising settlement, intermarriage, destruction of cultural artifacts, and repression of Khmer customs.

In Western writings, and in booklets produced and circulated in the refugee camps, emphasis was placed upon a supposed massive immigration of Vietnamese settlers and the systematic destruction of Khmer culture by the pro-Vietnamese regime. One resistance figure, Son Soubert, wrote that Vietnam's intention was "to colonise and Vietnamise Cambodia through a process of 'de-culturating' the Khmer people." He estimated that 700,000 settlers, as well as troops and administrators, had entered Cambodia under Vietnamese auspices and commented: "By 1990, the change of demography will be completed as was done in Cochinchina, former Cambodian territory, during the eighteenth and nineteenth centuries."[9]

Another report claimed that the settlers had brought with them prostitutes, criminals, and beggars, as well as diseases such as syphilis and leprosy, reflecting a familiar image of Vietnamese corruption.[10] One Western commentator sympathetic to the resistance reported a plan to settle "several million [Vietnamese] settlers, approximately one million of whom seem to have been in place by the close of the 1980s," and linked this to a policy of "'ethnocide'—the destruction of culture within those who carry it," a concept that further promotes the notion of a foreign taint implanted into a Cambodian body.[11] The resistance-aligned Khmer Buddhist Research Centre spread stories that Khmers in Phnom Penh were adopting Vietnamese dress, music, and dance styles and that respect for the Buddhist religion was being undermined. The author of the study commented, "It is hard to conclude whether Cambodia is now the real Khmer country or a second Vietnam."[12]

The liberation rhetoric of the PRK and the "Vietnamization" scare stories of the border resistance, each circulated with generous funding from international supporters, were both mutually exclusive and panic-stricken. Claims and counter-claims regarding who was corrupt and who was pure, who was "foreign" and who was "authentic/original," who was Vietnamese and who was Khmer—and even regarding the distinction between brutality and righteousness—abounded and came to be appellated to the different sides of the civil war itself, with each side claiming the moral high ground. These concerns are not far removed from overarching discourses of the Cold War itself, certainly as this was applied to the "communist threat" in Asia. They also strongly resemble the split personality routinely ascribed to Asians by Orientalist discourses, and they certainly speak to French colonial rhetoric, including that pertaining to the Khmer and the "Annamites." However, for the purposes of this study, the question of where these discourses "came from" is less significant here than their implications for postwar Cambodia.

---

[9] Son Soubert, "The Historical Dimensions of the Present Conflict in Cambodia," in *Buddhism and the Future of Cambodia* (Rithisen: Khmer Buddhist Research Centre, n.d.), p. 20. Son Soubert is currently a member of the Constitutional Council in Cambodia.

[10] Khmer Buddhist Research Centre, "The Vietnamization of Cambodia: An Irreversible Act? (on the basis of information collected in Cambodia)," *Buddhism and the Future of Cambodia* (Rithisen: Khmer Buddhist Research Centre, n.d.), p. 93.

[11] Marie Martin, *Cambodia: A Shattered Society*, trans. Mark W. McLeod (Berkeley, CA: University of California Press, 1994), pp. 229, 230.

[12] Khmer Buddhist Research Centre, "The Vietnamization of Cambodia," p. 92.

For the resistance on the border, the presence of the Vietnamese in the Khmer land (*srok khmae*) offered them an easy rallying cry, both locally and internationally. Coupled with the hardship of life within occupied Cambodia and the availability of humanitarian relief on the border, the opposition's nationalist stance—and their rhetoric decrying the disappearance of the nation and Vietnamization—attracted a steady flow of refugees to the West. While the resistance was not able, from this position, to defeat the armies of the PRK, it remained itself unbeatable. A grinding stalemate ensued, promising to last for as long as the external powers were willing to maintain the flow of arms and funding.

The end of the Cold War ended external interest in the conflict; outside parties began in 1991 to pressure the Cambodian contenders to reach a peace agreement. However, the parties that came to the negotiating table in Paris differed from one another in one characteristic that was to prove decisive in postwar politics. For the resistance, a decade of international support in exile had produced an unproblematic dependence, in which a familiar local rhetoric of anti-Vietnamese nationalism coincided with Cold War tropes of anti-communism, in a manner that facilitated an unquestioned and essentially one-way flow of resources to resistance leaders and, through them, to the people they administered in the camps. For the Phnom Penh administration, dependence had been a much more difficult experience. As in many other Soviet-style administrations during the Cold War, intense administrative scrutiny and an inflexible state ideology that was largely divorced from everyday politics had combined with aspects of the local repertoire of traditional governance forms to produce administrative and political subcultures that were evasive, flexible, and highly personal, dependent upon networks of trust and loyalty between well-placed individuals to get things done, rather than upon Western-style institutions. By the end of the 1980s, the resistance was accustomed to heavy dependence, and a rhetoric of victimhood, whereas the Phnom Penh administration was accustomed to development of flexible mechanisms that could, whatever else happened, hold things together in the face of repeated legitimacy crises.

It is worth noting that each side attempted to nurture its respective modus operandi through the peace process. For the resistance, key provisions in the Paris Agreements, emphasized in the peace negotiations and revisited time and again during the implementation of the Accords by the United Nations Transitional Authority in Cambodia, related to the status of the Vietnamese. Continual revisiting of the question of whether Vietnamese forces had "really" withdrawn from Cambodia, as required by the terms of the accords, or were hiding in the jungles or among ethnic Vietnamese populations, was used as a means of undermining the legitimacy of UNTAC or "*yuon*-TAC," as the peacekeeping mission was dubbed by the border resistance parties.[13] Meanwhile, the Phnom Penh administration focused throughout the negotiations and the implementation of the Paris Accords upon retaining its administrative structures and armed forces intact and with as much freedom of operation as possible. While the Paris Accords mandated UNTAC to supervise all the administrative structures of the various parties to the conflict, the level of supervision UNTAC managed to exert over these was, in practice, minimal, hampered by shortages of Khmer-speaking personnel on the UN's side, as well as by

---

[13] *Yuon* is an epithet widely used by Khmers to refer to Vietnamese; it is usually considered to be derogatory.

stratagems that had been honed in the context of the far more intrusive Vietnamese presence on the side of the Phnom Penh administration.[14]

Both these positions in 2008 remain at the core of the political platforms of the parties that emerged from the resistance and the Phnom Penh regime. The Sam Rainsy Party (SRP), which remains the most viable opposition party in Cambodia, continues to mobilize a significant minority vote in every election, particularly in urban areas, largely on the grounds of its denunciation of the CPP-dominated state apparatus and military as not only corrupt and exploitative but as specifically "communist" and "Vietnamese." The CPP, however, has been effective in blocking the SRP from making major inroads in rural Cambodia because the CPP has maintained its highly flexible and impressively cohesive organizational structure, which operates concomitantly as a machine for patronage, protection, and, when required, intimidation and violence. For rural Cambodians, the CPP structure is ever present and inevitable, whereas the international support the SRP has repeatedly called for appears, from the perspective of the village, more distant and far less reliable.[15]

The remaining chapters of this study tell the story of how the CPP has achieved and sustained this effect under conditions of aid dependence, contrasting this performance with that of the FRETILIN (Frente Revolucionária de Timor-Leste Independente, The Revolutionary Front for an Independent East Timor) government in Timor-Leste, as a means to uncover the experience of aid dependence at the local level in post-conflict countries, and to illustrate how both the mass of the rural population and the elite stake out room to maneuver, within the modalities of the international aid regime. Within Cambodia, there has been a strong tendency among critics of the government to gloss the experience of the 1990s, along with the previous twenty years, in terms of a continued decline of the Khmer nation—a *longue durée* approach that emphasizes the corruption of the Khmer character resulting from foreign domination. A self-critical mood, which focuses on faults in the Khmer psyche, has led to a self-characterization of the Khmer as "extremists"—a population that is inherently unruly and prone to orgies of violence, and which thus requires a firm hand on the tiller, whether that hand belongs to the "strongman" Hun Sen or the technocrats of the World Bank and United Nations Development Programme.[16]

However, this study will argue that the performance of the CPP in using the advent of a neoliberal aid regime in the early 1990s as a means to shore up its crumbling patrimonial structures—structures developed from traditional repertoires in the context of an occupying regime expressing specifically Soviet-style ideological

---

[14] Michael Doyle, *UN Peacekeeping in Cambodia: UNTAC's Civil Mandate* (Boulder, CO: Lynne Rienner, 1995).

[15] I have written at length about this, and about the way in which traditional patron-client relationships have been adapted to meet the challenges of contemporary electoral politics, in a previous monograph entitled *The Political Economy of Cambodia's Transition, 1991–2002* (London: RoutledgeCurzon, 2003).

[16] The attribution of the crises of contemporary Khmer history to a "Khmer mentality" has surfaced in a variety of writings and statements. The Cambodian interviewee quoted at the beginning of this chapter represents one example; another is a book published in California by a Cambodian-American with a doctorate in psychology, which attributed to the Khmer a split personality that veered unpredictably between passivity and uncontrollable rage. See Bit Seanglim, *The Warrior Heritage: A Psychological Perspective on Cambodian Trauma* (El Cerrito: Bit Seanglim, 1991).

preferences—suggests not a fatal flaw in the Cambodian national character, but the profoundly counterproductive impact of neoliberal aid regimes themselves. The next chapter discusses the nature of neoliberal aid regimes in detail. They are characterized by a focus on "rolling back" the state and subjecting its activities to rigid and purportedly technical evaluations derived from ideals of "good governance." The latter are based upon ideological assumptions about the beneficial workings of "the market" and its superiority to the state in promoting efficient economic growth. This is a view that leaves little room for the deployment of resources in the interests of politics. Yet, in Cambodia, politics was needed to create a basis upon which distinct regimes could reunify and to relegitimize centralized authority. Consequently, in Cambodia, the pressing power of neoliberal donors became one more occupying force, which not only could be evaded, but had to be evaded to create political space for the kinds of accommodations that would end the war and restore order to the country. Neoliberal aid regimes, as explained in the next chapter, resemble Soviet-style communist regimes in that they are particularly bad at producing a living, breathing, and effective politics. Both systems, in operating from abstract templates that pay no heed to reality on the ground, require the emergence of an informal politics that can lubricate the system and plug its more gaping holes. In recognizing this failure of neoliberal regimes, I do not intend to elevate the informal system that emerges in compensation to a status of cultural or functional legitimacy. Rather my aim is to point out that the application of dogma does not preempt local creativity, but does preempt useful discussion of the pros and cons of possible alternatives. The neo-patrimonial politics of the CPP is often regarded as the cultural "Other" that neoliberal aid seeks to displace. While acknowledging the historical record that suggests patron-clientism enjoys a degree of cultural authenticity, this study argues that the continued expansion of neo-patrimonial politics in the 1990s represents an exploitative, often violent, but, in the circumstances, necessary prop to neoliberal policy, in a context where possible alternative forms of development and politics are not discussed, in a conspiracy of silence that benefits elites and donors alike.

THE WAR IN TIMOR

In Timor-Leste, the FRETILIN government of 2002 to 2007 came to power in circumstances that more closely resembled those of the Cambodian resistance than those of the CPP. Most of the FRETILIN central committee members who survived Indonesia's brutal twenty-five year occupation of the country were those who had spent the war in exile, although FRETILIN's External Delegation did not benefit from the kind of international assistance available to Cambodia's resistance leaders—quite the contrary. When FRETILIN's exiles returned, they found that their notion of Timorese nationalism was significantly out of step with that of the resistance at home. Indeed, FRETILIN's exiled leaders and its rank-and-file members and supporters within East Timor emerged from the war with sharply different perspectives on the question of nationhood and political participation. Unlike in Cambodia, where anti-Vietnamese nationalism held the resistance together for several years despite internal division, for FRETILIN, the contending perspectives could not be conveniently glossed through the bandying about of racist epithets.

Unlike Cambodia, which was characterized broadly by ethnic homogeneity and a unified system of precolonial government, East Timor is a country of great diversity. According to Elizabeth Traube, the various ethno-linguistic groups of Portuguese Timor took pride in their difference from their neighbors; however, they were linked by a complex and highly ritualized web of exchange obligations, which had given rise to political alliances across ethnic lines, to the widespread use of Tetum as the *lingua franca,* and to the common practice of traveling for trade or social interaction. Portuguese colonialism, until the late nineteenth century, took the form of trading posts that inserted themselves forcibly into this complex of exchanges, disempowering some groups within the system, but empowering others.[17] Power in pre- and early-colonial Timor resided in the hands of those who were influential in ritual systems of tribute and the organization of marital alliances. The entry of the Portuguese into this system added cloth, guns, and iron tools to the mix, but essentially left the system intact.[18] The Portuguese ruled indirectly until the late nineteenth century, awarding military positions to existing local kings (*liurai*) and maintaining the kings' loyalty through practices of divide and rule.

Although this was a process that involved considerable violence, it was not a process that drastically transformed the nature of Timorese economic and political action, and rebellions did not take on an explicitly nationalist form.[19] The CAVR (Comissão de Acolhimento, Verdade, e Reconciliação de Timor-Leste, Commission for Reception, Truth, and Reconciliation in East Timor) report says of this period in Portuguese history, "For the Portuguese, the price of this policy of divide and rule was persistent localized resistance to Portuguese authority. For the East Timorese, the price was perpetual weakness and disunity."[20] Uprisings were highly varied in form, including rebellions against local chiefs, wars among clans or ethnic groups, and revolts by followers of messianic cults, as well as assaults upon Portuguese power per se.[21]

However, as Geoffrey Gunn, John Taylor, and Elizabeth Traube all point out, the shift in Portuguese rule towards ambitions for territorial administration in the late-nineteenth century, combined with rapid advances in Portuguese military technology, entailed that Portuguese rule became more intrusive as the twentieth century began. Portuguese attempts to introduce territorial administration, and to increase its exploitation of the economy via the introduction of coffee as a cash crop for export, created more widespread discontent than had previously been the case. Furthermore, the division of the territory into *sucos*—the level of princes rather than kings in the traditional system—undercut the position of the *liurai*. This move was staunchly resisted by the *liurai*—the 1912 uprising was put down at the cost of 25,000 lives. Once the 1912 rebellion had been crushed, and Portuguese territorial administration fully established, the territory entered a period of quiescence that

[17] Elizabeth Traube, "Mambai Perspectives on Colonization and Decolonization," in *East Timor at the Crossroads: The Forging of a Nation,* ed. Peter Carey and G. Carter Bentley (London: Cassell, 1995), pp. 44–45.

[18] John Taylor, *East Timor: The Price of Freedom* (London: Zed Books, 1999), pp. 4–5.

[19] Geoffrey Gunn, "The Five-Hundred-Year Timorese *Funu,*" in *Bitter Flowers, Sweet Flowers: East Timor, Indonesia, and the World Community,* ed. Richard Tanter, Mark Selden, and Stephen R. Shalmom (Sydney: Pluto, 2001), pp. 3–14.

[20] Commission for Reception, Truth, and Reconciliation in East Timor (CAVR), *Chega!,* Final Report of the Commission for Reception, Truth, and Reconciliation in East Timor (Dili: CAVR, 2005), online at http://www.etan.org/news/2006/cavr.htm, accessed September 10, 2007, Pt. 3: History of the Conflict, p. 9.

[21] Gunn, "The Five-Hundred-Year Timorese *Funu,*" p. 7.

lasted through to 1975. The single major armed challenge to Portuguese rule during the period is the Viqueque uprising of 1959, and it is interesting to note that this uprising appears to have been initiated by Indonesian exiles, rather than by the Timorese themselves.

Liurai hung on, existing in an "uneasy truce" with the Portuguese administration, usually exercising influence on who would be appointed to local positions. Meanwhile, the emergence of the fascist New Order regime in Portugal produced the Colonial Act that imposed new categories of citizenship upon colonial subjects. These were divided into "assimilated" and "unassimilated"—"assimilated" characterized those who had reached a "Portuguese standard" of civilization. In denying the unassimilated the same rights as the assimilated, the Act had the effect of intensifying the oppression of the majority of the population who were found to be "unassimilated." A 1950 census found that only 1,541 persons of the indigenous population were "civilized," compared to 434,907 "*nao-civilizado.*"[22] Along with around 2,000 "*mestiço*" (mixed blood) persons and fewer than 4,000 non-indigenous (including Europeans, Chinese, and Goans), only this tiny number were awarded voting rights in colonial Timor, or the right to study in government schools. For the rest, life was harsh. Jill Joliffe suggests that forced labor and brutal corporal punishments, including whipping and caning, continued until after the Second World War.[23] Gunn describes East Timor in 1975 as a Latinized-creolized society par excellence,[24] with deep social cleavages dividing a Portuguese-oriented, and partially Portuguese-descended, elite, who bore Portuguese names, adopted Catholicism, and spoke Portuguese, from the "Maubere" mountain people, who retained traditional names, animist beliefs, and local languages. James Dunn describes 80 percent of the population as living, in the 1960s, in conditions little different from those that prevailed at the start of Portuguese colonization.[25] Portuguese colonialism did little to promote either institutions or infrastructure that might advance a national identity or a nationalist cause. Apart from a few roads in Dili, none of the highways were paved. Although primary school enrollment increased tenfold between 1950 and 1970, only ten East Timorese held university degrees in 1964. In the early 1970s, 90 percent of the Timorese people were illiterate, and only one public high school existed in the territory.

In 1974, the Carnation Revolution in Portugal suddenly raised the question of independence for East Timor. Aside from discussions among a handful of elite individuals, the question of independence had barely been raised at home, but within a mere eighteen months political parties were formed, a right-wing coup against the Portuguese administration had taken place, this coup had been militarily challenged by a leftist party that quickly prevailed after a short but destructive civil war, and independence had been declared. Xanana Gusmão, in his autobiography, described the experience of this process as being "hurled into a pit of

---

[22] Donald Weatherbee, "Portuguese Timor: An Indonesian Dilemma," *Asian Survey* 6 (1966): 684. Cited in Jill Joliffe, *East Timor: Nationalism and Colonialism* (St. Lucia: University of Queensland Press, 1978), p. 42.

[23] Joliffe, *East Timor*, pp. 47–48.

[24] Gunn, "The Five-Hundred-Year Timorese *Funu*," p. 12.

[25] James Dunn, *East Timor: A Rough Passage to Independence* (Double Bay: Longueville, 2003), p. 25.

independence."[26] It lasted only a few months; on December 7, 1975, the neighboring Indonesians, under cover of the Cold War, launched a devastating and bloody invasion and occupied Timor for the next twenty-four years.

Arguably, it was the war against the Indonesians, led by the small nationalist movement that emerged in 1974–75, rather than the experience of Portuguese colonialism, that has provided the grist for a specifically national Timorese identity, although it is noteworthy that the division between the party of the right—the União Democrática Timorense (UDT)—and the party of the left—(FRETILIN)—persisted almost to the end of the occupation. The UDT was partly duped and partly coerced into supporting the invasion early on, and even once their relations with the Indonesians had turned more or less publicly sour, intense mutual distrust between UDT and FRETILIN persisted. The two parties did not unite organizationally until April 1998, only a month before the resignation of Suharto and the beginnings of Indonesia's withdrawal from East Timor.

However, the Indonesian occupation did produce a concerted and breathtakingly determined national resistance effort, which was as united in its goal as it was divided in terms of its organization and ideology. The brutal Indonesian attack of 1975 presaged twenty-four years of further bloodshed and atrocity, perpetrated by Indonesian troops against an isolated Timorese population. Resistance to the Indonesian Occupation comprised three main phases. During the initial period, from 1975 to 1979, the territory was divided between an Indonesian-held area in the north and a FRETILIN-held area in the mountains and the south. Fighting took place along front lines between FRETILIN's armed wing, the Forças Armadas da Libertação Nacional de Timor-Leste (FALINTIL, Armed Forces of the National Liberation of East Timor) and the Indonesian military. During this period, FRETILIN continued to administer the majority of the population and saw itself as a legitimate government under attack, rather than a resistance force. However, massive assaults on its bases, the consequences of air attacks on the civilians under its control, and the death of FALINTIL's commander, Nicolau Lobato, at the end of 1978 brought about a new phase, during which FRETILIN relinquished control of territory and FALINTIL retreated to secret hideouts in the mountains, from where its members mounted sporadic guerrilla raids on the Indonesian army.

The period from 1979 to 1987 was the most difficult for the resistance movement, which was still largely based upon a conception of military struggle. During this time, the strength of the military force was reduced from around 5,000 fighters in 1979 to about 100 in 1987, reflecting the immense military power brought to bear on the situation by the Indonesians and the lack of any kind of material support from outside for the guerrillas. During this period, Xanana Gusmão, appointed commander-in-chief of FALINTIL and president of the National Council of Revolutionary Resistance in 1981, began to reorganize the resistance, breaking the guerrilla forces away from FRETILIN and forming a nationalist united front, the National Council of Maubere (later Timorese) Resistance. By the end of the 1980s, the guerrilla movement was almost exhausted, but the issue of independence was kept alive by a growing activism, in the form of protests and demonstrations, among students and young people in Timorese towns. This shift coincided with the end of the Cold War and the emergence of a new international agenda focused on issues of

---

[26] Xanana Gusmão, "Autobiography," in Xanana Gusmão, *To Resist Is to Win!*, ed. Sarah Niner (Richmond, Victoria: Aurora Books, 2000), p. 34.

human rights and democracy promotion. Wider international publicity of the intense sufferings of the Timorese, of whom about a third had by this time been killed, exerted new pressure on the Indonesians, despite continued support by countries such as the US and Australia for the Suharto regime.

In the end, events in Indonesia shifted the balance in Timor's favor. The Asian financial crisis in 1997 and the fall in 1998 of General Suharto, Indonesia's president for thirty years, weakened Indonesian resolve to pursue the struggle. The Indonesians granted the Timorese the choice, through a popular consultation organized by the United Nations, between continued integration with Indonesia and independence. The Timorese voted for independence by a majority of almost four to one, unleashing an orgy of violence by Indonesian troops that razed to the ground the capital city, Dili, along with many other towns and villages. Intervention by an Australian-led peacekeeping force, and subsequent UN administration, paved the way for independence in 2002.

As in the case of Cambodia, the story of East Timorese independence is a story of home rule bestowed in a hurry in an atmosphere of regional tension and international intrigue. In Timor, as in Cambodia, the success of nationalist movements elsewhere dictated the timing of independence. In both countries, colonial policy had created an elite that was tiny, ideologically polarized, and ill-equipped to orchestrate a coherent national response to external pressures.

Like the elite in Cambodia, the Timorese elite was deeply divided along Cold War lines. The UDT was the first Timorese party to form, and it was formed primarily of pro-Portuguese plantation owners, including the Carrascalão brothers, whose father was a Portuguese *deportado*. FRETILIN also drew its membership from the elite, incorporating a pro-Western group, represented by José Ramos-Horta, as well as a group of students who had returned from study in Portugal, who had been heavily influenced by Marxism and represented the radical wing, with Mari Alkatiri as their spokesperson, and also a third group, made up of soldiers from the Portuguese colonial army, led by Nicolau and Rogerio Lobato. The common ground among these various groups was the influence of African nationalism, an influence that prompted the choice of the acronym FRETILIN, inspired by the Mozambiquan movement FRELIMO (Frente de Libertação de Moçambique).

FRETILIN's narrative of the nation in the early years is difficult to pin down, in part because of the wide range of opinions espoused by its small group of leading members. Some much-debated issues include FRETILIN's declaration that it was "the sole representative" of the East Timorese people, a claim based on FRETILIN's "belief of the allegiance of Timor-Leste's indigenous-agrarian majority."[27] The association of this claim with the emergence of the ideology of Mauberism quickly awarded FRETILIN an image as the representative of the poor, as opposed to the landowning elite who comprised UDT.

Mauberism was an ideology that identified the nation with the *Maubere*—poor peasants in the hills—and, to a great extent, an idealized vision of the relationship forged between FALINTIL—an armed force that brought together soldiers from the Portuguese colonial army and the urban nationalists of 1975—and the mountain people, a relationship that has formed the basis of Timorese national identity. The practice, on the part of FALINTIL leaders, of taking on Timorese names—Alexandre (Xanana) Gusmão adopted the name Kay Rala, while Francisco Guterrez adopted the

---

[27] CAVR, *Chega!*, Pt. 3, p. 27.

name Lú-Olo—and participating in a variety of animist rituals permitted the bridging of elite Portuguese-Timorese nationalism with a nationalized version of "traditional culture" associated with the so-called Maubere. The adoption of the song *O Foho Ramelau* (Oh, Mount Ramelau)—a hymn to Timor's highest peak—as the FRETILIN anthem reflected an idealism that regarded the mountains of the interior as the source of Timorese strength and character. Xanana Gusmão, who was born into an educated family living in Laleia in the east, not far from the sea, describes his first foray into the mountainous interior, shortly after the Indonesian invasion:

> This was my first immersion in the belly of my Homeland! I experienced an atmosphere I had never known: welcoming fogs that took us into their cool embrace and imparted a soft hue to the ochre-brown earth that sustained and gave life to enormous *ai bubur*, eucalyptus trees. I learnt to truly appreciate the songs of my Homeland one night in an old hut, harmonies disappearing out into the cold darkness, the old men and women competing with the passionate but not yet tempered voices of the youth. I celebrated my first real encounter with my pure mountain origins, genuinely pure, by eating *koto Moruk*, bitter bean, and drinking *daulorok*, palm wine, to which the suffocating smoke of the fires lent a human breath.[28]

Xanana concludes this passage in a manner that highlights the importance of the war by noting how it spurred the elite to embrace a conception of the nation as defined by "Mauberism": "It was a bitter delight to find an identity amongst the crumbling explosions of war, a war that had pushed me into this open space of the Homeland, confused, tired, and searching for my place to fight."[29]

Despite these flights of rhetoric, the relationship of Mauberism, as produced during the war against the Indonesians, and the nationalism of the elite that had formed under Portuguese rule was a tense one. In one essay, written during the resistance era, Xanana Gusmão specifically delinked the Maubere identity from Portuguese influence: "We energetically repudiate that the struggle, and the suffering of our people, can be limited to 'the preservation of Portuguese culture,' and it is our repudiation that constitutes the principal defining aspect of the Maubere People's historical identity."[30] In making this statement, Xanana rejected the major cleavage in Timorese society under colonialism—the cleavage between the tiny Mestizo elite, which spoke Portuguese and took Portuguese names, and the ethnically diverse peasant population, which used traditional languages, names, and religions. In the context of the nationalist struggle, Xanana asserted, "It is all the people of East Timor who resist the barbarian occupation of their homeland"—thus asserting the equal contribution of all sections of society, from the FALINTIL guerrillas in the mountains, to the clandestine movement of urban activists in the East Timor's towns, to Timorese students studying in Indonesian universities across the archipelago, to the External Delegation in Lisbon and Lusophone Africa. This

---

[28] Xanana Gusmão, "Autobiography," p. 44.

[29] Ibid.

[30] Xanana Gusmão, "A History that Beats in the Maubere Soul," in Xanana Gusmão, *To Resist Is to Win!*, ed. Sarah Niner (Richmond, Victoria: Aurora Books, 2000), pp. 85–126.

vaunted equality, asserted by revolutionaries like Xanana, remained a significant legacy of the era of Indonesian occupation.

This was particularly so because of the socio-economic changes wrought by the period of Indonesian rule. Two aspects of the Indonesian occupation contributed to transforming the links between towns and villages in East Timor: the military and the developmental. Military operations required the construction of infrastructure to facilitate the movement of troops; this construction contributed to establishing what Benedict Anderson calls a "skein of journeys through which [the state] was experienced."[31] Constructed for the military, the road network, as it emerged, entailed new types of mobility for locals, which paralleled the pyramid of subdistrict, district, and provincial/national hierarchies of power.

At the same time, human rights abuses were visited indiscriminately on the population, on a wide scale, without respect for ethnicity, class, or political orientation. The ethnic ties proclaimed by the pro-independence party Apodeti before the invasion offered no protection from Indonesian assault; rich mestizos and penniless Maubere were similarly threatened. Anderson suggests that this equalizing violence emerges from "a deep inability" on the part of Indonesia "to imagine East Timor as Indonesian," given the problematic nature of Indonesian identity itself and the strong connection between the imagined community of Indonesia itself and Dutch colonial boundaries.[32] While it was somewhat awkward for many Indonesians to conceive of East Timorese as fellow citizens, the violence inflicted on East Timor did become a key element of Indonesian nationalism, particularly from the perspective of the military. The violence in East Timor justified the military's paramount role in New Order politics and gave an aura of unity and heroic purpose to an organization that might otherwise have appeared bloated and fat.

On the Timorese side, the same violence encouraged a new equality that transcended any preexisting social cleavage, as it was based on a common narrative of the Timorese nation as the collective victim of Indonesian atrocity. From the earliest days of the invasion in 1975, a new sense of unity among Timorese was confirmed. The mass displacement triggered by the invasion caused hundreds of thousands of civilians to flee into the mountains "with FRETILIN." FRETILIN established itself as the territorial government in the mountainous "liberated zones." Thanks to the brutality of the Indonesian invasion, upwards of 300,000 people migrated into these regions, and whole towns were left practically abandoned.[33] Although some of this migration represented spontaneous departure for ancestral areas, in other places it was specifically organized by FRETILIN, on a voluntary or compulsory basis. Testimony received by the CAVR underlines the importance of the liberated zones for the process of "nation-building" that had been so sorely missing up to that point. According to one FRETILIN cadre of the time, the argument for compulsory evacuation went as follows: "If we don't prepare the people

---

[31] Benedict Anderson, *Imagined Communities: Reflections on the Origin and Spread of Nationalism* (London: Verso, 1991), p. 115.

[32] Benedict Anderson, "Imagining East Timor," *Arena Magazine* 4 (April–May 1993), republished in *Lusotopie,* 2001, online at http://www.lusotopie.sciencespobordeaux.fr/anderson.pdf, p. 234.

[33] CAVR, *Chega!*, Pt. 7.3, p. 17.

politically, morally, and mentally, then we will not be able to maintain our legitimacy and fulfill our duty as the main party in Timor."[34]

In the *bases de apoios* (logistics bases), FRETILIN organized food production and education services. Health care was organized, based upon traditional herbs; youth and women's organizations taught hygiene and literacy and buried the dead. Cadres from different areas took responsibility for organizing people they recognized from their home regions. The priority was the provision of political education, through "enlightenment programmes" designed to "encourage the spirit of nationalism and support the national liberation struggle."[35]

The programmes reflected the dual aim of FRETILIN to raise a specifically nationalist, East Timorese consciousness among a population accustomed to locating its identity within a variety of intricate social hierarchies and cleavages, and, in the process, to foster a social revolution that would not merely secure independence from the Indonesians and the Portuguese, but also would liberate the country from the forces of "obscurantism." As such, cultural forms originating from different regions of the country were promulgated, alongside political consciousness, as a specifically national heritage, in a manner intended to break down divisions among Timorese from different regions and backgrounds and to encourage their solidarity in the face of the *malae* (foreigners, in this case Indonesians).

However, this period of FRETILIN control was short-lived, as the Indonesian army closed in and the bases were ultimately destroyed, leaving the resistance, and FRETILIN, in disarray, with many of its founding members dead. A new Central Committee was convened in 1981, comprising Xanana, Mau Hunu, and nine new members. At this conference, FRETILIN decided to ratify the Marxist-Leninist position put forward at a previous conference in 1977. The CAVR reports that it was unable, during its investigations of this period, to find any evidence at all about the organizational structure of the party at this time; the report speculates that "it is possible that [the party] consisted only of the Central Committee, which had no subordinate organs operating below it."[36]

Equally, the Revolutionary Council of National Resistance, created during this same meeting as a united-front umbrella organization to encourage contributions from a broader resistance, appeared practically nonexistent beyond the few FALINTIL cells left in operation. While it officially claimed to maintain structures at the district, subdistrict, and even village level, in many places no such structures existed below the central council. One activist described the movement as "just a kind of tactic to signal that an armed front [of the] Resistance, which wanted to continue the struggle, still existed."[37]

FALINTIL itself was forced to disaggregate into cells of three or four people, which were kept on the move. Cadres worked to build links between these cells and the population; these links primarily involved provision of logistical support. This subordination of the civilian wing to the military wing moved FALINTIL to the center of the resistance struggle, with FRETILIN playing a subordinate role. Decisions were increasingly made on the hoof by FALINTIL commanders, and

---

[34] Mario Nicolau Dos Reis, FRETILIN cadre in Baucau, 1975, testimony to the CAVR. See CAVR, *Chega!*, Pt. 7.3, 20.

[35] CAVR, *Chega!*, Pt. 5.2, 10.

[36] Ibid., Pt. 5, p. 27.

[37] Ibid., Pt. 5, p. 28.

Xanana, as the commander of FALINTIL, organized a restructuring of FALINTIL in 1984 without consulting the party. From this point onward, the struggle began to be oriented towards influencing international public opinion. There was little hope of achieving the unilateral expulsion of the Indonesians. Rather, FALINTIL operated as a symbol of Timorese resistance, and a reminder to the outside world of the illegality and brutality of the Indonesian regime.

Recognition of this shift, and of the importance, consequently, of gaining the support of other parties, such as UDT, and of forging a closer alliance with the Catholic Church, led to a further rethinking on the part of Xanana and some others within FRETILIN. In 1984, Marxist-Leninism was dropped as the ideology of the resistance, and the idea of separating FALINTIL from FRETILIN was mooted. In 1987, FALINTIL was taken out of FRETILIN, and, as its commander, Xanana resigned his FRETILIN membership. At the same time, the National Council of Maubere Resistance was formed. The CNRM (Conselho Nacional de Resistência Maubere) increasingly took the lead in promoting the struggle for independence on the international stage, under the auspices of José Ramos Horta from 1989.

Paradoxically, as the ideological orientation of the struggle moved away from theoretical Marxism and towards a broad notion of a primordial nationalism, conceived of as "Mauberism" and based upon the cultures of the mountain peoples, in the mid-1980s, the nature of the struggle became at once more urban and more international. By the end of the 1980s, there were fewer than one hundred FALINTIL guerrillas left, and military victory was out of the question. Greater efforts were made from this time onward to organize and mobilize a clandestine movement in Timor's villages and towns. This clandestine movement had long been used to feed and provision the guerrillas, but it was increasingly used to political effect, as a way of showing the outside world the strength of Timorese resistance to the annexation of their land, particularly following the Indonesian policy of opening up Timor to settlement and visits by non-Timorese, which was ongoing from 1989.

The activism of the clandestine movement through the 1990s primarily reflects the courage and tenacity of thousands of Timorese people. However, it also reflects the policies of the Indonesians themselves and the ways in which the Indonesian occupation had changed and politicized Timorese society. As one veteran of the clandestine movement put it:

> ... most Timorese-educated people were educated in the Indonesian time— almost 100 percent. From the Portuguese time, you can count on your fingers the number of people educated. Not more than two hundred went through university. But mostly we were educated by the Indonesians. From our generation, we fought against Indonesia, but we were educated by the Indonesians. We had our eyes opened because they sent us to school. That's how we won independence.[38]

A combination of violent and indiscriminate repression, the *Panca Sila* ideology,[39] and hearts-and-minds campaigning via new developmentalist policies on the part of

---

[38] Benedeito Barros, personal interview, Dili, April 2005.

[39] The fivefold principles of Panca Sila are regarded as the philosophical foundations of the Indonesian state. They are: belief in one true God, universalism, nationalism, consensual democracy, and social justice.

the Indonesians were all significant factors in promoting secular nationalism from a minority sport in 1974 to a mass movement in the 1990s. East Timor had always been the poorest province in Indonesia; over 42 percent of its people were estimated to live below the poverty line in 1996, as compared to an Indonesian average of 18 percent. The vast majority of the population lived off subsistence agriculture; agricultural productivity was low, and off-farm income scarce. The majority of the population were poorly educated, not to mention politically suspect by Indonesian officials, and consequently could not gain access to well-paid jobs in public administration. Because unskilled labor was not in demand, they remained "trapped in unproductive self-employment in subsistence agriculture."[40]

As a province with a large military and civil service establishment, moreover, East Timor suffered from one of the largest rates of consumption inequality.[41] Indonesian military and civil officials were paid, and lived, just as well as their colleagues in other provinces. The Timorese, by contrast, were on average poorer than other provincial populations. This inequality achieved extra salience through its coincidence with the nationalist boundary of identity between "Indonesian" and "Timorese." Equally significantly, in terms of its radicalizing effect, in the 1990s, following the opening-up campaign, opportunities for urban Timorese, at least, suddenly expanded. Economic growth rates reached 10 percent per year. Educational opportunities grew, as Timorese students began to be sent all over the Indonesian archipelago for higher education, and growing numbers of Timorese were imbued with Indonesian ideas concerning the importance of independent nationhood, as publicly celebrated in the twenty-seventh province on Indonesia's Independence Day every August 17. Through the education system, also, the Indonesians promoted the status of both Bahasa and Tetum as national and local languages, easing communication in a territory that boasts eighteen mother tongues. They built roads, schools, and clinics throughout the territory, exposing mountain people to the benefits of statehood. And as if to ensure that these efforts bore political fruit, the Indonesian army in the meantime pursued a relentless and indiscriminate campaign of horrific atrocities and abuse, forcing the question of independence onto the agenda in every village in the land.

The coincidence of changes in administration and society with the promotion of the nationalist ideology of "Mauberism" galvanized urban Timorese into increasingly open opposition to the Indonesian occupation. The links between urban protestors and mountain guerrillas was expressed precisely through the imagining of a national community based upon Mauberism; as one member of the Timorese Student Movement commented, from 1987, FALINTIL "existed in the mountains as a symbol, not as an important tool to directly challenge the Indonesian forces and win the war."[42]

Concomitantly, the diplomatic front became more important as a means to mobilize international support, particularly after the Santa Cruz massacre in 1991.

---

[40] This characterization is taken from Anne Booth, "Africa in Asia? The Development Challenges Facing Eastern Indonesia and East Timor," *Oxford Development Studies* 32,1 (2004): 19–35.

[41] Inequality measured by household consumption. Ibid.

[42] Constancio Pinto, "The Student Movement and the Independence Struggle in East Timor: An Interview," in *Bitter Flowers, Sweet Flowers: East Timor, Indonesia, and the World Community*, pp. 31–42.

The incarceration of Xanana Gusmão in Cipinang jail from 1992, initially seen as a major blow for the resistance, turned out to be a blessing in disguise. Compared to FALINTIL's remote mountain redoubts, Cipinang turned out to be a far better base from which Xanana could mobilize international attention and support, operate as a figurehead for Timorese nationalism, and organize the various branches of the resistance.[43] In the aftermath of the broadcast on the evening news of the atrocity at Santa Cruz, in 1991, a number of elements came together—a courageous and highly mobilized mass movement in the towns; a heroic guerrilla force representing the spirit of the Timorese nation in the hills; a Nelson Mandela-like figure in jail in Jakarta; and a scandalized international community—and the pressure on the Indonesians began to build.

Ongoing repression, however, meant that the resistance continued to operate in a very ad hoc way. According to FRETILIN leaders interviewed in 2005, many Timorese simply assumed that the resistance was equivalent to FRETILIN because the Indonesians consistently drew this connection. FRETILIN's secretary-general commented on this matter:

> When the Indonesian Army arrested someone they always said, "You are FRETILIN"—so this became a rumor that the only party that liberated the country was FRETILIN. The only party that fought for independence was FRETILIN.[44]

The reality was more complex than this. Not only had the CNRM replaced FRETILIN as the main vehicle for nationalist struggle by the end of the 1980s, both at home and abroad, but the CNRM itself constituted a highly varied and poorly coordinated set of forces. The clandestine movement, in particular, was actually a wide variety of more or less formally organized movements, some of which identified with FRETILIN, some with CNRM, and some with other parties and ideals. Many of these movements were actually no bigger than cells, formed spontaneously by groups of friends looking to contribute to the national cause. Some were linked into national and international networks, through FALINTIL, FRETILIN, or CNRM, but others were more autonomous. Even those who identified themselves as FRETILIN did not necessarily have any direct connection to the FRETILIN leadership, nor did the FRETILIN leadership have a particularly clear overview of the movement as a whole, and of who was doing what within it. According to Hernani Coelho,

> Between 1980 and 1999, the relationship between the party and the people was more one of spirit. The party initiated the resistance, but it wasn't well-structured. It didn't play a political role—its only objective was liberation … From 1982, many grassroots organizations emerged, some within FRETILIN, others were new. Some were closely linked to FRETLIN, some to other political parties … We didn't really control them, even now we can't really control them.[45]

---

[43] Irena Cristalis, *Bitter Dawn: East Timor, A People's Story* (London: Zed Books, 2002), p. 6.

[44] José Reyes, Secretary-General, FRETILIN, personal interview, Dili, May 2005.

[45] Hernani Coelho, Central Committee Member, FRETILIN, personal interview, Dili, May 2005.

In contrast to the disarray of the various political movements, another institution was building its strength as a bearer of national identity and was becoming ever more deeply embedded across the country. This was the Catholic Church. The Church was imported into East Timor during the era of Portuguese colonialism, and for much of the colonial period was strictly the preserve of the elite. The CAVR report describes the colonial Church as "an adjunct of the ultra-conservative Portuguese administration."[46] Only 20 percent of Timorese were Catholics at independence in 1975. Church schools were an important source of education for the children of elite Timorese; indeed, the seminary at Dare produced many of the leaders of the resistance. For many of these leaders, nationalism and religion conflicted, and they regarded the Church that had educated them as part of the oppressive colonial enterprise. As FRETILIN espoused a Marxist stance in the late 1970s, tensions between the party and the Church increased. However, on a wider scale, the image of the Church shifted dramatically between 1975 and 1999. Under the Indonesian occupation, it became a key institution maintaining a sense of separate Timorese national identity, as well as an active participant in the independence struggle, and 90 percent of Timorese belonged.

This change occurred for a number of reasons. For one thing, *Panca Sila* required that every Indonesian espouse one of five registered religions, which included Catholicism. As Timorese animism was not a permitted option for the forcibly incorporated Timorese, and as "relations between the Church and indigenous religious groups had historically been friendly,"[47] many registered themselves as Catholics. Furthermore, the Vatican made the surprising decision after 1975 to rule the Dili Diocese directly from Rome, rather than routing its administration via the Indonesian Bishops' Conference. This entailed that the Church became the only Timorese institution to have direct links with the outside world.

The internal face of the Church also changed somewhat under occupation. The appointment of the first Timorese Bishop of Dili, Bishop Belo, in 1983, indigenized the institution, as did the increase in the number of Timorese priests during the course of the occupation, until these numbered about a third of the body of the clergy. Prohibited by the Indonesians from continuing to use Portuguese for mass, the Vatican authorized the use of a Tetum liturgy, which emphasized the Church as something distinctly Timorese. The spaces of Church buildings offered symbols of sanctity and safety, which, Kohen reports, were largely respected until 1999, when a number of Church massacres occurred in the orgy of violence carried out by the Indonesian military and associated militias around the time of the popular consultation. Furthermore, churches represented the only places in which Timorese could congregate as a community without arousing the suspicion of the Indonesians.

Many Timorese priests played a role in passing messages or material support to resistance fighters. In 2005, villagers interviewed for this study recalled the role of the Church in organizing collections from villagers to support the resistance. In 1999, the Church was active in rallying villagers to resist the intimidation surrounding the popular consultation and to vote No in response to Jakarta's autonomy proposal. For these reasons, not to mention Bishop Belo's Nobel Peace Prize, the Church emerged from the occupation with a larger flock and was now associated by the people with

---

[46] CAVR, *Chega!*, Pt. 3, p. 98.

[47] Arnold S. Kohen, "The Catholic Church and the Independence of Timor," in *Bitter Flowers, Sweet Flowers*, p. 49.

the struggle for independence, an alignment that had been severely lacking in 1975. It is important to note also that the involvement of the Church as an active player in the independence struggle has entailed a politicization of the Church hierarchy and a willingness to use its moral authority to intervene in politics. The Church's moral stature, association with national identity, and its organizational presence throughout the territory put it in a position to engage in politics to great effect.

If the Church had gained stature as a visible symbol of Timorese nationhood, FALINTIL remained an invisible reminder of nationalist aspiration. The mobilizations of the clandestine movement sporadically produced highly charged demonstrations of East Timorese aspirations. However, the prospects for achieving coherent organization for nationalist movements were very poor—for secular nationalists, there were no institutions resembling the Church's network of parish priests available to provide an organizing structure. Furthermore, the very rapid disintegration of Jakarta's will to hold Timor, following the Asian financial crisis of 1997, entailed that when the opportunity for restoration of independence came, it took the Timorese unawares, rather as it had the first time around in 1974. The suddenness of the offer of a referendum, following the fall of Suharto, in the midst of ongoing brutal repression of independence activists on the ground, created a situation in which the resistance had no real window of opportunity to organize itself better in readiness for post-Indonesian politics.

The situation was further complicated by the nature of the violence in 1999. Much of the violence was carried out by paramilitary organizations of Timorese, sponsored by Kopassus; difficulties in recruiting members of these militias led to practices of forced conscription. Timorese youths were forced out of their homes at gunpoint to join militia activities and given what were called "crazy dog pills"—pills that apparently made them "see human beings as animals"—washed down with whiskey. They were then armed with automatic weapons and encouraged to fire indiscriminately. Equally, the mandatory practice, during the worst weeks of destruction, of wearing militia colors to avoid being killed meant that it was difficult for anyone involved to know who—beyond the obvious core of committed fighters—was "really" militia and who was just pretending.

During the years of clandestine resistance and during the chaotic violence surrounding the popular consultation, it was difficult for leaders outside the country, and even inside the country, to keep track of who was involved in the independence struggle; who sacrificed themselves for the cause, and in what capacity; who collaborated with the Indonesians; which persons collaborated out of altruistic motives, which merely for the sake of self-preservation; and which "collaborators" cost other Timorese their lives. As one interviewee described the situation: "Actually, the reality is we don't know who did what for the resistance. We only know we are a nation of heroes."

This comment encapsulates two aspects of Timorese politics. First, as in Cambodia, there is a strong sense of disorientation associated with society's emergence from warfare. Festering wrongs and guilts, suspicions concerning what different individuals' loyalties might "really" have been in a situation where everyone was forced to dissemble, and competition for recognition of sacrifice are common features of post-conflict situations. But where postwar Timor differed from postwar Cambodia is in the powerful sense of victory and purpose it bestowed on the post-independence political milieu. In Cambodia, many people emerged from the war appalled at the atrocities their society had proved capable of visiting upon itself, and distrustful of one another. In postwar Timor, nearly everybody regarded—or claimed to regard—himself or herself as a hero, each with responsibility for winning independence equal to that of others who had been involved. Timorese society, like all societies, has its social cleavages and regimes for justifying inequality, including class cleavages, traditional status systems associated with the *liurai* structure, and sharp gender disparities. However, thanks to the war, these came to exist alongside a powerful sense of the idealized Timorese, who represents a force for freedom in the world, a moral beacon penetrating the grimness of *realpolitik*, and, questions of local precedence and hierarchy aside, a person entitled to equal concern and respect in the post-conflict nation.

This highly mobilized and self-confident nation comprised citizens keen to step forward and claim their place at the table of independence politics. However, this orientation was directly antithetical to the approach of interveners and donors, who regarded East Timor, at the end of 1999, as a wasteland bereft not only of buildings and institutions but also of talent and expertise. Meanwhile, the returning FRETILIN elite, who had spent the past twenty-five years steeped in international diplomacy, Portuguese activism, and African nationalism, brought with them a set of attitudes towards their fellow citizens and a set of political ideals that had little to do with the *Panca Sila* nationalism imbibed from Indonesian education and development strategies. A clash of perspectives emerging from the diverse struggles glossed under the category of Mauberism during the war was soon evident within the nation of heroes itself; confined within a straitjacket of neoliberal development policy, this clash was to prove impossible to reconcile.

CHAPTER III

"MASTERS OF INDEPENDENCE": WAR-TORN COMMUNITIES IN INTERNATIONAL POLICY

"It might sound as though I am … against … noble standards of democratic participation. I do not mind if it happens in the democratic minds of people. What seems to be absurd is that we absorb standards just to pretend we look like a democratic society and please our masters of independence."
Xanana Gusmão, December 31, 2000

As "post-conflict" societies, Cambodia and East Timor found themselves inserted into conceptual frameworks for international action and intervention that were subject to rapid change during the course of the post-Cold War era and which differed significantly from those used at home. Cambodia's peacekeeping operation took place between 1991 and 1993. It was one among the rash of international interventions that sought to deal with civil wars that staggered on as a legacy of the Cold War era. East Timor's operation took place between 1999 and 2002 in different circumstances; post-Cold War optimism regarding a democratic peace based upon elections and civil society had been knocked by events in Somalia and Bosnia, and the more circumspect "good governance" approach of the international financial institutions was in the ascendant. Both interventions took place before the implications of September 11th fed through into international politics, sparking a new set of state-building projects associated with "regime change" and the War on Terror.

This chapter situates the conflicts and the peace in Cambodia and Timor in the context of international thinking in the 1990s, seeking to contextualize the presumptions and ambitions of international actors intervening in Cambodia and Timor. The discussion that follows tracks the policy discourses of post-conflict reconstruction from their origins in post-Cold War euphoria for a Kantian democratic peace. It discusses the presuppositions of this position, and its implications for interventionary practice, before continuing to investigate the rise of the "good governance" agenda, strongly promoted by the World Bank as it staked out its own position in the context of post-conflict reconstruction in 1998. The chapter proceeds to examine the way that ideas of "good governance" have been defined in opposition to a construction of civil wars—and the states and populations that engage in them—as deviant and pathological. It concludes by showing how developed countries, multilateral organizations, and aid agencies became increasingly confident in asserting rights to intervene across state borders, and that this inclination combined with their strong predilection against the spread of populations venturing in the opposite direction—outside those state borders. The demonization of war-torn states and societies has led to a view of refugees and migrants from them as potentially dangerous and destabilizing, leading to interventionary practices that seek to promote the salience of international boundaries, even while violating them. In making this case, the chapter charts the emergence of a discourse that is found across a wide range of policy documents associated with the various types of development "consensus." This analysis lays the foundation for the discussion in subsequent chapters of how policies of intervention and post-conflict reconstruction were framed in Cambodia and Timor-Leste.

POST-COLD WAR ASPIRATION

In the early 1990s, international policy-makers in multilateral agencies and states of the North were greatly excited over the prospects for resolving long-running conflicts in various parts of the global South that had been prolonged and fueled by superpower rivalry. Liberal democracy as the triumphant ideology was regarded by a broad range of policy-makers, humanitarians, and academics as providing the conceptual tools for ending these conflicts and establishing new modes of international cooperation that could provide "better standards of life in larger freedom." The post-Cold War doctrine of "peacebuilding" formalized transformations, in conceptions of peace, from the Cold War "traditional peacekeeping" approach, to the post-Cold War preference for "comprehensive, political settlements." Peacebuilding was defined in a resolution of the United Nations General Assembly in 1993 as "sustained cooperative efforts by the United Nations to deal with the underlying economic, social, cultural and humanitarian causes and effects of conflicts in order to promote a durable foundation for peace" and "the creation of a new environment to forestall the recurrence of conflicts."[1]

In delineating this position, UN Secretary-General Boutros Boutros-Ghali was drawing upon, and to a considerable extent reifying, the radical tradition in peace research associated with Johan Galtung.[2] Galtung advocated a reconceptualization of peace, shifting away from its negative definition as the absence of war and towards a conception of "positive peace" that aimed at becoming "ever more holistic and ever more global." The peace research agenda also proposed that the conceptualization of violence be extended away from agency-based models and towards a structural approach that regards violence as harm done over the long term, through the normal operation of structures of power, which, unintentionally or unthinkingly, cause misery and hardship.

Galtung's approach was radical in that it prompted a shift in perceptions of the ethical dimensions of violence and peace research, shifting attention away from the immediate motivations of an aggressor, and toward the broader structures that allow or foster the build-up of aggression. Galtung coined the term "peacebuilding" to refer to the promotion of a positive peace that tackled structural violence over the long term, as opposed to "peacekeeping," which simply sought to silence the guns. Boutros-Ghali appropriated this terminology and transposed it into his analysis of a situation in which "structural violence" was implicitly associated with the

---

[1] United Nations General Assembly, "An Agenda for Peace," General Assembly Resolution, UN document A/RES/47/120, September 20, 1993, reprinted in Boutros Boutros-Ghali, *An Agenda for Peace, 1995,* 2nd ed. (New York, NY: United Nations, 1995), p. 92.

[2] See, for example, Johan Galtung, "Twenty-Five Years of Peace Research: Ten Challenges and Some Responses," *Journal of Peace Research* 22,2 (1985): 141–58.

superpower rivalry of the Cold War—"the immense ideological barrier that for decades gave rise to distrust and hostility."[3] In an analysis that reflected the immediate post-Cold War zeitgeist, Boutros-Ghali described the violence of the Cold War as having "crippled" the United Nations and undermined its prospects of maintaining peace, justice, human rights, and social progress.[4] He proclaimed the demise of the Cold War to be an "opportunity [that] must not be squandered" to "address the deepest causes of conflict: economic despair, social injustice, and political oppression" via the spread of "democratic practices—such as the rule of law and transparency in decision-making."[5] As such, positive peace became associated with the spread of liberal democratic institutions of state, in a context of globalizing neoliberal economic relations.

Although peacebuilding therefore confronts the vexed relationship between the boundaries of sovereign autonomy and the boundaries of humanitarian concern, in the *Agenda,* Boutros-Ghali locates the solution in the good sense of governments that are invited to give their consent to United Nations assistance to build peace:

> The time of absolute and exclusive sovereignty ... has passed; its theory was never matched by reality. It is the task of leaders of States today to understand this and to find a balance between the needs of good government and the requirements of an ever more interdependent world.[6]

According to Boutros-Ghali, states can be socialized into this new role by the promotion of their sovereignty, territorial integrity, and independence, as a foundation for "democratic principles at all levels of existence."[7] These can permit the institutionalization of peace within communities, and, consequently, within states, and internationally.

This association of peacebuilding with a peaceful and ordered society, specifically composed of *states,* emerged in the early 1990s from the reformulation of Kantian "democratic peace" theory[8]—a theory that predicted that the emergence of a community of internally democratic states would reduce the incidence of war. Democratic peace theory surfaced in both the *Agenda for Peace* and the Clinton administration's "democratic enlargement" doctrine. Thus, Boutros-Ghali stated, "Democracies almost never fight each other. Democratization supports the cause of peace"; while US Secretary of State Warren Christopher opined, "Democratic nations are far less likely to go to war with each other and far more likely to respect international law."[9]

---

[3] Boutros Boutros-Ghali, *An Agenda for Peace, Preventive Diplomacy, Peace-Making and Peace-Keeping,* Report of the Secretary General, UN Document No. A/47/277-S24111, June 17, 1992, online at http://www.un.org/Docs/SG/agpeace.html, accessed September 20, 2008, para. 8.

[4] Ibid., para. 3.

[5] Ibid., paras. 3, 15, 59.

[6] Ibid., para. 17.

[7] Ibid., para. 19.

[8] See for example, Michael Doyle, "Liberalism and World Politics," *American Political Science Review* 80 (1986): 1151–63; Daniele Archibughi, "Immanuel Kant: Cosmopolitan Law and Peace," *European Journal of International Relations* 1 (1995): 429–56; and Stanley Hoffman, "The Crisis of Liberal Internationalism," *Foreign Policy* 98 (1995): 159–77.

[9] Boutros Boutros-Ghali, "An Agenda for Peace: One Year Later," *Orbis* 37 (1993): 329; Warren Christopher, "America's Leadership, America's Opportunity," *Foreign Policy* 98 (1995): 10.

This view of peacebuilding prefigured the form of dispassionate state-building that later came to be advocated by international financial institutions. The idea that one could differentiate scientifically between "good" and "bad" states entailed the emergence of ever more specific distinctions between the healthy and the dysfunctional.[10] As elections in places like Algeria and the Balkans indicated the insufficiently liberal nature of many societies in conflict, the nature of good states was increasingly regarded as a scientific, rather than a democratic, issue. A number of related developments led to ever more penetrating interventions. These developments included the increased incidence of state collapse, as the superpowers' clients failed to meet the challenges of life without foreign sponsorship; the replacement of breathless admiration for East Asian developmental states with denunciations of "crony capitalism"; and the phenomenon of ethnic persecution and religious zealotry pursued by floundering leaders in collapsing states. These new interventions were meant to correct manifestations of political deviance and to generate, from the wreckage of deviant democracy and failing statehood on the periphery, states reflecting the solid world citizenship ethos celebrated in the *Agenda*.

Oliver Richmond describes the emergence of a peacebuilding consensus from these elements of the liberal tradition, but points out that the elements of the contemporary liberal peace "all depend upon external actors' intervention" and place international interveners, whether these are foreign militaries or international NGOs, "in an almost omniscient position in relation to the peace they construct."[11] Richmond argues that attempts to achieve a form of positive peace involved not merely the establishment of a clear victory for one side or another, but also attempts to bring marginalized actors out of the shadows and "bring to light the hidden factors which give rise to violence."[12] In so doing, Richmond points out, the peacebuilding consensus puts external actors into a privileged position as conflict managers; and this condition, he comments, "rapidly expanded to include the multiple interventions of a variety of international agencies, organisations, and non-state actors."[13] According to Richmond, identifying an ideal construction of the concept of peace made peace seem "technically plausible," producing an "epistemic community providing the necessary expertise." It necessitated "multiple third party interventions aimed at redefining the discourses, practices, and structures of the conflict environment." But, he adds, there is a "tension" in the "gap between the interveners' understanding of peace and their recipients' expectations and interests"—a gap that has been little considered in the peacebuilding literature.[14] Richmond suggests that liberal regimes of peace combine "outside-in" construction of peace by external actors employing "technical" expertise with "inside-out" negotiations by disputants "according to their own interests, cultures, and frameworks."[15]

For Richmond, convergence on an ideal of peacebuilding masks fundamental dissensus over what the ideal peace should look like. The technocratic approach to

---

[10] Francis Fukuyama, *State Building, Governance, and World Order in the Twenty-First Century* (New York, NY: Profile, 2005), pp. 30–43.

[11] Oliver Richmond, *The Transformation of Peace* (Basingstoke: Palgrave, 2005), p. 51.

[12] Ibid., p. 101.

[13] Ibid., p. 102.

[14] Ibid., p. 103.

[15] Ibid., pp. 103–4.

peace denies the need to negotiate relationships among international actors and those on the ground, yet the experience of peacebuilding—which involves the erection of power relationships both among peacebuilding professionals and between peacebuilders and local actors, and in which the ongoing negotiation of these relationships in a context of divergent cultures and interests is evident—suggests that apparent ideological consensus masks a reality of significant dissensus among the various actors. The ongoing need for coercion in peacebuilding, and the importance of debates over the nature of "consent," are symptoms of this dissensus. Advocates of liberal peace proclaim its universal appeal, but that appeal does not hold in reality, giving force to critiques of peacebuilding as a new form of disciplinary governance.

Boutros-Ghali's initial formulation of peacebuilding as a policy option in 1992 occurred at a time when international attention, responding to the "people power" revolutions of Eastern Europe, was focused on democratization and the power of the individual to topple dictatorship through enlightened, self-interested, consumerist action. Cambodia's own experiment with democracy, in the form of the 1993 elections, appeared to support this view. Despite the persecution of ethnic minorities and political opponents and the bullying of voters by unreconstructed communist warlords and repressive village chiefs, the Cambodian electorate showed what appeared to be a magnificent faith in their own democratic power, walking long distances and queuing in the sun for hours to cast a vote for their first elected government in thirty years. Excited commentators reported that Cambodians had voted most determinedly against the ruling party in areas where it had been most oppressive; that they had braved the most atrocious threats to exercise power; and that the rise to democratic consciousness of the people had generated unstoppable momentum for better government in the future.[16]

However, this faith in electoral democracy as a set of political procedures that would generate a virtuous cycle of increased participation and better governance quickly lost its shine, as other populations failed to follow suit. The rise of "illiberal democracy" in some instances ignited ethnic conflict and facilitated the rise of political Islam, prompting arguments about cultural difference and denting enthusiasm for democracy promotion in the West.[17] The failure of electoral procedures to precipitate a convergence around liberal peace supports Richmond's unease over the adequacy of the model when applied universally; however, as the discussion of politics in Cambodia and East Timor in subsequent chapters will suggest, this disappointing outcome—the emergence of an "illiberal" hybrid democracy—should not be regarded as a simple consequence of "cultural" resistance but as an outcome of the impact of victors' politics on the democratic ideal. Implementing a victor's peace entails the exercise of considerable naked power by

---

[16] See, for example, MacAlister Brown and Joseph Zasloff, *Cambodia Confounds the Peacemakers* (Ithaca, NY: Cornell University Press, 1998); and Janet Heininger, *Peacekeeping in Transition; United Nations in Cambodia* (Washington, DC: Brookings Institute, 1994), for optimistic accounts.

[17] See, for example, Clark D. Neher, "Asian-Style Democracy," *Asian Survey* 34,11 (1994): 949–61; Terry Lynn Karl, "The Hybrid Regimes of Central America," *Journal of Democracy* 6,3 (1995): 72–86; Fareed Zakaria, "The Rise of Illiberal Democracy," *Foreign Affairs* 96,6 (1997): 22–43; Charles Taylor, "The Dynamics of Democratic Exclusion," *Journal of Democracy* 9,4 (1998): 143–56. These articles are part of a vast literature that developed from the mid-1990s on various types of "defective" and hybrid democracy.

external actors, thus violating central democratic principles and putting the issue of sovereign autonomy onto the electoral table. This is a situation that in no way resembles any "cultural" or "traditional" precedent; however it does make an ostensibly "cultural" politics, in which political leaders are reduced to spouting sterile arguments about their own and their opponents' "authenticity" in contending attempts to win support, far more likely.

Alongside the rediscovery of liberal peace theory in international relations, public economists reviewed and reconsidered a decade of neoliberal orthodoxy to conclude that "institutions matter" in the context of development.[18] Reevaluation of the role of governance in the trajectories of underdeveloped countries was the most significant shift in peace and development thinking in the 1990s, and it has contributed directly to the expansion of global governance as a perceived antidote to the activities of aberrant states. In the 1980s, the neoliberal ideological mantra adopted by the international financial institutions headquartered in Washington, DC, insisted on the rollback of the state in every area of its activities across the developing world. This approach, known as the Washington Consensus, saw the International Monetary Fund coercing states in crisis into blanket programs of privatization and of contracting out, if not dismantling, welfare systems.

From the mid-1990s, the Washington Consensus was qualified by a new emphasis on institution-building. The World Bank's reformulated view of the state as expressed in the 1997 World Development Report highlights the need for states not only to practice fiscal responsibility and impose a tight monetary policy, but also to establish effective tax regimes that can promote "growth with equity," in particular to defuse potentially explosive ethnic or regional grievances; for states to attend to investment in human capital such as health and education; and for states to implement strong measures to guard against corruption. In the lexicon of the World Bank, these requirements in post-conflict contexts were incorporated in a definition of "reconstruction" now regarded as extending beyond physical infrastructure to encompass the *enabling conditions* for a functioning peacetime society."[19] A revitalization of statehood in order to manage these problems has been high on the agenda of international actors in post-conflict societies, advocated as a means to promote greater integration of post-conflict societies into global markets.[20]

The focus on governance led the bank, along with United Nations specialized agencies, bilateral donors, and even NGOs, into new forms of intervention that involved micromanaging the reordering of state agencies. Doing so required expansion of intervention, in terms not only of the content of policy prescriptions, but also of closeness of supervision, coordination of international expertise, and time frames over which these were to be continued. While these concerns might be

---

[18] Shahid Burki and Guillermo Perry, *Beyond the Washington Consensus: Institutions Matter* (Washington, DC: World Bank, 1998), online at http://www-wds.worldbank.org/external/default/WDSContentServer/WDSP/IB/1998/11/17/000178830_98111703552694/Rendered/PDF/multi_page.pdf., accessed May 22, 2007.

[19] James Boyce, "The IFIs, Post-Conflict Reconstruction, and Peacebuilding Capacities," paper prepared for the High-Level Panel on Threats, Challenges, and Change Seminar entitled "Strengthening the UN's Capacity on Civilian Crisis Management," Copenhagen, June 8–9, 2004. Online at http://www.cic.nyu.edu/archive/conflict/Boyce%20-%20IFIs%20&%20peacebuilding%20-%20June%202004.pdf., accessed Sept 17, 2007, p. 1.

[20] World Bank, *The World Bank and Post-Conflict Reconstruction: An Evolving Agenda* (Washington, DC: World Bank, 2002), p. 6.

regarded as preferable to those emphasized by the Washington Consensus, as they acknowledge the need to respond to inequity and other social and political phenomena, this approach also entailed a much closer scrutiny of, and far more intrusive intervention into, local political affairs.

Cambodia and Timor-Leste were inducted swiftly into these new orders of intervention and post-intervention scrutiny. The peacekeeping operations mounted by the UN in each country represented a significant expansion of anything that had been attempted before; subsequent activities with respect to scrutiny of aid also expanded, with significant consequences. Almost every aspect of government activity in Cambodia has remained subject to increasing levels of donor inspection. Over the past nine years, the Cambodian government has participated with its major donors in regular meetings of eighteen "Joint Technical Working Groups," covering a wide range of policy areas from Health, Education, and Agriculture, to Land, Public Administration Reform and Public Financial Management, to Gender and National Strategic Development Planning. Within each field, the government has committed itself to a series of Joint Monitoring Indicators that represent a road map for policy reform. This extraordinarily long-lasting, wide-ranging, and detailed regime of collaboration has not proved particularly successful in determining government priorities or actions, from the donors' point of view, but the mere fact of the erection of this framework, and the amount of time spent on it by government, is itself indicative of the extent of donors' claims to rights of supervision.

Two presumptions underlie these approaches: first, that an optimal path to development and security exists; and, second, that this path must be followed from the earliest stage of international engagement to minimize the prospects of deepening poverty and exacerbated conflict. Much of the debate on post-conflict reconstruction has revolved around identifying the optimal path in a confused and chaotic situation. Much less of the debate has questioned whether such an optimal path does objectively exist or whether any kind of envisaged post-conflict trajectory is necessarily political, pitting a variety of different and incommensurable interests against one another, offering different options that would empower different types of actors, and requiring political accommodations among coalitions. The predilection towards casting post-conflict reconstruction as a difficult, but essentially technical, task of jolting states onto "correct" political and economic trajectories has resulted in a dearth of critical commentary on post-conflict reconstruction. Rather, it has fostered the growth of an interested epistemic community that is geared towards overseeing post-conflict reconstruction according to "international best practice."

In response to a proposal from the High Level Panel on Threats, Challenges and Change, convened after September 11th, one part of this epistemic community has been institutionalized in the form of a UN Peacebuilding Commission, whose central tasks are "to integrate system-wide peacebuilding policies and strategies, develop best practices, and provide cohesive support for field operations."[21] The four specific objectives of the peacebuilding commission, stated on its website, reflect the axes along which global governance has expanded over the past fifteen years: namely, tighter integration of strategic thinking by international actors; more effective mobilization of financial resources to empower these strategies; extension of the "period of attention by the international community"; and the development of

---

[21] High Level Panel on Threats, Challenges, and Change, *A More Secure World: Our Shared Responsibility* (New York, NY: United Nations, 2004), p. 84.

models of "best practice" to enable closer collaboration among different types of actors in the political, military, humanitarian, and development fields.[22]

In sum, global governance, as a concept and practice outlined by those engaged in providing assistance to post-conflict countries, has been born as the successor to the structural adjustment programs and ad hoc humanitarian relief operations of the 1980s, which were typically conducted at arms-length. The global governance doctrine comprises a consolidated set of concerns implemented by a wider range of actors, better coordinated than their predecessors, speaking a common technocratic language amongst themselves, and reaching much deeper into a wider range of states, over a longer time frame, than did the policies of the 1980s. As such, responsibility for post-conflict reconstruction has broken out of the confines of the Department for Peacekeeping Operations at the United Nations—a department that found itself under severe strain in the 1990s due to increasingly holistic and ambitious ideas of what peacekeeping missions could and should achieve—and into the domain of new UN departments, development agencies, international financial institutions, nongovernmental organizations, militaries, and foreign policy agencies. The goals of post-conflict reconstruction, in consequence, have shifted from the minimal ambition of monitoring ceasefires to the broader aims of promoting security locally, regionally, and globally; jump-starting development processes; improving governance by state institutions and encouraging participation by empowered publics; and providing for restorative and retributive justice, if necessary, through international tribunals and through establishing institutions responsible for law, order, and enforcement of property rights.

This holistic approach has resulted in the proliferation of concerned parties and the broadening of their mandates, well beyond Cold War precedents. The World Bank has retreated from its macroeconomic focus and its declarations that politics is none of its business, to engage in new areas of policy such as demobilization of soldiers and community-driven development and to perform "conflict sensitivity" assessments of its own aid distributions to test their impact on politicized cleavages such as those of ethnicity, region, or religion. At the same time, emphasis on coordination and multilateralism have led to proliferating, flexible, and mutually reinforcing relations among international actors and their local "partners." The "four pillars of conflict resolution"—security, governance and participation, social and economic well-being, and justice and reconciliation—cited in many policy documents thus constitute a broad-based approach to reconstituting relationships among actors in post-conflict societies, in line with international standards. The overall thrust of all this activity, however, remains focused on the same perennial goal—the closer integration of peripheral societies into the global economy. As such, it remains in line with a long-standing ideologically driven concern, on the part of the World Bank and the rest of the UN system, to further the advancement of economic growth and its recognition as the *sine qua non* of progress. Greater attention to the issues of governance has prompted not a critical examination of the nature of power relations in post-conflict countries, but ever greater "technical" interventions aimed at producing the right sort of politics: a politics that is, above all, compatible

[22] Website of the Peacebuilding Commission, United Nations, http://www.un.org/peace/peacebuilding/, accessed August 22, 2006.

with the expansion of the market.[23] Subsequent chapters will demonstrate the effects of this predilection in relation to issues of democratization and governance in post-conflict Cambodia and Timor-Leste.

"NOT THE AMERICAN CIVIL WAR": DYSFUNCTIONAL STATES AND DYSFUNCTIONAL SOCIETIES

During the 1990s, the growth in interest in governance just described was accompanied by growing concern, among policy-makers in the North, regarding the dysfunctionality of whole nations, civilizations, or ethnic groups engaged in civil war. The failure of oppressed populations to embrace unproblematically a liberal agenda led many international actors to retreat rather quickly from advocating the comparatively optimistic democratic peace thesis, as exemplified by the reaction of Western governments to the victory of Islamist parties in a series of elections from Algeria to Palestine. At the same time, the good governance agenda was given urgency by new analyses that linked conflict with "failed states"—states that had failed due their own incompetence to retain legitimacy and police their populations, and which, therefore, not only fell into civil strife at home, but caused security problems for their neighbors and internationally.

Consequently, a series of academic, media, and policy-oriented analyses began to advance the thesis that some states failed because the societies over which they presided were exceptionally unruly; often such generalized unruliness was said to be caused by "cultural" attributes that had precluded assimilation of the attributes of modernity. For example, concerns over "Serb aggression" in Kosovo and "Islamic extremism" in many other places in the world fueled new ideas about intervention, ideas that prescribed the reengineering, not merely of states, but of societies, too. The new institutionalism gave short shrift to structural accounts of underdevelopment, prompting exclusive focus on the internal dysfunctionality of states and of non-state institutions such as clans, tribes, or religious establishments in societies in conflict. Alongside this tendency, the "securitization" of development prompted aid organizations, donors, and policy-makers to define these dysfunctional states and societies as threats, not just to themselves, but to "us."

This portrayal of conflict bolstered international intervention and imposed two overarching "security" objectives, both of which operated in the service of the market. The first objective was the restoration of the territorial integrity and coercive power of the disrupted state as a means to cordon off the causes of conflict—defined a priori as local in origin—and to keep unruly populations safely at home. The second objective was to use mechanisms of state-society interaction to try to reengineer societies themselves, in a manner that would break up deviant non-state authority structures, regarded as perpetuating pathological cultural practices, and replace these with societies of atomized individuals, ready to compete in the global market.

An example of this characterization of failing states and dysfunctional population is found in the World Bank's 1998 account of its own role in post-conflict reconstruction. In this document, the bank's emphasis upon "cultures of armed

---

[23] See for example, Kofi Annan, *"We the Peoples": The Role of the United Nations in the Twenty-First Century,* Millennium Report of the Secretary-General to the United Nations (New York, NY: United Nations, 2000), p. 21.

warfare and violence" that purportedly feed on, and exacerbate, "ethnic or religious competition," encouraged a view of conflict as increasingly an endemic condition.[24] A cycle of violence emerges that is embedded in a local context and that increases in its complexity with every round, entailing that "there is no pattern of single causal agent in any given case, and outside actors have only a limited ability to influence the course of events in specific countries."[25] Paul Collier's research for the bank on the causes and consequences of war refined this thesis, suggesting that economics was more important than social structure in prompting conflicts, and offering greater scope for corrective intervention as a result. Yet the way in which his finding was couched still emphasized the agency of the local rather than the global—in this instance, "Africa"—in producing this condition:

> Far from Africa's conflict problem being deep-rooted in its social structure, it is a consequence of the disastrous deviation of African economic performance from that of other developing countries that set it apart during the 1970s and has proved persistent. Of course, Africa's distinctive social composition may have contributed to its poor economic performance, but this is a different issue.[26]

In Collier's writings, poor economic performance, resulting in what he describes as marginalization from the world economy, is always regarded as a failure that is generated by states themselves, rather than by the global economic structures with which states interact. The aside, quoted here, remarking that social composition may turn out to be the cause of bad policy in Africa, suggests that it is the state-society itself that needs to be realigned; such an agenda leads directly to solutions based upon policy interventions in the field of governance. Discovery of the "conflict trap" underlines the need for external interventions, as those with the capability to intervene observe disrupted countries embarking upon a downward spiral of social division, poor governance, poor economic performance, and further social division.

Similar concerns are evident in United Nations documents surrounding the Millennium Campaign. Kofi Annan, for example, in his Millennium Report, lays the blame for poor economic performance in Africa firmly in the laps of African governments. In terms of economic policy, he states, "economic regimes tend to be tightly controlled and inefficiently managed by the state. This results in high trade barriers and poor delivery of public services. It also means that corruption is widespread."[27] According to Annan, such poor policy making in the economic arena is exacerbated by political obstacles to development, evident in "a winner-takes-all attitude to political competition, the control of society's wealth and resources, and to the power of patronage and the prerogatives of office." The locus of necessary change is clear: "Only Africans ... can break out of these vicious cycles." Yet international pressure is called for, Annan writes, as the will seems to be lacking: "...

---

[24] World Bank, *Post-Conflict Reconstruction: The Role of the World Bank* (Washington, DC: World Bank, 1998), p. 2.

[25] Ibid., p. 17.

[26] Paul Collier, *Breaking the Conflict Trap: Civil War and Development Policy* (Washington, DC: World Bank, 2003), p. 117.

[27] Kofi Annan, *We The Peoples: the Role of the United Nations in the 21st Century* (New York: United Nations, 1999), p. 31

inexplicably, even today, few African governments show the necessary commitment to poverty reduction in their national economic and social policies."[28]

In fact, the nature of African politics is not entirely "inexplicable." There is a large body of literature, of which, one presumes, Annan was aware, that lays out, in cogent and rational terms, the various schools of thought, many of which provide perfectly good explanations for the particularities of politics and government in a variety of African countries.[29] Indeed, a major strand of scholarship links issues such as corruption and neo-patrimonialism clearly into the structures of international trade and aid into which colonial and postcolonial African economies and states have been inserted, raising directly the question of whether it is "only Africans" who are implicated in the problem and their potential solutions.[30] The use of the term "inexplicable" to characterize African politics and government is rhetorical; its effect is to present African governments as the problem and to concentrate more normative power into international hands. Annan presents a particular and partial narrative, in which the cause of the problem is local, cyclical, and intransigent; the responsibility for solutions rests in local hands, but because of their "inexplicable" reluctance, technical interventions by expert international actors is mandated, along with strategies to provide sufficient international leverage to overcome local lack of will.

Much of the UN's reform program, as envisaged by the High Level Panel on Threats, Challenges, and Change, is oriented to this agenda. In regarding the problem as intractable and responsible local partners as unenthusiastic, overseers of global governance create an alibi for their own potential failure, along with a justification of a further tightening of networks of surveillance and control. As a number of commentators have pointed out, the global governance agenda outlined above relies for its force on the attribution of "economic dysfunctionalism" to objectified societies "in their pre-conflict, conflict, and post-conflict stages."[31] In so doing, it reserves professional expertise and technical knowledge for the use of individuals and agencies who form the "networks of global governance" described, demarcating their "functionality" from the inherent "dysfunctionality" of the "beneficiaries" of their policies and, thus, empowering them to remold political processes towards externally imposed targets, such as Millennium Development Goals, in societies in conflict.[32]

Further empowering the agenda of global governance is an explicit rejection of the idea that conflict might be fruitfully regarded as efforts by the poor to challenge their own governments to raise their game. In the late 1990s, the emergence of the "greed" thesis on intrastate conflict, which regarded the emergence of vested interests in conflict, particularly associated with rebel capture of lootable natural resources, as potentially significant in understanding the dynamics of conflict in Africa, reflected this rejection. Paul Collier's team members at the World Bank were

---

[28] Annan, *"We the Peoples,"* p. 31.

[29] Patrick Chabal and Jean-Pascal Daloz, *Africa Works: Disorder as Political Instrument* (Oxford: James Currey, 1999), p. xvii.

[30] See, for example, Jean-Francois Bayart, *The State in Africa: The Politics of the Belly* (Harlow: Longman, 1993); Robert Fatton, *Predatory Rule: State and Civil Society in Africa* (Boulder, CO: Lynne Rienner, 1992).

[31] Mike Pugh, "The Political Economy of Peacebuilding: A Critical Theory Perspective," *International Journal of Peace Studies* 10,2 (2005): 24.

[32] Ibid., p. 23.

at the forefront of promoting the "greed" thesis, arguing that there is no statistical correlation between objective measures of grievance, such as inequality, and the outbreak of civil war.[33] While acknowledging that rebel leaders usually offer some narrative of grievance, Collier and his associates reject the integrity of these proclamations on the grounds that "political opposition to governments is not usually conducted through military organizations. The normal vehicles for political opposition are political parties and protest movements."[34]

Collier attributes civil war primarily to "the lure of imagined wealth" for political leaders and to the irrationality of followers:

> The people who join rebel groups are overwhelmingly young, uneducated males. For this group, objectively observed grievances might count for relatively little. Rather they may be disproportionately drawn from those easily manipulated by propaganda and who find the power that comes from the possession of a gun alluring. Social psychologists find that around 3 percent of the population has psychopathic tendencies ... and this is more than is needed to equip a rebel group with recruits.[35]

Furthermore, according to Collier, the proliferation of child soldiers supports their thesis, as "obviously children do not join rebellions because of objective social grievances."[36]

This analysis colludes in empowering external actors at the expense of local ones by portraying resistance to the "inexplicable" callousness of African governments as irrational and poorly informed, at best, and childlike, if not psychopathic, at worst. In an unsupported flight of rhetoric, which promotes the objectification of governments and societies in conflict, and further reifies their essential difference from the rationality and social-minded purpose of the architects of global governance, Collier and his associates conclude: " ... hence most modern civil wars are not remotely like the nineteenth-century American civil war that ended slavery."[37]

By criminalizing and attributing undiluted local origins to non-/un-Western warfare, such analyses empower an agenda that is preoccupied with the quarantine of civil war within local state boundaries and the reengineering of society to remove the sources of violence. However, there is a further distinction in policy discourse on societies in conflict between the merely dysfunctional and the positively predatory. Some innocent local parties must be identified, in whose name intervention can be mounted and governance reconstructed. Thus the poor as a vulnerable group that is preyed upon by "conflict entrepreneurs" has loomed large in the development agenda, and, as a category of victims, "the poor" does considerable normative work in justifying the derogations of sovereignty and autonomy inherent in the practices of global governance. Because of this, running alongside the discussions of "new

---

[33] Collier, *Breaking the Conflict Trap*, p. 65.

[34] Ibid., p. 56.

[35] Ibid., p. 68.

[36] Ibid., p. 69.

[37] Ibid., p. 32.

Barbarism" in the international literature is a view of the "innocent poor" in whose name interventions may legitimately be conducted.

The Secretary-General's report to the Security Council on the Protection of Civilians in Armed Conflict notes that in the "new wars" of the 1990s, "the dividing line between civilians and combatants is frequently blurred,"[38] as armed gangs and paramilitaries take up arms in pursuit of a variety of interests. The policy literature seeks to reassert distinctions between the criminal combatant and the innocent civilian, as a corollary of the "greed" thesis, which promotes the view of mass action as being perpetrated by unwitting dupes in the service of a cunning and self-interested elite. The greed thesis removes rationality from conflict for all but the least scrupulous, and thus awards a role of victimhood to the "helpless civilian." For example, the Secretary-General's report begins by noting that

> ... hardly a day goes by when we are not presented with evidence of the intimidation, brutalization, torture, and killing of helpless civilians ... Rebel factions, opposition fighters, and Government forces continue to target innocent civilians with alarming frequency.[39]

Throughout the policy literature, similar distinctions are routinely drawn. Refugees yearning for home, rescued child soldiers, former combatants waiting to "reintegrate into civilian life or a legitimate, restructured military organization," farmers and merchants, parents, women, and unemployed youth appear regularly as groups of innocents who are preyed upon by conflict masterminds, "spoilers," terrorists, and their henchmen. An influential report produced by the International Commission for Intervention and State Sovereignty, devoted to the staking out of new normative ground in support of intervention, describes the plight of "civilians seeking shelter" or "caught in the crossfire," "people in need," "child soldiers," and "ordinary people" going about their "daily lives." The report specifically aims to "refocus ... the international searchlight back where it should always be: on the duty to protect communities from mass killing, women from systematic rape, and children from starvation."[40]

Such rhetoric supports the view that civil war is not a problem inherent in the condition of modern statehood on the periphery of a global economy characterized by structural violence; rather, it is a deviation from "normality," and once the rotten apples have been dealt with, ordinary life can resume. The rhetoric continues to proffer the hope that weak and oppressed, but determinedly liberal, individuals hide among the rubble in civil war battle zones, awaiting the helping hand of the international community to lead them out into the light of day so that they can begin the task of enacting a responsible politics and a market-oriented economics.

This is an analysis that achieves many rhetorical objectives. It erects a purported alliance between international interveners and oppressed and innocent liberals in war-torn states, thus legitimizing intervention. It posits war as a local and criminal phenomenon, a disruption that must be contained for the security of the rest of us,

---

[38] Kofi Annan, "Report of the Secretary-General to the Security Council on the Protection of Civilians in Armed Conflict," UN Doc. S/1999/957, September 8, 1999, para. 9.

[39] Ibid., para. 2.

[40] International Commission for Intervention and State Sovereignty, *Responsibility to Protect* (Ottawa: International Development Research Centre, 2001), p. 17.

thus further legitimizing specifically international action and promoting the resurrection of the territorial state that can effectively police its population and its borders as a priority for intervention. It develops a model of "good governance" as a technical matter, justifying far-reaching intervention into state agencies by international experts. Finally, it attributes state failure in part to dysfunctional non-state institutions within society, further justifying measures to break down preexisting constituencies and collectives through the imposition of procedures and processes that require the individual to respond *as an individual,* weakening preexisting bonds of solidarity and mutual assistance. As such, it constructs the problem of warfare in such a way that neoliberal models of governance appear to be the obvious solution to problems typically posed by civil conflicts in the 1990s.

BARBARIANS AT THE GATES?

A striking feature of the policy discourse enshrined in these documents is that the presumption of victimized innocence awarded to civilians in war zones is swiftly withdrawn if those civilians attempt to leave behind the scene of their terrorization and to find a safe haven "over here." A final aspect of contemporary policy discourse, and one that has a significant effect on the predispositions of international interveners and interventionary mandates, is the way in which the policy discourses characterize the dangers of people in flight from conflict situations. Concern expressed for the poor and victimized in a post-conflict situation has been singularly disconnected from any willingness to harbor these victims in an era during which increasing numbers of refugees have found respect for their rights declining. Several of the policy documents noted above demonize war-torn states and societies, a predilection associated with the policy-makers' concern to reinforce the borders that keep the populations of these states segregated from the rest of the world, in an era in which economic globalization threatens those borders.

Thus, the United Nations' High Level Panel on Threats, Challenges, and Changes articulates explicitly the sense of threat associated with greater mobility among wider sections of the global population:

> The technological revolution that has radically changed the worlds of communication, information-processing, health, and transportation has eroded borders, altered migration, and allowed individuals the world over to share information at a speed inconceivable two decades ago.[41]

These policy documents share a concern that populations on the move will prove difficult to govern, and a concern that the dysfunctional populations of the war-torn South may, through their mobility, spread the contagion of "insecurity." Thus the High Level Panel comments that "the security of the most affluent States can be held hostage to the ability of the poorest State to contain an emerging disease."[42] Meanwhile, Collier and his associates discuss the economic "burden" of accommodating refugees, along with the social effects of this accommodation. Their assertion that "large-scale refugee flows put people into crowded conditions in the

---

[41] High Level Panel on Threats, Challenges, and Change, *A More Secure World,* para. 16.

[42] Ibid., para. 19.

asylum countries without access to clean water and food, making the camps a perfect environment for the spread of disease" is notable in loading responsibility firmly onto the refugees.[43] The movement of refugees, rather than the restriction of their movement implicit in the camp system, is placed in the frame.

In the same report, Collier and his team point to a correlation between refugee movements and increases in malaria incidence. The unregulated movement of refugees through jungle areas where they come into contact with unfamiliar strains of the disease, against which they have no resistance, is regarded as rendering their bodies a threat to the wider world. Furthermore, Collier asserts, the movement of refugees not only promotes the spread of HIV/AIDS but actually caused the global epidemic. Collier cites research suggesting that HIV began as a sporadic contagion on the Uganda/Tanzania border, but changed into an epidemic infection "because of the continuous rape, promiscuity, and dislocation during and after the war."[44] Once the epidemic started, refugees spread it further, as their sexual behavior and health were affected by poverty, by disruption of family and social structures and of health services, by increased sexual violence, and by increased socioeconomic vulnerability. Collier's report offers a similar account of the international drug trade. Civil war is regarded as creating havens for the production and movement of hard drugs. According to Collier's analysis, these conditions create demand in industrialized countries, triggering the associated problems of dependency, crime, and death "among young people in Australia, the United States, and Europe." As with HIV/AIDS, the spread of drug use is entirely discussed as a problem emerging from the behavior of people in war-torn societies, rather than from the behavior of people in affluent ones.[45]

Similar preoccupations carry over into policy documents specifically concerned with issues of migration. The Commission on Human Security begins its 2003 report with remarks celebrating the "movement of people across borders," a phenomenon that is held to reinforce the "interdependence of countries and communities" as well as enhancing diversity, facilitating the transfer of skills and knowledge, stimulating economic growth and development, and creating "new opportunities for pleasure or business."[46] However, the report's analysis of the impact of migration begins with a discussion of the effect of movements of people on state security and with the comment that "massive population movements affect the security of receiving states, often compelling them to close their borders and forcibly prevent people from reaching safety and protection."[47] The report continues with a discussion of the link between movement and development, which it regards as "complex," and of the human security needs of migrants, including displaced persons. Throughout, the report draws a distinction between the "human security of people" and "national sovereignty, security, and development needs," suggesting that these are in incipient contradiction and need to be balanced.[48] The way to balance these concerns, the

---

[43] Collier, *Breaking the Conflict Trap*, pp. 36–39, 41.

[44] Ibid., p. 47.

[45] Ibid., p. 44.

[46] Commission on Human Security, *Human Security Now* (New York, NY: Commission on Human Security, 2003), online at http://www.humansecurity-chs.org/finalreport/English/FinalReport.pdf, accessed September 17, 2007, p. 41.

[47] Ibid., p. 42.

[48] Ibid.

commission concludes, is through multilateral approaches to "promote ... orderly and predictable movements of people." The commission suggests that an "international migration framework of norms, processes, and institutional arrangements" is necessary to "ensure such order and predictability."[49] Within this framework, "the sovereignty and security of states would be balanced by the human security of people."[50]

In the commission's view, the movement of people is inevitable within, and even essential to, the operation of the global economy; this perception of migration as key to international commerce similarly occupies the subsequent report of the Global Commission on International Migration (GCIM).[51] In this respect, and in its concern to "empower" people to "fend for themselves" using their innate "entrepreneurial spirit," the human-security approach reflects a neoliberal agenda, combined with concern for "protection" envisaged in terms of a basic level of respect for human rights.

At the same time, since their reports regard "protection" as best ensured by "multilateral approaches" adopted by states and international organizations, both the Commission on Human Security and the subsequent Global Commission on International Migration emerge as proponents of expansions of networks of global governance, which leave power in the hands of states, and, particularly, Northern states. Both commissions consequently distinguish sharply between "regular" and "irregular" migration, and call for immediate action to expand networks of governance to minimize the scope for "irregular" migration, in the name of the security of the migrants themselves. Both seek to expand the extent to which the practice of migration itself conforms to the global governance agenda of promoting efficient globalized production, and both seek to promote oversight of migrating people by the state or by multilateral organizations.

The status of the migrant as a person out of place remains a worry in both these reports, which retain a strong attachment to the view that stasis is the norm. Migrants are viewed in a form of double vision, which locates them as unusual economic and social actors in terms of static conceptions of the place they have left behind and of the place they are entering. For example, there is a strong predisposition towards incorporating the activities of migrants into the logic of global governance, with respect to their continued links with their homeland. In its report, the Global Commission on International Migration advocates greater control over remittances sent by migrants to their countries of origin, demonstrating the extent of its ambitions to administer the circulation of migrants and their resources. Both reports note that the total volume of private remittances exceeds the volume of overseas development assistance to developing countries, and see this as an opportunity for promoting development and hence security at home.

Thus, the GCIM advocates the regularization of these transfers through the formation of Home Town Associations, which can combine remittances to serve the public good at home, and through provisions whereby migrants themselves would

[49] Ibid., p. 47.

[50] Ibid., p. 52.

[51] Global Commission on International Migration (GCIM), *Migration in an Interconnected World: New Directions for Action* (Geneva: Global Commission on International Migration, 2005), online at http://www.gcim.org/attachements/gcim-complete-report-2005.pdf, accessed September 17, 2007.

have the option of remitting in the form of goods and services already purchased, "rather than leaving such transactions in the hands of family members."[52] The GCIM report shores up the nexus between development, security, and governance by reiterating that "without sound financial systems, stable currencies, a favourable investment climate, and an honest administration, even large-scale and long-term remittance receipts are unlikely to contribute to sustainable growth." Indeed, as the report asserts, without the conditions of good governance, remittances "may actually be a disincentive to the introduction of reforms that would provide a more effective basis for long-term economic growth."[53] In this formulation, despite the portrayal of migrants as potentially bridging the gap between North and South, the gap itself is reasserted in the implicit assertion that the migrant, with his or her entrepreneurial spirit and exposure to the rational world of the developed North, is a better judge of household priorities than the family left behind, and that the efforts of the migrant are likely to come to nothing if the feckless governments of their countries of origin are not similarly exposed to rational economic practices.

Yet when the discussion turns to the question of the migrant as he or she figures in the receiving country, the portrayal of the migrant changes. Here, the emphasis is on social cohesion and integration—migrants must not, in effect, be permitted to disrupt the coherence of the country in which they work. They must make extra efforts to familiarize themselves with the rational principles of the rule of law, understanding that in return they will be granted respect for their rights and the extension of the shade of the umbrella of governmental protection over them. This dual vision of migrants entails that the migrants themselves are viewed as possessing a double character: they figure both as a potential source of development back home, thanks to their exposure to the rational practices of developed countries, and to their access to work and income, but also as a potential source of disruption to those rational practices themselves, thanks to their underdeveloped origins. By investing the migrant with this sense of double displacement, the gap between static conceptions of North and South is reiterated, a state-centered vision of development and underdevelopment is reasserted, and a view of movement as subordinate to the natural condition of stasis is confirmed.

Underpinning this policy discourse, then, are a number of complementary oppositions that support a particular and highly state-centric view of intervention and post-conflict reconstruction, focusing on the state as the lynchpin of any form of order. In this way, the discourse ignores the potential inherent in Kantian liberalism, perhaps, for shaping a more cosmopolitan approach to the post-Cold War World. Peace and war are associated with liberalism and illiberalism; development and underdevelopment; modernity and savagery; rationality and barbarism; the global and the local. As such, certain actors are privileged—most specifically those "development experts" representing "global" institutions and knowledge regimes, who intervene to promote peace through the construction of liberal institutions of state. At the same time, others—in particular poor peasants moving on unregulated pathways through shadowy border zones and engaging in informal economic transactions—are stigmatized. The solutions implied are clear: the deployment of international interventionary task forces to engage in the business of reconstructing

[52] Ibid., p. 26.
[53] Ibid.

states that can contain, and ultimately discipline, their unruly populations in the interests of economic integration.

The impact of these ideas about civil wars and the people who prosecute them has, arguably, been far-reaching. The view of conflict zones as isolated wastelands, devoid of meaning, and peopled by psychopaths and trauma victims, was taken into post-conflict countries as a means of legitimizing far-reaching international intervention that exceeded mere peacekeeping. Furthermore, I will suggest that the prevalence of this view has significantly problematized relationships between international interveners and local populations, who, as the previous chapter suggested, regarded their struggles in rather a different light. The clash of paradigms that ensued forms the context within which the political strategies described in this study were formulated and pursued.

CHAPTER IV

"FULL OF MALARIA AND TOO REMOTE": CONSTRUCTING AND POLICING THE BOUNDARIES OF HOME

"[A Ministry of Interior official] said we should go to Ratanakkiri province where there is a lot of open land for farming ... But I will not go because Ratanakkiri is full of malaria and it is too remote."

Illegal migrant, describing his plans after deportation from Bangkok to Cambodia, 2003.

The discursive construction of peoples, societies, and states in conflict as dysfunctional, and the interventionary drive to render them amenable to governance and economic integration, resulted in two key policy goals evident across a range of policy documents produced by different international actors, namely, the construction of borders to keep the poor and war-afflicted in their place, and the atomization of populations within these borders to facilitate both their control by states and their competitiveness as market players. There are two problems with these efforts. First, the promotion of policies in both these areas simultaneously is paradoxical: on the one hand, the construction and policing of borders involves the promotion of particular subjectivities associated with idealized conceptions of nationhood and citizenship. On the other hand, the atomization of populations within these borders requires that collective identities remain in the realm of the ideal rather than forming a basis for a practical politics. Second, the cases of Cambodia and Timor both suggest that, empirically speaking, the ideal of peasant farmers yearning, above all, for a piece of land they can call "home" is not uniformly recognized by individuals in post-conflict situations as applicable to themselves—indeed, many such individuals routinely and strenuously resist it. While the devastating effects of displacement are clearly recognized in the policy literature, the desire of many displaced persons to avoid return, or of many individuals who remain at home to leave, is passed over in silence, and, thus, delegitimated by contemporary post-conflict policy.

Policies that differentiate "at home" from "displaced" are invariably portrayed as self-evidently in the interests of the "innocent victims" of warfare. While it is clearly the case that many people benefit from such policies, the self-evidence of their value requires critical scrutiny since it involves a considerable exercise of power. The ways in which power is tacitly exercised on the ground in post-intervention countries, to reinstitute boundaries and thus shore up the unequal power relations inherent in liberal peacebuilding, is the subject of this chapter. In this regard, two types of boundaries are examined: the territorial boundary between the state and its neighbors, and the conceptual boundary between the "local" and the "international" in the context of intervention.

It is a cliché of contemporary political science that the fragmenting impact of globalization mounts a challenge to the nation-state project. Indeed, the "new wars" are recognized as a symptom of this; Mary Kaldor notes a distinction between "old wars" of national liberation, which "presented themselves as emancipatory, nation-building projects," and wars based around identity politics, in which leaders advance a "claim to power on the basis of labels."[1] While noting the power of nostalgic discourses of home and the past, Kaldor also points out that these localized wars "involve a myriad of transnational connections so that the distinction between internal and external, between aggression (attacks from abroad) and repression (attacks from inside the country), or even between local and global are difficult to sustain."[2] Similarly, Mark Duffield refers to "network wars" that "typically oppose and ally the transborder resource networks of state incumbents, social groups, diasporas, strongmen, and so on."[3] Political economy approaches generally have noted the extent to which new wars are sustained by the ability of combatants to tap into networks trading in natural resources.[4] This new focus on networks in intrastate warfare has illustrated the extent to which borders are transgressed and identities manipulated for political gain in the dynamics of conflict, thus compounding the difficulties faced by those attempting to consolidate nations and states.

The distinction between new and old wars has been criticized on the basis that real warfare defies such neat categorizations. Edward Newman, for example, comments that all wars contain elements of both these categories.[5] While neither Cambodia nor East Timor fits the "new war" model precisely, they both contain elements of it that are worth bearing in mind in the context of interventionary exercises attempting to restore bounded sovereignty as a basis for peace.

In both Cambodia and East Timor, the wars were ostensibly about nation-building. In the case of Cambodia, contention between parties was framed in the ideology of the Cold War and, closer to home, was portrayed as a conflict about the achievement of Khmer autonomy, reclaimed from regional players who threatened that autonomy, prominently including Thailand, China, and Vietnam, which were said to have rapacious designs on the ancestral *srok Khmae*.[6] As the Cold War wound down, the latter portrayal came to dominate at the expense of the former, while the inclination of external observers to sympathize with Khmer claims that Chinese, Thai, or Vietnamese expansionism was a genuine strategic concern—rather than dismissing those claims as fictions born of ethnic paranoia—has markedly declined.

---

[1] Mary Kaldor, *New and Old Wars: Organised Violence in a Global Era* (Cambridge: Polity, 2001), pp. 6–7.

[2] Ibid., p. 2.

[3] Mark Duffield, *Global Governance and the New Wars: The Merging of Development and Security* (London: Zed Books, 2001), p. 14.

[4] David Keen, "A Rational Kind of Madness," *Oxford Development Studies* 25,1 (1997): 67–75; Philippe LeBillon, *Geopolitics of Resource Wars: Resource Dependence, Governance, and Violence* (London: Frank Cass, 2005).

[5] Edward Newman, "The 'New Wars' Debate: A Historical Perspective Is Needed," *Security Dialogue* 35,2 (2004): 173–89.

[6] "Khmer land." The nature and extent of this territory, and claims that it has been lost to neighboring peoples over the centuries, have constituted a central nationalist trope in Cambodian political rhetoric since boundaries were drawn during the colonial era.

This gave a "new war" feel to a rhetoric of ethnic antagonism that in fact changed little from the early 1980s to the turn of the century. The decline of superpower and regional material support transformed the financial aspects of the conflict, as militaries on both sides relied increasingly on illicit and transnational sales of national resources to fund their campaigns. Gems and timber, exported to Thailand and Vietnam by entrepreneurial military commanders without supervision from civilian authorities, permitted the parties that formed the post-1993 Cambodian government to purchase the defection of a number of Khmer Rouge commanders— and to do so on a competitive basis. The Cambodian People's Party's consolidation of power from 1997 was, to a great extent, the result of its success in winning the loyalties of defecting Khmer Rouge, at the expense of their former resistance allies in the Front Uni Nationale pour un Cambodge Indépendent, Neutre, Pacifique, et Coopératif (National United Front for an Independent, Neutral, Peaceful, and Cooperative Cambodia), better known as FUNCINPEC.

In East Timor, elements of the "new wars" are more difficult to find; yet, as with Cambodia, the shift in the nature of the conflict from 1991 onwards does reflect the "globalization" of civil conflict. Although members of the resistance movement in East Timor were never able to tap into lucrative transnational commodity networks, they did tap into transnational networks of activism and concern, appealing to a range of constituencies for support. In Australia, for example—a country that led the world in its diplomatic recognition of the Indonesian invasion and did not waver from this policy until the very end—a web of civil-society initiatives in support of East Timor emerged in the 1990s, attracting support from organizations as various as the Roman Catholic Church, the Returned Servicemen's League, and a variety of trade unions. Indeed, the resistance struggle became increasingly oriented towards capturing the attention of the media, rather than scoring military victories, as international interest grew. Although the Timorese resistance were motivated by aspirations for national independence, the war was won through its appeal to contemporary issues—primarily the issue of human rights—animating a self-declared "international community" of transnational activists. In these respects, the war in Timor bears the marks of normative cosmopolitanism, if not globalization. In both Timor and Cambodia, ostensibly nationalist wars had the effect of significantly thickening a variety of transnational linkages and importing foreign actors and networks into the intimate web of domestic politics.

Much of the post-conflict reconstruction literature has responded by focusing on the need to choke off transnational connections as a means to end new wars by "cutting the rebel financial jugular."[7] However, the hybrid, unbounded nature of "new war" models reflects not so much an aberrant feature of contemporary reality, but, instead, a broader shift in the way that reality is understood. This shift in understanding exemplifies the creativity with which human agents, in conditions of both war and peace, transgress borders and boundaries that are invested with power as "social facts." This creativity has been recognized in anthropological studies where the once foundational idea of the territorial "community," available for scrutiny via ethnographic methods deployed in "single sites and local situations," has largely disappeared in favor of a focus upon "the circulation of cultural

---

[7] Paul Collier, *Breaking the Conflict Trap: Civil War and Development Policy* (Washington, DC: World Bank, 2003), p. 141.

meanings, objects, and identities in diffuse time-space."[8] The impact of globalization in fragmenting the "world system" as an overarching metanarrative within which "lifeworlds" can be situated has prompted scholars of ethnography to pursue new paths and connections, moving towards the "speculative course of constructing subjects by simultaneously constructing the discontinuous contexts in which they act and are acted upon."[9] The idea of the closed, ahistorical community, echoing through the annals of anthropology since colonial times, has been replaced by a notion that lived worlds are fragmentary and constructed by the movement of individuals through a range of discontinuous contexts. The historical and cultural contingencies of birth may be a significant source of identity, but certainly not a determining one.

Even within international relations, the reified conception of the state as a unitary actor in an international states system has been attacked by critical theorists evincing a sharper awareness of the political, and consequently contingent, nature of the international. Thus Richard Ashley declared in 1989, as international relations theorists watched their world crumble,

> A domestic community, a linguistic convention, a *lebenswelt*, a social system, an economic sphere, a political sphere ... none of these is ever simply given as an undisputed, sharply bounded, already completed project to which one need only give a name. None exists prior to or independent of the play of practice within history."[10]

These positions give rise to new questions in the analysis of communities, nations, and states. Ashley asks, "How, by way of what practices, by appeal to what cultural resources and in the face of what resistances is [the] boundary imposed and ritualised?"[11] Arguably, this question implies another—"who determines whether imposition and ritualization have been achieved and whose interests they serve?" As such, some anthropologists increasingly question the extent to which the "local" has ever truly been local, viewing individuals as primarily, rather than marginally, travelers, networkers, and self-inventors, rather than rooted citizens.[12] This perspective places international intervention in a different light—not as a set of actions seeking to restore a normality lost during civil war, but as actions imposing a "normality" that perhaps has never been either practically realized or particularly salient.

Furthermore, the reality of international intervention itself, both as it is created through peacekeeping operations and through subsequent international reconstruction efforts, becomes an element that survivors in post-conflict countries consider when choosing their own global and transnational strategies, and, in consequence, this reality also shapes their imagining of community. For these

---

[8] George Marcus, "Ethnography In/Of the World System: The Emergence of Multi-Sited Ethnography," *Annual Review of Anthropology*, 24 (1995): 96.

[9] Ibid., p. 98.

[10] Richard K. Ashley, "Living on Border Lines: Man, Poststructuralism, and War," in *International/Intertextual Relations: Postmodern Readings of World Politics*, ed. James Der Derian and Michael J. Shapiro (New York, NY: Lexington, 1989), p. 262.

[11] Ibid.

[12] James Clifford, *Routes, Travel, and Translation in the Late Twentieth Century* (Cambridge: Harvard University Press, 1997).

reasons, the attitudes of post-conflict survivors towards the interveners who arrive to assist them are significant. To the extent that post-conflict survivors focus upon the fact of intervention, rather than the myth of restoration of sovereignty, they challenge the project of constructing a rigid divide between the global and the local, and they make plain the hypocrisy inherent in denigrating those who cross borders in the other direction (i.e., from inside to out, instead of from outside to in) as potentially or actually either criminal or diseased. Further, the ways in which post-conflict survivors resist the instruction to stay still and rebuild a particular territorial entity designated as their "home" have evoked far-reaching efforts by international interveners to reinforce and police the divide between those allowed to be mobile and those condemned to stasis. These efforts are prompted by a continued attachment, on the part of interveners, to traditional conceptions of governance that underpin notions widely accepted as universally beneficial—notions such as state sovereignty and democracy. However, in the context of a globalizing world, these notions have become ideological to the extent that they mask practices of coercion designed to shore up inequalities in the world order, a process described by, among others, Robert Cox and Mark Duffield in their work on aid and the function of the state in the contemporary world.

There is, then, a clear mismatch between the interests of social theory and those of peacebuilding policy. Social theorists increasingly seek to chart the ways in which individuals transgress conventional notions of static identity and the ways in which new notions of identity transgress conventional notions of community boundaries, while peacebuilding policy-makers promote statist forms of peace that imply specifically modern ideals of nation and citizenship. From the policy-maker's perspective, idealized notions of nation and citizen are regarded as emerging as the end-product of development and institutional design rather than as results of self-invention or political agency at the local level. However, critical trends in social theory suggest that these ideals' relevance to the lived experience of ordinary people has perhaps always been overplayed in conventional political science, and is certainly under challenge from the accelerating pace of globalization and its impact on modes of warfare and post-colonial statehood. This raises significant questions regarding the stakes of this kind of interventionary policy.

On the one hand, it should be acknowledged that the promotion of static conceptions of a bounded political community offers an approach to security, autonomy, development, and identity—an approach that is predicated on the functioning of the state. Rob Walker points out that, despite all the problems with statism, it does provide an "elegant solution" to the problem of inside and outside.[13] While the elegance of this solution becomes much more questionable on the periphery of the state system, in places like Cambodia and East Timor, where state-building efforts cost the lives of millions, it is nevertheless the case that political science has yet to come up with much of a thinkable alternative.

Furthermore, in both Cambodia and East Timor, a state-building project conforms precisely to elite agendas, formulated in the name of the "people." Although the wars in both countries had "new" aspects to them, those people involved also espoused strongly nationalist rhetoric. The reestablishment of boundaries was the *sine qua non* of peace for local leaders as well as for international

---

[13] R. B. J. Walker, *Inside/Outside: International Relations as Political Theory* (Cambridge: Cambridge University Press, 1992), p. 53.

interveners; and it certainly had important resonances for the public as well, many of whom bought enthusiastically into nationalist aspirations with respect to the homeland, even while they may have harbored ambitions to operate, as individuals, on a wider scale.

It is worth asking who benefits from peacebuilding projects designed to convert nationalist aspirations into internationally sanctioned state-building operations. I ask this question not because I wish to suggest that the wars in Cambodia or Timor-Leste were somehow better than the peace that was achieved, but as a means to understand what kind of power was awarded by the peace, and to whom. As Mary Kaldor points out, the emergence of transnationalized wars offers entirely different opportunities to different sections of the population:

> The [new] wars epitomize a new kind of global/local divide, between those members of a global class who can speak English, have access to faxes, email, or satellite television, who use dollars or deutschmarks or credit cards, and who can travel freely, and those who are excluded from global processes, who live off what they can sell or barter or what they receive in humanitarian aid, whose movement is restricted by roadblocks, visas, and the costs of travel, and who are prey to sieges, forced famines, landmines, etc.[14]

Kaldor's comment underplays the extent to which poor people *do* move, taking the most appalling risks to do so, through war zones, across borders, and around road blocks, often in desperation, sometimes in the pursuit of profit. However, her comment also underlines the fact that, in a world where movement is power, and where networks of interventionary global governance supercede the role of the state in making choices regarding the real redistribution of resources, policies currently being promoted—which seek to use democratic procedures, internationally guaranteed boundaries, and promotion of national identities as a means to channel the aspirations, orientations, and activities of people in post-conflict societies into particular forms of peace—acquire a political, rather than a merely humanitarian, tenor. From this perspective, the practice of reinstating the lost statehood of societies in conflict becomes a much more complex business, both in terms of ethics and pragmatics. Restoration of sovereign statehood starts to look less like the emancipation of peoples now placed in control of their own destiny, as a modernist defense might suggest, and more like a device to facilitate their internment.

Notions of peace anchored in the resurrection of the territorial state, then, offer an interestingly one-sided take on the subject of globalization. Globalization is discussed intensively in terms of its impact on the rationale for intervention; for example, much theorizing about the rights and wrongs of intervention has focused on the emergence of globally oriented citizens in Western countries watching scenes of suffering on television and desiring to promote human rights for all their fellow human beings. The role of international organizations, transnational networks, and even diaspora communities in producing coalitions in favor of intervention and action has been widely discussed.[15] However, the impact of globalization on the

---

[14] Kaldor, *New and Old Wars*, p. 130.

[15] See for example, Stanley Hoffman, *The Ethics and Politics of Humanitarian Intervention* (South Bend, IN: University of Notre Dame Press, 1997); Nicholas Wheeler, *Saving Strangers: Humanitarian Intervention in International Society* (Oxford: Oxford University Press, 2000); Piers

ideas of people in post-conflict societies is less prominent in the peace literature. This is true despite the fact that, as United Nations peacekeepers roll into town, the locals are already queuing up for jobs in sports bars with import permits and satellite links to facilitate the sipping of Victoria Bitter while watching the Superbowl.

The project of peacebuilding ascribes to local populations a desire only for greater security at "home" brought about through renewed assertions of respect, on the part of potentially threatening neighbors, for the sovereignty (manifest in an "invitation" to the peacekeepers and the appointment of small elite bodies of local notables to "consult" with them) and territorial integrity of their homeland. Despite the evident presence of transnational networks, international donors, foreign investors, and expatriate "technical assistants," peace is essentially conceptualized as operating within—indeed, as in large part constituted by—the reasserted borders of the community. Prescriptions for development, justice, and the reestablishment of political authority reflect a concern on the part of international policy makers and local elites to cement the bonds that confine individuals within particular spaces. The institutions envisaged are either institutions of state, or institutions of civil society, the latter perhaps sustaining transnational contacts but nevertheless remaining wedged firmly "between the state and the family."

The disjuncture between the end of reasserting territorial sovereignty, on the one hand, and the means to this end, in which a powerful role is awarded to international interveners representing a cosmopolitan community abroad, is telling, and is evident from the most cursory glance along the street within any newly autonomous state. Rhetoric aside, the securing of borders is not primarily about constituting an autonomous and self-governing political community, but about securing the interests of external actors and the ideological power of the state project more widely. Intervention represents a challenge to a state-making process; confining a conflict within the borders of an already "failed" state rescues the logic of the wider state system from violation. As such, conflicts with significant transnational or international dimensions can be reimagined as problems concerning a single state's failure, rather than as problems involving the wider disjunctures that emerge from the violence of competitive state formation itself. Thus, in the context of Cambodia, the Paris Accords set out explicitly to de-link the ongoing war from broader regional state-making efforts, not only by including explicit provisions regarding the withdrawal of foreign forces from Cambodian soil, but by incorporating reassurances regarding the sovereignty of neighboring countries. Equally, the Security Council's refusal to contemplate sending peacekeepers to East Timor, once the Indonesians had denounced this option as an affront to Indonesian sovereignty and to the status of the Indonesian military, showed a continuation of long-standing tendencies to value Indonesian state-building projects well ahead of Timorese welfare.

The typical peacebuilding effort to reinstate boundaries does not simply involve ensuring that foreign forces do not enter a post-conflict territory, but also involves framing issues related to conflict so that resolving those issues becomes the responsibility of the emerging post-conflict state, working in partnership with international organizations. This tendency to shrink internationalized conflict back into a territorial box is a very powerful one, which has two effects. First,

Robinson, *The CNN Effect: The Myth of News, Foreign Policy, and Intervention* (London: Routledge, 2002).

reconciliation and resettlement become issues to be confronted within the post-conflict population, a process that cannot be allowed to affect neighboring states or the state system as a whole. As such, a border becomes a *cordon sanitaire*. Second, the integration of the post-conflict state into the global economy occurs via the erection of borders that privilege capital flowing in, and entrench the position of elites who can gatekeep with respect to these flows, but which put wider sections of the post-conflict population at a disadvantage in seeking economic opportunities, forcing them to submit to the "competitiveness" of the market.

The two policy areas discussed below illustrate well the ways in which policy-makers promote idealized conceptions of the bounded political community as the answer to transnationalized warfare, even while their policies expand the possibilities for far-reaching intervention in the post-conflict state and society. These are policies concerned with refugee return and policies regarding accountability for atrocity. These are discussed here as a means of connecting shifts in international thinking on post-conflict reconstruction with modalities of intervention in Cambodia and East Timor, and in exemplifying the ways in which "solutions" are experienced by the individuals who have to make them work.

REFUGEE RETURN

It is often remarked that the "new wars" of the 1990s saw an enormous rise in the numbers of refugees in the world. It is also the case that the 1990s saw a decrease in the number of asylum applications and in the number of refugees being resettled outside their countries of origin, and a dramatic increase in the numbers of refugees being returned "home." Large-scale repatriation was associated with a number of peacekeeping operations, particularly those designed in the early 1990s to deal with conflicts left over from the Cold War, such as the conflicts in El Salvador, Nicaragua, and Guatemala in Central America; Mozambique, Namibia, and Angola in Africa; and in Cambodia in Southeast Asia. In 2006, the United Nations High Commissioner for Refugees (UNHCR) reported that while refugee numbers worldwide had declined from the high point of the early 1990s, the amount of time that refugees spend as refugees is rising. The percentage of these refugees who are in "protracted situations"—meaning that they have lived as displaced persons for more than five years—has risen from 16.3 percent in 1993 to 61 percent in 2004.[16]

This change in the nature of refugee flows arises from a number of factors, including the impact that the "successful" repatriations of the early 1990s had on international perceptions of refugees. The 1990s saw a marked shift in policy discussions on refugees as compared to the 1970s and 1980s. In earlier decades, agencies such as the UNHCR typically emphasized providing refugees with opportunities for relocation, or the means for self-reliance in refugee camps, and assisting hosting countries with development projects intended to help counteract the burdens posed by the refugees. In the 1990s, however, and despite the growing proportion of refugees caught in protracted situations, debates over refugees were much more intensively focused on "rights of return" and upon repatriation and reintegration schemes associated with peacekeeping and post-conflict reconstruction. This change in focus, combined with the emergence of a discourse on conflict,

---

[16] UNHCR, *The State of the World's Refugees: Human Displacement in the New Millennium* (Oxford: Oxford University Press, 2006), p. 10.

described in the previous chapter, interpreted the causes of displacement as essentially local and agential, rather than structural, and thus defined them as eminently fixable with local good will and the kind of external advice that was newly available in the post-Cold War world.[17] Essentially, the solutions available to refugees dwindled to one—go home.

The UNHCR characterizes the change thus: "Whereas the older paradigm can be described as reactive, exile-oriented, and refugee-specific, the one which has started to emerge over the past few years can be characterized as proactive, homeland-oriented, and holistic."[18] This implies, according to UNHCR, a requirement for governments and humanitarian organizations "to take active steps to prevent, limit, and reverse the movement of refugees from their country of origin."[19] A key figure involved in developing and implementing this new approach was Sergio Vieira de Mello, who oversaw the forced repatriation of Vietnamese boat people from refugee camps in Hong Kong and Southeast Asia, and who subsequently headed the UNHCR's repatriation program in Cambodia.

Return in the context of peacekeeping fits well with the logic and rhetoric of liberal global governance. It offers a humane alternative to resettlement in third countries,[20] ensured by increasing scrutiny of and intervention in not only the process of return itself, but of the refugees' "reintegration" into society, and of post-conflict reconstruction of that society. Thus in the repatriation programs of the early 1990s, the UNHCR "remained actively involved in addressing the needs of returnees for longer periods than ever before."[21]

The assertion that going "home" is the "most appropriate solution," not only to a refugee problem, but to refugees' problems, has been widely criticized for reifying an entirely accidental relationship between the individual and territory where he or she was born not only into a source of identity, but also into a historical destiny.[22] Furthermore, the centrality to the state system of asserting a "historic fit between the group and the land"[23] prompted neglect of the actual experiences of returnees themselves throughout the 1990s, which the UN had termed the "decade of repatriation." As B. S. Chimni suggests, the "repatriation turn" emerged not as a "product of extensive studies of the complex issues involved, but [as] the outcome of

---

[17] See B. S. Chimni, "The Geopolitics of Refugee Studies: The View from the South," *Journal of Refugee Studies* 11,4 (1998): 351.

[18] UNCHR, *State of the World's Refugees, 1995: In Search of Solutions* (Oxford: Oxford University Press, 1995), p. 16.

[19] Ibid.

[20] "Third countries" is the term used to refer to the resettlement of refugees in a different country from either their country of origin or the country where they initially sought refuge.

[21] UNHCR, *State of the World's Refugees: Fifty Years of Humanitarian Action* (Oxford: Oxford University Press, 2000), p. 133.

[22] See, for example, Daniel Warner, "Voluntary Repatriation and the Meaning of Return to Home: A Critique of Liberal Mathematics," *Journal of Refugee Studies* 7,2–3 (1994): 160–74; Finn Stepputat, "Repatriation and the Politics of Space: The Case of the Mayan Disapora and Return Movement," *Journal of Refugee Studies* 7,2–3 (1994): 175–85; Naila Habib, "The Search for Home," *Journal of Refugee Studies* 9,1 (1996): 97–102.

[23] Warner, "Liberal Mathematics," p. 163.

a marriage between convenient theory, untested assumptions, and the interests of states."[24]

The claim that refugees just want to go home makes the problem reassuringly simple; it also reinforces some of the binary oppositions, outlined in the previous chapter, between the guilty and the innocent, the "spoiler" and the "victims" who just want to "rebuild their lives." People, whether guilty or innocent, are changed by war, and, consequently, solutions that are legitimized by an appeal to nostalgia are dangerously divorced from reality. Individuals who have survived, perhaps for many years, in war zones or refugee camps have done so by orienting their "ordinary lives" to these conditions, in terms of their livelihoods and in the strategies they use for protecting themselves, their families, and their property.

The expectation that refugees will return home and resume their "ordinary lives" significantly underplays the extent of these changes. In wartime, people lose old skills and develop new ones; they forge alliances and enmities in pursuit of what they regard as their vital interests; they lose touch with extended families, or have children of their own; they often lose and occasionally gain material assets; and, of course, they simply get older. All of these processes mean that the idea that they have a "life" to return to and get on with is a highly problematic one. Although people may aspire to an ideal of peace, whether nostalgic or forward-looking, individuals find it highly risky to reorient their behavior and act *as if* peace is now assured. To the extent that they continue to use strategies adapted to conditions of wartime, everybody has the potential to be a "spoiler." This legacy of war was recognized in a report produced by the UN Border Relief Operation, which noted that conditions in the border camps and Khmer strategies for coping with them "have failed to provide them [residents of the camps] with the skills necessary for adapting to the pressures of 'normal' existence."[25] Repatriation schemes routinely underplay the cost and difficulty of reorienting one's perspective, livelihood, and survival strategies to conditions of peace.

Given these problems, the UNHCR's assertion that 90 percent of refugees on the Cambodian border were eager to return "home" requires closer scrutiny. While conditions in the camps were certainly appalling, it appears that part of the rush to return to Cambodia had to do with the fact that refugees "quite correctly assumed that on return there would be fierce competition to secure access to the limited livelihood resources available for returning families."[26] Furthermore, following twelve years in camps during which refugees had effectively been held as hostages to a policy of containing Vietnamese expansionism, it is likely that the camp dwellers saw any alternative as preferable to staying where they were. What the returnees actually knew about Cambodia, by this stage, and the kinds of survival strategies they thought would work once they got "home," is far from clear. The ideas circulating in the refugee camps about a Vietnamization of the *srok Khmae* suggest

---

[24] Chimni, "Geopolitics of Refugee Studies," p. 364. See also Flora Cornish, Karl Peltzer, and Malcolm MacLachlan, "Returning Strangers: The Children of Malawian Refugees Come 'Home,'" *Journal of Refugee Studies*, 12,3 (1999): 265.

[25] Quoted in Grant Curtis, *Cambodia Reborn? The Transition to Democracy and Development* (Washington, DC: Brookings Institute, 1998), p. 113.

[26] Christopher McDowell and Marita Eastmond, "Transitions, State-Building, and the 'Residual' Refugee Problem: The East Timor and Cambodian Repatriation Experience," *Australian Journal of Human Rights* 8,1 (2002), online at http://www.austlii.edu.au/au/journals/AJHR/2002/, accessed September 18, 2007.

that information was highly politicized, if not positively inaccurate. Politicized misinformation was not the only source of confusion for the returnees. Refugees also had to contend with the simple lack of information about conditions in post-war Cambodia, so that it is unlikely many of them had an accurate picture of "home" to respond to in their decision making. Some had lived in the camps for more than a decade; children had been born and educated there. For many long-term camp residents, their memories of Cambodia were of a country that no longer existed.

The poverty of information available to returning Cambodians—as well as to the international agencies involved with UNTAC (United Nations Transitional Authority in Cambodia)—is illustrated by the problems that emerged when the UNHCR, in charge of the repatriation program, offered returnees a deal that would provide them with two hectares of farmland on their return, and asked them where they would like their farms to be. The most popular choice was a district called Rattanak Mondul, in Battambang province. This district was not, in fact, the "home" of most of the refugees who chose it. However, they wanted to go there because it was considered to be an area of fertile land, situated on a prosperous gem-trading route and close to the Thai border in case there was a need to escape from Cambodia again. However, when the UN made investigations, it was discovered that Rattanak Mondul had been destroyed by war; most of its residents were living in a displaced persons' camp; the ground was contaminated with land mines; and it had become the poorest district in the province—it remained the second poorest, with critical food security problems, in Battambang in 2004. The prosperous farming and gem-mining region that the refugees remembered, or had heard rumors of, was gone.[27]

Similar issues arose across Cambodia. The UNHCR's initial plan to resettle refugees as farmers had to be abandoned because although sufficient available farmland was identified initially, much of this land was subsequently found to be infested with land mines and, consequently, nonproductive. The "former peasant" refugees would have to find new ways of life. Lack of land entailed that the UNHCR had to allocate refugees to areas under the control of the Khmer Rouge, despite the fact that the Khmer Rouge were not cooperating with the peace process. According to one account, leaflets circulated to refugees in the camps in November 1992 said, "UNHCR is about to start movements to some new areas where previously UNHCR had no access" but did not inform the refugees that these areas were under the control of the Khmer Rouge.[28]

Finally, the UNHCR adopted the policy of giving people cash grants instead of land. This policy was criticized on the grounds that it was unlikely to result in refugees settling down somewhere in rural Cambodia; critics raised fears that refugees would end up as a shifting, homeless, and consequently unruly population on the streets of Phnom Penh. Initially, the UNHCR claimed that this was not the case and that most of the recipients of the cash grant option had chosen to live with relatives.[29]

---

[27] UNHCR, *The Problem of Access to Land and Ownership in Repatriation Operation* (Geneva: UNHCR Inspection and Evaluation Service, 1998).

[28] Samantha Power, *Chasing the Flame: Sergio Vieira de Mello and the Fight to Save the World* (London: Allen Lane, 2008), p. 112.

[29] Jeff Crisp and Andrew Mayne, "Review of the Cambodia Repatriation Operation," UNHCR Evaluation Report (Geneva: UNHCR, 1993).

This claim is rather tenuous given that, in the case of Cambodia, the UNHCR had difficulties expanding its mandate to incorporate a monitoring role, and therefore it had no empirical basis for such assertions. This organization's monitoring of the refugees proved to be inadequate, due to high rates of movement by the returnees once inside the country, and its performance as a monitoring agency was criticized. In part, the problems were due to bad weather—the northwest was hit by both floods and droughts in the early 1990s, so many attempts at farming failed.[30] In part, the difficulties were also linked to the ongoing security problems in Cambodia, and particularly in the northwest, where new bouts of displacement recurred until the war finally ended in 1999, particularly associated with the Khmer Rouge's determination to hold Pailin. The northwest region (and particularly the district of Rattanak Mondul, which was right on the front line) saw trench warfare and the back-and-forth movement of armies associated with repeated government assaults on Pailin and the gem-mining regions around it until 1996, when Ieng Sary, the Khmer Rouge leader who controlled the region, defected to the government. The failure of peacebuilding more widely entailed the failure of intervention to monitor and support displaced persons' reintegration, and it was later concluded that up to 40 percent of repatriated refugees in the region later moved on as a result of instability, poor economic opportunities, or land expropriation, a problem to which returnees were particularly vulnerable.[31]

Despite the instability of the northwest, and despite the fact that many refugees had no kin networks there, according to declarations made by refugees at destination centers in Cambodia—the last information received by the United Nations regarding the whereabouts of returnees—the northwest remained the most popular destination for returnees. One subsequent study of returnees in the northwest suggests that many avoided going back to their actual "homes" or families out of "shame of being destitute" or fear of "losing face in their village or being rejected by relatives"—a finding that directly challenged the UNHCR's claim that most refugees went back to their families.[32] In early 1990s Cambodia, indeed, the sudden unannounced arrival of a new mouth to feed is likely to have posed problems for many rural families. Land shortages, extraordinarily rapid population growth, and dependence on low-productivity subsistence farming with scarce access to capital and poor irrigation made livelihoods precarious across the country. Later, UNHCR reports concluded that early claims that refugees were going "home" to their families had been overly optimistic; in fact, the returnees, rather than going "home," actually became pioneers, some carving out new villages and farms for themselves, using skills barely remembered after perhaps a decade in a refugee camp, and on land that was previously heavily forested, or, often, infested with land mines.[33]

---

[30] Fernando del Mundo, "Cambodia: The Killing Fields Revisited," *Refugees Magazine* 112 (1998), online at http://www.unhcr.org/publ/PUBL/3b81031e4.html, accessed September 18, 2007.

[31] UNHCR, *The Problem of Access to Land*, para. 77.

[32] Ana Garcia Rodicio, *A Restoration of Life in Cambodia: 1992–93 Returnees in Banteay Meanchey and Siem Reap* (Phnom Penh: Jesuit Refugee Service, 2000), cited in McDowell and Eastmond, "Transitions, State-Building, and the 'Residual' Refugee Problem," footnote 13.

[33] UNHCR, *The Problem of Access to Land*, para. 75; Brett Ballard, *Reintegration Programmes for Refugees in South East Asia: Lessons Learned from UNHCR's Experience* (Geneva: UNHCR, 2002), p. 47.

The point at issue here is not whether the returned refugees were better off in camps in Thailand or "at home" in Cambodia. The border camps were characterized by a level of violence and squalor that was hard to beat; and the fact that there was no unrest associated with the refugee program suggests that the inmates were glad to get away. The point is to consider the way the rhetoric surrounding the refugee return program obscured the reality of what the returnees might face, rather than revealing it in order to enable a debate over the appropriateness of the policy and subsequent forms of assistance.

It is significant, also, that some returnees continued to live a mobile lifestyle under the new border regime that emerged following the repatriation. One reason for the popularity of the northwest is that it was close to the Thai border and hence offered returnees the option of renewed flight if things didn't go well in Cambodia. Many displaced persons did flee to Thailand during the government offensive on Pailin in 1994, and, in 1997, 45,000 people were displaced following military battles in Battambang and Phnom Penh between forces loyal to the coalition partners, FUNCINPEC and the CPP (Cambodian People's Party). In 1997, camps were reopened in the former Sihanoukist enclave of O'Smach; one UNHCR official, reporting on a visit to this camp, commented, "Many told a recent visitor why they were reluctant to return home today after their dreams had turned to nightmares when they had first gone back."[34]

But the inhabitants were repatriated again in 1998, as the UN mounted another monitoring effort to encourage the return of those ousted in the fighting so that they could take part in new elections the same year. Until the end of the war, the northwest remained split between those regions under government control and the "Khmer Rouge zones" that had refused to integrate under the terms of the peace process and that remained enclaves of insurgent administration until they were formally integrated at the end of the 1990s, greatly enhancing the security situation. Subsequent to this development, the northwest remained attractive, not only for returnees from the Thai border camps, but for transient populations from other parts of Cambodia seeking land or opportunities for illegal work in Thailand.[35]

Increasing land hunger in Cambodia has prompted continued internal migration towards the northwestern provinces and back into Thailand; those following this path usually cross the border not as refugees, but as illegal migrants. By 1999, one study estimated that 82,000 Cambodians were working illegally in Thailand, earning, on average, double what they would earn as day laborers in Cambodia.[36] The movement of illegal migrants across borders has become a business opportunity for Thai and Cambodian people-smugglers, who charge around US$70 to smuggle an individual across the border. This trade has grown despite periodic crackdowns imposed by the Thai government; a report in the *Cambodia Daily* in 2003 described the return of a group of almost one thousand illegal Cambodian workers from Thailand. Flown by the Thai authorities back to Phnom Penh, the workers were met by Ministry of Interior officials who warned the deportees not to go back to

[34] Del Mundo, "Cambodia: The Killing Fields Revisited."

[35] Michelle Legge and Thor Savoeun, *Nine Years On: Displaced People in Cambodia* (Phnom Penh: Ockenden International, 2004).

[36] Chan Sophal and So Sovannarith, *Cambodian Labour Migration to Thailand: A Preliminary Assessment*, Working Paper 11 (Phnom Penh: Cambodia Development Resource Institute, 1999), p. 4.

Thailand, but to settle down—to stay, in effect, at home. One returnee interviewed by the *Daily* commented:

> He said we should go to Ratanakkiri province where there is a lot of open land for farming ... But I will not go because Ratanakkiri is full of malaria and it is too remote.[37]

The newspaper report noted that the interviewee and his wife "have not ruled out returning to Thailand, when the crackdown on illegal immigrants subsides." Another returnee said he had "had enough of Thai prisons" and would remain in Cambodia; a third could not be interviewed because, the day after her return, she had set out again for Thailand.[38] The flow of illegal migrants into Thailand includes unaccompanied children sent by agents to work as beggars on the streets of Bangkok. A 2007 report discovered that 95 percent of child beggars in Bangkok were Cambodian nationals, earning between 100 and 200 baht (US$3–6) a day.[39]

The continued migration of peoples towards the northwest, and onwards into Thailand as refugees or illegal workers, belies the UNHCR rhetoric describing the repatriation programs of 1992–93 and 1998 that emphasized the people's aspiration for "return" and "reintegration"; this continuing flow of migrants exposes the idea that the refugees were just going "home" as a "chimera."[40] Certainly the refugees were desperate to escape the camp and seek better opportunities, but the UNHCR's citation of "homecoming" as a legitimizing trope bore a questionable relationship to reality. Furthermore, the insecurities these returnees faced, insecurities caused by renewed fighting, foraging for firewood in mined jungles, and feeding a family on what can be raised on a small patch of earth without amenities or support in some of the poorest districts in Southeast Asia, also raise questions about whose interests were served by the exercise in repatriation, the squalor of the refugee camps notwithstanding. When "home" is full of malaria and too remote, going there represents impoverishment rather than fulfillment. The effect of the discourse of homecoming was to legitimize the closing off of alternatives.

Three major interests can be discerned in this process, two of which were achieved. The first interest is that of reconstituting a picture of Cambodian sovereignty that could serve to legitimize the regime emerging from the peacekeeping mission and thus cement the process of reconstituting Cambodia as a functioning state in the international system. The election held by UNTAC in 1993 was crucial to this process. The 1993 election, like many elections tied to peacekeeping processes in the 1990s, had little to do with promoting democracy per se; the conceptual and practical links between elections held under conditions of international peacekeeping and democratic governance, broadly defined, are extremely slender. Rather, the election was intended as a founding moment for the

---

[37] Thet Sambath and Nick Engstrom, "On the Road Again: Deported from Thailand, the Headstrong March Right Back," *The Cambodia Daily*, October 23–24, 2003, online edition, http://www.cambodiadaily.com/

[38] Ibid.

[39] Friends International, *The Nature and Scope of the Foreign Child Beggar Issue (Especially Related to Cambodian Child Beggars) in Bangkok* (Phnom Penh: Friends International, 2006), p. 5.

[40] McDowell and Eastmond, "Transitions, State Building, and the 'Residual' Refugee Problem."

sovereignty of the post-conflict state—a sign that the state existed as a representative of a politically functioning community. The return of the refugees in time to cast a vote was vital to this process, given that the existence of the camps had been used for a decade to deny legitimacy, internationally, to the Phnom Penh regime. However, as subsequent chapters will suggest, this was a reconstruction of the political community that occurred in the context of power relations that significantly problematized the fiction of sovereign autonomy—with profound implications for the opportunities available to returnees.

The second important interest that figured in this process was that of Thailand. Thailand's concern to "turn battlefields into marketplaces" reflected a new interest on the part of capital-rich Thai entrepreneurs in exploiting cheap Cambodian labor on preferential terms. For this purpose, a demilitarization and reopening of the border to allow Thai capital in was important, as was the related emergence of a border-control regime that could police the outflow of Cambodians to Thailand. Lindsey French comments that this phenomenon represents a continuation of a longstanding relationship: "... the history of Thai/Khmer relations in Thailand and at the border is a history of transactions and transformations between ethnic identity and national citizenship, as these relate to the needs of the developing Thai nation-state."[41]

Both of these interests were achieved by the repatriation program. The first, in particular, was much trumpeted by UNTAC, which used the construction of returnees as "voters" as an opportunity to link the rhetoric of "homecoming" with an idea of empowerment and self-determination. Certainly, the movement of refugees out of enclosed camps, from enforced dependence on international hand-outs for the most basic necessities or life, and from the imposed control of various Cambodian resistance armies, offered new opportunities to these displaced persons. The opportunities available, however, were confined to those consistent with broader international objectives associated with the reconstitution of the Cambodian state as a facilitator for superpower withdrawal and for Thai investment and exploitation of Cambodian labor. The refugees themselves had little choice in the matter.

The third objective—and the one that was, arguably, not met in the repatriation program of 1992–93—was the objective of "reintegration." One UNHCR study defines "reintegration" as an achievement confirmed by "an individual's capacity for socio-economic self-sufficiency and ability to exercise citizenship rights consistent with neighbours and people in other communities."[42] "Reintegration," defined in this way, is measured through examination of "linkages"—between returnees and other individuals and households within their community, and, more widely, between returnees and "other communities and markets." According to one study, reintegration is important for state reconstruction on a number of counts: it promotes the well-being of returnees, thus indicating how well transitional states are managing development goals; it provides the state with human resources for development; it returns to the state the legitimacy that is denied when "a proportion

---

[41] Lindsey French, "From Politics to Economics at the Thai-Cambodian Border: Plus Ça Change ..." *International Journal of Politics, Culture, and Society* 15,3 (2002): 434.

[42] Ballard, *Reintegration Programmes*, p. 12.

of its population remains outside the territory it controls" and signifies confidence in the state; and it provides a civil society with which the state can develop relations.[43]

There is a strongly neoliberal tone to this argument, which regards returnees, ultimately, as economic and political resources for the state. Proper management of returnees is important in ameliorating the "danger" of "additional migration and displacement on return."[44] It assists in promoting the legibility and governability of society. The reconstruction of refugees as registered voters and landed farmers, integrated into a community and an economy, and tied to a national state via the status of citizenship, promotes the ability of both the state and international agencies to assess the returnees' needs, monitor their progress, and, ultimately, regulate their activities. The importance of "reintegration" is discussed at length in the next chapter, with reference to both refugees and demobilizing soldiers; here it is sufficient to note that, in Cambodia, the failure to end the war and the scarcity of workable land available for returnees severely compromised reintegration and, consequently, entailed that the transformation of mobile refugees into settled, governable citizens remained problematic and, ultimately, incomplete.

In East Timor, the refugee issue was rather different, although handled in a similar way. The lack of land borders, except into Indonesia, had made mass flight from Timor difficult during the occupation, with the result that there was no emergence of a refugee camp system like the one on the Thai-Cambodia border. However, mass population movements did occur during the conflict. In 1975, thousands of people fled the invading Indonesian army into the mountains with FRETILIN (Frente Revolucionária de Timor-Leste Independente, The Revolutionary Front for an Independent East Timor). Following the destruction of the *bases de apoio* in the late 1970s, most of those who had fled surrendered to the Indonesians, who consolidated their control over the territory during the early 1980s. During this period, many of the surrendered civilians were incarcerated in strategic hamlets.

Just as the retreating Khmer Rouge in 1979 herded civilians ahead of them to the border, in 1999 Indonesian troops put into operation a planned forcible evacuation plan, in the course of which 250,000 Timorese—almost a third of the population— were moved across the border to West Timor[45] as violence erupted following the popular consultation ballot. Like the similar response of the Khmer Rouge to the Vietnamese invasion of 1979, this herding of civilians across the border was intended to have a political impact on the new regime. Indonesia's representatives subsequently claimed that these refugees were pro-integrationists who feared reprisals from independence forces; it was clear that this was an effort to deny the Timorese independence leaders control over their people. "Call your Xanana. Tell him he can be president for dirt and stones. That is all that will be left in East Timor."[46]

The movement of refugees thus became a politicized issue associated not merely with the security situation on the ground in Dili, which was dire, but with the

[43] Sarah Petrin, *Refugee Return and State Reconstruction: A Comparative Analysis,* Working Paper 66, New Issues in Refugee Research (Oxford: Refugee Studies Centre, 2002), p. 5.

[44] Ibid.

[45] Irena Cristalis, *Bitter Dawn: East Timor, A People's Story* (London: Zed Books, 2002), p. 3.

[46] Militia threat, cited in Erin Trowbridge, "Back Road Reckoning," in *The New Killing Fields: Massacre and the Politics of Intervention,* ed. Nicolaus Mills and Kira Brunner (New York, NY: Basic Books, 2002), p. 221.

legitimacy of the popular consultation and the new nation. The significance of this politicization is implicit in the way that people who did not go to West Timor, but who sought refuge with the United Nations in Dili, were treated. While peacekeepers on the ground attempted as far as they could to offer protection and assistance to the refugees, international diplomats drew clear distinctions between "internationals," who required international protection, and "locals," who would just have to cope with the situation as best they could. One UN staff member described a statement by the foreign minister of New Zealand during the crisis, which exemplified this attitude: "What one hopes comes out of the Security Council, of course, is that you can somehow cordon off those UN-related people over there and give some kind of protection for them."[47]

As a matter of fact, many staff members in the UN compound resisted this "cordoning off" of refugees from UN staff; a group of eighty or so volunteered to stay when the evacuation was ordered. Yet the courage of these individuals, and their empathy and solidarity with the Timorese refugees, throws the presuppositions of UN managers and international diplomats, regarding the ineradicable difference between UN personnel and "locals," into even sharper relief and suggests even more strongly the power of the discursive construction of the boundary between international and local in determining action. In fact, this "cordoning off" of post-conflict territories advocated in international policy operates specifically as an ideological device designed to shore up conceptions of a state-centered and tightly bounded local community: conceptions whose importance and meaning are threatened by the sheer presence of thousands of international interveners and by the myriad human relationships forged between "internationals" and "locals" in these situations.

Part of the reason for the predisposition to "cordon off" those with UN status from mere would-be refugees was precisely the same kind of legitimacy concerns that exercised the UNHCR when it organized repatriation campaigns to Cambodia. The UN's ability to cast itself as an organization carrying out a mission to rescue the Timorese relied upon a construction of the Timorese as fixed within Timor. The fear that Xanana Gusmão might indeed find himself presiding over dirt and stones prompted extraordinary efforts to try to persuade the Timorese to stay in Timor during the very worst excesses of violence. In the context of the 1999 violence, these were efforts that suited the interests of Timorese political elites also, but which had disastrous impact on the threatened population.

Subsequently, UNHCR faced the task of returning those who had been forcibly displaced after the ballot from West to East Timor—a task that was not entirely straightforward. An evaluation report on the UNHCR operation notes that the composition of the refugees in West Timor was complex. The report points out that "a significant minority" of 21.5 percent, or almost 93,000 people, had voted for autonomy within Indonesia in the popular consultation. Even given the effects of intimidation, this entailed that possibly tens of thousands of the refugees in West Timor had gone there because they wished to live in Indonesia—an option that Indonesia held out to them. Others may have fled because they had been involved in the violence, either as willing accomplices or forced conscripts. Distinguishing these from people who had fled simply to escape the violence, or because they had been forced to move by militias and now wished to return, was difficult.

---

[47] Geoffrey Robinson, "If You Leave Us Here, We Will Die," in *The New Killing Fields*, p. 179.

In fact, once the violence had ceased, many of the refugees were keen to return to East Timor, and 126,000—about half the total number—came back in the first three months. Of these, the UNHCR organized about two-thirds, and about 43,000 people returned by themselves. Clearly these groups represented a population for whom return home was the obvious and desired solution. From early 2000, however, refugee flows dried up; over the next two years, only 5,500 people returned under their own steam. The UNHCR's objectives changed at this point "from how to deal with mass return to how to sustain it." As an evaluation report on the process commented, "this repatriation was not just a humanitarian intervention, it became a political objective."[48]

Political objectives existed on both sides of the equation. Within the refugee camps in West Timor, militia leaders wielded significant power over the population, and those who wished to leave were threatened and intimidated. The UNHCR adopted an "extraction" policy of hit-and-run evacuations, whereby a truck would arrive in the camps to collect returnees, who would then jump on board at the last minute and be whisked away before the militias could prevent them from leaving. This policy was a courageous one, which undoubtedly facilitated the return of many who were being held against their will in West Timor. However, for the UNCHR to engage in such a controversial policy—a policy that stands in sharp relief to the UN's refusal to act without Indonesian consent during the prior violence—indicates how high the political stakes were, for the UN as well as for the refugees, and how much pressure was exerted on the organization by the political imperative for return. The policy led to significant hostility between UNHCR and the militias in the camps, culminating in the murder of three UNHCR staff at Atambua in September 2000. Subsequently, the repatriation operation was suspended, and information gathering within the camps became impossible. The UNHCR shifted its attention then to promoting information to counter "unfavourable rumours and disinformation circulating in West Timor"[49] and to facilitating high-profile reconciliation activities, to persuade the remaining refugees that it was safe for them to return to East Timor without fear of retaliation.

Getting the refugees back was vital for the legitimation of the new government in Timor-Leste, and for the political elite also. Thus Xanana Gusmão visited refugee camps in West Timor in April 2002 to request that refugees return in time for the presidential elections in order to "experience the joy of independence along with their compatriots."[50] The existence of the refugee camps was perceived not only as a security threat, due to the presence of militias within them, but as an affront to Timorese independence and as a problem for the legitimacy of the Timorese leadership.

The fact that the repatriation was organized by a UN agency at a time when the UN, in the guise of the United Nations Transitional Authority in East Timor, held sovereignty over the new state entailed that the UNHCR was regarded from the Indonesian side as politically motivated. This concern was shared by UNHCR staff

---

[48] Chris Dolan, Judith Large, and Naoki Obi, *Evaluation of the UNHCR's Repatriation and Reintegration Programme in East Timor, 1999–2003* (Geneva: UNHCR Evaluation and Policy Analysis Unit, 2004), p. 1.

[49] Ibid., p. 18.

[50] "Gusmao Calls East Timor Refugees Home," *BBC News*, April 4, 2002, online at http://news.bbc.co.uk/1/hi/world/asia-pacific/1910863.stm, accessed September 18, 2007.

members, as the evaluation report highlights. The issue of separated children became particularly politically explosive as media reports suggested that perhaps more than two thousand Timorese children were stuck in Indonesia. The issue was problematic, due to the wide range of circumstances through which the children became separated from their parents. While some were clearly abducted or had been lost in the violence of 1999, others had been sent by their parents to patrons or family members for education and care, a common practice in East Timor, as in other Southeast Asian countries. The politicization of the issue rebranded all these children as hostages of the Indonesian state. The evaluation report cites a UNHCR staff member who commented that, at times, the UNHCR, under pressure to act on the issue, returned children to their parents in cases where the child had genuinely been sent away for his or her own betterment, and in which parents were not able to afford to support the child:

> It was commented that UNHCR was only interested in gaining publicity [from the fact that they] brought children home, then the family was suffering to take care of the additional children. Then, UNHCR did not care much; once the child was dropped off at home and photos were taken, they [the family] did not see UNHCR again.[51]

This over-zealous repatriation effort resembles the Cambodian program in its compulsory aspects, even though, in the East Timorese case, Indonesia did offer citizenship rights to those who did not wish to return to East Timor. The position of another group of reluctant returnees underlines the point that the UNHCR's activities with respect to Timor were not *merely* humanitarian, but *also* operated in line with a wider concern to promote the naturalization of links between a Timorese homeland and people of Timorese extraction.

Over the course of the 1980s and 1990s, significant communities of Timorese refugees had built up in Australia. These refugees were permitted to remain in Australia on temporary protection visas, and some had lived in Australia for a decade or more on this basis. In 2004, the Howard government announced a plan to repatriate approximately 1,650 Timorese who had been living in Australia for up to fifteen years on temporary protection visas, returning them to Timor-Leste where, according to the Australians' judgment, the threat of persecution had now passed. The refugees were informed that they had twenty-eight days to leave the country. This prompted the launch of a campaign called "Common Sense for East Timorese: Let Them Stay!" particularly in the state of Victoria, where a large community of Timorese is settled in the city of Melbourne and where the campaign won the backing of the state's premier. The campaign focused on the fact that the Timorese people in question were settled in Australia, with children in Australian schools, and were contributing to the Australian economy and community. Questions regarding the continued political stability of Timor were also raised.

There was a somewhat awkward silence on this issue, on the part of the East Timor solidarity campaigners, who felt that, in fact, any social or economic contribution to be made by the Timorese should be made within Timor-Leste, which needed help more than Australia did. The issue soured relations, to an extent,

---

[51] UNHCR staff member's comment, cited in Dolan et al., "Evaluation of the UNHCR's Repatriation and Reintegration Programme," p. 63.

between the Timorese diaspora and the Timorese government, which felt that the "Let Them Stay!" campaign presented conditions in Timor in a bad light and that the attitude of the Timorese in Australia was unpatriotic.[52] Some Timorese members of the "Let Them Stay!" campaign in Melbourne, who were interviewed for this study, justified their stance on this issue by arguing that they could better benefit Timor by staying in Australia and lobbying for pro-Timorese policies—an argument that clearly accepts, to an extent, the pressure imposed by appeals to their patriotism.[53] Although the Australian government ultimately backed down with respect to most of the individuals in question, in response to the campaign, and the Timorese government eventually said that, in any case, it would have difficulty supporting these returnees, the issue illustrated an official presupposition on both sides that Timorese "should" want to go "home," even in situations where their personal preferences and household interests were and are clearly better served by staying "in exile."[54]

TAKING THE BLAME

In the Timorese case, as in the Cambodian case, the UNHCR was criticized for insufficient efforts to follow up on the "reintegration" of returnees. The evaluation report notes this criticism, but comments that, through its "shelter programme" particularly, the operation in East Timor offered housing materials to 35,000 families. These were offered, not just to returnees, but to "vulnerable families" more generally.[55] The evaluation report on the Timorese operation notes the similar criticisms of the Timorese and Cambodian cases and suggests that the recurrence of some complaints reflects organizational problems within UNHCR. However, as the shift in emphasis of the shelter program suggests, it is also possible that, in both cases, the salience of the refugee issue dramatically declined as the post-conflict countries' continued aid dependence permitted the UN to scrutinize the workings of these Southeast Asian governments closely and gave it access, for the first time in a generation, to the broader population of Cambodians and Timorese. The UNHCR's evaluation of its own performance in Cambodia on this front is curiously fatalistic:

> Could the 1992–93 operation have been handled differently? Critics say UNHCR should have stayed longer to help the refugees before handing over its reintegration projects to development agencies. Others contend this was never a viable option in Cambodia where disasters, man-made and natural, began almost as soon as the refugees returned. After decades of war and natural

---

[52] Interviews with John Sinnott and Sieneke Martin, Melbourne, February 2004; interview with Jenny Drysdale, Canberra, May 2004.

[53] Interviews with Fivo Freitas and Ly Lay, Melbourne, February 2004.

[54] The Australian government's analysis of the situation is discussed in Kerry Carrington, Stephen Sherlock, and Nathan Hancock, *The East Timorese Asylum Seekers: Legal Issues and Policy Implications Ten Years On*, Current Issues Brief no. 17, 2002–03 (Canberra: Department of the Parliamentary Library, 2003).

[55] Dolan et al., "Evaluation of the UNHCR's Repatriation and Reintegration Programme," p. 20.

calamities, one of the world's poorest nations was never going to be rehabilitated overnight.[56]

This apparent denial of its own self-proclaimed responsibilities, in fact, fits with a different aspect of border reinstatement—the drawing, in post-conflict situations, of boundaries between the problematic domestic polity, which is assumed to be the perennial cause of turbulence, and the ordered and coherent international sphere, which is blameless when turbulence occurs. This kind of boundary has been erected, more generally, with respect to international memories of the conflicts in Cambodia and Timor as a whole, in which local causes of conflict have been significantly privileged over international causes.

Joseph Nevins gives an account of the independence day celebrations in East Timor that illustrates this effect. Former US President Bill Clinton was invited to the independence day celebrations, and Nevins describes the way Clinton attempted to avoid questions from journalists critical of the policy the US had followed with regard to Timorese independence up until the very last moment in September 1999. According to Nevins, Clinton downplayed the issue of American complicity with the Suharto regime and its actions in East Timor with one rather weak admission: "I don't believe America or any of the other countries were sufficiently sensitive in the beginning, for a long time"; with a dubious claim: " ... when it became obvious to me what was really going on ... I tried to make sure we had the right policy"; and with an outright denial of responsibility: "We never tried to sanction or support the oppression of the East Timorese." Clinton finished his response by arguing, "I think the right thing to do is what the leaders of East Timor said. They want to look forward, and you want to look backward. I'm going to stick with the leaders."[57]

Nevins points out that this kind of airbrushing of the past reflects the political import of history, and, in particular, accountability. It is a common aspect of post-conflict situations, and flows from the logic of reestablishing the state as a means to peace. For the state to operate as the anchor for a post-conflict pact requires that the causes of the conflict be relocated to the national level. The drawing of a symbolic line under the messy interventions of the past is a necessary adjunct to reconstituting statehood in a system of states that is itself both the product and the cause of problems of war. The wars in Cambodia and East Timor emerged in large part from processes of state-building enacted in neighboring states; a statist solution requires, at the very least, that those state-building processes should not be required to reverse. Thus the Paris Accords specified that UNTAC's efforts to marshal the support of neighboring states in ending the Cambodia conflict should "not infringe upon their sovereignty"; while a solution to the conflict in East Timor was only conceivable to key countries such as Australia, Japan, and the United States once the Asian financial crisis had already inflicted a fatal blow upon the Suharto regime and the powerful role it had awarded the military.

The speed with which external actors came to "forget" international culpability for East Timor's situation is indicated by a comment made by the commander of UN civilian police in East Timor during the transitional period and the protest it evoked. In an interview with a reporter for the Australian Associated Press in February 2001,

---

[56] Del Mundo, "Cambodia: The Killing Fields Revisited."

[57] Quoted in Joseph Nevins, *A Not-So-Distant Horror: Mass Violence in East Timor* (Ithaca, NY: Cornell University Press, 2005), p. 140.

as a date was set for general elections in August that year, Commander Gent expressed his concern over the potential for violence surrounding those elections, remarking:

> Their last experience [of an election], you know what happened there; they're still learning this process. The vast majority don't understand what democracy is all about, that you can have a contrary point of view. This raises conflict, and they don't handle conflict properly.[58]

This comment evoked a letter of protest from Timorese NGO leaders. They wrote:

> External forces caused the violence that plagued East Timor during 1999 (and for twenty-three years before that). The Indonesian government, its military, and militia proxies instigated and perpetrated virtually all the violence before, during, and after the 30 August vote. Most of the world's most powerful countries—all of which consider themselves liberal democracies—provided significant economic, military, and diplomatic support to Jakarta from 1975 to 1999, thus greatly facilitating Indonesia's crimes against the people of East Timor.[59]

The NGO leaders decried the "racist stereotypes" put forward by the police commander, which "replicate the false arguments put forth by the Indonesian military that blamed East Timorese for the violence fomented by an invading force."[60] Their letter was posted on the Internet; UN civilian police made no response to it.

The brevity of international memories regarding the conflict in East Timor reflects the powerful logic of post-Cold War attitudes to conflict, even conflicts that began and were sustained internationally through the entirely different logic of the Cold War itself. This suited external actors whose interests changed dramatically once the Cold War was at an end. It is further exemplified in comments made by Australian Foreign Minister Alexander Downer in 2001, commenting to an ABC television program on the increasingly hostile negotiations between Timor and Australia over the demarcation of their maritime boundary and associated division of significant oil resources under the Timor Sea. In his comments to the ABC *Four Corners* program, Alexander Downer expressed his surprise at Timor's stance on the issue, twice using the phrase "after all we've done for them" to refer to the intervention of Australian forces in September 1999.[61] This normative framing of the conflict in a manner designed to promote the image and interest of Australia at

---

[58] Rod McGuirk, "Police Expect Election Violence in Dili," *Australian Associated Press*, Dili, February 8, 2001.

[59] See Benjamen Sanches Afonso et al., letter to Commander Gary Gent, Chief of Civpol Operations, UNTAET, Dili, February 17, 2001; posted online at http:// members.pcug.org.au/ ~wildwood/01maretngos.htm

[60] Ibid.

[61] Australian Broadcasting Corporation, *Four Corners*, "Rich Man, Poor Man," May 10, 2004, transcript online at http://www.abc.net.au/4corners/content/2004/s1105310.htm, accessed September 18, 2007.

Timor's expense exemplifies the process of "forgetting" Nevins describes—in this case, a forgetting of Australia's well-documented complicity with the Indonesian invasion and occupation from start to end. Forgetting permits a reshuffling of responsibilities necessary to sustain the unequal relationship between interveners and the subject state. The logic of intervention requires that the international sphere be recast as not merely powerful but blameless and altruistic—operating out of an enlightened "responsibility to protect"—in contrast to the dysfunctional, war-torn domestic sphere.

A similar logic is at work in the Cambodian case, where the external drivers of the wars of the 1970s and 1980s have been little discussed internationally since 1991, and the presumed dysfunctionality of a "traumatized" and "brutalized" population has been made the basis for external intervention. The establishment of a tribunal process for trying perpetrators of crimes against humanity in Cambodia is a powerful example of the ways in which boundaries are constructed to frame conflict as a purely local affair. Initially instigated by a request from Cambodia's co-prime ministers, at a stage in the war when they were attempting to prompt defections from the insurgent Khmer Rouge, the idea was taken up by the Special Representative for Human Rights in Cambodia. The Special Representative asked the UN to "examine the request by the Cambodian authorities for assistance in responding to past serious violations of Cambodian and international law."[62] A group of experts was convened for this purpose and wrote a report that suggested a number of aims that might be met by a tribunal. The report stated that bringing the perpetrators of crimes against humanity to justice "… is a matter not only of moral obligation but of profound political and social importance to the Cambodian people" in order to provide survivors with "a sense of justice and some closure on the past." The report claimed that a tribunal would help in "repairing the damage done to that society by the massive human rights abuses and for promoting internal peace and national reconciliation." Finally, by virtue of identifying and punishing those responsible, a tribunal could ensure that "Cambodians can better understand their own past, finally place this most tragic period and those responsible for it behind them, and work together to build a peaceful and better future."

However, at the behest of the Cambodian government, and with the endorsement of the United Nations, the group of experts noted that their mandate "directs the Group to consider the human rights violations of the Khmer Rouge only during the period from 1975 to 1979" and commented that "the mandate is limited to the acts of the Khmer Rouge and not those of any other persons or, indeed, States, that may have committed human rights abuses in Cambodia before, during, or after the period from 1975 to 1979." This limitation was intended to focus attention on "the extraordinary nature of the Khmer Rouge's crimes."[63]

This limiting of the targets of the tribunal—to the "Khmer Rouge" committing crimes against humanity between 1975 and 1979—has rarely been questioned. Yet it is politically significant in that it takes a slice of Cambodian history out of context

---

[62] United Nations, *Report of the Special Representative of the Secretary-General on the Situation of Human Rights in Cambodia,* UN Doc. E/CN.4/1998/95, 20 February 1998, online at http://daccessdds.un.org/doc/UNDOC/GEN/G98/105/80/PDF/G9810580.pdf?OpenElement, accessed September 23, 2008, para. 6.

[63] Group of Experts for Cambodia, *Report Pursuant to General Assembly Resolution 52/135* (New York, NY: United Nations, 1999), online at http://www1.umn.edu/humanrts/cambodia-1999.html, accessed, September 18, 2007, paras. 9–10.

and frames responsibility in terms of individual agency, ignoring larger questions as to why Cambodian social and political structures were so severely disabled that such individuals were able to mobilize support, and then take and maintain power. In so doing, this framing cuts out of contention external actors who committed crimes in Cambodia—most notably the American government and military, who were revealed in 2000 as having begun their illegal and secret bombing campaign on Cambodia in 1965, four years earlier than previously thought. During the ten-year period from 1965 to 1975, the Americans dropped more bombs on Cambodia than the tonnage dropped by all the allies in the whole of World War II,[64] despite the fact that Cambodia was formally neutral for half of this time, a crime that surely qualifies as "extraordinary." Ignoring this prior circumstance makes the Khmer Rouge era appear to be a phenomenon that popped up from nowhere, other, perhaps, than the murky depths of the perennially tortured Khmer psyche. This latter is, indeed, the explanation favored by many accounts produced in the 1990s, which purport to trace, in contemporary Cambodian history, a reprise of the battles depicted in the stone bas-reliefs carved at Angkor. One account suggests: "One can glimpse the tragic predicament of Cambodia in 1998 reflected in the history of the Khmer Empire in the ninth century as well as in the authoritarian habits of a civilisation that flourished almost a millennium ago."[65]

It is interesting to contrast the construction of Cambodian politics in these postwar manifestations with that popularized in William Shawcross's study, *Sideshow*, published in the 1970s. Shawcross's book, subtitled *Kissinger, Nixon, and the Destruction of Cambodia*, was produced at a time when Western confidence was shaken by the defeats in Indochina, the disgrace of President Nixon, and the embarrassing exposure of flaws in American political institutions.[66] Clearly, history that attributes Cambodia's disastrous recent experience entirely to the actions of the US or the CIA is as partial as history that attributes it to the militarized culture of fourteenth-century Angkor. Penny Edwards has argued that preoccupation, in domestic political discourse, with an image of Cambodia as an innocent victim of external events has been profoundly disempowering, since it removes responsibility and consequently agency from Cambodians themselves.[67] While this is a perceptive point, conversely the "forgetting" of the criminal behavior of external actors is equally as politically charged, reinforcing and justifying sharp differentials of power between international and local actors under conditions of aid dependence.

---

[64] This comparison is drawn by Taylor Owen and Ben Kiernan at Yale University, in an analysis posted on the award-winning Cambodian Genocide Project website, and is based upon new information released by President Bill Clinton in 2000; see Taylor Owen and Ben Kiernan, "Bombs Over Cambodia," *The Walrus*, October 2006, online at http://www.yale.edu/cgp/Walrus_Cambodia Bombing_OCT06.pdf, accessed September 18, 2007.

[65] Frederick Brown and David Timberman, *Cambodia and the International Community: The Quest for Peace, Development, and Democracy* (New York, NY: Asia Books, 1998), p. 25.

[66] William Shawcross, *Sideshow: Kissinger, Nixon, and the Destruction of Cambodia* (New York, NY: Simon and Schuster, 1979).

[67] Penny Edwards, "Imaging the Other in Cambodian Nationalist Discourse Before and During the UNTAC Period," in *Propaganda, Politics, and Violence in Cambodia: Democratic Transition under United Nations Peacekeeping*, ed. Stephen Heder and Judy Ledgerwood (London: M. E. Sharpe, 1996), pp. 50–72.

The ways that international agencies and actors have organized the return of refugees and reframed responsibility for conflict have had important effects in promoting particular explanations for conflict and solutions for post-conflict reconstruction. Both activities strengthen the idea of "the local" as an objective referent sphere, promoting ideals of homecoming and essentially static citizenship at the expense of the lived experiences of border crossings, transnational appeals, and external interventions that characterize warfare. As such, these programs and discourses contribute to an ideological process of shoring up the boundaries of the putative national community, a prop to policies of "reconciliation" designed to underpin institution building and peace. They also reconstruct the "local" as dysfunctional in contrast to an enlightened "international" realm, justifying intrusion by the international into the local. This discursive construction masks a considerable exercise of power. With respect to refugees, the celebration of the success of repatriation is only sensible if one overlooks the intimate connection of this success with policies of incarceration and the incremental tightening of rights to asylum over the past two decades. The claim made by UNHCR that the refugees had "gone home" is only comprehensible if "home" is shorn of all associations other than the international designation of a particular territory as belonging to one state or another. Equally, the justice arising from the assignment of individual responsibility is merely ideological if it is divorced from a wider accounting for the structural violence of the state system that reverberates through and often shapes individual actions in war. The success of these policies owes much to the ability of implementers to frame out of consideration significant aspects of the lived reality of those targeted by them.

POLICING INDIGENEITY

The enactment of these kinds of solutions requires significant international intervention, not only in the form of "complex peacekeeping," but in subsequent supervision of politics during an extended period of aid dependence. During this period, large numbers of international actors are typically present in the country, wielding power, taking decisions, negotiating support, and spending resources, often working in relationships of asserted "partnership" with indigenous actors. Yet, the formal purpose of such interventions is the restoration of sovereignty, raising the question of how boundaries between the local and the global are constructed and policed in the context of dense, personal, everyday interactions between international personnel and local people. Again, this is a process that requires a considerable exercise of power, that begins with transitional administration and continues into periods of post-intervention dependence.

In Cambodia, UNTAC worked alongside state apparatuses that were termed "existing administrative structures." UNTAC exercised a rather poorly defined control function, rather than administering the country by itself. In East Timor, UNTAET (United Nations Transitional Administration in East Timor) exercised all the normal powers of a state, operating as executive, legislature, and judiciary, in a context of state collapse. The potential for renewed violence in Cambodia was greater than in Timor, and local elites were better organized, forcing greater reliance, on the part of UNTAC, on local players who could mobilize the population to participate in the peace process. Yet in both these contexts, issues of boundary construction and maintenance were paramount—UNTAC was a temporary and external entity, while the existing administrative structures were to form the basis of a new state.

In Cambodia, UNTAC promoted the boundary between the local and the international by insisting on observing the forms of diplomatic relations with "existing administrative structures," while refusing to acknowledge the wider social, political, and economic impact of its presence. This eyes-closed, diplomacy-oriented approach represented an attempt to maintain a public stance of "impartiality" and distance, while promoting a straightforwardly state-centered solution to the problem of peace. This approach was much criticized both within the mission and from outside it. Justified as the only practicable way of negotiating the intricacies of Cambodian politics, it nevertheless represented a façade rather than a reality of aloofness. In reality, UNTAC facilitated the transformation of Cambodian politics, economy, and society. Individual UNTAC members forged close relationships with local people and kindled new and dramatic changes in opportunities for many. In particular, the UN Volunteers in the Election Component, human rights workers in the Human Rights Component, and the many Khmer-speaking scholars of Cambodian history and society in the Information and Education Component made tireless efforts to forge relationships with ordinary people.

UNTAC's presence empowered some sections of society at the expense of others, and it made possible freedoms, for example in the media, that had been unthinkable just months before its arrival. Yet in the course of these dramatic changes brought about by its presence, UNTAC's senior policy-makers hid behind diplomatic rituals that frustrated staff members who desired deeper engagement; in this section, I argue that this was a strategy that enabled the UN to police the conceptual coherence of the "local" as opposed to the "international" sphere.

In East Timor, UNTAET went further, resisting all but the slenderest consultative relations with Timorese, while at the same time intruding into every aspect of the country's political, social, and economic life. Timorese actors both clearly perceived and loudly criticized UNTAET's retention of special privileges and exclusive decision-making power, not only in public life, but also in the context of working and social relations between international and Timorese staff within the mission. Local actors in Timor living under UNTAET faced different alignments of international and local power from local actors in Cambodia living under UNTAC. In both cases, however, the strategic concerns of local actors reflected approaches to the problematic issue of demarcating international-local boundaries in a context of intervention, and the sharp appreciation, locally, of the degree of power that international actors held.

The ambitious nature of UNTAC's mission in Cambodia, and the inclusion of previously untried elements, such as a Human Rights Component equipped with its own radio station, led many to conclude that the mission sought to represent the interests of the Cambodian people vis-à-vis oppressive elites, and to remake the Cambodian polity in a manner that would promote, above all, democracy and respect for human rights.[68] Many of UNTAC's own staff members saw this as their main purpose in Cambodia. However, their efforts to do so were consistently thwarted by the statist approach to intervention implicit in the Paris Accords, and

[68] This included UNTAC's own Human Rights Component; see UNTAC Human Rights Component, *Final Report* (Phnom Penh, UNTAC Human Rights Component 1993), pp. 10, 41, 72.

their subsequent interpretation by senior staff, as a means to police a distinction between the local and the international that would both lay the foundation for future aid dependence while giving free rein to Cambodian elites to perform the function of riot control vis-à-vis the poor. As a result, the main thrust of UNTAC's power was deployed straightforwardly in pursuit of these aims. Although individual members of UNTAC often acted to assist people in difficulties on a variety of bases, and components such as the Human Rights Component argued furiously for greater action to assist ordinary people suffering violence or intimidation, UNTAC's final policy decisions consistently prioritized the interests of elites, from whichever party, over those of the poor. UNTAC was accused by leaders of all parties of partisanship in its operation; yet, in fact UNTAC bent over backwards to accommodate the full range of elite demands. Where it committed politically interested acts of omission, it did so at the expense, not of one party or the other, but of the poor.

For example, the resistance parties accused UNTAC of failing to investigate political violence, and of failing to act against obvious violations of human rights and of the Paris Peace Accords, in cases where to do so would antagonize the State of Cambodia.[69] Judy Ledgerwood, who worked as an information officer for UNTAC, commented that UNTAC's failure to respond to reports of abuse from its own staff made UN officials "look foolish to their Cambodian counterparts."[70] Yet it appears, rather, UNTAC did respond to this kind of abuse—by offering to facilitate campaigning by former resistance party leaders. Prince Norodom Ranariddh, leader of FUNCINPEC, for example, was given rides to campaign rallies in UN helicopters. In some places, opposition party offices were protected by armed UN police. But the average FUNCINPEC voters, under the purview of increasingly violent village authorities, had to fend for themselves with the limited assistance that could be provided by an embattled and under-resourced Human Rights Component.

The Party of Democratic Kampuchea (the Khmer Rouge) strongly protested UNTAC's approach, yet it, too, benefited. In protest at UNTAC's inaction over alleged SoC (State of Cambodia) abuses, the Khmer Rouge refused to cooperate with the demobilization process or to allow UNTAC officials access to Khmer Rouge zones. The image of UNTAC officials turning back at the border of a Khmer Rouge enclave because their way was blocked by a single bamboo pole became infamous as a portrait of UN weakness and reluctance to confront the political leaders. Later, in an effort to tempt the Khmer Rouge back into the process after their return to insurgency, the UN stood by as thousands of ethnic Vietnamese fled Cambodia in panic, following massacres perpetrated by Khmer Rouge in ethnic Vietnamese villages.[71]

When the defection of the Khmer Rouge from the accords was confirmed, UNTAC allowed the SoC to maintain its own abusive and ill-disciplined armed forces as a means to defend "the country" from the Khmer Rouge. The SoC's ailing administrative apparatus was shored up with an aid package arranged by UNTAC. In so doing, UNTAC finally buried the notion, prevalent in 1991, that UNTAC would

---

[69] United Nations, *The UN and Cambodia* (New York, NY: United Nations, 1996), Doc. 62.

[70] Judy Ledgerwood, "UN Peacekeeping Missions: The Lessons from Cambodia," *Asia Pacific Issues: Analysis from the East-West Centre* 11 (1994): 8; online at http://www.seasite.niu.edu/khmer/Ledgerwood/PDFAsiaPacific.htm, accessed May 15, 2008.

[71] Jamie Frederic Metzl, "The Many Faces of UNTAC: A Review Article," *Contemporary South East Asia* 17,1 (1995): 85–96.

arrive as a "liberator" for a people caught between a variety of uninspiring and oppressive political parties.

The arrival of UNTAC's advance party, the United Nations Advance Mission in Cambodia (UNAMIC), had sparked a short-lived "Phnom Penh Spring" in 1991. One expression of this hopeful surge was a demonstration in December 1991, protesting corruption and the illegal sale of state-owned enterprises that had resulted in the laying-off of workers. Ministry employees whose wages were in arrears joined the protests, as did students. The house of Transport Minister Ros Chhun was attacked and burnt. The government made threatening noises, but the demonstrations escalated. Eventually, riot police fired on the crowds, killing nine demonstrators, and made numerous arrests. The affair represented a major crisis for the SoC government and a test for the human rights and democracy commitments enshrined in the Paris Accords; yet UNAMIC neither intervened nor commented on the matter, disappointing the demonstrators who had viewed the arrival of the UN as a sign that the international community was planning to sponsor change.

This disappointment presaged a broader reality check, as Cambodian expectations of UNTAC were revised downwards. Regarding the failure to address human rights abuse systematically, Amnesty International suggested that "human rights considerations may have been subordinate to the larger political and military objectives of UNTAC."[72] Indeed, the components that had most direct dealings with ordinary people—the Human Rights Component and the Electoral Component— were at a clear disadvantage vis-à-vis other components. The Human Rights Component was under-resourced and under-staffed and found that diplomatic objectives repeatedly blocked its efforts to gain arrests of human rights abusers, while the Electoral Component was reliant upon United Nations Volunteers, who ranked low in the UN hierarchy. Although individuals in these components worked hard to assist ordinary Cambodians, they were rarely able to bring the weight of the UN machinery to bear in support of villagers in contention with powerful members of the political elite or the military. Rather, the UN machine remained oriented towards the needs of the elite and tended to back away from assertive action in support of the poor.

Charged with controlling administrative structures, UNTAC was no more successful in quelling the explosion of corruption than it was in addressing human rights abuses. This additional failure had a significant effect on UNTAC's public image; one internal report commented on corruption within the Education Ministry: "For UNTAC to not see the corruption when everyone pays, or alternatively could not pay and had their child fail his or her examinations, seems to them [to be] ridiculous."[73] The same kinds of attitudes greeted UNTAC's failure to deal with a crime wave that hit Phnom Penh in 1992 and with the increase in fatal traffic

---

[72] Amnesty International, *Cambodia: Human Rights Concerns, July to December 1992* (London: Amnesty International, February 1993), p. 22.

[73] UNTAC Information/Education Division, "Report on Public Perceptions of the UN in the City of Phnom Penh," Analysis Report, September 18, 1992, in *Between Hope and Insecurity: The Social Consequences of the Peace Process in Cambodia*, ed. Peter Utting (Geneva: United Nations Research Institute for Social Development, 1994), online at http://www.unrisd.org/unrisd/website/document.nsf/462fc27bd1fce00880256b4a0060d2af/0989f68532e21da580256b6500558beb/$FILE/beet.pdf, accessed September 24, 2008, p. 102.

accidents associated with the arrival of hundreds of UNTAC vehicles.[74] Judy Ledgerwood concluded, "Disjuncture between UNTAC's outward signs of power— its obvious wealth, cars, helicopters, and so on—and its seeming impotence ... was mystifying to many Cambodians."[75]

Cambodians reduced their expectations as UNTAC's deployment neared its end. Willingness on the part of Cambodians to speak out about abuses started to decline, according to one staff member, while the pilfering of UNTAC property increased. Equally, towards the end of 2002, public complaints began to be raised about the behavior of UNTAC personnel. In particular, there were complaints that UNTAC personnel were involved in sexual misconduct. These complaints ranged from accusations concerning child abuse, rape, and abandonment of wives, to claims that the UNTAC operation as a whole had given rise to a dramatic increase in the number of prostitutes in Cambodia, encouraged increased openness in the conduct of the sex trade, and had sparked an HIV epidemic. The response of the Special Representative, who said that this kind of behavior was only to be expected of UN peacekeepers and would have to be accommodated, scandalized Cambodian public opinion; Cambodians saw the activities of UNTAC as an affront to Khmer culture.

Sandra Whitworth points out that while yards of analysis have been generated by the activities of UN peacekeepers, the analysis focuses almost exclusively on their official activities, rather than the impact of their off-duty presence.[76] Yet in Phnom Penh, in particular, this impact was huge. In the 1980s, staff members of Western aid agencies operating within Cambodia had been kept strictly segregated from Cambodian society, required to live in a particular hotel and prevented from socializing with Cambodian colleagues. UNTAC's peacekeepers, however, quickly developed relationships as customers, tenants, donors, colleagues, lovers, protectors, even prospective husbands or wives of Cambodians. The extraordinary rates of pay and the status, freedoms, and protection enjoyed by these "international" individuals awarded them an unusual level of personal power. The day-to-day relationships that naturally emerged between individual Cambodians and UNTAC members—and the fact that many UNTAC staff members *did* try personally to assist Cambodians they knew, if they had difficulties—had a powerful impact on perceptions of UNTAC. This made the official UNTAC's aloof, impersonal, diplomatic stance, which paid relatively little heed to ordinary citizens and failed to respond to the offenses caused by some peacekeepers' off-duty activities, all the more frustrating for Cambodians.

The Special Representative's lack of interest in the peacekeepers' off-duty activities is indicative of UNTAC's concern to retain a strict separation with respect to public and private interactions between peacekeepers and the host community. This concern is illustrated by the order that UN staff could visit brothels if they wanted to, but not in uniform, and they should not park their UN landcruisers right

---

[74] Nayan Chanda, "Easy Scapegoat, People Blame the UN for All Their Woes," *Far Eastern Economic Review,* October 22, 1992, p. 18.

[75] Judy Ledgerwood, "Patterns of CPP Repression and Violence During the UNTAC Period," in *Propaganda, Politics, and Violence in Cambodia,* p. 126.

[76] Sandra Whitworth, *Men, Militarism, and Peacekeeping: A Gendered Analysis* (Boulder, CO: Lynne Rienner, 2007). Simon Chesterman makes the same point with respect to the perverse economic impact of peacekeeping, which he describes as "one of the least studied aspects of humanitarian and development assistance." See Simon Chesterman, *You the People: The United Nations, Transitional Administration, and State-Building* (Oxford: Oxford University Press, 2004), p. 200.

outside the brothels. Private liaisons were inevitable, UNTAC acknowledged, but should be disguised so as not to disturb the clarity of boundaries between the international and the local sphere; they certainly should not be acknowledged as a policy matter for debate with local representatives. Similarly, attempts by Cambodian actors to negotiate the support of the obviously powerful UN in private matters, such as land disputes, or in public matters, such as human rights abuse and corruption, were problematic. Although individual UN members often tried hard to help, they found it difficult to mobilize the full weight of UNTAC behind these kinds of issues. These matters were viewed warily by the leaders of a mission that viewed embroilment in such issues as potentially breaking down the flimsy boundary between a "neutral" peacekeeping mission and a quagmire.

By maintaining this distinction, UNTAC obscured the intertwining of international and local power structures that emerged in the UNTAC era and persisted into the period of aid dependence.[77] UNTAC legitimated a new regime that would be aid-dependent and subject to international prescriptions for good governance. At the same time, by privileging the elite and giving priority to its dealings with them over its dealings with ordinary Cambodians, UNTAC set a precedent: from this point, it was intended to be very difficult for ordinary Cambodians to have any kind of formal access to or entitlement regarding the international sphere UNTAC represented, which would subsequently intrude so much into their lives. This required policing of activities associated with the peace process in a manner that paid relatively little official attention to ordinary Cambodians, outside particular set-piece rituals such as the election. It further required ignoring critical voices complaining against the more disastrous of the panoply of de facto direct and unequal power relationships enacted between UNTAC staff and local people on the ground.

In East Timor, a similar type of policing occurred, but it was expressed in a very different way. Here, the UN was given full executive, legislative, and judicial powers after 1999. Rather than operating as a peacekeeping mission engaging diplomatically with a sovereign state, the United Nations Transitional Authority in East Timor actually *was* the state for the two and a half years that preceded independence in 2002. This permitted UNTAET the luxury of remaining aloof from acknowledging its own social, economic, and political impact on the mass of the Timorese population, and, at last, the luxury of avoiding as far as possible any kind of engagement with East Timorese, an aloofness that engendered much criticism as UNTAET failed to consult and cultivate Timorese political society.

This failure has been attributed to a variety of contingent factors. For one, UNTAET was hurriedly constructed in the weeks of crisis following the destruction of September 1999. Furthermore, the operation took on peacekeeping attributes as a result of the violence, and consequently control was shifted away from the UN's Department of Political Affairs, to the Department of Peacekeeping Operations, which then implemented a plan inherited from Kosovo. These factors have all been widely cited. Astrid Suhrke suggests, also, that there was a strong desire on the part of the UN to avoid upsetting the Indonesians by awarding recognition immediately to the East Timorese resistance.[78] Jarat Chopra, who worked as a district

---

[77] Cambodia's aid dependent status is discussed in Chapter Five.

[78] Astrid Suhrke, "Peacekeepers as Nation-Builders: Dilemmas of the UN in East Timor," *International Peacekeeping* 8,4 (2001): 1-20.

administrator for UNTAET, discusses the impact of different aspects of internal UN culture, such as: a predisposition towards hierarchy; the reluctance of UN staff members on high salaries to cast their own competence or necessity into question by including Timorese in decision making; the staffers' unwillingness to let millions of dollars in aid slip out of their control; and the lack of institutional rewards for staffers who engaged in the mundane business of local "capacity-building."[79] Critics have blamed these factors for significantly retarding the business of grooming a Timorese elite for "state-building" activities. In fact, these characteristics of UN culture reflect the tensions between state-centered solutions, based upon the empowerment of an indigenous political elite, and the logic of intervention, which posits that even the most liberal and professional local elites in post-conflict societies are tainted with a variety of dysfunctional attitudes and ideological predispositions —ranging, in the Timorese case, from tendencies to corruption and cronyism, on the one hand, to radical nationalism or communism on the other.

Some of the explanations for UN failures advanced above accord with the broader analysis put forward earlier in this study: namely, that an entrenched view of conflicts in the South—their causes and consequences and the nature of their antagonists—has a powerful impact on the nature of intervention. Some authors have argued that interveners "should have" recognized the civil conflict in East Timor as different from the "new wars" of the 1990s, with their powerful dimensions of ethnic antagonism.[80] The distinctiveness of the East Timor conflict is sometimes said to derive from the absence of internal discord in that country during the resistance era—contrasted with the violent conditions in other countries emerging from civil war—which should have permitted rapid transfer of power to a local Timorese elite. It is alternatively regarded as derived from the "functionality" of the Timorese war of liberation, which is distinguished from a "dysfunctional" civil war. In fact, from the perspective of interveners, in East Timor, where an independent and functioning state apparatus had never previously existed, and where the level of physical destruction was extraordinary, interventionary ambitions were magnified, rather than tempered. Instead of representing an exception that required only a light touch, Timor was regarded as the ultimate laboratory for experimentation with post-conflict reconstruction. Sergio de Mello, Special Representative to the Secretary-General in East Timor, described the situation on UNTAET's arrival as "not just a ground-zero situation, but ... sometimes even below that." The blankness of the state, in the UN's eyes, was total:

> What we found was a devastated country. Humanitarian assistance was our top priority. But there was also no judiciary, no education system, no police, no defence force, no representative forms of government. Nothing, nothing, nothing.[81]

---

[79] Jarat Chopra, "The UN's Kingdom of East Timor," *Survival* 42,3 (2000): 27–39.

[80] Simon Chesterman, *You the People*, p. 256.

[81] Sergio de Mello, quoted in Fabien Curto Millet and Rathin Rathinasabapathy, "East Timor, the Building of a Nation: An Interview with Sergio Vieira de Mello," *Europa Magazine*, November 2001, online at http://users.ox.ac.uk/~ball1024/SergioVDM_interview.pdf, accessed September 18, 2007.

Because of this destruction, in de Mello's words, "the international community has, in East Timor, the unique opportunity and the responsibility to get the development of a country right from the beginning."[82] Although de Mello went on to acknowledge the difficulties associated with this task, as performed by the United Nations, and admitted later that the UN could have done more to include the Timorese elite in its efforts, this construction of East Timor as "a tremendous opportunity for us all"[83] strongly predisposed UN representatives towards solutions delivered by international technocrats possessed of international expertise. This required the marginalization of the Timorese, who might have had their own ideas about their future, and in this case, the UN indulged itself so far as to marginalize even the furious Timorese elite.

This alienation between the UN staffers and Timorese elites had a corresponding effect on the ability of ordinary Timorese to contribute. As Jarat Chopra points out, the claim that "nothing, nothing, nothing" existed in Timor was patently untrue in the districts, where various village-level organizations that had existed under the Indonesian regime, and clandestine organizations associated with the resistance, were accustomed to organizing their own affairs.[84] Members of the clandestine movement stepped forward to form village-level committees to organize reception and distribution of emergency relief supplies, village defense forces, and other affairs. While the clandestine movement was a fragmented movement, oriented towards resistance to Indonesian rule rather than the management of village affairs, it nevertheless had strong legitimacy and a high degree of enthusiastic local support. Given that leading members of the main political party, FRETILIN, had just arrived back in the country after long years of exile in Portugal, active leaders in the districts and villages of Timor were almost certainly far better organized and in tune with local sentiment than the Timorese elite was.

UNTAET, however, refused to recognize these local leaders and structures, preferring to insist upon the blank-slate metaphor, even as its falsity became increasingly obvious and East Timorese social and political structures revived after the chaos of 1999. The blank-slate approach allowed the UN to continue focusing on the perfect, internationally and centrally directed solution, negotiated with a tiny, select group of Portuguese-speaking returnees, ignoring wider sensibilities, interests, and allegiances among the local population. Where advisory committees were formed in the districts, they were given little power and were ultimately criticized as a "tokenistic" exercise.[85] UNTAET actions indicated its priorities and its conception of distributions of power in post-conflict Timor by the sequence of its actions: it organized itself first, then reluctantly conceded the need to admit the Timorese elite to the circle of power, only then moving to recognize grassroots politics and political actors.[86] This strategy allowed the Timorese political elite themselves to turn their backs on the grassroots organizations.

---

[82] Statement by Mr. Sergio Vieira de Mello, Special Representative of the Secretary-General in East Timor, Lisbon Donors' Meeting on East Timor, June 22–23, 2000, online at http://siteresources.worldbank.org/INTTIMORLESTE/Resources/Opening+Sergio.pdf

[83] Ibid.

[84] Jarat Chopra, "Building State Failure in East Timor," *Development and Change* 33,5 (2002): 979–1000.

[85] Chopra, "The UN's Kingdom of East Timor," pp. 27–39.

[86] Simon Chesterman, "East Timor in Transition: Self-Determination, State-Building, and the United Nations," *International Peacekeeping* 9,1 (2002): 67.

In compensation for its far-reaching intrusion into the realms of domestic governance, UNTAET policed international–local relations ever more stringently, in an attempt to shore up the image of an autonomous "domestic" sphere. In Cambodia, much of UNTAC's activity was classed as "diplomatic" and hence as belonging to an international sphere set apart from the mundane realities of government. In Timor, UNTAET faced no dangerous or delicate peace-brokering tasks: they simply did what a mixture of Indonesians and Timorese had previously done, only with less finesse and for far higher wages. The great disparities in pay, rather than any division of duties reflecting the proper limits of intervention, became *the* key distinction between the local and international participants in this effort, and as such became highly contentious.

This problem with unequal pay shaped UNTAET's approach to civil service formation. In an attempt to avoid the embarrassing situation of having international and local staff doing the same jobs for vastly different wages, UNTAET decided not to employ Timorese as civil servants within UNTAET during the transitional period when UNTAET exercised executive, legislative, and judicial power in East Timor. Consequently, a "two-track" approach was developed, whereby a Timorese civil service was employed independent from UNTAET, which actually exercised power. Because the formation of this independent civil service was to be handled by one of UNTAET's components, this approach required the UN staff to focus on recruitment to UNTAET before they dealt with recruitment to the civil service itself. Thus the first part of UNTAET's mandate was preoccupied with importing very expensive international staff. This process was justified by depicting the Timorese as "lacking capacity"—a designation that caused discontent among the Timorese. Furthermore, Timorese leaders quickly raised concerns about the quality of international staff, many of whom appeared to have little experience in government or administration at all, let alone in a poor, conflict-stricken country.[87]

This ploy did not avert confrontations over pay. UNTAET paid international staff thirty to forty times more than it paid local civil servants, once these were recruited. Within UNTAET itself, Timorese were only allowed to be employed as manual workers in order to preserve the integrity of the international-local border. The total allocation for local UNTAET staff salaries was less than 1 percent of the total UNTAET budget. This was similar to the proportion of the budget allocated to local staff in UNTAC's mandate; however, close similarity between the actual work done by local and international staff members made the issue explosive in Timor. From UNTAET's point of view, the disparity in pay was justified because it would avoid distortions in the local wage economy; UNTAET thus fixed local wages for different kinds of work at a level they assumed future governments would be able to "afford." Nevertheless, to local UNTAET staff faced with bills for reconstructing their houses, responsibilities for extensive networks of dependents, and the prospect of unemployment once the UN mission was over, the disparities appeared excessive, and local staff went on strike over the issue. Evidence suggests that there was local sympathy for the strikers; student postings on an Internet discussion board active during the strikes included telling comments on this and a range of other employment issues:

---

[87] See Joel Beauvais, "Benevolent Despotism: A Critique of UN State-Building in East Timor," *New York University Journal of International Law and Politics* 33 (2000–2001): 1149.

Each UNTAET member in East Timor has a big salary, and they receive US$109 per day for lunch money,[88] while Timorese worker does not earn this much money in a month.

UNTAET has created unemployment in East Timor, because Timorese do not have not an opportunity to get a job [*sic*], and UNTAET seems to pay no attention.

Some Timorese get work in UNTAET, but they must pay 10 percent tax to UNTAET. UNTAET [employees] don't pay tax. We think that idea is very bad, and UNTAET profits from Timorese workers.[89]

Similar comments were expressed on occasion by interviewees five years on, during my fieldwork in East Timor, indicating the depth of feeling that these issues had raised.

Not only were UNTAET staff members paid more, but they performed tasks that were perceived as specifically "local" at a time when unemployment in Timor was estimated by the Transitional Administration to have reached 80 percent.[90] Furthermore, UNTAET staff were exempt from tax, while local staff, as citizens of a new state that required a revenue base, were subjected to income tax despite their considerably worse economic situation.

Further strikes took place at a floating hotel brought in to house international UN staff. Workers at the hotel earned $3 a day in a hotel that charged the UN $160 a night for a room. Timorese criticisms of the floating hotel included complaints that the UN could have spent the money absorbed by the hotel in rebuilding local houses, which the owners could have rented to UN staff, rather than paying millions to a Singaporean company. The floating hotel symbolized not only the repatriation of much of the money spent on UNTAET to richer countries, but also the separation of UNTAET staff from the country they were administering. A report in *The Guardian* commented:

As if afraid to learn or take any initiative, many UN staff drove round from meeting to meeting with their windows up, appearing not to acknowledge the destitution and suffering around them. "After work people would not go out and speak to the East Timorese, to find out what they wanted," one UN staffer said. "They went and checked their email."[91]

---

[88] In fact, the $109 was the daily allowance, not the lunch allowance.

[89] Selected postings from IMPETTU Press, November 2000, supplied by Thierry Basset, IT Coordinator, NGO Forum East Timor, to the East Timor Activists Network, online at http://www.etan.org/et2000c/november/26-30/28impett.htm, accessed September 18, 2007.

[90] United Nations Information Service, "Head of UN Transitional Administration Briefs Security Council; Describes Improved Internal Security but Says Poverty 'Calamitous'; Asks for Quick Release of Resources," UN Doc. UNIS/SC/1181, February 4, 2000, online at http://www.unis.unvienna.org/unis/pressrels/2000/sc1181.html, accessed May 15, 2008.

[91] John Aglionby, "Bungled UN Aid Operation Slows East Timor's Recovery," *The Guardian*, August 30, 2000, posted online at http://www.etan.org/et2000c/august/27-31/30bungl.htm, accessed September 18, 2007.

The international media spoke of the emergence of a "UN consumer class" that pushed up prices for ordinary East Timorese by their free-spending habits off duty and by their tendency, while on the job, to spend a lot of time instituting new taxes for the Timorese from which they themselves would be exempt.[92] These concerns caused significant antipathy towards UNTAET, as evidenced in an episode in which around seven thousand Timorese who had queued for hours for jobs as UN drivers were suddenly told that no one would be considered who did not speak English. Infuriated that their time had been wasted, and their competence in Tetum, Indonesian, and Portuguese dismissed as irrelevant, the disappointed applicants began throwing stones at the UNTAET office.[93]

This sense of disenfranchisement spread to the private sector, where the Timorese involved in trade regarded UNTAET policies as designed to ensure that their integration into an international economy would take place on unfavorable terms. Demonstrators in Dili protested the UN's use of foreign contractors and workers and the importation of goods that could have been produced locally. They decried the fact that foreign businesses had come swiftly into Timor and opened highly profitable operations while Timorese were still reeling from the destruction and had no capital of their own with which to compete. The complicity of UNTAET in producing this inequality was suggested by the fact that UNTAET enforced a regulation limiting unskilled wages to $6 a day well before they began to focus on issues of business taxation.[94] An Australian Broadcasting Corporation radio program looking into the activities of a "Silver Circle" of well-connected, Darwin-based businessmen in East Timor in 2000 broached the term "profiteering" in an investigation of Australian business activities in Timor.[95]

At issue, however, was not merely the question of pay and profit, but how power was used to exclude and even criminalize Timorese who entered international spheres. Thus workers at the floating hotel complained not only about pay, but about having to undergo humiliating security searches of their possessions in front of passers-by on the jetty as they left for home.[96] Within UNTAET, policing of the divide between international and local personnel was evident in differential access to the tools for mobility and transnational connections. Local staff were not permitted to receive lifts in UN cars to and from work, whereas international staff were; local staff were not allowed to use UN cars outside of working hours, unlike international staff; and local staff were not given passwords to log on to the Internet or email with office computers, unlike international staff.[97] These kinds of practices represented attempts to keep the Timorese out of spheres designated "international" and to ensure that Timorese staff members became accustomed to the kind of low-paid,

---

[92] Kelly Morris, "Comment," *Guardian Online,* July 10, 2000, posted by Lao Hamutuk, online at http://www.laohamutuk.org/reports/news02.html

[93] Richard Lloyd Parry, "East Timorese Seethe at UN as Their Cities Remain a Wasteland," *The Independent,* January 29, 2000.

[94] Gerald Tooth, "Doing the Business in East Timor," ABC Radio *Background Briefing,* May 7, 2000. Transcript online at http://www.abc.net.au/rn/talks/bbing/stories/s125738.htm, accessed September 18, 2007.

[95] Ibid.

[96] "Staff at UN Floating Hotel Strikes for Better Pay," *Deutsche Presse-Agentur,* February 11, 2000.

[97] Former UN local staff member, personal interview, Dili, June 2005.

low-status work that the Timorese economy was likely to offer them in the future.

When tackled by reporters on the issue of the UN staff's grievances, UN officials suggested that the inexperience of the Timorese work force explained the pattern of disparities, rather than either UN unfairness in the way the emerging economy was being structured, or UN marginalization of the Timorese from political power. For example, an UNTAET official interviewed by *The Australian* on the subject of strikes by local staff, and the wider issue of Timorese dissatisfaction with the role allotted to them by the UN, gave a response that simply reemphasized the boundary between the international and the local that was the source of these complaints:

> The Timorese have no familiarity with any of these roles. All that experience left with the Indonesians. We, the donors and the international agencies, are having to train them virtually from zero.[98]

This response reinforces the divide between locals and internationals on the grounds of local incompetence and, consequently, the appropriateness of hierarchical relations in such cases. Thus, the "international" is represented as a sphere in which politically uncommitted and highly expert technicians visit various unpleasant conflict zones in order to do a dirty but necessary job that the locals cannot do themselves. For this effort, the international experts need to be rewarded at highly competitive rates. The "local," by contrast, is a sphere characterized by incompetence and underdevelopment, which must be repaired in an internationally prescribed manner.

To an extent, this logic is self-fulfilling: those workers whose abilities have been questioned tend to perform at a level commensurate with these low expectations. What's more, their problems at work are exacerbated by the extra pressures they face as "locals" in a post-conflict environment. An East Timorese judge, who had worked alongside international judges during the transition period, described this phenomenon:

> Nobody wanted to work with international judges, because we're not treated as on the same level. International judges are paid by the UN, and Timorese were paid by the government. ... And everything is very expensive, and I earned just $300 a month. I had to pay for taxis everywhere, and then they treated me badly —like for example, we spend an afternoon discussing something, and then I have to get a taxi home. They have a car, but they don't offer to drop me off. One day I came late, and they said, We can't work with you because you are always late. I said, I have a lot of difficulties—you have better conditions than I have. They said I had no background in how to work with others. But after two months, we learned to work together as a group. At the beginning I felt frustrated, but later on I loved it.[99]

---

[98] Peter Alford, "Peacing East Timor Back Together: Rebuilding East Timor is Proving a Thankless Task," *The Australian,* June 27, 2000, reproduced online at www.etan.org/et2000b/june/25-30/27theaus.htm

[99] Judge (name withheld for purposes of confidentiality), personal interview, Dili, July 2005.

The issue of "capacity" is widely used in both countries to justify international intervention and exercise of power in a local sphere. Yet the imposition of limits on the power and mobility of local staff applies even to those who do have capacity. This is evident in the orthodox doctrine, accepted by those engaged in international development efforts, which dictates that international staff should remain in country only while there are no locals sufficiently skilled to do the job; and that, therefore, capacity-building of local counterparts is a major part of any international aid worker's job. However, this presumption erects a barrier in the form of a glass ceiling between local and international roles—local counterparts are trained to take the local job but not the international job. While it is the case that occasionally talented locals are promoted to international status, there is a strong presumption against such promotions on the grounds that they lead to "brain drain." Similarly, international agencies in post-conflict countries frequently adopt informal policies against poaching talent from local non-governmental or governmental organizations, policies that, from a different perspective, resemble blacklists. As a result of these well-intentioned policies, opportunities for locals are restricted to those available within the territorial boundaries of the state; while international staff have access to the far better remunerated sphere of global post-conflict reconstruction work.

It is not the application of principles of meritocracy that justifies the boundaries between international and local; rather, the division is justified by an explicit, but ultimately arbitrary, assignment of individuals to "homelands," a pattern of discourse analyzed above in the discussion of refugee return. Individuals are expected to put their own immediate pressing concerns aside and to accept the fact that their indigeneity condemns them to a salary that is less than a tenth of their colleagues' on the grounds that doing so is in the best long-term interests of their country. Fundamental to this logic is the attempt, basic to UN interventions of this kind, to invest in a boundary between the international and the local that makes such distinctions natural. Although both UNTAC and UNTAET brought a promise of freedom, they each ended up, in different ways, operating above all to demarcate a "home" within which regimenting political and economic processes could be implemented and an elite—sooner in the case of Cambodia, later in the case of Timor—would be privileged through a process of state-building. State-building processes tied these elites into conditions of aid dependence, marked by unequal relationships between locals, who lacked resources and capacity, and internationals in possession of wealth and expertise. Cultivating the domestic political and economic spheres would be the next task.

CHAPTER V

"NORMAL AND SIMPLE MEMBERS OF THE COMMUNITY": DEMOBILIZING THE MOB

"Soldiers need to forget about the life of a soldier and become normal and simple members of their communities. They have to become ordinary villagers who can participate in commune activities."
NGO Worker, Battambang, 2000

The policing of the borders of political communities in the context of peacekeeping and aid dependency is one part of a two-pronged strategy, which also involves reconstructing the internal dynamics of those communities themselves. The politics of return and of indigeneity represented the construction of a delimited field of action within which international power could be effectively projected and individuals disciplined, to create not only new state institutions, but also a new society with which that state could engage in internationally sanctioned ways. Approaches to these goals altered over the course of the 1990s. In the immediate post-Cold War era, international policy-makers' attention was devoted to liberating societies on the assumption that they would pressure states to reform. From the mid-1990s, as the democratic peace thesis gave way to ideas of the new barbarism, attention on the part of the United Nations system shifted from using societies to police aberrant states towards promoting states as a means to police aberrant societies.

The mechanisms envisaged for these processes have been similar in both Cambodia and East Timor. In both cases, this chapter argues, a section of the elite has been ushered into power; subsequently, observable and activist social forces that might award that elite a domestic power base have been engaged as targets of demobilization. This is a strategy of atomization—one that privileges forms of engagement between state and society in which the individual is encouraged to act and make decisions as an individual, rather than as a member of a community or a collective. As such, it is a strategy that evinces a fear of collective action, perceived as mob action. The individual is encouraged to participate in a variety of impersonal political processes according to the dictates of "conscience" rather than in pursuit of consensus. The aggregation of individual consciences into a collective will is performed, not by social acts of accommodation or compromise, but via the rule of codified procedures to which loyalty and acquiescence are prescribed. Interaction with such procedures is required to be not only conscientious, but voluntary, conducted in isolation from others, and self-disciplined. Flexibility, creativity, or critical engagement are not encouraged, except by professional democracy promoters speaking on behalf of the poor. Beyond this form of political participation, the major role required of the individual and of local communities is the organization of social and economic self-reliance, in subservience to the dictates of the market.

This chapter examines the functioning of these mechanisms in the context of policies for demilitarization and democratization in post-conflict Cambodia and Timor-Leste. Designed to promote peace, in the case of the former, and responsive and accountable government, in the case of the latter, these concerns have been significant to peacekeepers and donors engaged in the post-conflict setting. As is true of those groups involved with the policies examined in the previous chapter, there is no doubt that international and local personnel alike share an interest in, and concern for, demilitarization and democratization. However, the way in which these processes have been set up with international assistance in Cambodia and Timor, and the particular outcomes generated, can be explained only with reference to distributions of power among international, national, and local actors negotiating over them. This chapter will argue that international promotion of demilitarization and democratization in Cambodia and East Timor has followed a neoliberal agenda that advocates economic self-reliance and political atomization and that regards peace as a function of the political emasculation of contentious constituencies, even when there might be significant wider disadvantages to such an approach. This has had a powerful influence on the types of politics deemed legitimate internationally and promoted locally. The way these look to national elites and local villagers, and the responses they have elicited, are the subjects of the final chapters of this study.

DEMILITARIZATION

The way in which various donors and international actors tackled the questions of disarmament, demobilization, and reintegration of armed forces is one example of the way in which a predilection towards atomization trumped all other considerations. In both Cambodia and Timor-Leste, this led to international donors providing aid and assistance for demilitarization strategies that were ill-informed and unworkable. In Cambodia, the outcome was that donors eventually abandoned the issue, leaving the Cambodian government to come to a quiet accommodation with the powerful armed forces in a manner that significantly affected the nature of the peace that emerged. In Timor-Leste, the issue of demilitarization became explosive and was intimately connected with a new outbreak of violence in 1996. In the discussion that follows, I show that the overriding faith in atomization as a solution, with the aim of transforming highly politicized networks of soldiers into "normal and simple" individuals interacting with the market, blinded international actors to a whole range of problems in both countries, many of which remain unresolved.

Timor-Leste gained its independence in 2002 with an army nobody quite knew what to do with. FALINTIL (Forças Armadas da Libertação Nacional de Timor-Leste, National Liberation Armed Forces of East Timor) had not been awarded any status by the May 5 Agreements between Indonesia and Portugal that led to the Popular Consultation; the Agreements stipulated that Indonesian security forces would be responsible for ensuring security during the popular consultation process. A subsequent Security Council Resolution created the United Nations Assistance Mission in East Timor (UNAMET), which was charged with organizing the ballot; this resolution called "for the laying down of arms by all armed groups in East

Timor, for the necessary steps to achieve disarmament and for further steps in order to ensure a secure environment devoid of violence or other forms of intimidation."[1]

Given the high level of ongoing militia violence, FALINTIL did not disarm. However, once UNAMET was deployed, FALINTIL moved into four cantonments and stayed there throughout the subsequent violence. FALINTIL commander Taur Matan Ruak believed that one goal of the militia violence was to tempt FALINTIL into renewed warfare, thereby escalating the violence, justifying a renewed Indonesian crackdown and jeopardizing external support. FALINTIL's "immense self-discipline"[2] under this provocation and its refusal to break its ceasefire was described by one UN military official as "an amazing act of restraint and strategic vision."[3]

The position of the Cambodian armed forces was rather different. Unlike FALINTIL, which in 1987 had broken away from FRETILIN (Frente Revolucionária de Timor-Leste Independente, The Revolutionary Front for an Independent East Timor) to espouse a specifically nationalist cause, represented by the CNRM (Concelho Nacional da Resistancia Maubere, National Council of Maubere Resistance), the Cambodian armies remained overtly tied to political parties. Under UNTAC's (United Nations Transitional Authority in Cambodia) auspices, these armies were supposed to be cantoned and disarmed in preparation for demobilization. However, the withdrawal of the PDK (Party of Democratic Kampuchea) from the Cambodian peace process entailed that its associated armed force, the National Army of Democratic Kampuchea, return to warfare. Other parties successfully lobbied UNTAC to halt demobilization, on the grounds that Cambodia needed to defend itself from the insurgency. The military, consequently, remained active and intrusive throughout the peacekeeping process and into the subsequent period of aid dependence. While UNTAC acquiesced to the cessation of demobilization as a means to shore up the state administration in the extremely insecure conditions surrounding the 1993 election, the continued status of the Cambodian military as a key political player in Cambodia today has prompted repeated efforts by donors to initiate new rounds of demobilization. These have been successfully resisted by the Cambodian military and the political elite with whom it is allied.

In East Timor, CNRM policy had long been that Timor would disarm completely at independence, relying thereafter upon diplomacy, rather than armed force, for protection. This stance was dropped after 1999, in part due to militia violence and continued concerns about border security following the flight of militia members to camps in West Timor. In part also, Timor's leaders anticipated that demobilizing FALINTIL would be perhaps more problematic than retaining it. The result was a partial and unsatisfactory demobilization, the failures of which were blamed for continuing security problems in post-independence Timor.

---

[1] Security Council Resolution 1246 (1999) on the Situation in Timor, UN Doc. No. S/RES/1246, 11 June 1999, online at http://www.un.org/Docs/scres/1999/sc99.htm, accessed September 28, 2008, para. 11.

[2] Edward Rees, *Under Pressure: Falintil-Forças de Defesa de Timor Leste, Three Decades of Defence Force Development in Timor-Leste: 1975–2004*, Working Paper no. 139 (Geneva: Geneva Centre for the Democratic Control of Armed Forces, 2004), p. 44.

[3] Michael G. Smith with Maureen Dee, *Peacekeeping in East Timor: The Path to Independence*, International Peace Academy Occasional Paper Series (Boulder, CO: Lynne Rienner, 2003), p. 49.

In both cases, lack of success was in part a function of tensions within liberal conceptualizations of what demobilization might mean in a post-conflict country. International policy regarded post-conflict armies as significant problems, best dealt with by downsizing and, if possible, complete dismemberment, followed, if necessary, by a new process of recruitment designed to establish a distinct, professional armed force, which would exist alongside an armed police force. The shift from militarization to policing is fundamental to liberal approaches to security in a post-conflict state.

The twin concerns of "professionalization" and "policing" conform closely to neoliberal policy discourse, which is inclined to promote the atomization of potentially unruly groups within society. A post-conflict army is distrusted as politicized and assertive and, consequently, as destabilizing for the fragile post-conflict state, which will be ill-equipped to resist the army's demands. "Professionalization," which generally implies the demobilization of most of the old forces and their replacement with new ones, is intended as a direct attack on institutional cultures formed of personal relationships of loyalty, obligation, and accountability that build up under conditions of conflict. Sending former soldiers home through demobilization and reintegration programs is intended to rupture old relationships, transforming the army from a powerful mass constituency into a set of atomized individuals amenable to policing and requiring assistance.

The establishment of a police force further reinforces this approach. Unlike an army which, even as a guerrilla force, represents mass resistance or contention, a police force deals with perpetrators of violence or instability on an individual basis. The shift to policing fosters conceptions of post-conflict violence as individual in cause and effect; it operates to reframe conflict, identifying it as the result of everyday disputes and transgressions rather than as a matter of mass contention over distributions of power. A transition from use of the military to use of the police to defend security is thus an ideological device, intended to delegitimate acts of violence and reframe resistance as criminality.

Such policy prescriptions disguise ongoing contention rather than defusing it. Demobilization entails a move away from accommodating powerful collective actors and towards policing individuals, who are consequently disempowered vis-à-vis the reconstituted state. However, this policy is likely to be clearly perceived and resisted by the constituencies to be demobilized; further, it is evident to elites who seek every opportunity to turn the process to their political advantage. As such, demobilization is not merely ideological in intent, but unavoidably political in implementation.

The failures of security-sector reform in Cambodia and Timor illustrate the problems. The failure of UNTAC to disarm the various armies in 1993 has affected Cambodian politics ever since. The military in Cambodia resisted subsequent donor efforts at reducing its size, the scope of its activities, and its tendency to carry out shocking acts of violence, not only against identified opponents, but against more or less anyone who crossed its path.

The Cambodian military has been used for three main purposes since 1992. First, it has been used to deal with the Khmer Rouge. Initially, failure to demobilize the armed forces during the UNTAC era was justified on the basis that the Khmer Rouge insurgency remained a real threat that needed to be defended against. The Royal Cambodian Armed Forces (RCAF), formed by integrating SoC (State of Cambodia) and non-Khmer Rouge resistance forces in 1992, performed this task. Later, the RCAF provided an institutional home for Khmer Rouge soldiers and commanders who had defected to the government. Throughout this period, it also functioned as a large income-generating and electoral machine, which created slush funds for commanders, cementing their loyalty to the center, and delivered financial and political support to the government while keeping the opposition weak through intimidation and threats. Finally, it acted as a welfare organization, which kept thousands of poor and unskilled men off the streets of urban Cambodia by incorporating them into entrepreneurial activities. The RCAF's engagement in illegal and destructive logging and smuggling, and in the sex trade, has been widely acknowledged in Cambodia.

The RCAF's performance of the first function—to resist the Khmer Rouge—was sanctioned by international donors, who were as unwilling as anyone else to see the Khmer Rouge make military gains. Donors accepted this role for the RCAF, understanding that military action would be paralleled by a sanitizing process—the establishment of a tribunal to judge former Khmer Rouge leaders. Donors have been less happy with the military's performance of its latter two functions, and, since the end of the war in 1998, a variety of demobilization schemes have been mooted, intended to reduce the size and increase the professionalism and quality of the RCAF; to reduce its tendency to engage in human rights abuse; and to allow transfer of limited government funds away from the defense sector and into the social service sector.

A World Bank-funded project to assist with demobilization of 30,000 troops was launched in 2001, following the government's pilot demobilization of 15,000 troops between 1999 and 2000. The scheme was halted, however, in 2003, following discovery of corruption in procurement activities associated with the program, and in the midst of wider concerns based upon rumors about who was being demobilized and why, and who was getting the lion's share of donor resources.

These problems arose, in part, from the Cambodian government's lack of cooperation, discussed in the next chapter; as it happened, the Cambodian People's Party (CPP) relied on the military for political support.[4] But in part, demobilization failed because the RCAF as envisaged by the authors of these schemes simply did not accord with the reality of the RCAF as a force. The viability of demobilization relied upon assumptions about the nature of the distinction between military and civilian, the popular appeal of ideas of "reintegration," and the potential for self-reliance among postwar Cambodians that did not relate to reality. As a result, the demobilization effort in Cambodia, as in East Timor, put not only the Cambodian government but also military commanders and ordinary soldiers into positions where they faced demands that were incompatible with their vital interests and perceived obligations.

The scheme was premised upon the assumption that demobilized soldiers could, and would, become self-reliant in civilian life, able to use the assets they were given when "discharged" from the armed forces productively, to support their families, and that they would be able to access civilian services on their own initiative in an appropriate way. These premises were somewhat at odds with the assertion that particularly vulnerable groups would be demobilized first, in order to relieve the armed forces of the least productive soldiers. The level of need of these soldiers was directly at odds with the assumption that they would learn to become self-reliant

---

[4] Dylan Hendrickson, "Cambodia's Security Sector Reforms: Limits of a Downsizing Strategy," *Conflict, Security, Development* 1,1 (2001): 67–82.

quickly, an assumption implicit in the reintegration strategy. Furthermore, donors presumed that demobilization could be achieved by severing institutional connections. In fact, the military as an organization comprised webs of personal relationships that either did not take a properly institutional form or would outlast the cutting of formal ties.

Participants in the demobilization scheme fell into three broad groups. First, there were "vulnerable groups"—sick, disabled, and elderly soldiers, and war widows living in barracks. These people were considered by donors to be unproductive and therefore dispensable, despite the fact that their prospects outside the armed forces were as unpromising as their prospects within it.

While donors discharged their duty to such individuals with cash payments, for commanders the relationship with these soldiers was more complicated. Commanders occupied the role of patron, with soldiers as their clients, and these were relationships that could not easily be severed. Whether the individuals concerned remained inside the armed forces or outside it, commanders would continue to bear an obligation towards them. Jettisoning the role of patron in favor of a more "professional" relationship would be difficult for these officers, in part because of the cultural and moral understandings that had been invested in these relationships over the long years of warfare, and in part because the status of patron, adopted by so many commanders, was central to ongoing relationships with soldiers staying on in the military. Commanders' attempts to abandon long-standing "clients" would seriously affect relations throughout the armed forces.

Second, there was a large number of fit and healthy soldiers who had access to productive assets outside the army and thus were the best candidates for "reintegration." However, many of these soldiers had effectively demobilized themselves and abandoned the armed forces, although their commanders were often still drawing their pay. But ongoing ties with the armed forces privileged such individuals in their villages, allowing them access to protection, support, and even weapons that were not available to others. The fact that many individuals enjoyed a "military" status even though they did not contribute on a day-to-day basis to the activities of the armed forces was a significant dynamic in the ongoing impact of militarization on Cambodian society, affecting such issues as weapons ownership, human rights abuses, and power relationships with other villagers.

A problem for donors was establishing how many individuals fell into each category. Donors were reluctant to give "reintegration packages" to soldiers who were already reintegrated; they also feared that the money for these packages would simply end up in the hands of corrupt military commanders, and tried to insist the "ghosts" be removed from the armed forces lists prior to the start of demobilization. The Cambodian government announced the removal of 15,000 "ghost" troops and more than 100,000 "ghost" dependents in 1999. However, there was ongoing contention over the status of the approximately 130,000 soldiers the Cambodian government claimed to be sustaining. Estimates of the actual number of active soldiers ranged between 40,000 to 70,000.

Donors found it difficult to verify the information they were being given by the Cambodian government as the demobilization process unfolded. Severance fees were paid—and probably ended up in the pockets of the commanders who had been appropriating "ghost" salaries—and names were removed from the military payroll, but there was little clear evidence to show what impact any of this had on the core of active military cadre because the distinctions among currently active soldiers, ex-soldiers, old soldiers, and civilians were blurred in the first place. This situation frustrated the external actors when the problems became apparent; some donors resented the idea that they were paying millions of dollars for a largely clerical exercise, and media criticism of this waste was a factor in the subsequent suspension of the demobilization program; the official explanation for this decision cited evidence of corrupt procurement practices. Brad Adams, a human rights activist who has spent many years following the human rights record of the Cambodian military, summed up this mood in writing: "Each non-soldier who is demobilized represents a missed opportunity to remove a real soldier from the RCAF's ranks, with all the costs to law and order and the country's economic future this entails."[5]

There was also little information available that would clarify the relationship of the military to the position of the "ghosts" themselves. If official demobilization was regarded by the ghosts and their former commanders as severing the de facto clientelist links that persisted between ex-soldiers and their units, then it would serve some purpose in altering the status of those ex-soldiers in the eyes of their neighbors, and thus might contribute to a demilitarization of wider society. This kind of impact was not monitored by the donor agencies. A further criticism voiced by Adams, concerning the failure of donors to challenge the army's decision that demobilized soldiers be allowed to continue wearing military uniforms, suggests that ex-ghosts identified themselves as "military" even after demobilization.[6]

The third group comprised the core of active soldiers, most of whom spent their time busily employed in the various entrepreneurial activities that the military engaged in: manning checkpoints on highways and borders; providing security for various operations such as logging; and taking part in logging, as well as the harvesting of other kinds of illegal forest products. Since commanders had strong financial interests in retaining both these last groups of soldiers, these were unlikely to be swiftly demobilized. Adams criticizes the fact that donors made few attempts to identify or insist upon the demobilization of human rights abusers among the armed forces.[7] Demobilization thus achieved the worst of both worlds—cutting loose individuals least able to cope outside the military, while leaving intact the most abusive, most secretive, and least "professional" parts of the military apparatus. In fact, the various demobilization projects that occurred dealt largely with old, disabled, and sick soldiers, and with "ghost" soldiers; resistance by the government to any internal restructuring ensured there would be relatively little impact on the actual structure and functioning of the military itself. While the demobilization of ghosts certainly saved on salaries over the long term, and contributed to an increase in spending on social services, the demobilization of the vulnerable groups merely shifted the burden of providing for their welfare elsewhere.

The donors' perceptions of elderly and vulnerable ex-soldiers, which were implicit in their demobilization schemes, also helped create a view of society distinctly at odds with Cambodian reality. First, the civilian services, such as health services, that the soldiers were supposed to rely on after demobilization were poorly functioning and highly corrupt. Civilians long accustomed to the vagaries of commune clinics and district hospitals, for example, found it extremely difficult to

---

[5] Brad Adams, "Demobilization's House of Mirrors," *Phnom Penh Post*, November 23–December 6, 2001, online at www.phnompenhpost.com, accessed September 17, 2007.

[6] Ibid.

[7] Ibid.

gain access to these services; finding transportation to the centers was difficult, hours of service were irregular, and the staff frequently demanded bribes. Demobilized soldiers were placed upon the same footing as other villagers, but often with fewer coping strategies or support networks; consequently they struggled.

These difficulties were partially recognized during the demobilization process, but were not addressed. For example, a World Bank study of a pilot demobilization project run by the government found that 74 percent of the discharged soldiers required ongoing medical treatment for various illnesses. This discovery prompted a scheme to provide soldiers with certificates they could take to health clinics to prove that they were entitled to treatment. However, this scheme was apparently poorly implemented; newspaper reports suggested that soldiers interviewed by reporters were unaware of the provisions for health care and didn't know how to gain access to them. It is tempting to speculate that this laxity was a sign of a lack of confidence in the certificate scheme, given the state of Cambodian health services more generally. A comment from an official interviewed by the *Phnom Penh Post* supports this interpretation. He remarked that it was likely an unknown number of soldiers had been infected with HIV, since the armed forces had long been specified as a high-risk group for HIV in Cambodia. However, demobilized soldiers were not being given an HIV test, as "it is too expensive and would require follow-up counseling," a service that demobilized soldiers would not find conveniently available in the civilian sphere.[8] While sending home sick and disabled soldiers is clearly a logical way of rationalizing the armed forces, this strategy did not address the needs of the soldiers themselves, nor did the reintegration of people living with HIV and other undiagnosed infectious diseases into a community with poor access to health care promote the security of that society, widely conceived. At best, it broke the problem up and spread it across the country.

Second, in a context marked by decreasing land ownership and high urban unemployment, some ex-soldiers found it difficult to become economically self-reliant. The heavy reliance upon subsistence in rural areas and the inflated urban economy entailed that microenterprise in either rural or urban areas offered only an extremely meager living. Interviews with demobilizing soldiers, conducted by the Working Group on Weapons Reduction (WGWR) in 2001, suggested that 70 percent were worried about their ability to support themselves in the future.[9] A report in the *Phnom Penh Post* noted that the most optimistic demobilizing soldiers were those with access to land or with relatives to care for them. Those who did not have access to land were unsure how they would survive. These findings were backed by evidence from more extensive studies, which suggested that soldiers who had no family members living in a village would find it difficult to integrate.[10] These

[8] Bou Saroeun, "Cambodia's Soldiers Start New Lives as Civilians," *The Phnom Penh Post*, October 26, 2001, online edition, at http://www.phnompenhpost.com/index.php/200110265971/National-news/Cambodia-s-soldiers-start-new-lives-as-civilians.html, accessed September 23, 2008.

[9] Working Group on Weapons Reduction, *NGO Report on the 2001 Demobilization Programme: Observations and Recommendations* (Phnom Penh: Working Group on Weapons Reduction, 2002).

[10] Prum Sam Ol, Peng Chiew Meng, and Elizabeth Uphoff Cato, *Starting Over: The Reintegration Experience of Returnees, Internally Displaced, and Demobilized Soldiers in Cambodia*, Cambodian Veterans Assistance Program Executive Secretariat Background Report (Phnom Penh: Cambodian Veterans Assistance Program, 1996).

concerns over the future were perhaps the reason why the WGWR survey of demobilizing soldiers in 2001 raised doubts about the extent to which soldiers had really disarmed. The WGWR study found that soldiers were aware that they were not permitted to take weapons with them into civilian life, and 95 percent of the respondents claimed that they had disarmed. However, two-thirds of respondents told the WGWR team that they believed others had kept their weapons, leading the WGWR to question whether disarmament had really been achieved.[11]

Related to the question of livelihood was the question of social status. The WGWR study also found that "fear that other civilians will look down on them after they lose their power as soldiers" was widespread among veterans.[12] This problem was not confined to the soldiers themselves; it concerned their families also. The idea that the soldiers had homes to return to, with waiting wives and children who would be glad of an extra pair of hands to help on the farm, was simply mistaken. Many soldiers' families lived on or near the base with them and depended upon the military for support; demobilization, to the extent that it occurred in the way donors planned, set the whole family adrift into an economy and society that was potentially hostile.

In this context, even once they were formally demobilized, ex-soldiers found it very difficult to cut their ties with the patronage networks that had always sustained them. Thus, one general commented:

> After the soldiers are demobilized, it is the burden of the local authorities to ensure their living conditions ... But many soldiers go to their former commanders instead and ask for help when they face difficulties. For instance, in Banteay Meanchey, some twenty families of demobilized soldiers are still living right outside the military base.[13]

Some of the soldiers interviewed by the *Phnom Penh Post* said they planned to beg for help from relatives. In both cases, whether these veterans sought support from former commanders or from relatives, the outcome was the shifting of the burden of care and support from the army as an institution to individuals within the army or outside it. Similarly, although both donors and villagers feared that demobilized soldiers were prone to become bandits or violent threats to their neighbors, or were likely to suffer from mental illness, nothing was done to address these threats, real or imagined. Thus, once again, problems were shifted away from the army as an institution to the private realm of extended families and villagers.

In the Cambodian case, three answers to these problems emerged. The first answer, put forward by donors and NGOs involved in the pilot demobilization process, was heavier involvement from "civil society" in providing reintegration support, particularly to vulnerable groups such as disabled or elderly former soldiers. However, this solution was never seriously pursued in a targeted way. Among competitive international funding organizations prepared to support

[11] Working Group on Weapons Reduction, *NGO Report on the 2001 Demobilization Programme*, p. 12.

[12] Ibid., p. 15.

[13] Gen. Bun Sen, Commander, Military Region 5, Royal Cambodian Armed Forces, quoted in Anette Marcher and Vong Sokheng, "The Day after Demob: Old Soldiers Find Themselves Left High and Dry," *Phnom Penh Post*, November 10–23, 2000, online at www.phnompenhpost.com, accessed September 17, 2007.

nongovernmental initiatives, the provision of outright welfare to disabled or sick ex-soldiers was not likely to be a high priority: former combatants are not considered with much sympathy, and the idea of welfare hand-outs divorced from some form of self-reliance does not play well with this audience. The government faced great difficulty meeting even the most basic of its commitments to provide food aid to veterans during an initial transition period; further efforts were few and far between and fell under general community development initiatives.[14]

The second, implicit, solution to the problems created by demobilization was to leave reintegration to market forces. The discipline of the market would force veterans to find a solution for themselves; and this solution, however personally disastrous, would be more efficient than any solution connected to the ongoing presence of a bloated, incentive-distorting military in the Cambodian economy. The fact that so little monitoring was carried out to assess the welfare of demobilized soldiers suggests that this laissez-faire approach was favored by international actors.

However, away from the spotlight of donor attention, the Cambodian military adopted a third strategy. Although assessments of veterans and their living conditions have not been undertaken on a large scale, it is clear that a number of the ex-soldiers returned to work for the private enterprises of their former commanders, but as private individuals rather than as subordinates in the armed forces. Some were awarded land by the government, or by their commanders, sometimes bringing them into conflict with local villagers. High-profile land disputes in Banteay Meanchey and Ratanakiri provinces have featured the claims of demobilized soldiers to land awarded them by their commanders and the counter-claims of dispossessed villagers; and in both cases, further disputes occurred when RCAF commanders later tried to sell the land for their own personal gain, dispossessing both sets of claimants.[15] While this absorption of ex-soldiers into the private economy reduced the size and cost of the military, the reincorporation of these individuals into economic activities connected with smuggling and the illegal harvesting of natural resources illustrates how market solutions, for Cambodia, tend to rely upon exactly the kind of violent and lawless shadow economies of unregulated international trade that demilitarization was supposed to combat. These activities in the shadow economy funded the patron-client relationships that ultimately took some of the strain off failed "reintegration" programs. Essentially, the Cambodian military took care of the problem itself, but in a manner that was not amenable to political scrutiny and that ultimately added to the economic and political power of the Cambodia's military commanders.

This success on the part of the military, juxtaposed with limited opportunities in the mainstream economy for young Cambodians, appears to have strengthened the Cambodian government's conviction that the military is useful. New plans to introduce compulsory military service for young people have been mooted in response to continuing high unemployment among urban youth and an alarming increase in indicators of social alienation, such as gang membership and violence. As

[14] Helen Brereton and Sok Chan Chorvy, *Gender Analysis of Cambodia's Pilot Demobilization Project and Gender Mainstreaming Recommendations for the Full Demobilization Project,* (Phnom Penh: World Bank, 2001), p.18.

[15] See Kenneth Fernandes, "A Summary of 2006 Evictions in Cambodia," *Cambodian Eviction Monitor* 1 (2006): 7, online at http://www.cohre.org/store/attachments/Eviction%20Monitor%20Jan-Dec%202006.pdf, accessed September 2, 2008; Erik Wasson and Yun Samean, "Villagers Vow to Fight Land Sale in Ratanakiri," *Cambodia Daily,* January 23, 2007, pp. 1–2.

a result, the thinking behind demobilization has been reversed. Advocates of demobilization envisaged the entrepreneurial and abusive military being disbanded and then reshaped through the salutary discipline imposed by a free market society. Now, the government proposes that those who might turn to violence and criminality—as a result of the failure of the political and economic order to provide significant opportunities, particularly to the landless—will be shipped into the military in order to provide them with some form of occupation and support.

Both international and Cambodian policy-makers were reluctant to perceive veterans as a political constituency, one that might have real problems that could be dealt with through political solutions. The problem posed by veterans was said to stem from their association with one another; their absorption into wider society was regarded as the solution to that problem. Yet it is unclear how successful that reintegration was for individuals who had lived for a long period apart from society, since reintegration policies themselves precluded any possibility of the veterans achieving a unified public voice. Some of these individuals ultimately chose to use their leverage as clients to make demands of their patrons and thus avoid the difficulties of genuine reintegration. Consequently, some ended up remaining attached to their former commanders in dependent relationships that offered them a degree of protection, but which neither presaged the chance for a new life nor resolved the main problems caused by widespread militarization—namely the negative impact of the military on social stability and the prospects for democratization.

International and Cambodian policy makers paid little attention to the reality of veterans as a political constituency—represented as *veterans*, rather than as "normal villagers." One official commented:

> ... when you have lived as a soldier for so long, it is a challenge to change your life to a civilian ... But the soldiers need to forget about the life of a soldier and become normal and simple members of their communities. They have to become ordinary villagers that can participate in commune activities. If that doesn't happen, they are not really demobilized. Physically and formally they are, but they will still want to live as a soldier. I don't think that is what anybody wants.[16]

While salaries could be stopped and names struck off rolls, breaking the personal relationships that linked members of the armed forces to one another (indeed, which to a great extent comprised the Cambodian armed forces) and normalizing the status of former soldiers in the eyes of their fellow villagers, and in their own eyes, were much more problematic affairs. Ultimately, demobilization reduced soldiers' choices to two options: they could continue to adhere to the military's patronage, on the one hand, or face isolation and poverty in a harsh economic and social environment, on the other. International policy-makers' fear of the veterans as an unruly group within society precluded discussion of alternative strategies that might have been able to deal with the specific problems faced by this group of people, and to maintain their

---

[16] Kung Munichan, program manager, Cambodia Area Rehabilitation and Regeneration Project, Battambang, quoted in Anette Marcher and Vong Sokheng, "The Day after Demob," online version.

support networks in a manner that was productive, rather than shadowy, violent, and located on the edges of the law.

   For the glorious FALINTIL, the liberators of East Timor, dilemmas associated with demobilization were even more acute than those in Cambodia. For these fighters, demobilization not only meant reorienting of attitudes, relationships, and livelihoods, but a significant loss of moral status. The international organizations' desire to undercut the soldiers' status was evident from their reluctance to award FALINTIL much respect in the first place. Despite the moral status of FALINTIL, not just locally, but internationally, interveners treated them with the same suspicion that they had showed to the combatants in any of the "uncivil wars" of the 1990s, perceiving them uniformly as an armed and potentially unruly constituency. This was not simply a mistake; the logic of the neoliberal order required that armed and potentially assertive constituencies be dismantled, lest they demand special treatment. Indeed, even following the rejection of the Indonesian occupation by the East Timorese at the polls and the evident complicity of the Indonesian army in the subsequent wholesale killing and destruction, incoming interveners drew a distinction, not between perpetrators and innocents, or those with public support in East Timor and those without it, but between forces associated with policing and those that were potentially "political."

   In the case of FALINTIL, this logic led the International Force for East Timor (InterFET), which had been deployed to restore order in 1999, to argue for the immediate disarmament of FALINTIL in conjunction with the disarmament of other "armed civilian groups"—namely, the pro-integration militias that had wrought such destruction while FALINTIL remained in cantonments. InterFET's rules of engagement called for the "disarming of armed elements,"[17] which they interpreted to include FALINTIL. However, the same rules of engagement ruled out disarming the Indonesian army, which was regarded as a legitimate security force. FALINTIL resisted disarmament, which led to "something of a standoff" between InterFET and FALINTIL.[18] FALINTIL's members argued that their weapons were vital for their own defense, given the level of insecurity and the continued presence of thousands of Indonesian troops in East Timor. The Australian Defence Force, whose troops comprised the bulk of InterFET, dismissed this argument and maintained that "all those armed militia groups of whatever persuasion should be aware that it [security] is InterFET's responsibility and leave it to InterFET."[19] This equation of FALINTIL with "armed militia groups" was considered deeply insulting by FALINTIL and members of the CNRT (Congresso Nacional da Reconstrução de Timor, National Congress for the Reconstruction of East Timor). Xanana Gusmão protested that FALINTIL should not be seen as "a group of bandits."[20] Subsequently, FALINTIL

---

[17] Australian Defence Force Spokesman for East Timor, Colonel Duncan Lewis, quoted in "InterFET Claims Mandate for Disarming FALINTIL," *The World Today*, ABC News Online, October 5, 1999, 12:20, online at http://www.abc.net.au/worldtoday/stories/s57097.htm, accessed May 13, 2007.

[18] Ibid.

[19] Ibid.

[20] East Timor Observatory, "East Timor Defence Force: The Price of Security," *Defence Dossier*, Document No. DEF01-17/05/2001eng, May 27, 2001, online at http://www/pcug.org.au/

commanders began to insist that they be included in a new security plan for East Timor. Commander Lere Anan Timor suggested: "We will propose we have a policing role and we must also be allowed to carry our arms as we have done for the last twenty-four years."[21]

While InterFET gave way on the issue of immediate disarmament, UN staff strongly promoted the idea, previously espoused by the CNRT, that East Timor could do without an army after independence. FALINTIL leaders, however, disagreed, arguing that ongoing militia activity suggested the need for their organization to remain intact. In public statements, FALINTIL commanders played upon the popularity and legitimacy of FALINTIL, clearly perceiving it to be either in the country's interests, or perhaps in their own, to prolong the existence of FALINTIL as a postwar actor and contributor to national reconstruction. Thus Taur Matan Ruak announced in a speech in 2001, "I affirm once again: there will be no destabilizing campaign that will annul the institution that is FALINTIL and its identity ..."[22] This approach was greeted with a great deal of nervousness by Western analysts and donors. Dennis Shoesmith, who acted as a consultant for the UN in East Timor, comments that "the political character of the army has grave implications for the Alkatiri government."[23]

The UN took a sharply different approach to the creation of a police service. Here, they privileged individuals who had previous experience serving with the Indonesian police service, even though it might be argued, in a parallel to the line taken on FALINTIL, that experience gained policing authoritarian rule over an occupied zone might be inappropriate and counter-productive in an independent democracy. Where FALINTIL members' public image as heroes of independence was regarded as potentially problematic, the public image of the Indonesian National Police (POLRI, Polisi Negara Republik Indonesia) as collaborators and brutal oppressors was not considered in the same way. Ludovic Hood points out that recruitment of these police, although accompanied by a vetting process, was conducted without consultation with East Timorese constituencies, that the recruiters had limited training, and the selection process was heavily biased towards criteria that primarily served the interests of UNTAET (United Nations Transitional Administration in East Timor), such as familiarity with English.[24] Emphasis on promoting the police at the expense of the military, even when the police patently lacked legitimacy in the eyes of the public, while the military had support among large sections of the population, suggests the overriding concern to subordinate the politics of nation-building to the disciplinary imperatives of state-building. UNTAET privileged the building of security forces that would be uninvolved in local political debates and, as evidenced by the English-language requirement, it also expected

~wildwood/01maydefence.htm, accessed September 17, 2007. East Timor Observatory is an NGO set up by two Portuguese solidarity groups to monitor East Timor's transition from Indonesian rule.

[21] Quoted in ibid.

[22] Taur Matan Ruak, address, Transition Ceremony from FALINTIL to F-FDTL, Aileu, February 1, 2001, online at http://members.pcug.org.au/~wildwood/febfalintil.htm, accessed September 20, 2007.

[23] Dennis Shoesmith, "Timor-Leste: Divided Leadership in a Semi-Presidential System," *Asian Survey* 43,2 (2003): 231–52.

[24] Ludovic Hood, "Security Sector Reform in East Timor, 1999–2004," *International Peacekeeping* 13,1 (2006): 64.

these forces to be compliant to the demands of experts and technical assistants supplied by donor countries; this last qualification was apparently more important than their legitimacy in the eyes of local people. The idea of a force that might regard itself as possessing a specifically political legitimacy was treated with great suspicion.

Because of this suspicion, FALINTIL remained officially cantoned in Aileu until February 2001, when a new defense force was formed following protracted negotiations. UN staff strongly promoted the idea, previously espoused by the CNRT, that East Timor could do without an army altogether after independence. The East Timorese leaders, however, changed their position in the light of ongoing militia activity on the border. UNTAET responded to the sensitive question of demobilizing FALINTIL with hesitation until the problem became a crisis. Conditions in the cantonment at Aileu deteriorated: as combatants, FALINTIL members were not eligible for assistance by humanitarian agencies, and UNTAET had no specific mandate to deal with them either. FALINTIL soldiers went hungry, and malaria and tuberculosis became rife in the camp. At the same time, disagreements emerged among different FALINTIL commanders, forced to deal with one another for the first time, and some left the camp. Among those leaving was a group associated with a commander named Cornelio Gama, or L-7, a rival of Xanana's from the war years.[25]

Finally, in mid-2000, UNTAET acted on this increasingly sensitive issue. UNTAET called on a team of consultants from King's College in London to advise them on options for the future of FALINTIL. The consultants produced a report that laid out three options for a future defense force. The option adopted, after further negotiation, provided for the demobilization of more than half the FALINTIL force and the retention of 650 soldiers to form Battalion 1 of the new Forças de Defesa de Timor Leste (FDTL, later renamed Falintil Forças de Defesa de Timor Leste or F-FDTL). FALINTIL High Command agreed to the demobilization only on condition that it be allowed to select which forces stayed and which demobilized.

Awarding control to the FALINTIL High Command considerably reduced the extent to which donors could monitor the process, as had been true in Cambodia under similar conditions. It also increased, rather than reducing, the likelihood of politicization from that point onwards. Those FALINTIL members who were recruited into the new FDTL were primarily those who were loyal to Xanana; as a result, the new force was dominated by the "*Firaku*"—people from the three easternmost districts of Timor. This process also entailed that those who were demobilized against their will regarded their fate as the consequence of a political affair, and the presence of disgruntled veterans groups was frequently regarded as a major threat to stability in the early years of independence.[26] Rees regards UNTAET as having been "manipulated" by FALINTIL in this matter, as donors were manipulated by the Cambodian government. Yet it is hard to see how any other outcome could realistically have been achieved. Since the donors had the ideas of "professionalization" and "reintegration" so firmly in mind, they mistakenly accepted the twin strategies of facilitating the entrenchment or recruitment of new FDTL loyalists, and marginalizing loose cannons such as Cornelio Gama, as solutions to post-conflict dilemmas, rather than the beginnings of a problem.

---

[25] This account is taken from Edward Rees, *Under Pressure*, pp. 44–49.

[26] See for example, ibid., p. 1.

These approaches to dealing with the security forces raised protest within East Timor, not only amongst FALINTIL veterans themselves, but also in the wider community. Some activists apparently feared the politicization of the new force: a FRETILIN-allied student group, the Organização de Jovens e Estudantes de Timor Leste (OJETIL), for example, sent a letter of protest to UNTAET over the decision, calling the dissolution of FALINTIL "a betrayal to East Timor's history." "East Timorese society feels sad," the students claimed, "that FALINTIL, as the Armed Forces of the Maubere People, has been sacrificed to accommodate the political interests of certain groups."[27]

Others had broader critiques to make. The monitoring NGO Lao Hamutuk criticized the failure of UNTAET to consult with FALINTIL representatives. The organization argued that the wide decision-making mandate given to UNTAET, acting as the executive and legislative authority in East Timor, and the narrow consultative function of the National Committee of Timorese that was set up to provide legitimacy to UNTAET's decisions, made it possible for UNTAET to draw up plans for the security sector "without any transparency or accountability to a) groups with interests in legislation like FALINTIL or b) the people of East Timor."[28]

Furthermore, the NGO argued, the demobilization plan adopted represented an attempt "to construct an army from a western perspective" and as such presaged "the disappearance of FALINTIL's identity." The NGO argued that FALINTIL "had a symbiosis with the people of East Timor, as seen in its concept of unity." Following its transformation into the F-FDTL, FALINTIL lost this identity. Lao Hamutuk activists suggest there was a concomitant loss of any emancipatory potential that might have come along with independence:

> FALINTIL was a National Liberation force. Freedom was born from a desire to change the reality imposed by Indonesia at the time. In this sense, the struggle for freedom was not just related to territory, but also to social and economic liberation from poverty. With FALINTIL's professionalisation, its identity has faded substantially. It is clear that F-FDTL is no longer a popular national army, but one with a more elitist orientation.[29]

The demobilization process imposed a rubric of "professionalism" on the recruiting process for soldiers that ruled out the possibility of exploring ways to encourage broad-based accountability to the wider community in favor of a process that gave responsibility for selection to a professional elite. The problem with this approach was that when that elite subsequently proved to be self-interested in its selection, there were few checks and balances, in the form of wider consultation or input, to prevent outright political partisanship from shaping the new East Timorese armed forces.

Following the demobilization process, getting soldiers to actually go home and reintegrate into society proved problematic. As in Cambodia, in Timor it was

---

[27] "OJETIL Protests the Dissolution of FALINTIL," *Timor Post*, February 1, 2001, original in Bahasa Indonesia, translation posted on http://members.pcug.org.au/~wildwood/febprotests.htm, accessed June 12, 2007.

[28] Lao Hamutuk, "An Overview of FALINTIL's Transformation to FDTL and its Implications," *Bulletin Lao Hamutuk* 6,1–2 (April 2005), pp. 1–6.

[29] Ibid.

difficult to establish definitive lists of those soldiers who had been released from service. Whereas in Cambodia this problem was largely the result of corruption within the military, in East Timor the problem arose in part from political and personal rivalries within FALINTIL, and from the difficulties of maintaining control of soldiers during the long period of cantonment. Some soldiers had already left the force, but they had no assistance to help them reintegrate; others were apparently deliberately left off the lists of those entitled to assistance. Different commanders disagreed as to who should be in and who should be out. According to James McCarthy, after July 2001 the FDTL tried to submit two hundred more names of veterans who were entitled to assistance but had been left off the initial list; unfortunately by that stage the funds had run out.[30]

The economic situation in East Timor made it difficult for older soldiers to find employment. As in Cambodia, many had lost touch with their families and relied on personal relationships with commanders and comrades for a support network. An evaluation report produced in 2002 found that "as many as 15 percent of the beneficiaries, or two hundred—generally older, more senior, or physically impaired—veterans appear to be experiencing more acute difficulties in the transition process from former combatants to civilian life." The report also described a further group of veterans referred to locally as "the Forgotten" who had been excluded either by accident or design from the assistance programs. The report suggested that these veterans had not reintegrated well and that "their relative vulnerability has both wider and potentially significant implications."[31]

Demobilization offered veterans a sum of money to go away; it did not seek—indeed, it was consciously aimed at avoiding—the institution of any political or social processes through which these veterans might be able to voice their concerns or needs. This frustrating condition, along with a strong sense of having been rejected by their former commanders, left veterans open to recruitment by dissident groups or by ambitious politicians, among them former FALINTIL commander Rogerio Lobato, who organized a public demonstration of several thousand ex-FALINTIL in Dili in May 2002. The demonstration was reportedly intended to show FRETILIN that Rogerio was a powerful contender in Timorese politics; if so, it worked. Lobato was made Minister of Interior a few days later.[32]

Those who were keeping watch over these developments were particularly concerned by the proliferation in Timor of so-called "security groups," which organized military-style parades and martial arts training, and which targeted former FALINTIL members for recruitment. Observers also voiced concern about other groups of veterans, such as Cornelio Gama's "Holy Family" group, which clung together as disenfranchised and discontented groups on the margins of national politics.[33] According to the UN inquiry into the violence of 2006, one such group, the Rai Los group, led by ex-FALINTIL soldier Vincente da Conceicao, was

---

[30] James McCarthy, *Falintil Reinsertion Assistance Program Final Evaluation Report* (Dili: International Organisation of Migration, 2002), p. 40.

[31] Ibid., p. 80.

[32] Rees, *Under Pressure*, p. 49; also cited in International Crisis Group, *Resolving Timor-Leste's Crisis*, October 10, 2006 (Brussels: ICG, 2006), p. 5.

[33] Ibid. See also James Scambari, Hippolito Da Gama, and Joao Barreto, *A Survey of Gangs and Youth Groups in Dili, Timor-Leste* (Dili: AusAID, 2006).

mobilized and armed illegally by the Minister of Interior, Rogerio Lobato, during the political crisis in Dili, to serve as a "security" force for a FRETILIN party congress.[34]

The extent to which real FALINTIL veterans were the driving forces in these "security groups" is, in fact, unclear, since some security group members apparently claimed "ex-FALINTIL" status on highly dubious grounds, and many FALINTIL veterans did not join these.[35] However, the difficulties inherent in the UNTAET approach to dealing with former FALINTIL cadre—namely, the way it gave priority to "reinsertion" as a strategy for dealing with veterans and neglected to award them any kind of representation *as* veterans—entailed that these martial identities could be exploited. The failure of the international administrators, in both Timor and Cambodia, to consult with veterans reflects a fear of politics as a means of resolving problems. Rather than awarding soldiers or veterans a voice, neoliberals advocated swift demobilization as a means to sever links among soldiers and thus to undermine their ability to organize as a force in society. However, this approach does not adequately comprehend the extent to which, first, links between former soldiers are personal as well as institutional, and may persist despite demobilization, and, second, the extent to which older ex-combatants would have a very hard time being rapidly "reintegrated" into a struggling post-conflict society and economy. In attempting to keep soldiers out of the political sphere as an organized force, liberal interveners, while claiming, in a rather well-worn phrase, to be replacing "bullets" with "ballots," in fact created powerful incentives for informal groups of veterans, marginalized from the political sphere, to stick together.

In Cambodia, as described above, former soldiers have retained their association with the military by continuing to operate—although on a rather more freelance basis than has been typical of Timor's soldiers—as security guards and other functionaries in military entrepreneurial activities. As such, they remain tightly woven into the militarized power base of the Cambodian People's Party. In Timor-Leste, disenfranchised veterans groups constituted a marginalized fringe of retired fighters, who came to represent a focus for grievance to many Timorese. The replacement of FALINTIL, regarded as representing the Timorese nation, with a politicized force in which cadres from the eastern districts were apparently privileged, produced grievances that were coopted and mobilized by competing politicians during the escalation of intra-elite rivalry in 2006, leading to dramatic violence. While the actual extent of involvement of former FALINTIL members is unclear, the crisis in part reflected the ease with which the issue of their treatment could be exploited.

Demobilization, then, can be criticized in terms of its aims, its assumptions, and its implementation. Its primary aim—the atomization of individuals deemed potentially "dangerous"—was not achieved in either case; a significant number of soldiers stuck together in private life, causing more problems outside the institution than they had within it. This treatment of the veterans and failure to accommodate them politically grew out of certain flawed assumptions: that severing institutional connections is sufficient to achieve such atomization, and that the post-conflict economy offers scope for reintegration and self-reliance, even to disabled, old, sick, or institutionalized individuals. In terms of implementation, in real life, the military

---

[34] United Nations Independent Special Commission of Inquiry for Timor-Leste, *Report,* Geneva, October 2, 2006, p. 39.

[35] James McCarthy, *Falintil Reinsertion Assistance Program Final Evaluation Report,* p. 80.

and associated elites had sharply different aims from donors, employed different assumptions, and pursued different interests; and ultimately they found it easy to manipulate, or outright resist, the donors' agenda.

Despite wide disparities in the character of FALINTIL and RCAF at the outset of demobilization processes in East Timor and Cambodia, respectively, both have emerged from this transition as forces that continue to be politicized—in fact, even more so than during the conflicts—and which have a high potential to destabilize and undermine civilian political processes. This politicization of disgruntled veterans' groups and of the armies they leave behind profoundly affects the post-conflict reconstruction process. In the case of Cambodia, the military has remained a politicized tool of the incumbent party, which has acted to protect military interests in return for political support. Cooptation of the military in this way has secured political stability. However, the ongoing politicization and impunity of the military has had a deleterious effect on the country's human rights record; has entrenched illegal business operations, including those associated with drugs, the sex industry, human trafficking and smuggling; and has had a deadening effect on voter decision-making in the context of elections.

In the case of Timor, and in sharp contrast to the widely applauded "discipline" of FALINTIL in 1999 and its immediate aftermath, both veterans and the army itself have become associated with dissidence and instability. Poor treatment of veterans and soldiers has contributed to a series of outbreaks of instability and violence, most notably in March and April 2006. UNTAET's failure either to reintegrate veterans, or to award them a platform from which they could participate politically in pursuit of their interests, left them marginalized and angry, while the politicization of the remaining army led to a row within the military in 2006, which escalated into an outbreak of violence that displaced up to a hundred thousand people, led to the resignation of the prime minister, and prompted Australian troops to intervene in the country once again. This instability has encouraged the development of politicized regional divisions in Timorese society. These divisions, which had little political salience in the Indonesian era, have hardened in large part as a result of disputes and rivalries internal to the armed forces and veterans' groups, and the way these translated into wider disruptions in a context of demobilization. It remains to be seen whether, having been provoked, these divisions can be swiftly repaired.

DEMOCRATIZATION

Democratization, in both Cambodia and Timor, represented an expansion of the logic of demobilization to wider civilian society. In both cases this process, as it was actually implemented, turned out to embody only a limited commitment to the idea of opening new opportunities for political deliberation. It was more visibly focused on atomizing potentially powerful constituencies and impairing their ability to organize collective action that could either advantage them in the marketplace or give them power over the state. Thus aspects of democracy that focused upon individual choice—such as the secret ballot—were emphasized to the detriment of aspects that focused on mobilization of and deliberation by the population. This was by no means inevitable: as Steve Smith has pointed out, debates about the best way of promoting democracy internationally have abounded in political science for thousands of years. Yet in contemporary donor discourses just one approach has dominated—an approach that, once again, encourages depoliticization of the public realm and citizens' engagement with politics as atomized individuals rather than as an empowered and engaged constituency.[36]

Cambodia and Timor-Leste offer good examples of this model. In both cases, while great efforts and significant amounts of funding have been poured into the ritualistic forms of democracy, the substance has been relatively neglected. Democratic deliberation has been heavily policed, if not directly discouraged. Donor agencies justified this approach with reference to fears of violence, yet it has the effect of reserving key questions of resource allocation for government and donors to decide. The consequences have been similar in both countries. Improved, more smoothly organized voting procedures have been implemented in successive elections, accompanied by grandiose rhetoric focused to a great extent on issues of status and identity, but public debate on issues pertaining to everyday life has been restricted and impoverished, leading to an atmosphere of political frustration in which individual citizens struggle to make themselves heard. The emphasis upon democracy as a means to manage conflict displaces concern for democracy as a means by which individuals call leaders to account or engage with questions of social justice. In line with a desire to demobilize "over-politicized" constituencies on the brink of violence, donors have encouraged ever more highly stylized rituals of political engagement. In Cambodia, two examples stand out that illustrate how the form of disciplined participation has been privileged over the substance of democratic deliberation: the campaign to promote the secrecy of the ballot, and the promotion of candidate debates.

United Nations staff initially emphasized the secrecy of the ballot as a guarantee to voters that they could safely vote against the State of Cambodia during the 1993 UNTAC elections, as security deteriorated and the "neutral political environment for free and fair elections" envisaged in UNTAC's mandate was patently not achieved.[37] UNTAC responded to the situation by downplaying the significance of a deliberative aspect of elections, while promoting the importance of the sovereign act of choice. Thus, voters were discouraged from discussing their preferences—encouraged, even, to join parties they did not intend to vote for and espouse allegiances publicly that they did not honor privately—on the understanding that, once alone in the polling booth, they could "vote according to their conscience."[38]

Clearly, in the case of the 1993 election, many issues were at stake, and the extreme precariousness of the peace accords in the lead-up to the election offers a justification for this approach. However, the focus on secrecy in 1993 was never revisited or questioned, in terms of its impact on broader understandings of democracy; rather, it set a precedent that was adhered to in later elections, when international democracy advocates continued to promote vigorously the importance of secrecy as opposed to discussion. This had a crippling effect, not only on the

---

[36] Steve Smith, "US Democracy Promotion: Critical Questions," in *American Democracy Promotion: Impulses, Strategies, and Impacts,* ed. Michael Cox, G. John Ikenberry, and Takashi Inoguchi (Oxford: Oxford University Press, 2000), pp. 63–83.

[37] The term "neutral political environment conducive to free and fair general elections" appears in the Paris Peace Accords, October 23, 1991, Part 1, Article 6, online at http://documents-dds-ny.un.org/doc/UNDOC/GEN/N91/361/63/img/N9136163.pdf? OpenElement, accessed September 13, 2008.

[38] Judy Ledgerwood, "Patterns of CPP Repression and Violence during the UNTAC Period," in *Propaganda, Politics, and Violence in Cambodia: Democratic Transition under United Nations Peacekeeping,* ed. Stephen Heder and Judy Ledgerwood (London: M. E. Sharpe, 1996), p. 126.

possibility that forums for democratic debate might emerge in the countryside, but on the potential for political parties to address rural concerns. A rhetoric of fear, adopted by all parties, significantly restricted policy debate and political mobilization, and privileged a long-standing rhetoric that warned against secret campaigns of infiltration and destabilization carried out by Vietnamese *agents provocateurs*. Conspiracy theories abounded and ranged from the conceivable—for example, that ballots were being secretly discarded, activists being murdered—to the improbable—that spy satellites were hovering in the sky and computerized pens being planted in polling booths to monitor voter choices; that thousands, if not millions, of Vietnamese were being registered to vote illegally and shipped across the border on polling day; and that Vietnamese tanks were hiding in the jungle ready to roll out if the CPP (Cambodian People's Party) were unseated.

Attempts by rural voters to use the election campaign to gain practical support from the parties in local political campaigns were condemned to failure by the policies of acquiescence promoted by the parties, international observers, and the press. While voters repeatedly raised local issues in meetings with party members, campaigning political leaders and National Assembly candidates—those outside the Cambodian People's Party—were poorly equipped to offer assistance in terms of leadership and organization; consequently, they preferred to cast voters in a passive role as listeners and victims, rather than as actors, even where voters themselves were taking great risks in demanding political freedoms.

For example, during the 1998 election campaign, Sam Rainsy ignored requests for assistance from a group of families that were conducting a campaign of non-compliance with the CPP's membership drive in Kraceh. Approached by a representative of the families on a campaign trip to Kraceh province, Rainsy reportedly "referred" the individual to a UN monitor, who reportedly told him that the families should abandon their efforts and cooperate with the CPP, adding the comment, "if you want to stay alive, you are better off doing that than being a strong dead man."[39] This remarkable response, which reinforced, rather than denounced, the threats and intimidation to which the families had been subjected, must have been profoundly dispiriting to the families involved. Yet this was a common response throughout the country, privileging the need for an orderly election over a broader conception of freedom. The approving reporting of the incident in an English-language newspaper suggests the extent to which expatriates in Cambodia considered this the appropriate way of promoting democracy in the country.

Other leaders of non-CPP parties campaigning in 1998 reported a similar response to their supporters who requested their assistance in resisting CPP cooptation:

> If they are forced, we tell them to do it now, because they get very much trouble otherwise. But at the moment of the voting they are free to choose who they like.[40]

> We have asked our supporters not to do anything which jeopardises their security ... We have our own network, but we will not do anything openly ...[41]

---

[39] Eric Pape, "On the River with Rainsy in Search for Votes," *Phnom Penh Post*, May 22–June 4, 1998, p. 14.

[40] Chrun You Hai, president, Khmer Reconstruction Party, personal interview, May 1998.

[41] Son Soubert, president, Grandfather Son Sann Party, personal interview, May 1998.

Similarly, in Kompong Cham, Rainsy called upon policemen to abandon their allegiance to the CPP and switch their loyalties to the Sam Rainsy Party, not openly, but "just in your hearts."[42]

The 1998 election, like the 1993 election, was surrounded by uncertainty and threats of violence; yet mass demonstrations followed the results, suggesting that Cambodians were prepared to take significant risks in order to protest. However, few efforts were made to support those Cambodians prepared to challenge the menacing CPP; in this way, international actors followed the lead of UNTAC, which had continually downgraded expectations for substantive democratic deliberation in the 1993 elections in order to maintain the momentum of the peace process. Such attitudes persisted in the 2003 election—Cambodia's most peaceful election yet. By 2003, the war had been over for five years, security was well established, and complaints of political violence were much reduced compared to previous elections. Furthermore, commune-level authorities had been elected a year previously, in an exercise that—even as it delivered an overwhelming victory to the CPP, which had controlled local level government since 1981—removed some of the more unpopular and abusive commune-level leaders from power. Arguably, there was an opportunity in 2003 to significantly reduce the level of fear surrounding election campaigns and to try to open up democracy to become a more substantive and interesting affair.

To an extent, efforts were made to do so. The parties' greater willingness to engage politically with their opponents permitted the organization, for the first time, of televised debates between party candidates. The format of these debates, which were organized and funded by the US-based National Democratic Institute (NDI), facilitated the participation of elite politicians in cross-party deliberation; however, old habits die hard, and the participation of ordinary Cambodians was heavily qualified.

The debates comprised spontaneous responses by candidates to questions posed by the debate organizers, following consultation with local people; questions posed by the parties to one another; and questions put by members of the audience. The purpose of the debates, as envisaged by their American sponsors, was outlined in an NDI briefing document: "create an opportunity for responsible candidates and voters to hold a public dialogue on issues facing their provincial and national constituencies so that voters can make a more informed choice when they go to the polls." NDI hoped that "these debates will demonstrate that, while candidates from different parties have diverse policies and opinions, they can discuss these differences in a productive manner, free from violence or retribution."[43]

However, in his introduction to the debate in Siem Reap Province, an NDI representative made a speech that, to a great extent, retreated from this participatory focus and exhibited a great deal of nervousness about allowing Cambodians to confront one another with contradictory opinions. As in 1993 and 1998, the attitude of international democracy promoters was to heavily privilege choice over debate; discipline and regimentation over spontaneity and emotion; and the atomized

---

[42] Sam Rainsy, campaign speech, Stung Trang District, Kompong Cham Province, July 5, 1998. Recorded and translated by Caroline Hughes and Sok Ty.

[43] National Democratic Institute for International Affairs, "2003 National Assembly Candidate Debates, Program Overview," internal document (Phnom Penh, July 2003).

individual over the collective. Thus the representative commented that the purpose of the debates was not to thrash out fundamental issues over the nature of Cambodians' problems, and to address the pros and cons of different possible solutions, but to "to open up the process so that you the electorate can receive more information to help you make your choice on election day."[44]

There was no suggestion, in this introduction, that the debates might give candidates a chance to listen to voters; rather,

> Candidate debates provide an opportunity for candidates and parties to express their views in a moderated environment in equal time. Most importantly, candidate debates give you, the voters of the country, an opportunity to hear the parties and candidates, assess their performance, and make a decision .... [45]

In this formulation, the roles awarded to candidates and voters were quite clear:

> Let me remind you that in a democratic society, all the candidates have a right to be heard. Whether you agree or you disagree, and you will hear things today with which you agree and you will hear things with which you disagree, please remember to treat all of the candidates and the moderator with respect. Please also remember to treat each other in the audience with respect.[46]

The debates clearly demarcated politicians from voters: the role of the politicians was to speak, to answer, and to be heard. This distracted attention entirely from the ground-breaking aspect of the debates. In this particular debate, the powerful CPP Minister of Commence, Cham Prasidh, appeared on the podium to speak directly to voters and answer their questions. However, rather than celebrating this event and encouraging voters to have their say, raise their grievances, and hold the minister to account for the government's performance, the NDI representative surrounded the whole event with such a heavy veil of caveats that the kind of specifically antidemocratic inequalities of power that the average Cambodian would expect to confront when attempting to engage with a minister ended up being reasserted and reemphasized. Voters were given an opportunity to ask questions, via the mediation of professional democracy promoters, however, their primary function was to listen, to be respectful, and, ultimately, to choose in secret: "It is your right as free citizens in a free Cambodia to come out and cast your vote to decide the future of your country. The ballot is secret. Do not be afraid."[47]

Interestingly, the NDI representative impressed upon the audience the importance of behaving in this way, not so much because it would contribute to some conception of national political culture, but because it would promote Cambodia's image in an international sphere:

---

[44] NDI representative, candidates' debate between CPP, FUNCINPEC, and SRP, Siem Reap Province, broadcast on Channel 9, July 25, 2003, 18:00–20:00, recorded and transcribed by Caroline Hughes.

[45] Ibid.

[46] Ibid.

[47] Ibid.

Today's debate is being taped for broadcast, and it will be seen by Cambodians all over the country. In fact, today's debate will be seen outside Cambodia as well. The international community is taking a very strong interest in the elections in your country. Please let us all remember to conduct ourselves in a way that will make Cambodia proud.[48]

By specifically removing the import of the debate from a national to an international sphere, the NDI representative again undermined the potential for empowerment inherent in public political exchanges. The debate is no longer about the relationship of government to voter; it is about the relationship of Cambodia to the outside world, and in this relationship, in a context of aid dependence, it is the expectations of the outside world that dominate in a manner that is entirely beyond the control of Cambodians. This approach to television debates fixes the roles inherited from authoritarianism, rather than challenging them with an inclusive, egalitarian approach to deliberation.

The highly stylized nature of the debates divorced them from the intense emotion, the sinister backdrop of violence, and the life-and-death consequences of politics in Cambodia's villages. Rather than offering an opportunity to channel this emotion so that voters might be empowered by the rules of debate, the ritual of this debate marginalized those aspects of the process that enable the public seriously to question its leaders. General questions were asked about health and education; candidates replied that their party, if elected, would ensure better provision of these services. No follow-up questions were permitted; politicians did not feel the need to expand upon their comments or confront fundamental questions of corruption, access, the difficulties of mobilizing the sclerotic and dysfunctional state apparatus, or the question of how to prise funds away from the military for diversion into social services. Nor were the politicians in much of a position to outline broad trajectories for the future, since these remained dependent upon aid donors, whose future priorities could not necessarily be discerned. The content of the debate, consequently, shed little light on how Cambodia's future might be shaped under one party or another. What it clearly did, however, was reinforce a culture in which little is expected in terms of meaningful accountability from politicians. Further, like the campaign to promote the secrecy of the ballot, the format of these debates clearly illustrated the privileging of disciplined participation over creative deliberation, on the part of international democracy promoters, to the extent that deliberation was rarely even envisaged as a key aspect of democracy whose absence might have important effects on the nature of governance.

Similarly, in East Timor, Tanja Hohe reports that in the 2001 elections, a list of prohibitions on particular types of political campaigning were far more widely recognized than the content of party platforms themselves. She comments that the atmosphere in East Timorese districts was "rather apolitical," and she remarks:

Party representatives at the subdistrict or village level were often not aware of party programmes or even the differences between their parties. Often the only information they could provide was to recite the "don'ts" which they had received from the party leadership: "don't force anybody, don't go from door to

---

[48] Ibid.

door, don't promise anything, don't ask for donations, don't raise flags on the village level, don't cause any problem with other parties."[49]

It is indicative that, aside from the first and last, these prohibitions comprised fairly standard means by which political parties typically communicate with voters, and vice versa. For new parties attempting to build a support base in a country with many remote areas, low levels of literacy, and limited mass media coverage, prohibitions on local level canvassing, fund-raising, flag waving, or the making of election promises left little scope for them to make any connection with the voters at all. Although rallies and flag-raising ceremonies were held at the district level, and often attracted large crowds, these were spectacular events, in which the role of the voter was to watch and listen, rather than engage, inform, and insist. As in Cambodia, the relationship of voter to party, as envisaged by international administrators, was to be conducted at arms-length and based upon very slender contact. The desire to avoid stirring things trumped a desire for genuine voter-candidate interactions, thus preventing the emergence of links of representation based upon familiarity, contactability, and debate.

Hohe describes the atmosphere in Timorese villages as "rather apolitical," as a result, in terms of party allegiance, even though it was "highly politically charged" in terms of contests over local leadership.[50] This pattern strongly resembles electoral trends in Cambodia, where elections are won or lost not on the basis of national policy platforms, but on the ability of candidates to connect at the local level through control of village and commune chiefs, and through the ability to deliver local development assistance. In both countries, observers have criticized the vacuity of political platforms and the strong tendency of parties to continue to rely on heroic wartime narratives long after the war is over. Yet arguably, the nature of post-conflict elections, as promoted by international interveners, provides strong incentives for political parties to do just this. The heavy emphasis upon form rather than substance, and the strong desire to avoid contention that might get out of control, entail that international democracy promoters privilege forms of electioneering that limit debate rather than broadening it; meanwhile, the "choiceless" nature of policy making in an aid-dependent polity means that there is not much to debate anyway.

Democracy promotion has not, of course, been limited to the promotion of elections. In both Cambodia and Timor-Leste, international advocates of democracy have paid attention to the promotion of "civil society"—a sphere that is specifically intended to offer opportunities for deliberation, advocacy, and debate. In the context of international democracy promotion, such a "civil society" was regarded as giving rise to forces for democratization, and the manner in which this might occur was the subject of great interest among scholars of democratic consolidation in the early to mid-1990s. These scholars expected that the voluntary association of individuals in groups would help voters better press their interests with government, and they argued that "civil society" could perform key democratic roles: limiting, monitoring,

---

[49] Tanja Hohe, "Totem Polls: Indigenous Concepts and 'Free and Fair Elections' in East Timor," *International Peacekeeping* 9,4 (2002): 73.

[50] Ibid.

democratizing, and, ultimately, strengthening the state; and stimulating, training, socializing, representing, and informing the citizen.[51]

Once again, however, as with other potentially democratic exercises and procedures, the activities of "civil society" were limited within pre-set, internationally sanctioned disciplinary boundaries. In both Cambodia and Timor-Leste, support for civil society was associated with a considerable degree of policing, enabled by the offer of funding on a selective and competitive basis.

Civil society organizations in conditions of aid dependence, and in a context where democracy is being internationally promoted, tend to become heavily dependent themselves on international, rather than local, sources of funding. Through their funding decisions, international organizations, donors, and international NGOs have a far-reaching effect on the development of local civil society.

One effect is the immediate formation of a divide between social collectives that have international support, in the form of funding, training, or "partnership," and those that have none. In Cambodia, the latter barely existed: Cambodia has never had the degree of associational life at the village level found, for example, in neighboring Vietnam. Some traditional associations were documented in the pre-war years—associations for regulating the sharing of water resources and communal items for use in festivals, such as large cooking pots; loose networks of labor exchange; and pagoda committees—but these were destroyed under the Pol Pot regime. Continued lack of tolerance for non-state organizations under the PRK (People's Republic of Kampuchea), combined with the weakness of the tradition in any case, entailed that few organizations emerged prior to the influx of international funding. International agencies looking for non-governmental or community-based organizations to work as their partners largely had to create their own, beginning with the support given to human rights organizations by the Human Rights Component of UNTAC. However, during the course of the 1990s a variety of Cambodians did start to initiate new forms of collective action that could have assisted in empowering poor communities and imbuing democracy with a deliberative element, for example in the form of trade unions. Yet international actors have shown little support for such forms of collective action. Rather, the Cambodian government has moved swiftly to directly repress such movements, and international actors have paved the way for this by promoting the same kinds of atomizing strategies noted above rather than offering the kind of positive support that the Cambodians involved might have hoped for.[52]

In Timor-Leste, many more local organizations existed on the ground: the Church acted as a major organizing force in society, while various women's, students', and youth organizations associated with the clandestine movement were also widespread, although highly fragmented. Under the Indonesian regime, a variety of youth clubs, particularly sports and martial arts clubs, had existed, along with some NGOs; the legal aid organization Yayasan Hak was a prominent example. Many of these organizations played an active part in the emergency relief operation in 1999, following the arrival of InterFET.

---

[51] Larry Diamond, "Rethinking Civil Society: Toward Democratic Consolidation," *Journal of Democracy* 5,3 (1995): 45–14.

[52] The case of the labor unions that emerged in the garment factories of Phnom Penh in the mid-1990s is discussed below.

In both Cambodia and Timor-Leste, however, the impact of international funding was overwhelming, far outstripping the kinds of resources that could be mobilized locally and creating a strong imperative for organizations to orient themselves towards the competitive search for international partnership and sponsorship. This applied equally to service delivery and advocacy organizations.

On the donors' side, incentives are mixed. On the one hand, concern to establish a presence, stake out turf, and spend the money that has already been raised promotes open-handedness. As the representative of one local NGO in Timor-Leste commented: "The organizations like to be represented—they are like businesses looking for market share. And this is a profitable business to be in."[53]

On the other hand, international donors also desire to control where funds are going and to show results. The balance between these objectives shifts over time and in response to external events. In Timor, international appeals for public donations as part of the relief effort immediately after the disaster of 1999 brought millions of dollars into the country. Donors were under pressure to spend it fast. As one INGO worker commented, "People want to know that the money they have raised is helping immediately."[54] As a result, any group of well-intentioned individuals could set itself up as an NGO and get a cash grant: "Any NGO putting a request in got the money, and never had to report on it. They bought equipment, motorbikes—nobody knows where they are now."[55]

Equally, the ability of local NGOs to use international money is constrained by the fact that the amount of money they have to spend is likely to vary dramatically in response to external factors. For example, NGO workers reported:

> The impact from the tsunami [on aid to Timor-Leste] was huge—money we had been verbally promised was reduced.[56]

> Last year, one donor unloaded $450,000 in two months. We had to write proposals in two days for the money—we were buying the staff motorbikes and computers … The donors don't know what they are getting from one year to the next—they have to keep accounts at their end, and things are subject to political changes.[57]

> This year, the Spanish government has changed, and now they want to focus on training so we have to present new projects. We have to figure out our new projects—find NGOs with a human rights focus to be trained, for example, in skills for NGOs. If you want to do something, you need a local partner that has capacity in the area.[58]

---

[53] NGO worker, Asosiasaun Hi'it Ema Ra'es Timor (Association for the Equality of the Disabled People of Timor, or ASSERT), personal interview, Dili, May 2005.

[54] INGO worker, Catholic Relief Services, personal interview, Dili, April 2005.

[55] Ibid.

[56] NGO worker, ASSERT, personal interview, Dili, May 2005.

[57] NGO worker, Judicial Sector Monitoring Project, personal interview, Dili, April 2005.

[58] INGO worker, Fundeso (Fundación Desarrollo Sostenido, Sustained Development Foundation), personal interview, Dili, April 2005.

Both Cambodia and Timor saw significant reductions in funding for NGOs following an initial bonanza, as donors turned their attention elsewhere and focused the funds they offered on a narrower set of NGOs. One donor in Timor commented,

> Now the emergency situation is over, and they have to be accountable. Donors are tightening up … all the donors have come together and taken a stand. We have discussed it at various meetings. Local NGOs are more used to it—they know that's the game now … Now we can see a core of established NGOs who through their reputation are able to maintain themselves—this is a natural and healthy process.[59]

Different kinds of funding give different kinds of latitude for organizational development, but most are entirely project based, offering little money for organizational overhead expenses. In between projects, NGO staff go without salaries, or go to work in other jobs, coming back together when further funding is available. However, this traps NGOs in a cycle that is difficult to break out of, in terms of relations with donors. Too often, the local organizations are viewed as unprofessional, over-generalized, and ad hoc. According to a representative of an international NGO,

> Local NGOs are very project driven … There were some NGOs that came to us— they had done HIV, civic education, puppet theatre—they had no idea what they were going to do next, what their constituency is.[60]

A local NGO staffer who had managed to escape from the project-funding trap described the challenges as follows:

> It is difficult to develop the organization—sometimes we can't do anything because the 10 percent for administration is not enough to make the organization bigger and to develop new program… It depends on the program. If you have a program, then the organization lives, if not the organization dies. We try to discuss this with our partners, but they don't want to pay for administrative costs.[61]

Yet it is precisely this organizational development that donors are looking for when they decide who should be funded. For local NGOs, the development of a strong reputation among donors is the most important credential in an aid-dependent environment, and acquiring this reputation entails not only the establishment of effective programs, but also the ability to respond to donor demands in terms of meeting deadlines, producing and sticking to organizational constitutions, demonstrating financial accountability, and writing effective reports at the conclusion of a project. While donors are prepared to tolerate weaknesses initially, the functioning of local NGOs is evaluated to a great extent on these terms, and inadequacies are expected to be addressed.

---

[59] INGO worker, Catholic Relief Services, personal interview, Dili, April 2005.

[60] INGO worker, Concern, personal interview, Dili, April 2005.

[61] NGO worker, Caritas Dili, personal interview, Dili, April 2005.

There is a powerful incentive for organizations to orient themselves ever more closely towards international priorities and prescribed modes of working and to look strategically for partners who will help them build reputations and credibility. This orientation inclines local NGO staffers to rely upon, for example, international volunteers to provide training to local counterparts: "I do gain experience from my colleagues from New Zealand—they contribute their experience to me and build my capacity to make proposals and follow the criteria of the donors."[62] It also encourages local staffers to be strategic in applying for funds to particular donors whose approval increases their credibility; a Spanish aid worker commented, for example, that getting a grant from the Spanish Development Agency is a coup for local NGOs and consequently worth devoting considerable attention to, because "it is CV-building vis-à-vis other funders."[63] Thus local NGOs are encouraged to adopt the issues that are of concern to the most prestigious funders and to refrain from deviating from agreements in the course of implementation: "We are happy because donors can trust us, and we try our best to train our staff members to follow the proposal—follow the rules in the proposal. I have to do what I said I was going to do."[64] In Cambodia, the NGO Forum has instituted an NGO certification program, precisely for providing such quality assurance to donors. To gain a certificate, NGOs have to show that their organizational systems reach an approved standard, and their previous or existing donors are interviewed to verify this accomplishment. The certification program entails NGOs policing one another for the sake of the donors' interests; the equation of NGO integrity with accountability to and approval from donors illustrates the internalization of donor values in the NGO sector.[65]

For those who are outside the loop defined by donor confidence and approval, the difficulties are many, but the orientation remains the same:

> It is difficult to find funds—we have to try to lobby by ourselves. If we know someone inside an international agency, we have the opportunity to know about funds that are available, but if we don't know anybody, it is really difficult to confirm whether we have got funds or not. Also, there is only support for activities, because we are voluntary workers, so we don't get salaries ... It takes time to produce a proposal due to a lack of electricity.[66]

A perverse effect of the international funding market is the dissipation of the energies of volunteers in proposal writing, rather than in actual activities. The relationship between the economy and the polity that liberal democracy promoters advocate in liberal civil society models—whereby economic actors take up political action in pursuit of their economic interest—is reversed. In aid-dependent societies, political action, if it accords with the interests of powerful external actors, becomes a way of supporting oneself in an environment where the economy offers limited opportunities. In Timor, the 2004 census revealed the importance of the NGO

---

[62] NGO worker, PRADET (Rekuperasaun no Dezenvolvimentu ba Trauma no Psiko-sosial iha Timor-Leste, Psychosocial Recovery and Development East Timor), personal interview, Dili, July 2005.

[63] INGO worker, Fundeso, personal interview, Dili, April 2005.

[64] NGO worker, PRADET, personal interview, Dili, July 2005.

[65] NGO worker, NGO Forum Cambodia, personal communication, Madrid, March 2007.

[66] NGO worker, Justice and Peace Commission, personal interview, Liquiçá, June 2005.

movement in the job market, indicating that NGO jobs comprised almost a fifth of paid employment available.[67] The fact that NGO activists are also dependent upon NGO jobs in a job market where little else is available creates heavy pressure to toe the donor line, so that finally the energies that NGOs invest in building their reputations with donors distract from the business of serving constituencies. Indeed, on occasion, the power of donors over civil society runs specifically counter to the articulated interests of local constituencies. This is particularly the case when constituencies are potentially or actually unruly and contentious.

This was evident in the case of the Cambodian trade union movement. The labor movement emerged in the second half of the 1990s from a wave of wild-cat strikes among workers in the newly flourishing garment industry in Phnom Penh. These strikes drew the attention of the opposition Sam Rainsy Party (SRP), which had been launched in 1995, and which was, at the same time, seeking a support base in preparation for elections in 1998. The party facilitated the establishment in late 1996 of a trade union—the Free Trade Union of Workers of the Kingdom of Cambodia (commonly referred to as the Free Trade Union, FTU). This trade union enjoyed a close relationship with the party throughout the late 1990s, when it actively mobilized followers for participation in SRP demonstrations and protests on a range of issues, and in return received the support of the party in turning spontaneous walk-outs into a concerted and successful campaign for improvements in conditions and a higher minimum wage.

This activity swiftly attracted the attention of international actors, including anti-sweatshop campaigns, international unions, and international organizations. By 1998, these actors were also providing assistance to the Free Trade Union, and other unions that established themselves in Cambodia, some of which were sponsored by the CPP and some of which were sponsored by employers. Buyers for designer labels also entered the fray, promulgating codes of conduct for garment factories that had to be followed in order to retain the contract.

All this activity had a salutary effect on the garment industry. Conditions in factories improved, as did wages, which rose by a remarkable 66 percent from $27 a month in 1996 to $45 a month in 2000. However, government and international actors quickly became concerned about these protest activities. There was much discussion about the effect of the strikes and the pay raises on Cambodia's international competitiveness. Equally, the workers' militancy, and the activism of the Sam Rainsy Party on the streets of Phnom Penh—in large part due to its ability to mobilize workers on a wide range of issues—prompted concern over instability, particularly within the government. From around 2001, two trends were notable: a decreased willingness on the part of the government to tolerate public protest of this

---

[67] Calculated as a percentage of paid positions in which the worker is employed by others—i.e., the statistic does not include the self-employed or subsistence production sectors. The census recorded 6,509 individuals (2 percent of the total labor force) working for NGOs, as compared with 17,412 (5.5 percent of the labor force) working for government; 3,121 (1 percent of the labor force) working for the UN system; and 9,832 (3 percent of the labor force) working for private industry. A further 10 percent of the labor force was self-employed; 2 percent was looking for work; and 76 percent was engaged in subsistence farming or fishing. Direcção Nacional de Estatistica, "Table 6.1: Timor-Leste: Population in Private Households, Fifteen Years of Age and Older, by Age Groups According to Sex and Current Economic Activity," *2004 Census,* online at http://dne.mopf.gov.tl/census/tables/national/economic_activity/table6_1.htm, accessed May 22, 2008.

kind, and concern on the part of international agencies to impose greater discipline on Cambodian trade unions.

International organizations criticized the relationship between the FTU and the SRP, requiring the union to loosen its connection with the party in return for continued international recognition—a demand that was deeply resented by the FTU leaders, who were fully aware of the political connections that unions cultivated in other countries.[68] Furthermore, the International Labour Organization (ILO) moved in 2001 to impose new structures and constraints on labor relations in Cambodia. It launched its Garment Sector Project, now renamed "Better Factories Cambodia," which made two innovations: first, a standing negotiating committee to incorporate trade union representatives and employers; and, second, an international inspection regime to monitor compliance by both garment factories and trade unions with the Cambodian Labor Law.

The negotiation committee was disastrous for the FTU in a number of ways. For one thing, it awarded the FTU just a single seat on the committee, alongside other unions that were more or less openly affiliated with the CPP or that were creations of the employers. As such, the FTU representative sat on the committee as an isolated minority of one, even on the trade unions' side of the table. In return for this representation, the FTU was required to acquiesce to negotiating procedures designed to replace the militant activism of the workers themselves for deals brokered within the committee.

Meanwhile, the ILO's inspection regime, which inspected factories to monitor conformity with international and national legal labor standards, operated to delegitimize considerably the militancy of the workers' movement in Cambodia by declaring that conditions in the factories were relatively acceptable. Inspection reports found that Cambodian factories did not indulge in the worst forms of exploitation, such as slavery, child labor, or violence. While a range of infringements of health and safety standards were identified in different factories, and while it was accepted in the reports that union representatives were frequently harassed or discriminated against, the overall finding that Cambodian factories weren't as bad as factories in other countries stood out. The result was that Cambodian Ministry of Commerce officials soon began to talk about "ethical branding" of Cambodian garments. Minister of Commerce Cham Prasidh told the *New York Times* in 2005, "If we didn't respect the unions and the labor standards, we would be killing the goose that lays the golden eggs."[69]—a theme that was picked up by international anti-sweatshop activists.[70]

---

[68] Chea Vichea, president, Free Trade Union of Workers of the Kingdom of Cambodia, personal interview, Phnom Penh, July 2001.

[69] Elizabeth Becker, "Low Cost and Sweatshop Free," *New York Times*, May 12, 2005, online at http://topics.nytimes.com/top/reference/timestopics/people/b/elizabeth_becker/index.html?offset=20&s=newest, accessed January 10, 2007.

[70] See, for example, Lora Jo Foo and Nikki Fortunato Bas, "Free Trade's Looming Threat to the World's Garment Workers," Sweatshop Watch Working Paper, October 30, 2003, p. 8, online at http://www.sweatshopwatch.org/media/pdf/SWtradepaper.pdf, accessed December 4, 2005; Ethical Trading Action Group, "Lessons from Corporate Social Responsibility Initiatives in the Apparel and Textile Industries," Submission to National Roundtables on Corporate Responsibility, Toronto, Canada, Sept. 12, 2006, online at http://en.maquilasolidarity.org/sites/maquilasolidarity.org/files/ETAGsubmission0906.pdf, accessed September 12, 2007.

While this was going on, outside the factories and the negotiating committees, the Cambodian government launched a comprehensive crackdown on public protest. Workers who continued to go on strike were met with increased police brutality on picket lines. In 2004, two FTU leaders, including the organization's charismatic president, Chea Vichea, were shot dead by unknown assailants in Phnom Penh's streets. Vichea's wife, seven months pregnant at the time, was denied medical care in Phnom Penh hospitals and was forced to flee into exile. Interestingly, a month later, the ILO's Garment Sector Project issued a synthesis report on working conditions in Cambodian factories, which failed to mention Vichea's murder at all, despite the fact that 40,000 of his union's members worked in garment factories. Remarkably, the report claimed "some improvement in ensuring freedom of association and protection against anti-union discrimination, though this remains a problem in a small number of factories."[71] Significantly, these innovations have not succeeded in further improving wages. Indeed, a study in 2006 suggested that real wages in the garment sector were declining. In 2005, they fell by 8 percent, in a year when garment exports rose by 20 percent. Garment factories were shifting the terms of employment from permanent jobs to short-term contracts and piece-rate work.[72] The competitiveness of Cambodia's industrial sector was rescued at the expense of the position of workers.

Across these various policy areas, two common policy strands stand out and may be summarized as policies of atomization and policies of regimentation. Post-conflict polities are regarded by international administrators and donors as requiring demobilization as a means of rendering conflict amenable to management by state or international structures. This drive for demobilization corresponds to the prescriptions of neoliberal governance, which are predicated upon a notion of bounded statehood, atomized citizenship, and minimal government action, all implemented to facilitate the smooth functioning of the market. Within the market, individuals are expected to pursue their interests and derive, not only their satisfactions, but their aspirations and their identities.

There are two major problems with this approach. First, it is doubtful whether, even if the goals are admitted as valid, the means are sufficient to achieve them. The disciplinary mechanisms described above are weak. While they may effectively break up groups that have mobilized for action, the evidence that they can exert the power to restructure individuals' perceptions of their interests, aspirations, and identities is slight. The pressure placed on individuals to "reintegrate" belies the reality, in post-conflict settings on the periphery of the global economy, of divided societies on the edge of subsistence. There is little evidence that the forging of specifically liberal individuals out of unruly populations of autonomous agriculturalists has ever been achieved by the mechanisms of demobilization, civic education, and electoral exercises. The so-called "established liberal democracies" of

---

[71] Garment Sector Monitoring Project, Eighth Synthesis Report on the Working Conditions Situation in Cambodia's Garment Sector, Feb. 2004, online at http://www.betterfactories.org/content/documents/1/8th%20Synthesis%20Report%20-%20English.pdf, accessed December 1, 2006, p. 6.

[72] Chan Vuthy and Sok Hach, *Cambodia's Garment Industry Post-ATC—Human Development Impact Assessment* (Phnom Penh: Economic Institute of Cambodia and United Nations Development Programme Regional Centre in Colombo, 2007), online at http://www.eicambodia.org/UNDP/download/UNDP_Cambodia_Garment_Post_ATC_table_content.pdf, accessed February 19, 2007, p. 10.

the developed world were created through the sustained application of coercion over long periods, in contexts of urbanization, industrialization, and state expansion. In the absence of these or similar tectonic pressures, the demobilizing mechanisms described can scatter constituencies, denying them recognition, but there is little evidence to suggest that perceptions of political interest are transformed as a result—in fact, the remainder of this study will suggest the opposite. Marginalizing such groups without restructuring their political affiliations—in a manner, indeed, that reduces their ability to pursue their interests effectively via collective action—compounds, rather than resolves, the problem, leading at best to alienation, at worst to the lingering existence of groups with an interest in destabilization.

A second problem relates to both the means and the goals. If a shortcut to an emancipatory—rather than merely ritualistic—democracy is to be found, then it requires the active participation of interested constituencies rather than their marginalization. The approaches described above show a fundamental lack of faith in political solutions requiring discussion, debate, and mutual accommodation among people. Potentially unruly constituencies are dealt with, with varying success, by efforts to split them up, to silence them, or to regiment, limit, and police their activities—a matter that is considerably facilitated by the ability of international agencies to offer glittering prizes in the shape of external funding. Yet in so doing, these same international agencies, despite their declared interest in democracy promotion, collude with sometimes abusive national elites to withhold power of any meaningful kind from the very individuals upon whose rationality and public spirit liberal democracy depends. Under such conditions, the stated means and the goals are in contradiction, raising a question about the extent to which the goals offer a genuine prospect, rather than merely a prepared script, for emancipation. The experiences of workers in Timor and Cambodia strongly suggest that atomization in the context of the market is not a prelude to self-realization, but to exploitation.

CHAPTER VI

"DILIGENT AND OBEDIENT BOYS": DEPENDENCE AND DISCRETION IN ELITE POLITICS

"We are between these two great expectations—that of the rich world that aids us and wants us to be diligent and obedient boys, and that of our people, living in extreme poverty, waiting for results from the government and to reap the benefits of Independence."
Mari Alkatiri, Prime Minister of Timor-Leste, May 18, 2004

The concern, on the part of interveners, to install states that can effectively atomize and thereby discipline unruly populations while facilitating the smooth functioning of the market posed a significant problem to elites in aid-dependent societies. As discussed in the previous chapter, the atomizing mechanisms advocated by interveners were of dubious effectiveness in assuring stability. State policing was mandated, in accordance with imported ideas of "good governance," conceptualized as essentially comprising the necessary institutional support for "sound macro-economic policy." Various interventionary agencies imposed tight surveillance over a variety of aspects of state functioning and policy in an attempt to pursue this goal. However, the specifically political basis of the triangular relationship among three key sets of actors—the state; cross-cutting global networks of interveners, investors, and donors; and the mass of the impoverished population—thus operated awkwardly and in a state of extreme tension. State elites, as Alkatiri commented in the quotation above, were squeezed between demands by donors for facilitation of the market, including tax breaks and other sweeteners for foreign investors, and demands from easily mobilized social forces for redistributive policies at home. Given the importance of international resources in a post-conflict environment, the pressure upon elites to conform to international prescriptions was intense; yet the precondition for success from the perspective of donors and investors was the ability to deliver political stability, which entailed accommodating pressures from below.

International resources were imperative to elites in the post-conflict era. The scale of international assistance, and the potential rewards it offered, entailed that elites could not afford to be marginalized from the process by which these resources were distributed. However, in soliciting and distributing these resources, local elites were focused not merely on questions of economic rationality, but of political cohesion—and in particular the cohesion and allegiance of their own support base. To win and hold support, they found it necessary to distinguish themselves from the international sphere and carve out spaces for autonomous action that would provide them with political latitude in dealing with their internal rivals, their constituents, and their international "partners." Typically they sought to take advantage of international assistance in order to dismantle the support bases of rivals, while defending and supporting their own. The comparative cases of Cambodia and East Timor suggest that elites in both countries were acutely aware of the difficulties inherent in this challenge. There were some important differences, but also some telling similarities, in the way that various sections of the elite in each country pursued this project.

THE NATURE AND SCOPE OF AID DEPENDENCE IN CAMBODIA AND TIMOR-LESTE

With UNTAC's (United Nations Transitional Authority in Cambodia) departure and the passage of the new constitution, Cambodia moved into a new era. The war continued until 1998, but political and economic reforms were ongoing, and huge quantities of international aid—more than US$7 billion between 1992 and 2007, and currently about half a billion US dollars a year—flowed into the country, marking a new era of aid dependence. In 2005, ranked comparatively by the World Bank, which measured aid as a percentage of total imports, and aid as a percentage of Gross National Income, Cambodia came in twenty-third and thirtieth, respectively, out of countries ranked in the table. However, where government spending was concerned, aid equaled 112.6 percent of the Cambodian central government's budget—a level exceeded only in Afghanistan—out of the countries for which figures were available in 2005.[1] This situation has prompted concerns among economists that aid "distorts the economy and the government's response to economic problems."[2] It also distorts political relations within the national community.

A recent study by the Cambodian Development Council found that, as measured by the number of donors and the distribution of market share among them, Cambodia is one of the most competitive aid markets in the world.[3] From 1993 onwards, Cambodia attracted large numbers of donors, dividing their assistance among a range of sectors. The involvement of so many donors has been viewed in different ways by observers. Some observers, particularly those unsympathetic to the political platform and claims of the CPP (Cambodian People's Party), have complained that it is difficult for external actors to coordinate pressure on the Cambodian government in such an environment. Persistent calls from opposition figures asking that donors attach conditions to their gifts and require that these conditions be met as a sanction against the Cambodian government has indeed been largely resisted by donors, even in the face of blatant affronts by the national government to international concerns.

However, it is not the case, therefore, that the government has managed to manipulate donors into dancing to its own tune. Indeed, donors have been

---

[1] World Bank, World Development Indicators, Table 6.11, "Aid Dependency," online at http://siteresources.worldbank.org/DATASTATISTICS/Resources/table6_11.pdf, accessed September 19, 2007.

[2] Martin Godfrey et al., "Technical Assistance and Capacity Development in an Aid-Dependent Economy: The Experience of Cambodia," *World Development* 30,3 (2002): 355–73.

[3] Council for the Development of Cambodia, *The Cambodia Aid Effectiveness Report 2007* (Phnom Penh: CDC, 2007), online at http://www.cdc-crdb.gov.kh/cdc/aid_management/AER-Report-2007-FINAL.pdf, accessed September 19, 2007, p. 6.

remarkably united and consistent in their distrust of the Cambodian government. A Cambodian government review of donor–government relations, produced in 2004, commented on the weakness of the Cambodian government in its relationship with donors, regarding development cooperation as "donor-driven" and characterized by "insufficient attention to Cambodian ownership," a situation that creates "heavy dependence on donor aid." The Cambodian government blamed its failure to take control of government–donor relations on the preoccupation of the first post-UNTAC national government with fighting the ongoing insurgency at the time when donors flooded into Cambodia.[4] The relationship between the Cambodian state and international interveners from the departure of UNTAC to the formation of the second government at the end of 1998 was consequently largely confused, distrustful, and conducted strictly at arms length.

From the end of 1998 onwards, there was a shift in the relationship, coinciding with changed thinking internationally and a view prevalent throughout the donor community in Phnom Penh that the new government, in which the CPP was the senior partner following its election victory in 1998, had the potential for greater effectiveness than the unstable coalition that had been formed in 1993. This led to new efforts to promote donor–government cooperation. From the side of Western and multilateral donors, and in negotiation with the Cambodian government, efforts were made to promote "national ownership" through the development of a National Strategic Development Plan, a variety of government strategies, and "harmonization" through a raft of coordination committees and Technical Working Groups, with donor-government representation, for which Joint Monitoring Indicators were established to assess progress.

A number of indicators released in 2007 by the Cambodian government as part of its aid-effectiveness review show a continued reluctance, on the part of donors, to trust the Cambodian government with their money. Examples include the continued channeling of large quantities of international assistance through NGOs rather than through the government. Figures are not available to show the amount of aid channeled through NGOs in the 1990s, but in 2006 almost a fifth of development assistance was channeled through the nongovernmental sector.

Even when they channeled development assistance through the government, donors adopted modes of engagement that attempted to segregate their activities from the political sphere of the state. This tendency persists. For example, the government's 2007 review noted (as had reviews conducted in 2001 and 1999) that aid was predominantly invested in fixed-term projects with clear objectives and timetables, to the exclusion of programmatic or sector-wide approaches. For example, only 2 percent of assistance to agriculture in 2007 was disbursed via programs rather than through projects. Projects are simpler for donors to monitor, as a means to evaluate the return on their investment, but the focus on projects makes it harder for the government to link up various types of assistance into long-term developmental strategies. The 1999 review of Cambodian aid had commented on the impact of this pattern with regard to a case study of projects in the health sector in Battambang province: "The contrast between the affluence of even the most modest

---

[4] Government–Donor Partnership Working Group, Sub-Working Group no. 3, "Practices and Lessons Learned in the Management of Development Cooperation: Case Studies in Cambodia," Phnom Penh, January 2004, online at http://www.cdc-crdb.gov.kh/cdc/aid_management/practices-lessons-learned.pdf

project and the poverty of the average government office at the same level is embarrassingly striking."[5] The drive, on the part of donors, to control the spending of aid money led to sharp discontinuities within government, between favored but highly disjointed sectors that were subject to the close surveillance and intervention of donors and sectors that were left underfunded and ignored.

The donors' inclination to oversee the distribution of their funds and avoid awarding discretionary power to the government, noted in these various studies of aid dependence, was marked by typical strategies: funding agencies were generally unwilling to use Cambodian government public financial management systems; agencies relied excessively on expensive foreign consultants for policy advice; and such agencies tended to establish and use project implementation units, through which they could supplement the salaries of seconded civil servants in order to secure their loyalty and set them to work in units that paralleled the existing structures of the Cambodian state.[6] Some success stories were mentioned in the studies. Reviews generally agreed that positive collaboration, and effectiveness and transparency in the use of funds, had been demonstrated within the health sector, which in 2006 received almost a fifth of all aid donations as a result. Even here, however, international aid flowed disproportionately to certain powerful vertical structures that had managed to achieve a level of independence from the wider structures of the ministry. Other structures, faced with equally pressing problems, found it much harder to attract funds. The National Council for HIV/AIDS and Dermatology (NCHADS), for example—which under the leadership of its director, Mean Chivun, had managed to gain a degree of independence from the broader ministry, had developed a variety of donor-friendly mechanisms for dealing with money, and was one of only a few government departments to submit to independent auditing—received twenty-five times more funding in 2006 than did the maternal and child health sector. This imbalance persisted despite the fact that maternal and child health is a key area for achieving Cambodia's Millennium goals, and despite the fact that mother-to-child transmission is expected to become the leading source of HIV infection in Cambodia over the next few years. Despite its importance, Maternal and Child Health did not have the same dynamic leadership and institutional independence as NCHADS and was passed over as a result.

Encouraging the fragmentation of ministries in this way makes surveillance by funding agencies easy, but actual government difficult. For example, the departmental director at the Ministry of Health commented:

At the referral hospitals, sometimes there is a microscope only for HIV or only for malaria. So how can that microscope be used across the responses? If there are different programs—for example, we have a car for the Global Fund, but for the Avian Flu Outbreak, we don't have a car. Can we use the car from the Global Fund? Donors need to be flexible on how we use our resources. In 1998, there

---

[5] Godfrey et al., "Technical Assistance and Capacity Development in an Aid-Dependent Economy," p. 362.

[6] Council for the Development of Cambodia, *The Cambodia Aid Effectiveness Report 2007;* Michael Hubbard, "Cambodia: A Country Case Study," report produced for the OECD-DAC Task Force on Donor Practices, Birmingham, 2002, online at http://www.idd.bham.ac.uk/research/Projects/oecd/country_reports/TFDP_Cambodia_6%20Dec.pdf; Godfrey et al., "Technical Assistance and Capacity Development in an Aid-Dependent Economy."

was cholera in Takeo, and it was difficult to send information to the center. The Public Health Department had a fax machine, but the fax was only supposed to be for that organization, and the donors asked, "Why have you used these resources for other things?"[7]

Because funding agencies distrusted the Cambodian government, they preferred this state of affairs to one where money would be poured into the country, to be used at the government's discretion and diverted to political objectives that were not sanctioned by donors.

In other sectors, notably those pertaining to justice, natural resource management, and public administration reform, any efforts at collaboration foundered on the mutual distrust and incompatible objectives of government and donors. On the donors' side, "good governance" implied the promotion of rational-legal forms of public administration across Cambodian territory, in a manner that would facilitate the functioning of the market. On the government side, however, the key goal was the maintenance of the state apparatus as a sphere of discretionary political action and an instrument of political control. The judiciary, civil service, and natural resources sectors were crucial to government strategies, since they formed the basis for the emergence of a shadow state based upon discretionary control of natural resources and other informal revenues, a network that could be used to pursue political strategies outside the boundaries of donor surveillance. Hence the highest echelons of government acted consistently to prevent donor reform strategies from influencing these sectors. In less crucial areas, such as health and education, donors found "reform-minded individuals" within ministries and were able to use these partners in pushing through certain types of reform, within the overall constraints imposed by the culture of the public service.

Timor, similarly, became heavily aid dependent following 1999, due not only to the destruction wrought by the departing Indonesian armed forces, but also to the effect on the Timorese economy of its suddenly being wrenched free of the Indonesian economy. East Timor had always been the poorest province in Indonesia; at the end of the 1990s, conditions worsened as a result of many factors: the financial crisis that hit Indonesia in 1997–98; the destruction visited upon East Timor in 1999; the shock to the Timorese economy resulting from its sudden divorce from Indonesian subsidies and markets; the influx of high-spending UN personnel and their subsequent departure; and the shift of Timor's currency from the rupiah to the dollar. The size of the real economy in 2001 was only about 88 percent of its size in 1997,[8] and, following independence and the wind-down of UNTAET (United Nations Transitional Administration in East Timor), it contracted further. Donor assistance to East Timor peaked in 2002 and subsequently tailed off, as international staff began to leave, taking their earnings with them. The GDP (excluding revenues from oil) fell by 6.7 percent in 2002 and 6.8 percent in 2003. Low positive rates of

---

[7] Departmental Director, Ministry of Health (name withheld for reasons of confidentiality), personal interview, Phnom Penh, April 2006.

[8] RDTL Government in consultation with Development Partners, "Poverty Reduction Strategy Paper—National Development Plan, Road Map for Implementation of National Development Plan, Overview of Sector Investment Programs—Strategies and Priorities for the Medium Term," Washington, DC: International Monetary Fund, 2005, online at http://www.imf.org/external/pubs/ft/scr/2005/cr05247.pdf, p. 18.

growth were posted in 2004 and 2005, although as population growth increased to about 3 percent a year, overall per capita income fell. A further contraction in total non-oil GDP was attendant upon the violence of 2006.[9]

In the first years after independence, around half the Timorese government budget was funded by external assistance, and aid amounted to about 60 percent of the country's GDP.[10] In sharp contrast to the Cambodian government, Timor-Leste's government, under the leadership of Mari Alkatiri, pursued efforts to end its aid dependence as quickly as possible.[11] In part, this was due to rapid dwindling of donor interest, so that even before independence the finances of the government were precarious. As early as June 2001, the government was already struggling to finance its budget from donor pledges, predicting a deficit of US$15 million in an overall budget of only US$65 million.[12] This danger was averted, although the government was forced to limit its spending plans due to lack of other options: through the first two years of independence, donors continued to supply almost half the central government's budget directly through budgetary support. This level of support fell to just over 25 percent of the budget in 2004–05 and then to 8 percent in 2005–06, as oil revenues began to flow in. However, Timor remained a heavily aid-dependent country. Public expenditure from all sources leveled off from 2002 at around US$225 million a year; technical and development assistance peaked at around US$180 million in 2001–02, but nevertheless, in 2004–05, this type of assistance was still worth US$154 million.[13]

Like Cambodia's government, the Timorese government at independence was confronted with a large number of international aid donors, including multilateral, bilateral, and nongovernmental organizations, channeling money through different funds and for different purposes. Some of these funds were available to the government, for projects and budget financing; others were spent directly by the agencies, with more or less coordination with government, depending on the donor. A Timorese director of an INGO project in Timor in 2005 commented:

> International aid here has been a very wide, complex thing. There has been a flood of international organizations with no clear mechanism. Every organization is trying to impose its own basis here.[14]

Another Timorese nongovernmental observer wrote, regarding the relationships established between donors and government:

---

[9] Ibid.

[10] World Bank, *Timor Leste Education: The Way Forward* (Dili: World Bank, 2003), p. 15.

[11] See Xanana Gusmão quoted in Thomas Crampton, "Ex-Rebel's Vision for East Timor," *International Herald Tribune*, November 1, 2001, online at http://www.iht.com/articles/2001/11/01/t5_0.php

[12] Mari Alkatiri, speech on the occasion of the ceremony of the swearing-in of members of the transitional government of East Timor, Dili, September 20, 2001.

[13] Nicolau S. Neves Guteriano, "The Paradox of Aid in Timor-Leste," presented at the seminar on "Cooperação Internacional e a Construção do Estado no Timor-Leste," Brasilia, July 25–28, 2006, online at http://www.laohamutuk.org/reports/06ParadoxOfAid.htm, accessed September 19, 2007.

[14] Bendito Freitas, Stromme Foundation, personal interview, April 2005.

Aid does not come as cash alone, but arrives with government agencies and international staff whose way of thinking is very far from that of the Timorese. In reality, even though our government signs contracts, the donors' government agencies have more power to control the money than the Timor-Leste government. In some bilateral projects, our government is not allowed to make decisions, and is limited to ceremonial functions.[15]

Timor faced considerable problems in revitalizing its economy after 1999. The extent of reliance on subsistence agriculture, the level of physical destruction, the difficulty in restoring basic state services, and the distorting effect of the UN presence on the economy all took their toll. Furthermore, the considerable amount of capital investment undertaken by international agencies in East Timor during the UNTAET era did not improve the economic situation much. It had a relatively small multiplier effect because of the funding agencies' tendency to tender internationally for contracts and to conduct procurement in Australia. Much of the reconstruction work in Timor was done by foreign workers for foreign companies using foreign supplies, and consequently much of the money injected by international organizations ended up flowing straight back out of the country. This failure to engage Timorese workers and vendors was highly controversial—the World Bank faced angry protests from local carpenters when it attempted to import plastic furniture from overseas to refurnish East Timorese schools. The furniture was commissioned via a tendering process that involved complicated legal contracts in English and restriction of tenders to registered businesses, which excluded many Timorese carpentry shops. Even when the World Bank changed its policy and decided to award a certain percentage of the contract to "national" businesses, most of this work went to international firms or NGOs with a local presence, rather than to truly Timorese outfits.[16]

The same was true of the money spent on UNTAET itself, which, to the extent it was spent locally, was invested in a service industry constituted of hotels, restaurants, and supermarkets that were Dili based and foreign owned, which imported their products, and which repatriated profits. According to one study, less than 10 percent of UNTAET's budget went into the local economy, and around 80 percent of that was spent in Dili, which was also the focus of most other aid agencies' assistance.[17] As a result, although UNTAET's presence generated a degree of economic activity as foreign firms entered East Timor to cater to UNTAET staff, and as UNTAET itself employed local people, it left little in terms of sustainable economic infrastructure behind. With UNTAET's departure, and as international donors' priorities shifted elsewhere, the Timorese government faced a precipitous economic decline. In particular, the focus of international activity upon Dili had prompted rapid urbanization and, following UNTAET's departure, there was a crisis in the urban economy. This unsustainable expansion of the urban sector was an important factor in the violence that engulfed Dili in 2006.

---

[15] Guteriano, *Paradox of Aid*.

[16] Lao Hamutuk, "The Provision of School Furniture: Assessing One Component of the World Bank's Emergency School Readiness Project," *Lao Hamutuk Bulletin* 2,5 (2001): 12–15.

[17] Michael Carnahan, William Durch, and Scott Gilmore, *Economic Impact of Peacekeeping*, Final Report (New York, NY: United Nations Department of Peacekeeping Operations, 2006).

RESPONSES TO AID DEPENDENCE: NEGOTIATING SPHERES OF AUTONOMY

The responses to aid dependence in Cambodia and Timor differed sharply. The first Timorese government, under Alkatiri, adopted two distinct approaches. One of these, particularly evident in the speeches of Jose Ramos-Horta, then foreign minister, focused upon Timor's vulnerability to compassion fatigue. For Ramos-Horta, it was not aid dependence per se that was a problem, but the question of Timor's competitiveness vis-à-vis other needy countries. Consequently, in Ramos-Horta's approach to the question, as foreign minister, as prime minister (after 2006), and as president (after 2007), there is a strong focus on "branding" Timor-Leste as a capable performer and reliable partner for international aid donors. This approach was based upon erecting a reputation for Timor as pliable and responsive to international concerns, and above all, as non-corrupt.

For example, in mid-2001 Ramos-Horta published an opinion piece in the *International Herald Tribune*, which was essentially an appeal for international aid. The piece was entitled "East Timor Is Worthy of Your Help," and in it, Ramos-Horta emphasized the strengths of the Timorese aid environment. Foremost among these were Timor's asserted willingness to adapt and its responsiveness to donor concerns:

> We have made mistakes but have learned from them. East Timor benefited from the experience of other countries that have achieved independence. We realized early on that we would have to manage within our own resources.[18]

In his statement, Ramos-Horta acknowledges donors' concerns regarding financial management, while emphasizing the importance of raising revenue within Timor:

> We have tried to create a capable public administration with strong financial management that will make the best use of international aid and our own taxpayers' funds. Recognizing the dangers of corruption in new and fragile institutions, we have put in place mechanisms that provide for transparent decision-making and effective financial controls.[19]

At the same time, he proffers an exit strategy:

> East Timor has natural resources on which sustainable economic growth can be based. In addition to our traditional farm production, including the production of premium-grade coffee for export, revenue from oil and natural gas projects in the Timor Sea, along with increased domestic revenues, should, by around 2005, eliminate our dependence on international support to fund the core operations of government.[20]

In this short statement, Ramos-Horta manages to touch most of the bases of donor concern, showing an astute awareness of the "aid effectiveness" doctrine that had become increasingly important in the calculations of funding agencies. Given

---

[18] Jose Ramos-Horta, "East Timor Is Worthy of Your Help," *International Herald Tribune,* June 14, 2001.

[19] Ibid.

[20] Ibid.

Timor's small size and lack of intrinsic interest to many international donors—with the exception, perhaps, of neighboring Australia and Timor's former colonizer, Portugal—this approach represented an effort to promote aid to Timor on the grounds that dollars spent in Timor would yield a larger return in terms of measurable development. The article includes two references to the devastation of 1999. Ramos-Horta comments:

> When I returned in late 1999, after representing the independence movement abroad during the Indonesian occupation, I was shocked by the destruction, and part of me believed that the country would never recover.

Later he adds:

> The reconstruction may not seem impressive to visitors seeing the country for the first time, but they should realize that 18 months ago East Timor was little but scorched earth.[21]

However, there is no mention of human development indicators or the fact that Timor-Leste has become one of the very poorest countries in the world. Rather, the article is resolutely upbeat, focusing on the Timorese people's "resilience" and the "responsibility" of public servants. It focuses on what has been achieved rather than what has been destroyed. It does not ask for compassion from donors, recognizing that this sentiment tends to be fleeting; rather it offers a solid rate of return on investment.

Similarly, in a lecture given at Oxford University in 2002, Ramos-Horta praised the generosity of donors and commented that "the real question is: will the Timorese meet the expectations of the international community?"[22] Ramos-Horta stated that it was incumbent upon the Timorese to "prove we are deserving of international support" through promoting democracy, judicial independence, freedom of the media, and "transparent, accountable government."[23] Acknowledging the important contribution of the "international community" in helping Timor to attain independence—"Timor is free thanks to the international community, not only thanks to Timorese determination"—he added that because of this, "we have a responsibility to the international community... [International assistance] places an enormous burden upon us. Would I have the courage to face my friends in Portugal or Washington if we become yet another rotten corrupt country?"[24]

In outlining this approach, Ramos-Horta focused on Timor's small size and weakness—factors which, he argued, entailed the need to "sometimes swallow our principles for the sake of the national interest." This included rapid normalization of relations with Indonesia; support for the stance of the United States, which refused to extradite US citizens to an International Criminal Court; compromise with Australia on the Timor Sea dispute—which was especially important, he noted, "when our

---

[21] Ibid.

[22] Jose Ramos-Horta, "East Timor: The Challenges of Independence," special lecture, Asian Studies Centre, St. Anthony's College, Oxford, June 10, 2002, recorded and transcribed by the author.

[23] Ibid.

[24] Ibid.

security is being protected by Australian troops"; and a resolutely forward-looking stance with respect to the atrocities committed by Japanese troops in East Timor during World War II, as well as acceptance of the heavily "tied" nature of Japanese aid. With respect to this last point, he commented, "It's their money. Why would they give it to us to spend on American goods?"[25] This attitude of tolerant pragmatism for the inequitable and coercive aspects of international aid politics was designed to make virtue of necessity, as Ramos-Horta talked the donors' language and reassured them that Timor was prepared to play the game.

Prime Minister Alkatiri concurred with Ramos-Horta's approach, at least at the level of rhetoric. In speeches to donors, he continually emphasized Timor's reputation for "prudence," and his government's policies during the first few years of independence focused upon promoting this image internationally to reassure donors and maintain their commitment to Timor-Leste. At the same time, Alkatiri acknowledged the different pressures coming from above and below during these years: "We are between these two great expectations—that of the rich world that aids us and wants us to be diligent and obedient boys, and that of our people, living in extreme poverty, waiting for results from the government and to reap the benefits of Independence."[26] The policies carried out by Timor's government between 2002 and 2006 suggest that the government responded more directly to the expectations of "the rich world" than to those of the poor at home.

This was surprising, since Alkatiri had long enjoyed a reputation for "economic nationalism." Some of the decisions taken by the Alkatiri government do exhibit this economic nationalism. Its approach to developing the public health system, and its successful collaboration with the Cuban government—a collaboration that prompted protests from the US Ambassador to Timor-Leste—both show a commitment to the nation's welfare and economic independence. Such opportunities were the exception, rather than the rule, however; as it turned out, most of the opportunities for economic nationalism that presented themselves in the post-independence environment were those that made life more onerous for the poor rather than less. The Timorese government found itself trapped in an economic context in which their efforts to achieve greater independence simply entangled them deeper in the dilemmas associated with dependent governance.

One important example of these dilemmas emerged as Alkatiri sought to end Timor's aid dependence as quickly as possible, while acknowledging it as inevitable over the short term. In particular, the Alkatiri government was adamant in its insistence that ebbing aid flows after 2002 should not be replaced by the loans and debt that the World Bank was encouraging the government to sign up for. While this approach was regarded by some as evidence of his unreconstructed socialism, in fact it went down very well with many donors, since the budget gap that resulted was dealt with by the imposition of "drastic"[27] austerity measures. The willingness of the government to impose these cuts on an already desperate population in order to avoid deficit financing was regarded by international financial institutions as a masterly display of fiscal responsibility and neoliberal minimalism. Thus, in 2002, when shortfalls in the budget were identified, the government cut the budget rather

---

[25] Ibid.

[26] Mari Alkatiri, remarks at opening session, Timor-Leste and Development Partners Meeting, May 18, 2004.

[27] Ibid.

than borrow money. Again, in 2004, Alkatiri announced to donors the imposition of "a number of stringent measures to arrest potential drift in expenditures," including reductions in the use of vehicles and telephones and travel expenses for the government.[28]

A second element of this policy was its strong focus on maximizing revenue. Some initiatives to increase revenue had a similar effect to the imposition of austerity budgets. Rapid and aggressive moves were initiated to collect user fees for, for example, electricity. The position of the electricity generating authority was quickly improved by swiftly expanding the installation of electricity meters and collection of payments in and around Dili. This was a policy that, in a climate of economic collapse, was poorly received at home. Alkatiri himself admitted in 2004 that the policy of installing pre-paid metres into 10,000 houses connected to the electric grid "initially met considerable resistance."[29]

In other areas, the government's economic nationalism was not regarded as favorably by donors. This was particularly true when the government attempted to impose fees and taxes on foreign investors and agencies. Timor-Leste established a steeply progressive income tax system after independence, and made collection of tax arrears an early priority, largely achieved by 2004. Offenders included international companies contracted by the UN—the owners of the floating hotel that housed UNTAET staff were leading examples—who resisted payment, arguing that, as UN contractors, they should be exempt from Timorese tax. Their interpretation was endorsed by UN headquarters despite the disastrous impact it would have on Timorese government revenues. Ultimately, the Timorese government was successful in winning this battle, but its general weakness in pursuing and enforcing nationalistic economic policies was somewhat exposed when it was later forced to reduce tax demands made in negotiation with oil companies operating in the Timor Sea.

Numerous reports were produced that compared the competitiveness of Timor-Leste unfavorably with that of other countries—especially Indonesia. Excessive red tape and high taxes were widely criticized; Jose Ramos-Horta, after election to the presidency in 2007, raised the possibility of abolishing taxation on foreign investment and turning Timor into a second Hong Kong. In these battles, the government's economic nationalism stood it in good stead in eliciting revenues; however, tax policy and concern to regulate foreign investment, as a means to promote state autonomy, combined with the weakness of post-conflict administrative structures to give the country a bad reputation among investors. While it enjoyed positive branding in international aid circles, by 2006 Timor was second from the bottom in the World Bank's perception-based "Doing Business" survey rankings. In the entire world, only the Democratic Republic of the Congo was regarded by investors as a worse place to do business.[30]

In any event, the amount of revenue raised through taxation of foreign companies were miniscule compared to the potential revenues that might be made available to the Timorese economy through sale of oil and gas reserves in the Timor Sea worth an estimated US$30 billion. At independence, these reserves were being

---

[28] Ibid.

[29] Ibid.

[30] World Bank Doing Business Project, online at http://www.doingbusiness.org/map/, accessed September 18, 2007.

exploited unilaterally by Australia as a result of a treaty signed with Indonesia in 1991 that established a joint exploration and exploitation regime in the so-called "Timor Gap"; terms of this agreement were highly favorable to Australia. As a newly independent country, Timor had no established maritime boundaries. The appropriate position for the boundary became a point of intense disagreement between Timor—which was holding out for equidistance—and Australia, which claimed a larger share owing to the greater extent of its continental shelf. Legal experts disagree on the rights and wrongs of the case, which has not been tested in court, owing to Australia's refusal to submit to arbitration.

Following 1999, UNTAET made a new, but still controversial, deal with Canberra and reestablished the Joint Petroleum Development Area in the Timor Sea, including some, but not all, of the disputed oil and gas fields, the rest of which remained under Australia's sovereign control. Within the Joint Petroleum Development Area, Australia and Timor were to share the revenues, although Timor claimed exclusive entitlement to these, under their reading of international law, since they were on Timor's side of the half-way line between Timor and Australia. After independence, negotiations, often acrimonious, continued between Dili and Canberra, with Timor persisting in claiming a legal entitlement to 100 percent of the disputed fields, and Australia refusing to concede the point while continuing to pump the oil as fast as it could and earning around US$1 million a day in the process.

In its negotiations with a recalcitrant Australian government, the Timorese suffered from an important handicap—namely, the skepticism with which their quest for oil was viewed by international experts. Fears that Timor would be overtaken by a "natural resource curse"[31] were widely voiced by international economists, who regarded the Timorese state as too fragile to manage revenues that, if Timor were awarded all it claimed, could reach twelve billion US dollars over the course of the next three decades.

The reality of the "resource curse" in other oil-rich countries was acknowledged by the Timorese government:

> We are very aware that, unless well managed, petroleum has the potential also to be a curse instead of a blessing for us, too. But we are doing this within our own national context, that is, within the context of our constitution (which is widely recognized as a progressive and modern one), and within the context of the need to strengthen the institutions established by our constitution and to consolidate our achievements to date in building up our governance institutions.[32]

---

[31] The "natural resource curse" thesis holds that the exploitation of large amounts of valuable natural resources can undermine economic and political institutions, owing to the distorting effect on the rest of the economy; the potential for large fluctuations in revenue; and the likelihood that political constituencies at home will engage in aggressive contention in an attempt to capture the profits. See, for example, Jeffrey Sachs and Andrew Warner, "The Curse of Natural Resources," *European Economic Review* (2001): 827–38; Ian Bannon and Paul Collier, eds., *Natural Resources and Violent Conflict: Options and Actions* (Washington, DC: World Bank, 2003).

[32] Mari Alkatiri, speech to the Extractive Industries' Transparency Initiative Conference, London, March 17, 2005, online at http://www.laohamutuk.org/Oil/Transp/05PMtoEITI-UK.htm, accessed September 18, 2007.

The question of the natural resource curse imposed important restrictions on the Timorese government's plans for spending the oil revenues it regarded as rightfully its own. Australia's obstructive position on the question of who owned the oil reserves made these restrictions more acute. In order to shame Australia into sharing the revenues more equitably, the Timorese government embarked on an international publicity campaign on the issue. But for the Timorese, getting international support for its position on the question of sovereignty and revenue sharing entailed showing a willingness to conform to international prescriptions regarding management of the money in a manner that would avoid the resource curse. Once again, the Timorese government's aspiration for economic nationalism was limited by the reality of starkly unequal relations of power between the Timorese and their international supporters.

There was a strong resemblance between this situation and the internationalization of the struggle against Indonesia in the 1990s. This resemblance, indeed, was highlighted by the Timorese, who hoped to shame Canberra by comparing its actions to those of Jakarta. The publicity campaign had a clear impact, including within Australia itself, where solidarity groups condemning the Australian government's position on East Timor had been active since 1975. The Timor Sea Justice campaign, indeed, gave new impetus to these groups, which had lost their raison d'être since 1999, and who now picked up the new challenge with enthusiasm. Advertisements were run on Australian television condemning the Australian government's intransigent position and bullying tactics. The Australian government refused to back down on its essential position regarding sovereignty and the position of the maritime boundary; however, it did make a series of concessions over distribution of revenues from certain oil fields in disputed areas. Whereas the "arrangement" concluded with UNTAET in 2000 granted Timor 23 percent of total revenues from Timor's side of the half-way line, a subsequent interim treaty signed with the government in 2002 raised the share to 42 percent. In 2006, with an election looming and under pressure to demonstrate progress, the Alkatiri government signed another treaty, in which the Timorese agreed to shelve sovereignty claims for fifty years (until after the oil reserves are exhausted) in return for a 60 percent share of revenues.[33]

Concern to reduce the country's aid dependence both drove—but also, to an extent, inhibited—the Alkatiri government's negotiating position on the revenues. The goal coincided with the economic nationalist agenda: interest on oil revenues alone would more than finance the central government budget for decades. The issue was highlighted in publicity issued by the Timorese government's Timor Sea Office, whose summary fact sheet begins by stating:

> An agreement on permanent boundaries, and the consequent ability to derive revenues from the development of offshore petroleum and other resources, is essential for securing Timor-Leste's economic independence. These resources

---

[33] East Timor and Indonesian Action Network, "Statement on the East Timor-Australia Maritime Agreement," January 15, 2006, *Action in Solidarity with Asia and the Pacific Website*, online at http://www.asia-pacific-action.org/statements/2006/etan_onetaustraliamartime agreement_150106.htm, accessed September 18, 2007.

will allow Timor-Leste to avoid long-term aid dependency as it goes about alleviating mass poverty and rebuilding the nation.[34]

But the need to internationalize the issue in order to win further concessions from the Australian government forced the Timorese government to conform further to international prescriptions regarding development policy, in order to maintain a moral high ground as it fought for access to these resources. In Timor, the question of the resource curse was subordinated, in public discussion, to the question of sovereignty and relations with Australia. In Australia, much was made of the suggestion that unimpeded access to the oil could leave East Timor worse off than before, ruining its economy, corrupting its institutions, and generating a predatory elite. This was clearly a self-serving discourse, but one that played well internationally.

At the same time, international oil companies—in particular, Woodside, the company developing the Greater Sunrise Field from which Timor expected to benefit—insisted on the rapid conclusion of a treaty, threatening to pull out of oil exploration if this were not achieved. A further constraint imposed upon the Timorese government related to petroleum processing. While the revenues negotiated in Australia would provide a welcome source of cash for the Timorese government, the development implications would be magnified if Timor could claim a share of the processing industry. This required efforts to convince oil companies like Woodside to pipe the gas to Timor, rather than Australia, and build a processing plant there, to provide Timorese jobs. In this situation, the Timorese government's negotiations with oil companies ran in direct competition to Australia's. As one analyst put it:

> Timor-Leste, as a new country with a tragically violent history, has not had time to establish an investment-friendly reputation of peace, stability, and adherence to the rule of law. As a result, oil companies are wary of relying on on-shore facilities or Timor-Leste regulations.[35]

Because of these constraints, the Timorese government found itself facing few options where economic policy was concerned. Getting access to oil revenues and the wider benefits associated with an onshore processing industry would reduce its dependence on aid and permit the government to continue to pursue its own, cautious approach to self-reliant development. At the same time, winning the international sympathy and confidence needed to prise concessions out of Australia and capital investment out of Woodside and its partners required an even stricter adherence to deflationary policies and neoliberal principles than would be imposed by mere aid dependence, this in an economy still reeling from the destruction of 1999 and the collapse following UNTAET's departure. Concern to burnish its international image in this way prompted the minister for natural resources, Jose Teixeira, to tailor the government's position to insure that Timor did not appear to

[34] Timor Sea Office, "Fact Sheets—Summary," online at http://www.timorseaoffice.gov.tp/summary.htm, accessed September 18, 2007.

[35] Charles Scheiner, "The Case for Saving Sunrise," submission to the government, July 28, 2004, posted online at http://www.laohamutuk.org/Oil/Sunrise/04sunrise.html, accessed September 18, 2007.

relish the prospect of an oil bonanza. It was a matter of principle only, he said; in fact, the Timorese government was unable to spend the oil money and "would rather leave the oil in the ground," regardless of the political price the electorate might exact for such parsimony.[36]

The government responded to international concerns about its own competence by setting up a Petroleum Fund, to be maintained outside Timor, to hold oil revenues in trust for the next generation. Meanwhile, the government would spend the interest generated by the account, funds expected to amount to perhaps 3 percent of the revenues—an amount that would be sustainable in perpetuity. This approach was lauded by international donors, although there was less enthusiasm for a plan to permit the government, with the approval of parliament, to withdraw money from the fund's principle for investments in free education and free health care, and to establish public enterprises. This proviso did, however, prompt applause from economic nationalists within Timor, who compared the architects of the plan with Hugo Chavez of Venezuela.[37]

It subsequently became clear that spending the interest alone would not reliably cover the government's planned budget, and the need to continue "branding" the country as a safe destination for capital to impress both the donors and the oil companies constrained policy even further. Internally, the government was under close scrutiny from NGOs that were much influenced by "resource curse" fears, while it also faced criticism from nationalists who argued that agreeing to a pragmatic split of resource revenues with international companies entailed selling off Timorese sovereignty. Clearly, the policy of relying on the interest from its oil revenues did not contribute much to Timor's economic independence. The Alkatiri government was left with very little room for maneuver; to avoid indebtedness, it needed to access revenues quickly. This required gaining the moral high ground in negotiations with the Australians, to achieve the maximum possible return immediately. This, in turn, required signing away sovereign rights, accepting a lesser share than nationalists believed Timor was due, and making a commitment to spend only about 3 percent of the revenues generated by these compromises. For an economic nationalist, it was a poor deal, but, given Australia's stance, it was better than nothing at all.

Yet, at the same time, while the Alkatiri government demanded its due in revenues, its approach to spending them was cautious, technocratic, and highly centralized. After UNTAET's departure, it quickly became clear that budgetary constraints were only part of Timor's problem: between 2002 and 2006, the Timorese government had great difficulty spending the small budgets it was allocated at the central level because of administrative bottlenecks brought about by a highly centralized public administration and very inexperienced staff members. The Timorese government, like UNTAET, gave priority to achieving a highly bureaucratic form of "capacity," in which the activities of civil servants were rendered "accountable" and "transparent" through the rigorous implementation of a

[36] Jose Teixeira, remarks at the seminar on "Avoiding the Resource Curse: Challenges to Sustaining Development in Timor-Leste, Australian National University, Canberra, March 25, 2004, recorded and transcribed by the author.

[37] Grupu Estudu Maubere (Maubere Students Group), "A People's State Against a Capitalist State," discussion paper, May 23, 2006, posted on "Back Door Newsletter on East Timor," http:///www.pcug.org.au/~wildwood/06may23gem.html.

large number of rules. This bureaucratic structure was designed to support a "zero-tolerance" policy towards corruption.

While this probably helped to keep corruption at bay, at the same time it added exponentially to the difficulties of getting the newly recruited and inexperienced civil servants to deliver goods to the population. Pressure to avoid corruption and demonstrate transparency to donors regarding what had happened to their money worked in direct opposition to facilitating swift delivery of funds and services to citizens at the local level. The World Bank remarked in its 2006 Country Assistance Strategy,

> Timor-Leste performs well on fiduciary accountability, but this comes at a high cost to service delivery ... Budget execution is very slow ... due to heavy centralization of expenditure management, tight expenditure and procurement controls, weak capacity in ministries, and poor communication between the MPF [Ministry of Planning and Finance] and line ministries.[38]

At the same time, the government's claims that it would try to curtail corruption did not play well among the population at large, since just about the only patronage that was available—patronage regarding appointments into the public service in a situation of high unemployment—was distributed in a highly politicized manner. The stacking of the public service with FRETILIN (Frente Revolucionária de Timor-Leste Independente, The Revolutionary Front for an Independent East Timor) loyalists was widely remarked, and linked with corruption through the Indonesian aphorism, KKN (*korupsi, kolusi, nepotism*, or corruption, collusion, nepotism). Equally, publicity surrounding gains in the Timor Sea negotiations, and reports of donations apparently flowing in from bilateral or multilateral agencies, convinced people that a great deal of money was being channeled to the Timorese elite, in sharp contrast to the meager funds trickling down to the local level. This prompted many villagers, accustomed to the mechanics of Suharto's New Order regime, simply to assume that the small amount of money channeled to the villages was inversely proportional to the depth of politicians' pockets.[39] In fact, however, there was little hard evidence of corruption in the Timor-Leste government between 2002 and 2006, despite persistent rumors and intense scrutiny by international officials.[40]

From the government's point of view, preoccupied as it was with accountability to donors rather than accountability to villagers, decentralization could not be achieved without risk of corruption until a huge amount of work had been done to ensure that local-level officials were familiar with rules that were still causing problems at the central level. As Mari Alkatiri remarked in a speech to donors in 2004:

[38] World Bank, *Country Assistance Strategy for the Democratic Republic of Timor-Leste for the Period FY06–FY08* (World Bank: Dili, 2006), pp. 9–10.

[39] These observations, taken from village surveys conducted in 2005, are discussed in more detail in Chapter 9.

[40] During my fieldwork in Timor-Leste in 2005, I heard many such rumors and met a number of different individuals who had come to Timor to work for different agencies with a specific anti-corruption mandate. Yet concrete evidence of any systematic or large-scale corruption within the Timorese government at that time has never come to light.

Before a global administrative decentralization occurs, which will take time, we understand that we can and should embark on de-concentration and decentralization tests in some of the more developed sectors in our administration. But, even here, there is some need for caution regarding the development of the resources-management system in order to prevent the inappropriate use of those very same resources and the risk of public assets being privately appropriated.[41]

Decentralization of budgets was urged upon the Timorese government by donors in an attempt to overcome the problem of underspending on already austere budgets. This prompted the government to begin establishing an administrative framework for five newly established "regions" of the country. The solution implemented merely initiated the process of imposing a new layer of administration over the top of the district structure, rather than actually empowering the districts themselves, and requiring new influxes of international trainers and technical assistants. In this, as in other areas of policy making, donor concerns imposed straitjackets on the Timorese government from which it could not free itself. The result, in the first years following independence, was sclerosis at the center and penury in the villages.

The deflationary effect on the economy was compounded by the refusal, on the part of donors, to countenance the use of aid to establish state enterprises in the areas of rice production and fisheries. The government was encouraged—particularly by the Asian Development Bank, but also by individuals within the World Bank—to focus on facilitation of the private sector, as a solution to unemployment, rather than attempting much active intervention in the economy. This policy eschewed short-term gains in favor of purported long-term benefits, but in a deflated economy, when many Timorese were already suffering desperately, these policies did little to boost either the fortunes of the population or the popularity of the government. The suffering imposed on the people by this development strategy was acknowledged by Prime Minister Alkatiri in 2004:

The recovery of the economy in the final two years of the Plan period, that is fiscal years 2005–06 and 2006–07, is expected to be modest. The net effect is that the economy would be largely stagnant during the five-year Plan period. At the same time, our population has been growing at about 3 percent per year, or by about 16 percent during the Plan period. The virtual stagnation of the economy and the growth in population would result in a significant increase in the incidence of poverty and the number of poor people. This is a serious concern for all of us.[42]

The Timorese government attempted to address this situation by starting work on Sectoral Investment Plans—development plans made by each ministry to identify areas in which donor projects could usefully contribute to human development and poverty reduction. These were based upon a "consultation exercise" carried out in 2001 and 2002, in which government officials held meetings across the country and

---

[41] Alkatiri, remarks at opening session, Timor-Leste and Development Partners Meeting, May 18, 2004.

[42] Ibid.

clarified the broad policy priorities of the general public. Unsurprisingly, the public was most interested in education, health, and agriculture. On the basis of this fairly broad prescription, the government then produced a series of policy documents culminating in the Sectoral Investment Plans. As one official pointed out, "It is important to highlight that these exercises were carried out in close cooperation with all Timor-Leste's major donors."[43]

Although the government made laudable efforts to include the population in planning at the beginning of the Sectoral Investment Plans initiative, the very broad and fairly obvious priorities mapped out were transformed into actual policy in collaboration with donors. This took a long time; the Sector Investment Reports were finally released in April 2005, four economically disastrous years after the consultation initially took place. The government then had to wait for donors to come forward with funding before the plans could be implemented. Meanwhile, progress on the ground was slow. Projects that were delivered quickly generally bore prominent signs attributing them to the generosity of one donor or another—but not to the government of Timor-Leste. According to Alkatiri, the government's solution to the desperate need across the country was "effective communication" with the people, to

> ... educate them on the issues of nation-building and to make sure they have a realistic understanding of what it will take to get our country where we want it to be, and the continued establishment of international best practice in all areas of development, tailored to the needs of Timor-Leste.[44]

Given that the government had just restricted its own use of cars and telephones and its domestic travel budget, and that progress on decentralization was glacial, it was not entirely clear how this "effective communication" was to be achieved. Estevao Cabral and Julie Wark suggest that "a certain division of labor" emerged between 2002 and 2006 in the Timorese government, in which the president—"the much more visible, among-the-people Xanana Gusmão"—represented the public face of the government, while Prime Minister Mari Alkatiri remained in a "world of facts, figures, and policy," in which he dealt largely with other officials and donors. In this world, Cabral and Wark argue, Alkatiri didn't "require charm or other PR skills,"[45] but rather needed the technocratic skills he had acquired during his studies in Mozambique during the resistance years.

Before either neoliberal or economic nationalist policies could provide any kind of political dividend, the government collapsed. In April 2006, with a political crisis already brewing within the military, unemployment still high, poverty increasing, and an election looming, the government announced a decision to reorient its policy,

---

[43] Hernani Coelho da Silva, Timor-Leste ambassador to Australia, "Four Years of Governance in Timor-Leste: An Overview," paper presented to the conference on "Beyond the Crisis in Timor Leste," Australian National University, Canberra, June 9, 2006, posted online at http://devnet.anu.edu.au/Timor-Leste_Beyond%20the%20Crisis_Seminar_Home.php

[44] Mari Alkatiri, address to forum hosted by Marion Hobbs in association with the Asia 2000 Foundation, Institute of Policy Studies, Centre for Strategic Studies and New Zealand Institute for International Affairs, New Zealand Parliament Buildings, Wellington, New Zealand, August 18, 2003.

[45] Estevao Cabral and Julie Wark, "Timor-Leste: Behind the Demonisation of Mari Alkatiri," unpublished manuscript, on file with the author.

and, in defiance of donor prescriptions, to use state resources to provide a boost to the economy. In a speech entitled "decision time," Alkatiri announced the policy to donors, remarking: "It is decision time, and the decision has been made: we will have the State make our economy grow."[46] He added, in a characteristic reference to Timor's international image: "Please do not accuse us of nationalizing the Timorese economy, led by some socialist influence that would characterize the decision-makers of this country."[47]

Decision time came too late. The breakdown of the political system that would lead to Alkatiri's own resignation under intense pressure in June 2006 had already begun. The years of decline had dissipated much of the goodwill the government had enjoyed in its first years; this was particularly the case in Dili, where the abrupt crash of the UNTAET bubble, following so closely upon the destruction of 1999, caused particular hardship, not to mention dashed economic expectations. As Alkatiri was speaking, a group of 597 former members of the Defense Force had taken up residence in an area of land named Taci Tolu, just outside Dili, from where they prepared to launch a demonstration outside parliament, protesting their dismissal for desertion of their barracks. The group had submitted a petition to Xanana Gusmão on January 11, 2006, claiming that they faced discrimination within the F–FDTL (FALINTIL–Forças de Defesa de Timor Leste). The group came from the western provinces of East Timor, collectively referred to as the "Kaladi" provinces; they claimed that the officer corps, predominantly Easterners, or "Firaku," were advancing their own fellow Firaku at the expense of the Kaladi within the army. When they received no response to their petition, the group abandoned their barracks, leaving their weapons behind, and went to Dili to try to meet with the president. The president ordered the group to return to their base, although he announced the establishment of a commission of inquiry to look into their complaints. However, following a week of activities by the commission, the petitioners were still dissatisfied and left their barracks again, prompting their dismissal by Defense Force Chief Taur Matan Ruak in the middle of March. Subsequently, Xanana made a televised address, in which he commented that the decision was unjust, and said that discrimination by Firaku against Kaladi was indeed a problem within the armed forces. Following this speech, at the end of March, rioting broke out in Dili between young men identifying themselves as Firaku and Kaladi. Subsequently the petitioners moved to Taci Tolu before launching renewed demonstrations outside the presidential palace in April.[48]

The dispute emerged from growing discontent within the armed forces, angered not only by the treatment of FALINTIL (Forças Armadas da Libertação Nacional de Timor-Leste, Armed Forces of the National Liberation of East Timor) during the demobilization exercise, but also by its subsequent fate. Within F-FDTL, there was a growing view that the armed forces were being sidelined from national development. Soldiers saw greater efforts and resources being put into establishing the police force—a police force manned by individuals that FALINTIL had fought against during the resistance era. They saw the police being awarded duties, such as

---

[46] Mari Alkatiri, "Decision Time," speech at opening session, Timor-Leste and Development Partners Meeting, Dili, April 4, 2006.

[47] Ibid.

[48] Account of events drawn from the "Report of the United Nations Independent Special Commission of Inquiry for East Timor," Geneva, October 2, 2006.

patrolling the border between Timor-Leste and Indonesia, which F-FDTL regarded as rightfully theirs. Most significantly, perhaps, they saw the police receiving better pay than the armed forces. As a result of these conditions, among others, problems with discipline and absenteeism had become more challenging within the armed forces, and among the petitioners were individuals who, their superiors alleged, had spent more time engaged in smuggling than in training. In itself, the demonstration was not necessarily either an outcome of or a challenge to the Alkatiri government; it represented a challenge to the F-FDTL leadership, which was more closely associated with Xanana than with Alkatiri. However, the escalation of the crisis was intimately associated with the unpopularity of the Alkatiri government among key groups, such as veterans' associations, and Dili residents more widely.

The attachment of the petitioners' complaints to an East–West, or Firaku–Kaladi, split, which had had little salience during the war, was highly problematic. The Firaku–Kaladi division is of uncertain origin, by all accounts; it corresponds to broad distinctions between the rice-growing and coffee-growing sections of the country; it also corresponds to the two different Indonesian commands in East Timor. It is certainly the case that, during the resistance, the Eastern and Western wings of FALINTIL were frequently cut off from one another, and that the Western wing lost more of its senior commanders in action, leaving the Eastern wing in charge when the troops came together in the troubled cantonment at Aileu after 1999. The Eastern commanders subsequently presided over controversial decisions regarding demobilization. Furthermore, the East quickly emerged as a FRETILIN heartland in terms of voting power, in both local elections in 2005 and subsequent national presidential and parliamentary elections in 2007. For these reasons, once the split had been politicized by the petitioners, and, by all accounts, manipulated by shadowy figures regarded as coordinating the violence, the conflict quickly drew in wider sections of the mixed Dili population, at the same time as it tested the cohesion of the police force.

As the petitioners proceeded with their demonstration, new groups, including groups of ex-veterans, arrived to join the protest. In the surrounding city, tensions rose and sporadic violence broke out, notably in the form of attacks on kiosks and market stalls identified as belonging to "easterners" or "westerners." On April 28, violence erupted at the demonstration site itself, in front of the government palace. Some of the police detailed to control the protest ran away, and others were attacked. The demonstrators began a march to Taci Tolu; along the way, houses were burned, people were assaulted, shots were fired, and tear gas unleashed. In the confused situation, military police and F-FDTL detachments showed up and engaged in fire fights with demonstrators. A rumor began to spread that F-FDTL units from the East had massacred demonstrators at Taci Tolu, although no evidence of a massacre was found by a later commission of inquiry. A group of military police also abandoned their post in early May, eventually ending up in the western town of Gleno, where a firefight took place between the group, led by Major Alfredo Reinado, and the police.

Sporadic fighting among different disaffected groups from different parts of the security services continued throughout May. The houses of political leaders came under attack. The home of relatives of the minister of the interior was attacked, as was the home of Defense Force Chief Taur Matan Ruak. As authority broke down, violence, looting, and arson spread through the capital, resulting in the destruction of more than 1,500 houses and the displacement of 150,000 people. Thirty-eight people were estimated killed and sixty-nine wounded.

Jose Ramos-Horta, addressing the United Nations in New York a month later to request a renewed UN presence in Timor-Leste, commented:

> The incidents in Dili last week were a wake-up call to us, the East Timorese leadership, as well as to the international community, that we must not take for granted the apparent tranquility in the country.[49]

The crisis of 2006 has often been attributed to the failures of security-sector reform or to the government's mistaken decision, in March 2006, to dismiss more than one-third of the entire defense force. Other analysts have pointed to the irresponsible and self-interested actions of individuals—notably Roque Rodrigues, the defense minister, who subsequently lost his job, and Rogerio Lobato, who went to jail, but also Alkatiri, Xanana, and Ramos-Horta—in pursuit of old rivalries dating back to the split between FALINTIL and FRETILIN or before.[50] It has been suggested that covert intervention by the Indonesians intensified the conflict, particularly given that one of the acts of violence that took place comprised an attack on the Serious Crimes office and the burning of records.[51] Similarly, questions have been raised about Australia's role, suggesting that Australia certainly has more intelligence about the situation in Timor than it has been willing to share.[52]

While all these elements contributed to producing the shape and timing of the crisis, its extent—and the serious deficiency of legitimate resources the government found it had at its disposal to deal with it—reflects broader political and economic failures, which result from the nature of aid dependence as much as particular policy decisions. Since 1999, both the UN and the Timorese elite had regarded a variety of East Timorese expressions of discontent as evidence of "unrealistic expectations" regarding the potential fruits of independence.[53] However, the management of expectations, unrealistic or otherwise, comprises the stuff of politics, and a political system that lacks the resources to reward at least some key constituencies will never attain stability. The failure of Timor-Leste and its donors represented the failure to realize, until too late, that the tight economic policies they were pursuing left little room for accommodating the political and economic demands of a range of easily mobilized, well-organized, and self-reliant groups accustomed to independent

---

[49] Jose Ramos-Horta, speech at the Security Council, United Nations, New York, NY, May 5, 2006, online at http://www.pm.gov.tp/speech5may.htm

[50] See in particular Sydney Jones, "Resolving Timor-Leste's Crisis," International Crisis Group Asia Report No. 120, Brussels, October 10, 2006, online at http://www.crisisgroup.org/library/documents/asia/timor/120_resolving_timor_lestes_crisis.pdf

[51] Richard Tanter, "Ten Questions about East Timor for Which We Need Answers," paper delivered at the workshop on "East Timor: Beyond the Crisis," Australian National University, Canberra, June 9, 2006, online at http://devnet.anu.edu.au/Timor-Leste_Beyond%20the%20Crisis_Seminar_Home.php, accessed September 19, 2007.

[52] Ibid.

[53] See for example, Jean-Marie Guehenno, Under-Secretary General for Peacekeeping Operations, cited in United Nations, "Recent Violence, Rise in Armed Groups Threaten Success in Timor-Leste, Peacekeeping Under-Secretary-General Tells Security Council," Press Release SC/7683, New York, March 10, 2003, online at http://www.un.org/News/Press/docs/2003/sc7683.doc.htm, accessed September 19, 2007. See also Mari Alkatiri cited in Shawn Donnan, "Complications Follow the Painful Birth of Timor," *Financial Times,* December 4, 2003, online at http://www.etan.org/et2003/december/01-6/04compl.htm, accessed September 19, 2007.

political action. Trapped between "these two great expectations," as Alkatiri presciently put it in 2004, the Alkatiri government, against its better judgment perhaps, bent too far towards the "rich world that aids us and wants us to be diligent and obedient boys," with disastrous consequences.

The crisis of 2006 resulted from a combination, then, of political and economic failures, in a context of intense international pressure. In economic terms, the takeoff that could have made tropes of self-reliance meaningful and subjected political groups to the atomizing influence of the market failed to occur. In political terms, the government, in accordance with the advice of donors, assumed the existence of passive citizens who could be prevailed upon to tolerate catastrophic levels of economic hardship over an extended period of time. This was an assumption starkly at odds with the highly activist, swiftly mobilized society of self-proclaimed heroes that actually lived in Timor-Leste. Members of the government found themselves constrained and unable to accommodate either powerful or potentially troublesome domestic interest groups through the formulation of policy. Despite its formally democratic nature, the Timorese political system had emerged as one in which too much power was concentrated in the hands of groups that had either no connection with the Timorese popular mood, in the case of the donors, or an increasingly limited connection with it, in the case of the government, which was increasingly preoccupied with the expectations of international funding agencies.

Aid Dependence in Cambodia

The Cambodian government's response to aid dependence was radically different from the Timorese government's and, from the point of view of the government itself, far more effective. Like the Alkatiri government, and in contrast to Ramos-Horta, the Cambodian government saw the intrusions of donors into policy making as inhibiting, and it sought to minimize these as far as possible. It did so by expeditiously erecting and stabilizing a machine for the circulation of resources that could operate off the books, and which was, consequently, both opaque to donor scrutiny and highly effective in brokering accommodations with powerful groups politically. This was a mechanism that focused on expanding to the greatest possible extent the government's freedom to maneuver politically through the generation of large slush funds for buying off rivals and supporters alike. Unfortunately, this strategy largely freed the government from acknowledging or seeking to abide by the juridical concept of accountability. This lack of accountability undermined tentative steps towards democracy, entrenched the threat of violence as an ever-present prop to the system, and produced, alongside a creditable record on poverty reduction and human development indicators, widespread social and political alienation and staggering inequalities between the powerful and the poor.

When UNTAC (United Nations Transitional Authority in Cambodia) entered Cambodia, the State of Cambodia was just emerging from a formative experience of dependence upon an unpopular and highly intrusive patron: the Vietnamese. The State of Cambodia's suspicions of outsiders combined with a reluctance on the part of donors to engage intimately with the state administration to produce an arms-length relationship of mutual suspicion between donors and the state between 1993 and 1999. At the same time, the ongoing insurgency gave the government a certain degree of latitude in undertaking unpleasant tasks that donors did not particularly want to know about.

From 1989, the State of Cambodia had implemented a raft of economic reforms designed to shore up the Cambodian state and economy in the context of the withdrawal of the Vietnamese army and advisors, the shrinking and then disappearance of material aid from the Soviet Bloc, and the political uncertainty surrounding the peace operation. Economic reform offered government officials an opportunity to abandon the unpopular rhetoric of socialism and to consolidate the state apparatus, which had always been weak, by the simple expedient of allowing state officials to supplement their salaries through the private sale of state assets and the acceptance of bribes. Although corruption had been a fact of life in Cambodia in the 1980s, in the 1990s it became institutionalized and systemic, linked to the reconstitution of the Cambodian People's Party in an era of electoral competition.

The return of resistance parties and their supporters to the territory of Cambodia and the mainstream of political life was regarded, and portrayed, by the CPP as a threat not only to the party hierarchy but to the state apparatus and the nation itself. This threat could be managed only by entrenching the party more firmly in the bureaucracy and military, through efforts to strengthen and protect chains of clientelism within these organizations. Civil servants and soldiers, in conditions of intense uncertainty, galloping inflation, and widespread violence, were encouraged to look to their patrons within the public service to protect and provide for them. In return, they were expected to vote for the party and share their takings from various informal and extralegal activities with their superiors. Much of the internal politics of the state, the military, and the CPP since 1991 has revolved around the entrenchment and rationalization of this shadow system, through a range of mechanisms: promotions and appointments; public denunciations and dismissals; turf wars and pay-offs; the calling in of debts and favors; arranged marriages between sons and daughters of key individuals; arrests and pardons; and the murders and exiling of people. These activities have produced a powerful shadow network of patron-client links that underpins the state, party, and military apparatus, while also entailing the superficiality of its rational-legal veneer.

In the Cambodian case, unlike the Timorese case, a series of pools of resources became available to the elite that could be exploited largely independently of donors, to provide immediate resources for the growing shadow government. Initially, intensive exploitation of Cambodia's forest resources served as a major source of funds. Government officials, ranging from provincial governors to the two prime ministers themselves, awarded lucrative logging concessions to commercial logging firms in return for bribes and kickbacks. Members of the military, widely deployed across the country's forested regions, were able to cut and transport logs themselves, to elicit bribes in return for permitting illegal logging from non-concessionaires, as well as to charge fees in return for their services as security guards to those who had been awarded concessions by one authority or another. Collaboration in this enterprise generated money for a wide range of actors through the early to mid-1990s. Subsequently, a "crackdown" on logging, launched ostensibly at the behest of multilateral donors, led to the rationalization of the system, monitoring illegal activities within the forests and ensuring that concessions could only be awarded at the central level. However, as Andrew Cock has documented, rather than providing the basis for more inclusive or sustainable development, this anti-corruption strategy merely ensured that a greater proportion of the bribes and fees made their way up to the highest levels of the system, enhancing central control over an economy that remained in the shadows, as far as the fiscal authorities available for donor oversight were concerned.[54]

The forests were not the only resources to be sold off in this way. Fisheries, mineral deposits, and water resources were all privatized with abandon by any official with sufficient backing to be immune to challenge. Even land—the foundation of the rural subsistence economy—was disposed of in this manner. In 1989, the CPP had privatized land through a "land to the tillers" program, which resulted in the distribution, on a fairly egalitarian basis, of rights to register land ownership to farmers across the land. Unfortunately, due to the difficulties and expense of engaging with a corrupt state administration, few farmers were able to navigate this process successfully. The unwieldy and corrupt system opened the way for an avalanche of land grabs and land disputes, in which, thanks to the corruption of local authorities and, as a last resort, the court system, the rich and well-connected invariably won the day. In addition, there were distress sales of land, extremely common in a country where, in the early 1990s, more than 40 percent of the population lived in absolute poverty, and in which the majority lived in highly precarious circumstances. As a result of these conditions, the distribution of landholdings was transformed from a relatively egalitarian process, typical in 1989, to a highly concentrated pattern of distribution by 2006, by which time 70 percent of the land was held by the richest 20 percent of the population. In an economy based upon subsistence farming by households, this represented a considerable dispossession of the poor. This mass privatization had two effects. First, it released enormous resources to the government, which could use the funds to buy support from key constituents. Second, it generated a close and mutually accommodating relationship between sellers and buyers, privileging a newly emerging Cambodian business class.

Some of this revenue was used to end the insurgency. From 1996, the government offered generous pay-outs to defecting Khmer Rouge, a policy that enjoyed rapid success. Defecting commanders, rather than being demobilized and integrated into society, were left in charge of their zones and simply given large sums of money to ensure their loyalty. Competition over the loyalties of these commanders led to intense friction between the two coalition parties within government: FUNCINPEC (Front Uni National pour un Cambodge Indépendent, Neutre, Pacifique, et Coopératif, or National United Front for an Independent, Neutral, Peaceful, and Cooperative Cambodia), the winner of the 1993 election, which had faced great difficulties in achieving any control of the state or military apparatus at all, and had consequently been frustrated in its efforts to govern; and the CPP. FUNCINPEC's leader, Prince Norodom Ranariddh, decried the exclusion of FUNCINPEC ministers from control of their ministries and the overt political loyalties of village and commune chiefs across the country who had been appointed in the 1980s, all conditions that hobbled the efforts of his party. The prince briefly attempted to build up his party's military forces and to attract Khmer Rouge support for a confrontation to force concessions from the CPP. However, his efforts were preempted by a CPP military assault that defeated those units of the military that

---

[54] Andrew Cock, "The Interaction between a Ruling Elite and an Externally Promoted Policy Reform Agenda: The Case of Forestry under the Second Kingdom of Cambodia, 1993–2003," (PhD dissertation, La Trobe University, 2007).

were loyal to FUNCINPEC. Ranariddh fled to Bangkok, and Hun Sen's ascendancy was ensured.

Other portions of this funding were used to finance political campaigns. The CPP's style of campaigning from 1998 onward depended heavily on dishing out goods to the population. A particular focus was the provision of public amenities, such as roads, schools, temples, and various kinds of training centers. These invariably were presented as personal gifts of CPP political leaders, and the scale of this largesse was such that the new buildings soon came to dominate the rural landscape. These gifts, combined with carefully targeted campaigns to place intense pressure on those identified as opposition supporters (who were threatened with the loss of their land, of security protection, and of development assistance if they voted the wrong way) were crucial in winning the CPP increasing shares of the vote in national elections in 1998 and 2003, and in local elections in 2002 and 2007.

The arrival of peace and the victory of the CPP in the 1998 elections initiated a new phase of donor engagement, during which international agencies attempted to cooperate with, and reform, the CPP-dominated state apparatus. Before its election victory in 1998, when the CPP had been part of the 1993–97 government coalition, acting as the junior partner to the royalist FUNCINPEC, Hun Sen had been confrontational in his relationship with donors. For example, in 1995 Hun Sen threatened to organize demonstrations against the US embassy following US criticism of the arrest and exile of a FUNCINPEC leader. At the time, the Americans were considering whether to renew Cambodia's Most Favored Nation (MFN) trading status. Hun Sen remarked to the press:

For Americans, if they talk too much about Cambodian affairs, we'll stage another demonstration demanding them to pay us compensation [for the war] ... We're not going to die depending on whether they give us MFN or not ... During the State of Cambodia era, we lived in a time when they attacked us, they surrounded us, they imposed sanctions against us. We survived [then], why can't we survive now?[55]

From 1999, with the CPP acting as the senior partner in the government, this tone was swiftly abandoned in favor of a much more conciliatory line, and donors became hopeful that their efforts were bearing fruit. The 1999–2003 Cambodian government established a set of mechanisms, such as the Joint Working Group structure, to organize contact between government and donors. The government also produced a set of policy-strategy documents, such as the National Poverty Reduction Strategy, which were heavily influenced, if not written, by donors and, consequently, conformed closely to donor expectations. However, after the reelection of the CPP in 2003, and the twelve months of limbo that followed, as the parties wrangled over how to form a government, donors became increasingly impatient. The CPP had proved intransigent and uncooperative on key issues: public administration reform to combat corruption; judicial reform to end the climate that allowed the rich and well-connected to engage in corruption with impunity and that made it impossible to establish a stable contractual environment for investment; and far-reaching reform to natural resource management.

---

[55] Hun Sen, speech, Kandal Province, December 5, 1995, quoted in Jason Barber and Ker Munthit, "Hun Sen Talks Tough to the West," *Phnom Penh Post*, December 15–28, 1995, p. 3.

Regarding the civil service, while both the CPP and FRETILIN used public appointments as a form of patronage for supporters, the CPP favored the retention of bloated, poorly paid, and poorly functioning organizations, in contrast to the Timorese leaders, who, following the World Bank's advice, cut their civil service to a third of the size it had been during the Indonesian era. The Cambodian civil service has endured miserly salaries, set well below a level employees needed to survive, prompting public servants either to stay away from the office in order to pursue second jobs or to attend the office in order to make money from various types of corruption. Cambodia's Joint Working Group on public administration reform set out a series of steps that had to be achieved in order to reform the civil service, including mapping of personnel and functions; rationalization, including the removal of "ghosts" from the books; and a shift to a structure in which good performance is rewarded with promotion and higher pay. However, moving ahead with this agenda would threaten vital government interests in maintaining the civil service as a foundation of its sphere of discretionary action. The reform agenda risks establishing an ethic of professionalism and meritocracy that might disable the civil service as a mechanism for generating slush funds and stalling further reform in wider fields of governance. As a result, the Cambodian government avoided, and continues to avoid, sharing sufficient information with donors to allow rationalization to begin, and it has announced an annual rate of civil service pay increases that would require almost a decade before the average bureaucrat's salary reached the bare minimum on which one might be able to survive in Phnom Penh. In a Government Donor Cooperation Committee meeting in February 2007, the Australian ambassador summed up the donors' mood on the issue, commenting: "We are surprised and disappointed that there has been such little progress, and appeal to the Government to consider how this work can be reinvigorated."[56]

Donors expressed similar frustration with regard to the passage of the anti-corruption law. A National Anti-Corruption Law was first mooted in 1994, at a time when international NGOs highlighted the huge bribes received by Cambodia's two prime ministers in return for allowing the destruction of Cambodian forests. Little progress was made in the years of instability that followed, but the issue reemerged on the agenda in 1999, following the stabilization of the political situation under a CPP-led coalition. In 1999, the law was reported to be imminent, however, parliamentary committees watered it down, then sent it back to the Council of Ministers, where it languished for several years. In 2002, Hun Sen promised donors that the law would be passed by July 2003, but it had still not emerged from the Council of Ministers by the time parliament was dissolved in advance of national elections in 2003.

These elections did not lead to the successful formation of a government, and no government was established until 2004, a condition that delayed the legislation still further. In 2004, the UN made passage of this law a "Joint Monitoring Indicator," a marker to be used by donors and government to measure progress on reform, with implications for aid. Cambodia's prime minister then ordered the establishment of a new drafting committee to revise the 2003 draft of the legislation. In 2005, the

---

[56] Her Excellency Lisa Filipetto, Ambassador of Australia, Joint Development Partner Statement on Public Administration Reform, Ninth Meeting of the Government-Donor Coordination Committee (GDCC), Phnom Penh, February 12, 2007, online at http://www.cdc-crdb.gov.kh/cdc/ gdcc/ninth/ninth_australia.htm, accessed September 23, 2008.

government held a public seminar for consultation on the provisions of the draft legislation. Participants in the seminar produced a new draft of the law, but it was criticized by donors for awarding insufficient autonomy and powers to the Anti-Corruption Board that had been designated to investigate allegations of corruption. In 2007, thirteen years after the process began, the law had still not been passed. The head of the drafting committee, former Hun Sen advisor Om Yientieng, placed the blame for this squarely on the donors: "When the national assembly sent [the law] back to the government … the same NGO[s], the same foreigner countr[ies] start[ed] to [get] involve[d], to review everything. When someone blocks this procedure and says please go ahead, what can we do?[57] Pressed by donors to conform to "international best practice" on the issue, but unwilling to commit themselves to legislation which, if it were implemented, could erode the basis of the government's discretionary power, and which, if it were not implemented, could provide a focus for campaigning by opposition groups at home, the government simply stalled.

This pattern of inaction was repeated across a range of policy issues that affected the government's sphere of discretionary action. Land reform and natural resource management were areas in which the government strongly resisted donor scrutiny. In the area of natural resources, the government agreed in 1999 to accept international monitoring of the work of a new Forest Crimes Unit; however, when the international monitors began to publish evidence of extensive collusion among those who had been charged with preserving Cambodian forests from illegal logging, they were fired from their positions, and individual members were threatened and attacked. In the case of land reform, the government delayed making information regarding land concessions publicly available. In the case of judicial reform, despite a series of cases in which corruption or politicization of the court system was manifest, no action was taken.

The ability of the CPP to flout donor demands in this way was a result of three factors. First, the scale of Cambodia's aid dependence is not accurately reflected in the figures quoted at the start of this chapter. The official budget, used to calculate aid dependence, represents only a part of the total amount of money available to the government, a fact that becomes clear when secret slush funds are taken into account. Opposition leader Sam Rainsy claimed in 2003 that US$400 million a year had flowed into "the pockets of the group of corrupt people" and been sent to offshore bank accounts.[58] Sums of this size permit a substantial degree of government action that takes place beyond the purview of either international donors or local opponents. From a different perspective, to the extent that this flow of money shores up the system, it can be said to represent the continuing high price of stability. The CPP has been adept, during past crises, in appealing to its supporters to use their considerable profits, gained from the privileges they have been awarded by the system, to bail out the government. There is no doubt that the amount of unofficial funding available to the government, at least on a temporary basis, considerably outweighs the amount of international aid that might be cut by donors determined to establish conditions that the Cambodian government repeatedly fails

---

[57] Om Yientieng, ABC Radio Australia, "Cambodia Says Anti-Corruption Law Delayed by Foreigners," January 3, 2007, online at http://www.abc.net.au/ra/news/stories/s1820635.htm

[58] Sam Rainsy, responses to callers, "2003 Election Campaign Radio Call-In Show," Cambodia Women's Radio, FM 102, July 2003, recorded by FM 102, translated by the author.

to meet. These internal, undocumented sources of funding give the government considerable leeway in resisting donor demands.

This leeway has expanded recently, as two new sources of funds have materialized: namely, the People's Republic of China, and oil reserves in the Gulf of Thailand. Since Hun Sen expelled the Taiwanese diplomatic liaison office in Cambodia immediately following the 1997 fighting in Phnom Penh, the relationship between the CPP and the Chinese government has become increasingly close. In the same year, as the reconstituted Cambodian government, with Hun Sen de facto in charge, faced condemnation around the world and a few donors moved to restrict aid pending new elections, China responded to Hun Sen's gesture with a shipment of weapons for the Cambodian military. In 1999, Hun Sen visited Beijing and received the equivalent of US$218 million in aid from China—the largest amount of aid ever donated by the Chinese, at that point, to any country in the world. Between 1997 and 2005, China has reportedly provided US$600 million in investment, aid, and loans; in 2004 China emerged as Cambodia's most significant investor, as well as its most generous military donor, and in 2005 it overtook the United States to become Cambodia's second source of bilateral aid, behind Japan. In contrast to the United States, which channels 50 percent of its aid through NGOs, China provides 100 percent of its assistance directly to the Cambodian government. In 2006, bilateral agreements were signed between Cambodia and China involving US$250 million in development assistance.[59]

Chinese aid and investment is perceived by the Cambodian government as political support for the CPP, and the supportive approach of China is compared favorably with the stance of Western donors, who tie aid conditionally to the recipient's willingness not so much to take action on reform as to engage in endless dialogue about it. But although Chinese aid is not tied to issues of neoliberal governance, it is not disinterested either. China's generosity reflects an interest in the economic and strategic potential of Cambodia as an ally. China has been active in redeveloping Sihanoukville, on the Gulf of Thailand, possibly with the intention of using the port as a docking place for Chinese naval vessels in the future. China is also interested in securing rights to drill for Cambodian oil, which would meet China's pressing need for a friendly and nearby source of fuel, whose delivery could not easily be blocked by other countries.[60] Chinese companies have also been granted large land and forestry concessions in Cambodia, and projects have been established in the logging sector in close cooperation with such politically powerful Cambodian companies as Pheapimex. Meanwhile, improved transport links between Cambodia and Yunnan province have prompted an influx of Chinese migrants, setting up small businesses in various parts of Cambodia.[61]

Oil reserves discovered offshore in the Gulf of Thailand constitute the second potential new source of funding for Cambodia, promising to enrich the country in the same way the Timor Sea does for Timor-Leste. Cambodian oil could double

---

[59] Council for the Development of Cambodia, *The Cambodia Aid Effectiveness Report 2007*.

[60] Shawn Crispin, "Cambodia's Coming Energy Bonanza," *Asia Times Online*, January 25, 2007, online at http://www.atimes.com/atimes/Southeast_Asia/IA26Ae01.html, accessed February 9, 2007.

[61] David Fullbrook, "China's Growing Influence in Cambodia," *Asia Times Online*, October 6, 2006, http://www.atimes.com/atimes/Southeast_Asia/HJ06Ae01.html, accessed February 9, 2007.

Cambodia's GDP. Estimates of annual oil revenues for the government range from US$170 million in 2011, to a peak of US$1.7 billion in 2021. The latter amount would equal almost three times the amount of aid pledged annually through the Cambodia Development Cooperation Forum process at present.[62]

In contrast to the Timorese approach, all the signs at present suggest that the Cambodian government plans to remove oil and gas revenues from public purview as quickly as possible, in order to expand to the maximum extent its discretionary power over them. A state agency, the Cambodia National Petroleum Agency, which has coordinated Cambodian imports of petroleum in the past, has been moved out of the Ministry of Industry, Mines, and Energy and into the direct control of Deputy Prime Minister Sok An, a member of the Council of Ministers. This suggests the political importance of oil and gas from the government's perspective; Sok An is Hun Sen's right-hand man and has presided over a number of economic sectors that are of central financial importance to the party. Under Sok An's chairmanship, the Cambodia National Petroleum Authority has emerged as a secretive institution, which reveals little to the public either about the amount of oil and gas thought to exist under the Gulf of Thailand or about terms and conditions negotiated with international oil companies. One Canadian oil company has reportedly withdrawn from the competition for contracts, claiming it was asked to pay large bribes for permits that never materialized.[63] Institutions that could scrutinize the use of oil revenues are missing, and the government has published no plans to establish any. This behavior stands in stark contrast to that of officials in Timor-Leste, who agonized over what kinds of people could possibly form a sufficiently incorruptible committee to serve as overseer of the Petroleum Fund there. Indeed, the Cambodian government's staunch refusal over the last decade to raise public salaries, pass anti-corruption legislation, or empower nonstate actors to fulfill any kind of oversight function paves the way for political leaders to spend oil money, as they have spent timber money, entirely at their own discretion, unhampered by the law.

A second reason for the Cambodian government's ability to retain room for maneuver in an aid-dependent context is international donors are unlikely to move from merely pressing for reforms to implementing and enforcing their own conditions. Hun Sen has achieved a degree of moral authority in the eyes of donors precisely because what he is doing appears to them to be working. Despite the fact that Hun Sen's style of governing in a range of policy areas remains antithetical to the neoliberal ideal of good governance, donors have few grounds for insisting on concerted punishment of his government, for his regime has demonstrated impressive achievements: a sound record on macroeconomic stability; success in restoring political stability in the wake of the 1997 battle; the ability to win elections with a lessening degree of violence; and, more recently, the delivery of respectable figures in terms of economic growth, human development, and poverty reduction. In periods of national crisis in Cambodia during the 1990s, donors were divided over how best to respond. While the Americans in the 1990s militantly insisted on democratization (responding to the lobbying of opposition politicians within

---

[62] Susan Postlethwaite, "Oil Spigot Set to Flow in 2011," *Phnom Penh Post*, September 7–20, 2007, online at www.phnompenhpost.com, accessed September 20, 2007. The total amount of aid pledged at the Cambodia Development Cooperation Forum in 2007, including aid from China, amounted to US$689 million.

[63] "Cambodia Finds Oil and Changing Fortune," *Bangkok Post*, December 17, 2006.

Cambodia and opposition-aligned diaspora groups in California), the French, Japanese, and Australians were much more inclined to be flexible in recognition of the stabilizing power of the CPP.

Since 2001, this approach has become more widespread. Indeed, a presentation by a group of international and local analysts to a group of donors, outlining the starkly illiberal basis of Cambodian governance in 2007, prompted a somewhat panicked World Bank official to intervene rather defensively with the question: "Anyway, where is the evidence to show that good governance is related to economic performance?"[64] thus retreating from ten years of well-established World Bank policy. The emergence of the discretionary sphere of the shadow economy, so regularly decried by donors, in fact represents a useful device to plug the gaping political holes that open up in a context of donor-prompted, neoliberal reform on the periphery of the global economy. The two are complementary, rather than incompatible; it is the combination of coerced political and economic stability and patrimonial relations among the government, the military, and investors that produced, for example, the success of the garment industry in Cambodia, which now contributes about 16 percent of GDP.[65]

A third factor that helps the Cambodian government resist pressures for reform has resulted from the demobilizing tactics of donors themselves, with respect to Cambodian society. In the early 1990s, the emergence of a vibrant civil society in Cambodia was explicitly envisaged by then-UN Secretary-General Boutros Boutros-Ghali as a check on the government's abuse of power. Subsequently, donors have been keen to fund Cambodian NGOs in training, advocacy, and service-delivery functions; however, as the previous chapter demonstrated with respect to Cambodia's trade union movement, they have done so in a manner that has left these organizations weakly defended against government tactics that combine the engagement in "participatory" forums encouraged by donors with a significant degree of background violence. Indeed, since 2001 the government has orchestrated a sustained crackdown on public protest that has included, at various times, violent police attacks on strikers and demonstrators, with many reports of beatings and shootings; the prohibiting of protest marches; the establishment of checkpoints on national highways that prevent provincial groups from entering Phnom Penh to present their grievances to the government; and the assassination, arrest, and imprisonment of oppositional civil-society leaders and of opposition members of parliament. This overall governmental strategy has made it extremely difficult for civil society to hold the government to account. The Cambodian government is clearly culpable, and subject to a sharp liberal critique, for failing to protect the human rights of its citizenry, but in post-September 11th Southeast Asia, most bilateral donors prefer to occupy themselves with improved poverty figures and economic growth rates.

The starkly different responses to aid dependence in Cambodia and Timor, and the implications of these responses for forms of politics and development, suggest that financial dependence upon advocates of neoliberal governance represents a trap for poor countries. Neoliberal governance prescriptions are predicated upon notions of bounded statehood, atomized citizenship subject to market discipline, and

---

[64] Author's observations, donor meeting, Phnom Penh, February 2007.

[65] Royal Government of Cambodia, *National Strategic Development Plan, 2006–2010* (Phnom Penh: Royal Government of Cambodia, 2006).

minimal government action. Neoliberal theorists expect this last condition to facilitate the smooth functioning of the economy, within which individuals pursue their interests and from which they ideally derive not only satisfaction, but aspirations and identity. However, comparisons between Cambodia and Timor-Leste suggest that this solution is untenable without significant bolstering through the sort of patronage and politics of the kind that the Cambodian government has excelled at. In the contentious atmosphere of post-conflict polities, neoliberal prescriptions offer few immediate solutions to specifically political problems resulting from the expectations of highly mobilized and often armed constituencies. All they can offer is the vague hope that a prosperous economy, over the long term, might encourage these groups to dissolve themselves so that the various members can disperse, go home, and each get a job.

For the governments concerned, however, negotiations and accommodations were required. The Cambodian government carried out this exercise more effectively than the Timorese government, mainly because of the Cambodian government's success in carving out a sphere of autonomous action for itself, within which it could deploy resources, accommodate the demands of the potentially contentious social forces representing the losers in Cambodia's post-war development trajectory, and, essentially, buy support from the powerful. Cambodia's politicians achieved this feat by the simple expedient of removing a large proportion of the de facto government budget from the books and distributing it through a shadow state comprising patronage networks that linked the party, the bureaucracy, and the military ever more tightly as time went by. This was a highly effective strategy in terms of promoting political stability, and this stability in turn prompted economic growth and poverty reduction at respectable levels.

Unfortunately, economic success involved very heavy costs, from which it is hard to see Cambodia recovering any time soon. These costs were: an administration that has come to be entirely opaque, not only to donors, but also to locals; continued militarization of politics, the economy, and society, associated with a continuing and pervasive sense of menace; entrenched corruption that has taken a heavy toll on the population and the environment; soaring inequalities dividing rich and poor; and the further impoverishment of already ritualized conceptions of democracy. However, a comparison between the Cambodian and the Timorese cases suggests that Cambodia's heavy-handed approach to both coercion and cooptation did not result from the failure of neoliberal reforms, but instead should be recognized as the cost of holding the country together following the imposition of market logic. The lack of flexibility on the part of donors, their failure to encourage debate or permit experimentation over different forms of development, and their general complicity in the suppression of civil society, have facilitated the ascendance of the most secretive, most violent, and most corrupt section of Cambodia's post-war elite, which now enjoys greater freedom from internal scrutiny than, arguably, it did in the early 1990s.

In Timor-Leste, by contrast, the political leaders' discretion of action was minimal. The finances of the government were transparent for all to see, and the bureaucratic program implemented to prevent misappropriation of funds entailed not only a generally clean administration but the failure to spend a large percentage of the government's miniscule budget on anything at all. Whereas the Cambodian government continually dared donors to cut their aid, Timorese government officials made an effort to be "branded" as excellent performers, but, in so doing, they left themselves no room to respond to constituencies at home. Indeed, repeated austerity budgets pushed more and more Timorese into poverty. The jarring contrast between the dream of independence and its reality was so evident as to be entirely politically untenable. All that was required to start a rebellion was a suitable rallying cry, and the petitioners' demonstration supplied this. Yet there is, of course, more to legitimacy than poverty reduction. The next chapter examines the ways that elites in the two nations presented themselves and their status to local people, and the ways in which they maintained their authority in an aid-dependent context where external actors were so clearly in charge.

CHAPTER VII

"KHMER WHEN IT'S EASY, AMERICAN WHEN IT'S DIFFICULT": GATEKEEPING AND THE POLITICS OF AUTHENTICITY

> If we want to take responsibility for the nation's fate, we must be responsible before the people ... We must dare to take responsibility, to live and die with the people. Don't say you are Khmer when it is easy and "American" when it is difficult.
>
> Hun Sen, Prime Minister of Cambodia, 1996

The strategies adopted by elites hoping to capture international resources and mobilize local support put those leaders in a peculiar position with respect to the domestic polity and the international sphere. The elites act as gatekeepers, straddling the border between the local and the global. To legitimize this position, they must promote their own status as leaders, uniquely qualified to represent the local sphere in a global arena and to control global inputs into the domestic setting.

Consequently, the legitimation strategies of dependent elites are Janus-faced in orientation, with international legitimacy, as well as domestic legitimacy, at a premium. To an extent, these two forms of legitimacy conflict, as the previous chapter demonstrated. International elites require "diligent and obedient boys," while the poor want an open-handed government that will expedite the business of "reap[ing] the benefits of independence." Complicating this difficulty is the fact that, in dependent communities, the entanglement of the international and domestic spheres entails that international and domestic legitimacy are not only mutually incompatible but are also mutually determining, to an extent. International legitimacy, in part, determines local legitimacy; for dependent populations, the ability of domestic elites to negotiate with, control, and manage international donors successfully is a crucial qualification that determines their capacity for government. Above all, elites must be able to keep the aid flowing in. Similarly, the pledges made by donors at annual funding conferences are sensitive to demonstrations of local legitimacy on the part of governments. While donors demand that governments respond to donor demands, they also require governments to be "responsive" to local populations, and they use this responsiveness as a measure of "good governance." At the same time, donors require that a government's responsiveness to the national community remain compatible with their own interests and priorities.

The previous chapter examined how domestic elites attempt to carve out spheres of international action that award them leeway in responding to local demands from key constituencies, as well as to donor demands. This chapter examines how elites attempt to legitimize their position through the cultivation of particular ideas regarding the shape of the community and the roles of different sections of the elite within it. Investigation of the Cambodian and Timorese cases suggests that detailed policy debate has limited effect in a situation where international aid donors visibly hold the power. However, there are two broad groups of strategies that present themselves to dependent elites: the politics of gatekeeping and the politics of authenticity.

The politics of gatekeeping represents that elites assert a unique ability to operate successfully in an international sphere by virtue of special knowledge of that sphere, a knowledge that their compatriots do not share. This claim is particularly appealing to returnees who have spent many years abroad, or to negotiators who have spent much time dealing with international agencies during peace negotiations or peacekeeping operations. It is a claim supported by the extent to which an elite individual can cite instances when he or she has received personal support from international actors vis-à-vis rivals, or can claim friendship with leaders from powerful donor nations. It is an elitist politics which demands that local constituencies place their trust in the leader's connections with powerful external actors, rather than mobilizing to formulate domestic solutions to domestic problems. The politics of authenticity, by contrast, rests on the assertion of a unique knowledge of the local sphere. Claim to such knowledge is achieved through two means: through blood and descent, on the one hand, with the emphasis upon ties of ethnicity and, in the case of traditional rulers, dynasty; and through the sharing of the hardships of war, on the other. Elites who use either form—or both forms— typically adopt populist stances that appeal to a notion of democracy as inherent in the shared cultural values of the people, and that asserts these values against international power, raising allegedly culturally inspired objections to various donor demands.

In the entangled political spaces of dependent communities, these two claims cannot be relied upon exclusively. The most successful elites present themselves as mastering both—as embodying, through their personal leadership, the merging of a potentially overwhelming international technology and international resources with a potentially uncontrollable national energy, in a manner that neutralizes the negative and enhances the positive in both. The account offered of the Timorese and Cambodian experiences, below, suggests that there is a strong possibility that elites who attempt this strategy will fail. The politics of gatekeeping is an unpredictable business. At the same time, the politics of authenticity is potentially divisive and dangerous.

Gatekeeping requires that dependent elites present themselves as having special leverage in relationships with donors, when, in fact, they are the junior partners in any such relationship. Overreliance upon international support, as Cambodia's former resistance parties have found, can leave individuals dangerously exposed if international actors let them down—something they are prone to do, since their calculations are not inclined to privilege particular elite actors except in special circumstances. Equally, overreliance upon authenticity is problematic in the aftermath of conflict, when the emergence of contending narratives of the nation can make the nature of the "authentic" an unstable and highly politically charged issue locally, and during a period when cultural institutions that might deliver support have their own agendas. Coming up with a story that can inspire support at home and marginalize contending stories, without putting off donors, requires a mastery of the art of political manipulation of the sort that Hun Sen has amply demonstrated over the past fifteen years, but that Mari Alkatiri, between 2002 and 2006, did not.

GATEKEEPING: SEDUCTIONS AND REJECTIONS

In 1998, the mandate of the government brought to power by the UNTAC (United Nations Transitional Authority in Cambodia) elections expired, and new elections were held, this time organized by a newly established Cambodian election agency. The elections were held in a climate of violence and intense distrust among parties, following closely upon the battle in Phnom Penh in 1997, in which the two coalition partners, CPP (Cambodian People's Party) and FUNCINPEC (Front Uni National pour un Cambodge Indépendent, Neutre, Pacifique, et Coopératif, National United Front for an Independent, Neutral, Peaceful, and Cooperative Cambodia) had turned on one another. FUNCINPEC politicians, along with colleagues from the opposition Sam Rainsy Party (SRP), with whom they had concluded an alliance, returned from Bangkok, the haven to which they had fled in 1997, to participate in the elections. The July fighting had delivered the armed forces directly into the hands of the CPP, which had denounced FUNCINPEC and the SRP as national traitors, spies, and agents provocateurs. It seemed unlikely in this setting that the military would accept a transfer of power to either of these parties following the elections, despite Hun Sen's assertion that he, personally, would step down if defeated. There was much speculation locally about what would happen and what the "internationals" might be counted upon to do in this circumstance. One elderly FUNCINPEC supporter encountered on the campaign trail speculated: "I heard that the day before the election, the internationals are going to take all the politicians out of the country, and only the winners will be allowed to come back."[1] It was as good an idea as any.

In fact, the CPP won the election, although by a slender margin and with insufficient votes to rule alone. Following the elections, opposition supporters—some frightened, some angry—gathered in Phnom Penh both to seek refuge from anticipated CPP reprisals against them in the villages and to complain about an election process they suspected had been fraudulent. A sit-in protest ensued in front of the national assembly building that turned into something more akin to a refugee camp and remained in place for three weeks.

In addresses to party supporters and the crowd at the protest site, Prince Ranariddh and Sam Rainsy, leaders of FUNCINPEC and the SRP respectively, made the following remarks:

> I would like to tell you that the United States, now, is the only superpower in the world … Only the US is a superpower, in terms of money and in terms of weapons. And America is a real democratic country. The US Congress helps Cambodian democrats very much … Recently a powerful US Senator wrote a letter to Secretary of State for Foreign Affairs Madeleine Albright, warning that America should not recognize the [would-be CPP] government that stole the vote … [Reads the letter in English and translates.] We have the big one to support us! … This is not me speaking. This is the message from the US. "We are

---

[1] Noted in my field notes, Lvea Aem District, Kandal Province, June 1998.

leaders of the free world"—that means they don't support us right or wrong, they support us because we are right—"in the struggle for freedom." They stand with Cambodian people … [He translates further.] Long live the US! … The superpower does not agree [with the victory of the CPP], and they may storm in. Only the US can send planes and arrest the president of another country. In Panama, they stormed in and arrested the president and kept him in the US. Noriega was sentenced to jail for forty-four years in the US. So he's already forty years old, and he has to stay in jail for forty years, so maybe he'll die there.[2]

A few weeks later, Sam Rainsy expanded on this point in a speech to demonstrators outside the National Assembly Building:

What are the Americans waiting for? Send the special air forces and remove Tuol Krasang [Hun Sen's home and bodyguard base in Kandal]. When the Americans waged war in Iraq, they didn't have to send their armed forces in on foot. They just sent their air forces, aircraft that can fly very fast, that are invisible because they fly very high, equipped with laser missiles … Hun Sen is a terrorist, so there is no point in America waiting any longer. Please fly in the planes to attack Tuol Krasang.[3]

Though fantastic, these claims were not entirely incredible. The year 1998 saw the US bombing of Kosovo, Afghanistan, and Iraq as the prelude to the wave of non-UN interventions that continued up to the invasion of Iraq in 2003. In 1998, it was as yet unclear whether Hun Sen's security crackdown would be successful or whether the Khmer Rouge insurgency was really over. By the time the 1998 elections were held in Cambodia, the majority of donors would breathe a sigh of relief and validate the results with unseemly haste, but the Americans, who had insisted on their own independent election-monitoring exercise, instead played hard to get. With key senators, whose constituencies in the US included thousands of active expatriate SRP and FUNCINPEC supporters, taking an interest in Cambodia's affairs, it was possible that the US government might exert serious pressure on the CPP to offer a new candidate for the prime ministerial post, in place of Hun Sen.

In Phnom Penh, a stronghold of opposition support, the prospect of an American invasion was taken seriously and viewed with apparent excitement. Students demonstrated outside embassies and the European Commission headquarters, appealing to international officials to reject the election results. Demonstrators raised placards in English, with messages like "UN and US Must Save Cambodia." A leaflet circulated stating:

Bill Clinton … has decided to save the Khmer people on the basis of the request of the US Congress. This action will help to liberate Cambodia, and the Cambodian people, from dictator Hun Sen, the puppet of the Vietnamese … Submarines are now ready to be deployed. So are battleships that carry all types

[2] Prince Ranariddh, speech to party supporters, FUNCINPEC Headquarters, Phnom Penh, August 8, 1998, recorded and translated by Caroline Hughes and Sok Ty.

[3] Sam Rainsy, speech to demonstrators, Democracy Square, Phnom Penh, August 26, 1998, recorded and translated by Caroline Hughes and Sok Ty.

of aircraft and armed troops. They will act in cooperation to arrest Hun Sen and his group to be sentenced for crimes against humanity.[4]

Much of Phnom Penh waited breathlessly for liberation.

Of course, there was no deployment of submarines, and it is extremely unlikely that Rainsy or Ranariddh believed their own rhetoric. Yet these statements and the tactics that accompanied them were a staple of opposition politics in 1990s Cambodia. Rainsy, in particular, and Ranariddh, on occasions when he was out of power, spent much time traveling the world, testifying before the Senate Foreign Relations Committee in the US, appealing to multilateral organizations and INGOs for assistance, and addressing bilateral donors on the urgent need to establish conditions that the new Cambodian government would be required to fulfill. While the purpose of international agencies in sending UNTAC to Cambodia had been to assist with the repatriation of Cambodian politics to Cambodian soil, Rainsy and Ranariddh devoted much energy to trying to make sure Cambodia's political condition remained a global concern, for two related reasons. First, Rainsy and Ranariddh hoped to undermine the international legitimacy of the Hun Sen government, thus putting pressure on the patronage networks that underpinned it and prompting internal dissent within the CPP. Cracks within the shadow state system could offer opportunities to the opposition to strengthen their presence in certain areas of rural Cambodia.

Second, the opposition representatives hoped that if they could mobilize an international show of support for their own position as political players, they could display this accomplishment to villagers as a means of overcoming their main image problem: the perception that they were weak compared with the strong CPP. This was an unsuccessful strategy, in part because it was based on a misreading of the degree of international engagement and concern. Donors desired the promotion of neoliberal governance in Cambodia; but cordoning off Cambodian politics within Cambodia's borders was their first priority. They were not willing to invest the additional effort required to trigger regime change, with the associated risk of renewed refugee flows and broader instability. Gestures of international support were made following the fighting of 1997—UN monitors were dispatched to follow opposition politicians as they campaigned and to monitor their safety, and the US ambassador attended a couple of opposition party rallies. However, while opposition candidates trusted that these actions demonstrated real support for their cause, the international community understood them to be essentially token gestures.

More importantly, this political strategy of citing and seeking international support was also unsuccessful because it failed to take into account the extremely slender connection between the international sphere and Cambodia's villages. International engagement, since UNTAC, had been more important to Cambodian politicians for its image than for its actual effectiveness. During the early stages of the UNTAC era, the former resistance parties were able to capitalize on the feeling that there was a new player in town: that the "international community" constituted a real and present advocate for individuals promoting change. UNTAC representatives were visible across the country, visiting government and new NGO

---

[4] Leaflet, circulated by demonstrators in Phnom Penh, September 1998, translated by Caroline Hughes.

offices, driving large cars, and promising change via Radio UNTAC broadcasts. While many voters came to feel that the initial promise of UNTAC had not been fulfilled, there was no doubt that UNTAC represented a new force in the country. The voters' faith that they had the option of delivering electoral victory to FUNCINPEC in 1993 arose in large part from UNTAC's presence.

However, this effect was fleeting. Cambodians' faith that UNTAC could effectively change the nation's politics declined precipitously during the period of the UNTAC's presence in Cambodia and did not last into the era of aid dependence. By the time UNTAC departed, Hun Sen was back in power, as second prime minister, and FUNCINPEC had done little to capitalize on its election victory. Indeed, for the next three years, many rural voters went back to business as usual. Little aid percolated down to the rural level in the first years of reconstruction; although farming received a boost from land distribution and improved security in some areas, economic growth beyond an immediate peace dividend was largely confined to urban centers. The National Assembly deputies elected in the 1993 election found they much preferred Phnom Penh to the campaign trail. The war did not end, although its intensity lessened in many parts of the country, and local-level officials did not change as a result of the elections. Aside from the appearance of the occasional NGO staff member, and some repairs to the main roads, life changed very little. The risks taken by citizens who had voted for FUNCINPEC in the election did not appear to have paid off, particularly when renewed fighting between FUNCINPEC and CPP broke out in 1997.

For those members of the elite who came from the resistance movement into government in 1993, however, the situation looked very different. They had long relied upon international assistance in their struggle against "communists," and their status had been transformed by the UNTAC operation. Now, in addition to enjoying diplomatic recognition, they had posts in a real, functioning, aid-receiving state. They sat in parliament, made and listened to speeches, plotted political maneuvers against one another, took bribes in many cases, and distributed patronage. They observed the emergence of a stratum of NGO representatives in Phnom Penh who engaged regularly and actively in international events. They addressed donors at Consultative Group meetings, in which donors expressed concern over particular political developments. By 1996, however, it became apparent that this internationally sponsored arena of "multiparty democracy," in which international support could be used to pressure and balance the power of the CPP, was confined to certain forums in Phnom Penh and was not spreading outwards. Complaints began to build that the government posts given to FUNCINPEC did not translate into real power, even within the ministries, let alone across the rural heartland.

In March 1996, Ranariddh denounced the power-sharing agreement, claiming FUNCINPEC's role was merely that of "first puppet prime minister, puppet vice-prime minister, puppet ministers, puppet governors, and deputy governors,"[5] in a reference to FUNCINPEC's impotence in affecting governance. He threatened to withdraw FUNCINPEC from the coalition if real power-sharing were not instituted throughout the state organization, to the local level. The CPP reacted by threatening use of armed force in the event of a FUNCINPEC withdrawal.

---

[5] Prince Ranariddh, quoted in Jason Barber and Ker Munthit, "'Puppet' Ranariddh Lashes Coalition," *Phnom Penh Post*, April 5–18, 1996, p. 10.

For both parties, real power at the local level was essential for getting out the vote as the 1998 elections approached. FUNCINPEC's concern was that, within the villages, unelected but powerful village, commune, and district chiefs openly supported and campaigned for the CPP while intimidating FUNCINPEC supporters. In denouncing the CPP's local control, FUNCINPEC attacked an aspect of the CPP that had constituted one of its traditional strengths—its politicized administrative network, which covered almost all Cambodian territory and which ensured CPP dominance in village politics.

A pro-CPP White Paper on the July 1997 fighting, produced by the Ministry of Foreign Affairs and International Cooperation, claimed later that CPP's advantage in the local areas was due to FUNCINPEC's own failure to "party build":

> In early 1996, FUNCINPEC faced a bad situation. Since 1993, it had done little in the way of party building. It had not held a party congress since 1992. Few of its officials engaged in outreach to the provinces. In some areas of the country, it did not exist at all ... [6]

This criticism is partly justified. While FUNCINPEC retained supporters, these supporters were neither organized nor active locally, nor were they securely linked to the party center, a state of affairs that was partly due to FUNCINPEC's failure to maintain and develop organizationally the momentum of support it had engendered during the 1993 election campaign. Ranariddh himself, at the start of the 1998 election campaign, admitted that FUNCINPEC had "forgotten" its local organizers during the years of the coalition government.[7] The White Paper contrasts FUNCINPEC's inactivity in this area with the busy efforts of the CPP and Hun Sen:

> As a political party, [the CPP] was active in every province of the country. In 1995, the CPP and Samdech Hun Sen initiated rural development programs designed to help meet the basic needs of the people. The CPP had promoted humanitarian programs to assist flood victims. It had strengthened its position in the government. In short, it was well prepared for the next election.[8]

However, it was also the case that the CPP had consolidated its power at the local level in a deliberate bid to exclude other parties. The SRP, when it tried to open offices in the provinces, found that its staff members were attacked and its signboards pulled down and shot at by local authorities. Efforts by the SRP to call international attention to these events met with limited success, although, after the crisis of 1997, a letter signed by Hun Sen under pressure from the UN and foreign diplomats guaranteed that all candidates be granted unimpeded access to rural Cambodia, and these guarantees were monitored by UN staff as a condition for international recognition of the 1998 elections.

Overall, politicians' attempts to engage an "international community" represented desperation rather than a winning strategy. The opposition hoped that

---

[6] Ministry of Foreign Affairs and International Cooperation, "White Paper, Background on the July 1997 Crisis: Prince Ranariddh's Strategy of Provocation," Phnom Penh, July 9, 1997, p. 2.

[7] Prince Ranariddh, speech to supporters, Ta Khmau, Kandal Province, May 27, 1998, recorded and translated by Caroline Hughes and Stephen Tong.

[8] Ministry of Foreign Affairs, July 9, 1997, p. 2.

UN monitors would be regarded as powerful backers, thereby shifting the balance of power within the country, in a situation where the military was clearly backing the CPP. A key question among voters in the 1998 election was how an opposition victory might be translated into effective control of the country, and especially control of the armed forces, which, since 1997, had been clearly loyal to the CPP. In portraying themselves as gatekeepers for UN or American intervention, opposition leaders proffered one answer to their own dilemma. Continued emphasis on international support was thus essential to encourage voters to support the opposition, first in elections and then in demonstrations, even though the likelihood of that support materializing was small.

For Sam Rainsy, in particular, his continued reference to international actors was a way of presenting himself as a link to a wider world of Western-style democracy, where things were done differently, and better, than they were in the world of Hun Sen's Cambodia. Hun Sen's Cambodia was portrayed not as outside of the global system, but as caught up in its sinister underbelly—trapped in the violence and criminality of the borderlands. Much of Rainsy's election campaigning focused on his ability—by virtue of his alleged access to American support, his understanding of international law, and his familiarity with the reputable systems of "progressive" (*choeun loeun*) countries—to drag Cambodia out of the twilight zone and into the light of democratic capitalism. In the 1998 election, this campaign message involved calling for direct US intervention. In the 2003 election, Rainsy compared Cambodia unfavorably with the Philippines, which had recently jailed Joseph Estrada, and Thailand, a "progressive" country with "real efficiency [*prosetthapheap*], where their national assembly, their courts, their commission against corruption work very well."[9] Cambodia, Rainsy claimed, had been designated a "mafia state" by the US; he claimed that corrupt CPP-aligned elites had expropriated US$400 million a year and stashed it in offshore bank accounts. One of Rainsy's key electoral claims was that, should his party win the election, it would resort to international law to reclaim expropriated money and distribute it to the people:

> We will force the banks that have the money of the corrupt group of people, we will force them via international law to send back the money that the corrupt group has stolen from the country and sent all over the place—the Sam Rainsy government will find the money and bring it back in order to rebuild the country, restore the Khmer people, and rebuild the people and the nation.[10]

In this statement, Rainsy portrayed himself as the antithesis of Hun Sen. While promoting himself as a repository of international knowledge and a representative of enlightened international opinion, he portrayed Hun Sen as internationally reviled, as a communist anachronism, and as a gangster reliant upon organized crime and, in a perennial refrain, Vietnamese power:

> If we still have Hun Sen, I firmly believe that our country will increasingly suffer, the people will be increasingly poor, corruption will be increasingly

---

[9] Sam Rainsy, responses to callers, "Election Call-In Show," broadcast on FM 102, July 2003, recorded by FM 102, transcribed by Ritthy Duong, translated by Caroline Hughes.

[10] Ibid.

heavy, the *yuon*[11] will take more and more Khmer land, the *yuon* will increasingly pour into Cambodia, because Mr. Hun Sen is the representative of one regime that is old, that destroys the country, that serves foreigners … [12]

The strategy of claiming that domestic problems are the result of misaligned international relations, to be resolved by appeal to international institutions, is a long-standing feature of Cambodian politics. However, its utility to politicians such as Rainsy in the post-Cold War era faded fast. This message played well in Phnom Penh, where evidence of international intervention and concern was—and is still—ubiquitous, in the large numbers of foreign personnel and the blue-signposted offices of international agencies, and where the impact of an international presence since 1993 continues to be great, economically and socially as well as politically. However, from the perspective of residents in the rural villages, the international community seemed a long way away, while the commune chief's office loomed large.

CONTENDING AUTHENTICITIES: VIETNAMIZATION VS. REBUILDING

Sam Rainsy's desire to drag Cambodia out of its backwardness and isolation reflected the ways in which he, like many others in the resistance, had perceived Cambodian experience during the 1980s. The idea that Cambodia had been "Vietnamized" during those years offered resistance members a role in rediscovering a form of Khmer authenticity that had not been tainted by Vietnamese domination, and had, in fact, been improved by exposure to the Western world.[13] Returnees such as Sam Rainsy presented themselves as capable of both restoring and transforming Cambodia, ridding it of Vietnamese corruption, and modernizing the country so that it could again take its place in a world of modern nation-states. In conveying this message, the returnees posited a claim of authenticity by promising to act as guardians of an authentic Khmerness that had been nurtured in the free air of the diaspora and on the border, out of reach of Vietnamization. This claim directly undermined a key plank supporting the CPP's legitimacy: that the CPP had been the author of Cambodia's "second birth" following the destruction of the Democratic Kampuchea (DK) era, and that, during the period in the 1980s when it had ruled over most of Khmer territory exclusively, the CPP had successfully restored key elements in Cambodian society, including families, temples, festivals, farming practices, and schools.

The differences between the opposition's and the CPP's views of history, and their importance to Cambodian politics as the country emerged from the war, were expressed in three related disputes. One was the dispute over the January 7 holiday. This holiday, commemorating the fall of Phnom Penh to National Salvation Front and Vietnamese forces in 1979, was established in the 1980s. After 1993, returning resistance politicians objected to it, on the grounds that January 7, 1979, was not a day of "liberation," as it had always been commemorated, but was the start of the

---

[11] "Yuon" is a colloquial Khmer term for Vietnamese, commonly used in a derogatory way.

[12] Rainsy, responses to callers, "Election Call-In Show," July 2003.

[13] This is discussed in detail in Caroline Hughes, "Democracy, Culture, and the Politics of Gate-Keeping: the Transnation Returns Home," in *State/Nation/Transnation: Perspectives on Transnationalism in the Asia-Pacific*, ed. Brenda Yeoh and Katie Willis (London: Routledge, 2004), pp 197–217.

disaster and humiliation brought about by Cambodia's subjugation to Vietnamese rule. The CPP, however, fiercely defended the holiday's status, motivated by the centrality of the date to the myth of the CPP's founding role in the reborn Khmer nation. The result was the continued official observance of the January 7 holiday, accompanied by annual denunciations, boycotts, and, sometimes, protests by members of the opposition.

A second dispute was over the portrayal of the war in schoolbooks. Textbooks from the 1980s had reflected the CPP view of the DK regime, complete with line drawings of DK soldiers killing babies. In the early 1990s, in deference to the participation of the Party of Democratic Kampuchea in the peace accords, these books were withdrawn. From 1993 to 2002, the question of how to portray both the DK era and the subsequent rule of the Vietnamese-backed government remained highly sensitive. A new history textbook containing an account of the DK years was finally published and made available to students after a long delay, in 2002. The new book endorsed the status of January 7 as "liberation day" and characterized the resistance as follows:

> After liberation, the genocidal clique escaped into the jungle and brought insecurity to the people. With the support of the UN, the US, China, and Thailand, the guerrilla forces fought against the government and Vietnamese forces. Guerrilla forces cooperated and formed a front headed by Prince Norodom Sihanouk. The guerrilla group sat in Cambodia's seat at the UN, and the US and China persuaded ASEAN countries not to form relationships with Indochinese countries.[14]

After just a few months, the new book was withdrawn in response to complaints from FUNCINPEC. FUNCINPEC's specific complaint was that the new book did not mention FUNCINPEC's election victory in 1993. Instead, the textbook stated merely:

> On October 23, 1991, the Paris Peace Agreement was signed. Representatives of all factions shook hands and agreed to have a general election supervised by UNTAC. Although the Khmer Rouge boycotted the 1993 election, it was held as planned. Twenty political parties took part. A constitution was adopted on September 24, 1993, from which a royal government was formed.[15]

The 1998 election is described in more detail:

> The royal government faced a number of secessionist zones controlled by the Khmer Rouge. Unfinished war, insecurity, and political instability continued in the country. [In accordance with] national reconciliation principles, these problems were abolished and the second mandate of the royal government, headed by Samdech Hun Sen as prime minister, was formed on November 30, 1998. An election was organized by Cambodians on July 26, 1998. Cambodia

---

[14] These extracts are taken from a translation provided by Pin Sisovann, "A Delicate History," *Cambodia Daily Weekend*, March 23–24, 2002, online at http://www.camnet.com.kh/cambodia.daily/selected_features/textbook.htm, accessed October 21, 2008.

[15] Ibid.

achieved national unity and political stability, without secessionist zones. People throughout the country lived safely and in peace.[16]

This account closely accords with the CPP's interpretation of their own key role in bringing peace to the country. FUNCINPEC's refusal to accept this story as authoritative prompted the removal of the new books. The result is that, with the exception of a few months in 2002, the history of the DK era has not been taught in the Cambodian curriculum for the last sixteen years.[17]

A third dispute related to the question of Vietnamese immigrants in Cambodia. The resistance claimed that the 1980s and 1990s saw the influx of up to two million Vietnamese into Cambodia; that these illegal settlers were given Cambodian identity cards by corrupt local officials; and that the immigrants' illegal votes were used to ensure that democratic elections expressed the will, not of the Khmer—who were attributed with a strong desire for an opposition victory—but of "Hanoi." Claims that Vietnamese were voting in Cambodian elections were raised repeatedly in elections from 1993. These complaints prompted the opposition parties to mobilize supporters to wait outside polling stations and, if possible, forcibly prevent anyone who looked, sounded, or was suspected of being Vietnamese from voting. Voters who exhibited a poor knowledge of Khmer history when questioned were considered suspicious. These activities were associated with consistent designation of the CPP, by opposition newspapers and politicians, as *ayong yuon*—Vietnamese puppets.

The question of authenticity was closely tied to the longstanding rhetoric of national disappearance. The CPP was portrayed not only as corrupting Khmer culture but as permitting gradual Vietnamese annexation of Khmer land. This was a potentially explosive political issue. In 2005, Hun Sen struck a controversial deal with Vietnam over the status of the border, prompting an outcry among nationalists, including human rights workers and trade unionists, at home. Their criticisms evidently hit the mark: Hun Sen responded by having the protestors thrown in jail.

Concern over these three issues—January 7, textbooks, and Vietnamese voters—is politically decisive, however, only among the Cambodian elite and the urban electorate. The opposition's assertions regarding Vietnam's annexationist ambitions possessed a mythical resonance bestowed by memories of decades, if not centuries, of similar concern in Cambodian politics. However, from 1993, despite the lingering tensions and fears produced by these disputes, the opposition has not been successful in winning an election; indeed, the CPP's share of the vote increased between 1993 and 2003, with decreasing reliance upon overt intimidation or violence. The opposition's approach to questions of national identity and aspiration has remained trapped in wartime rhetoric and has been largely abstract, divorced from

---

[16] Ibid.

[17] In 2007, a new history book was produced by a Cambodian author on the DK period, but although it responded to government concerns by employing "neutral" language, was endorsed by the government, and was made freely available to teachers and libraries, it was not specifically incorporated into the school curriculum. Ker Munthit, "New Text Gives Cambodians Glimpse of Khmer Rouge Period," *International Herald Tribune*, June 18, 2007, online at http://www.iht.com/articles/2007/06/18/news/cambo.php?page=2, accessed September 20, 2007. The book can be downloaded in English at http://www.dccam.org/Publication/Monographs/Part1.pdf and http://www.dccam.org/Publication/Monographs/Part2.pdf, accessed May 21, 2008.

the real life of the village. Meanwhile, the government has promoted its own account of authenticity, which has proved far more powerful in the rural context than that of the opposition by virtue of the fact that it played on the realm of everyday experience rather than the realm of legends and stories. For the CPP, authenticity was articulated in terms of the immediate power (*omnaach*) to control and defend the country. This power was something that the CPP had continually demonstrated since 1979, and which formed the mainstay of its political position.

The CPP strongly promoted the idea that the strength and solidity of the party assured the strength and solidity of the nation, and contrasted their competence favorably with the weak and insubstantial nature of the opposition, which, they claimed, tended to abandon both the land and the people when things got tough and seek shelter in other countries. Hun Sen stated in a major speech in 1996:

> If we want to take responsibility for the nation's fate, we must be responsible before the people ... We must dare to take responsibility, to live and die with the people. Don't say you are Khmer when it is easy and "American" when it is difficult.[18]

The disparagement of returnees as "part-time Khmers" who maintained second passports so they could leave if life became uncomfortable has been a consistent refrain for the CPP. The CPP defines itself as the party that remained with the people throughout, providing aid and combating enemies. This is a claim that is at once both reassuring and menacing, and is highly successful in capturing the rural vote. This message has attained force by virtue of the fact that the history of post-DK Cambodia has indeed been characterized by the periodic flight of opposition-party leaders, who have sought international support when under pressure from the CPP at home. Although this political strategy has been effective in preserving the lives and liberty of opposition party leaders, it has not done much either to reassure their followers or to establish these leaders as authentic challengers who might be able to claim and handle real power in the country.

For the opposition, the seductions of representing themselves as gatekeepers have undermined the specifically nationalist claims to authenticity that, in the early 1990s, were quite compelling locally. The CPP's success in developing its own sphere of discretionary action and the opposition's own mistaken belief that they could harness international donor power to win support for their party combined to undercut the opposition's options for maneuvering; by the mid-1990s, the opposition parties were divided and weakened, defeated militarily, and their organizational presence was largely confined to the urban centers, from where they competed at a severe disadvantage in local elections when these finally took place, in accord with the CPP's timetable, in 2002. As a result, these parties have appeared increasingly remote to rural people.

International support has kept most opposition leaders safe and preserved a facade of multiparty democracy at the national level. Crucially, however, at the same time, national-level politics has been gradually drained of significance by twin

---

[18] Hun Sen, speech, Phnom Penh Medical Training School, April 27, 1996, extract published in "Hun Sen: Live and Die with the People," *Phnom Penh Post* April 12–May 3, 1996, online at http://www.phnompenhpost.com/index.php/1996050319154/National-news/Hun-Sen-Live-and-die-with-the-people.html, accessed September 20, 2008.

strategies employed by the CPP: their cooptation of national institutions via policies of patronage and pressure, and their energetic promotion of the villages as the key site for development and reform—a local orientation that has increasingly been embraced with enthusiasm by international actors, also. The opposition's claims to authenticity in representing the nation cannot be translated into political power because the opposition has only a nebulous presence. Leaders frequently have to leave the country for their own safety, as well as for the fundraising and diplomatic lobbying that keep their parties viable. In the villages, opposition supporters are marginalized. The CPP, by contrast, has increasingly interposed itself successfully as a channel between international donations and local recipients. CPP leaders devote much of their time, especially in election years, to inauguration events for development projects, thus linking themselves with a form of international assistance that is less connected with fairy tales of national glory than with the real and immediate concerns of how rice will be irrigated and children educated.

A survey of voter attitudes conducted by the Asia Foundation in 2003 found that 30 percent of all Cambodian voters cast their ballots for parties they believed could "get things done," while an additional 24 percent voted for parties they believed could "keep the peace." In 2008, a survey by the International Republican Institute found that more than three-quarters of the population believed the country was "headed in the right direction." Asked why they thought so, more than three-quarters cited "more roads built" while almost two-thirds cited "more schools built."[19] These figures show that voters have become less interested in the nationalist mythology that brought so much disaster in the past and more interested in the everyday politics of what happens in the village. The CPP has both promoted and mastered this realm with a politics that links its claims to authenticity with an inescapable organizational presence and activity at the local level. As one local CPP official in a remote commune summed up in an interview in 2003:

> As for the people, now they understand a little bit about democracy. When we tell them they understand a bit. Seventy percent can't read. The children don't go to school. But they know about democracy, about the party that they love. They can see which party comes to help them. Big people come—then the people vote as they see. Who comes to solve their problems, build roads, build schools?[20]

Under conditions of aid dependence, the content of Cambodian political debate has been reduced to two essential issues: which party is most likely to be able to channel at least some aid to the villages effectively and reliably, and which party is able to maintain order most effectively? Caught between the stiff debates on health-care priorities and the anachronistic posturing of an opposition that cites abstract myths of Khmerness and monarchism, deliberation over real issues of historical injustice and future aspiration have been squeezed out of Cambodian politics. The cooptation of policy issues by donors, and the highly atomizing forms of procedural democracy promoted by them, have undercut the nation's potential to expand and

---

[19] International Republican Institute, "Survey of Cambodian Public Opinion," January 27-February 26, 2008, power point presentation, online at http://www.iri.org/asia/cambodia/2008%20May%2027%20Survey%20of%20Cambodian%20Public%20Opinion,%20January%2027-February%2026,%202008.pdf, accessed September 16, 2008.

[20] Commune chief (CPP), Ta Khaen Commune, Chuuk District, Kampot Province, personal interview, Ta Khaen, June 2003.

deepen larger debates about the distribution of actual existing resources in the name of social progress. In this sterile environment, the CPP's ability to reserve slush funds for distribution in the form of rural roads and schools proves decisive in eliciting voter loyalty. Efforts by the opposition to cultivate constituencies that could offer them the potential for representation of genuine interests, such as their effort to establish a relationship with the Free Trade Union, have been stifled by direct donor action. As a result, the politics that reaches down to the village is reduced to the issues of welfare and riot control—issues that the CPP has astutely made its own. The problem with this limited political discourse is that it offers little prospect for the revitalization of civic life, the control of corruption, or the tackling of inequality. As the next chapter will discuss, this is an uninspiring politics that has given rise to widespread alienation.

LUSOPHONE FEVER: FRETILIN AND THE LANGUAGE QUESTION

East Timor, like Cambodia, faced a postwar situation in which elites were divided into two camps: the homegrown and the internationally nurtured. The FRETILIN (Frente Revolucionária de Timor-Leste Independente, The Revolutionary Front for an Independent East Timor) external delegation—including Mari Alkatiri, Roque Rodrigues, Rogerio Lobato, Anna Pessoa, and Jose Luis Guterres, all of whom were shortly to figure in high-profile government posts—and the diplomatic front of the CNRT (Congresso Nacional da Reconstrução de Timor, National Congress for the Reconstruction of East Timor), personified by Jose Ramos-Horta, came back to East Timor in 1999 after twenty-five years in exile.

For the returnees, the situation they faced was in some ways similar to that faced by Cambodian resistance fighters who had gone into exile and later returned. Although FRETILIN did not have to contend with the highly organized and intransigent opposition that FUNCINPEC and the SRP confronted in Cambodia, it did have to deal with the decidedly unsympathetic and populist CNRT leadership, not to mention a vibrant array of independent and activist movements and institutions in society, and, following UNTAET's (United Nations Transitional Administration in East Timor) departure, an unfolding economic disaster. Both FRETILIN and FUNCINPEC could trade upon the nationalist image burnished by the resistance, which awarded them widespread recognition and a certain amount of access to resistance networks, although these were in both cases difficult to monitor and maintain. In both East Timor and Cambodia, this advantage was decisive in delivering initial election victories, although both these party alliances also subsequently found their position between an international sphere of donors and supporters and a local sphere of electors difficult to maintain past the first election cycle, a shared dilemma that ultimately led to the collapse of their electoral support.

Both the Cambodian opposition and the FRETILIN government in Timor-Leste faced charismatic opponents for whom authenticity was the central concern: in Timor, Xanana Gusmão emerged as the champion of the man-in-the-street by virtue of his years in the jungle and his close personal associations with the military leadership—all qualities he shared with Hun Sen.[21] Both these leaders also were not

---

[21] Samantha Power, in her recent biography of Sergio Vieira de Mello, claims that Hun Sen personally warned Xanana Gusmão and Jose Ramos-Horta against placing too much faith in the UN's legacy. This exchange reportedly took place in a chance meeting as the three of them happened to stand next to one another in a line waiting to meet US President Bill Clinton in

averse to criticizing foreign powers publicly, demanding recognition of the local people's contribution to ending conflict and demanding that local citizens have a say in the running of the country. Whereas for Hun Sen this stance reflects genuine suspicion of foreign intervention, Xanana was close to the UN, and particularly to Special Representative Sergio Vieira de Mello throughout the period of UNTAET administration. Yet, Xanana gained significant prestige at home through his championing of the cause of Timorization during the transition period. He appeared to reject explicitly a post-independence arrangement that would award the new government the trappings, but not the substance, of power, famously scorning, in one speech, a "legacy of cars and laws … of development plans for the future designed by [people] other than East Timorese."[22]

The FRETILIN government, by contrast, focused on building a central state that could deal with international donors, and elevated this concern as equal to the business of promoting reconstruction in the villages. An extract from a speech made by Mari Alkatiri in 2006 suggests this preoccupation:

> In three years, we have managed what other States take decades to achieve, and often in a shy way: we have a functional structure of State and respect for the law is a reality. In short: We have a State![23]

Alkatiri went on to list the ways in which the State of Timor-Leste might assist the people; yet FRETILIN would eventually founder in large part because the state institutions it established were more focused upon centralizing power than on distributing resources. Although the government made some very important gains in difficult circumstances, such as the reestablishment of functioning health and education systems, the level of public participation in state decision making was low and did not extend beyond elections. FRETILIN justified the establishment of the rule of law in terms of providing security to foreign investors, but this logic failed to impress much of the population because of the extreme inaccessibility of the court system to the majority of the citizens. The Petroleum Fund—the *"crème de la crème"* of state institutions, as Alkatiri called it in this speech—was similarly concerned with making funds inaccessible, rather than accessible, to the majority of the population; it was concerned with saving rather than spending. This was a highly technocratic approach designed to facilitate the capture of external resources rather than the grooming of domestic constituencies. As such, it pleased the donors. However, in the context of rapid economic decline, such technocratic claims rang distinctly hollow in the ears of the local population.

The technical knowledge of the outside world was regarded as necessary to reconstruct essential services, and both Alkatiri and Xanana frequently suggested that the need to harness this knowledge and gain external support necessitated unpopular moves at home. Xanana was able to use external pressures as a

---

New York in September 1999. Samantha Power, *Chasing the Flame: Sergio Vieira de Mello and the Fight to Save the World* (New York, NY: Penguin Press, 2008), p. 299.

[22] Xanana Gusmão, speech, quoted in *East Timor Observatory*, "Transition: Halfway to Independence," November 6, 2000, online at http://members.tip.net.au/~wildwood/NovTrans.htm, accessed September 20, 2007.

[23] Mari Alkatiri, "Decision Time," speech at the opening session of the Timor-Leste and Development Partners Meeting, Dili, April 4, 2006, online at http://www.Primeministerand cabinet.gov.tp/speeches.htm, accessed September 20, 2007.

justification for thwarting domestic interests, to an extent, because he was regarded by many as a man of the people. For example, he successfully rejected demands for a process that would deliver justice to victims of atrocities in 1999, a proposal that was widely demanded within Timor and recommended by the CAVR (Comissão de Acolhimento, Verdade, e Reconciliação de Timor-Leste, Timor-Leste Reception, Truth, and Reconciliation Commission) report. Xanana rejected the report's recommendations on the basis that pursuing close relations with Indonesia was more important than seeking justice for victims, an unpopular move that was tolerated because of his moral authority inherited from the war. Alkatiri lacked such moral authority and made rather little effort to court his people following his return to Timor. Consequently, even though Xanana, as much as Alkatiri, worked with foreign intervenors and bowed to foreign interests, it was Alkatiri who was criticized as a tool of foreign powers when he responded to external pressures in a manner that was severely detrimental to politically important constituencies at home.

Despite Alkatiri's official position as head of the first Timorese government and leader of by far the largest, best organized, and most recognized party in Timor-Leste, he faced a formidable political challenge in attempting to overcome the limits of his "returnee" status. Like Sam Rainsy in Cambodia, he portrayed his years of exile as having awarded him experience that could benefit the country. Like returnees in Cambodia, he attempted to assert the relevance of the experience of exile by claiming that those who had lived outside the country had been educated in the technical aspects of nation-building and also enjoyed a cultural authenticity that had not been tainted by years of occupation in the homeland itself. Like many returnees in Cambodia, he found that this position did not go down at all well with a good proportion of the locals.

The key cultural question in Timor, which pitted the group of former exiles directly against those sections of the population that had been educated under the Indonesian occupation, was the question of the official language. In line with longstanding FRETILIN policy, the constitutional council adopted Portuguese, along with Tetum,[24] as the national language of independent Timor-Leste. Portuguese was to be privileged, over the short term at least, in view of the "backwardness" of Tetum, which required "development and standardization" before it could be used officially.

The language question bound the issues of gatekeeping and of authenticity tightly together. Two broad defenses of Portuguese were raised: first, the idea that the use of Portuguese would tie Timor into the Lusophone community, thus awarding access to different kinds of assistance and aid; and, second, the idea that Portuguese was an integral part of Timorese identity. With respect to the former, Mari Alkatiri commented:

---

[24] Tetum is one of sixteen languages spoken in Timor. It is a member of the Austronesian group of languages and comprises four variants, one of which (Tetum–Dili) emerged as the *lingua franca* during the era of Portuguese colonialism. Currently, Tetum is the mother tongue of only 6 percent of the population of Timor, but 86 percent claimed some knowledge of the language in the 2004 census. According to the 2004 census, Tetum is spoken by a majority in Dili, and in parts of Manatuto, Baucau, Manufahi, and Covalima Districts, and by a significant minority (more than 20 percent) also in parts of Ermera and Oecussi. It is the language used by the Catholic Church in Timor. It is less widely spoken in the Eastern districts, where the most common mother tongue—Fataluku—is part of the very different Papuan group of languages.

We consider our membership and inclusion in CPLP [Comunidade dos Países de Língua Portuguesa, Community of Portuguese-Speaking Countries] to be of strategic importance. This desire is naturally derived from the history and culture shared with its seven member countries—Angola, Brazil, Cape Verde, Guinea-Bissau, Mozambique, Portugal, and S. Tome e Principe—and the sharing of a common language and the sentiments expressed by the use of this language. There are also other reasons. We will not forget that these countries were the oasis of solidarity in the desert for the Resistance for many long years. To us, it is a membership of strategic importance that extends the frontiers of East Timor far beyond its geographic borders.

The Lusophone community had harbored the exiles and lobbied on their behalf during the occupation. Alkatiri himself had lived, worked, and studied in Mozambique for much of the period. Roque Rodrigues did the same in Angola. Ana Pessoa and Jose Luis Guterres lived in Lisbon as expatriates.

The ideals of nationalist leaders in Portuguese Africa had been of formative significance for FRETILIN. Jose Ramos-Horta and Alkatiri visited Mozambique and Angola in the early 1970s, and what they saw there influenced the ideologies they promoted back in Timor. When the party's name was changed from ASDT (Associação Sosial-Democrata Timorense, Timorese Social-Democratic Association) to FRETILIN in September 1974, this was a direct result of Ramos-Horta's and Alkatiri's admiration of FRELIMO (Frente de Libertação de Moçambique, Mozambique Liberation Front) in Mozambique. The Marxist orientation of the party subsequently emerged as the result of the return of radical students, such as Abilio de Araujo, from Portugal.

The international experiences of its members had an enormous impact on FRETILIN in the early 1970s. Jill Joliffe, in her 1978 history of Timor, quotes from FRETILIN policy literature at the time, which emphasized:

FRETILIN defends the policy of closer international cooperation with Portugal, Brazil, Guinea-Bissau and the future countries of Portuguese expression, as well as the countries of the geographic area in which Timor is integrated.[25]

Joliffe comments that this foreign-policy position puts regional cooperation "in the context of a rather unreal stress on the primacy of the Portuguese African colonies."[26] Remarkably, that position still stood, as far as the returnees were concerned, in 2002. Indeed, their experience of Lusophone solidarity in an otherwise pitiless world had strengthened their allegiance to the language.

With respect to the question of Timorese identity, Jose Ramos-Horta, also a defender of the Portuguese-language policy, commented that the decision "had to do with preserving East Timor's national identity," adding that "the concept of the 'people of East Timor' doesn't make sense except in the context of Portuguese colonialism."[27]

---

[25] Quoted in Jill Joliffe, *East Timor: Nationalism and Colonialism* (St Lucia: University of Queensland Press, 1978), p. 75.

[26] Ibid.

[27] Jose Ramos-Horta, "East Timor: The Challenges of Independence," lecture, St. Anthony's College, Oxford, June 10, 2002.

In fact, a preference for Portuguese as the national language was shared across party lines because it was the one thing that the Timorese elite had in common.[28] In sticking to this line, however, the returnees faced the opposition of a new constituency that had emerged within Timor-Leste in the meantime—the young generation of Bahasa speakers, who were unfamiliar with the "common language and sentiments" of the Lusophone community, but whose nationalist credentials were impressive by virtue of their participation in the clandestine resistance movement of the 1990s. In 2002, UNDP reported that only about 5 percent of the population had a good knowledge of written and spoken Portuguese—namely, people who had been educated under the colonial Portuguese system, thirty years before—although the 2004 census reported that 38 percent had some knowledge of the language.[29] Either way, since the colonial regime had paid little attention to education, the number of people educated in Portuguese represented a very small proportion of the older generation. Most of this generation had not received any education at all, and they spoke local languages along with, often, Tetum.

Education had expanded dramatically under the Indonesians, however, so that by 2002 the vast majority of educated Timorese were below the age of thirty and had been instructed in Bahasa.[30] From the perspective of this generation, there were two problems with the Lusophone policy. The attachment of national identity to the Portuguese language made no sense to them, and appeared to disparage their own nationalism, nurtured in Indonesian, as less authentic than the Portuguese variety. Their distrust of arguments favoring Portuguese was compounded by the fact that the content of the ideology imbibed from Portuguese Africa—populist and progressive—was sharply distinct from the form of nationalism imparted by the Indonesians—conservative and religious. Second, the asserted importance of the Lusophone community as an "oasis of solidarity" may have reflected the strong sentiments of those former exiles who formed one branch of the resistance, but it had had little impact on the clandestine movement at home. Events such as the visit of the Pope in 1989 were remembered as far more significant in terms of expressions of solidarity.[31] In terms of Timor-Leste's contemporary needs, the Anglophone community, which included the Australians and the Americans as well as ASEAN and the South Pacific peoples, appeared more relevant to this younger generation of nationalists.

[28] I am grateful to an anonymous reviewer at Cornell SEAP Publications for raising this point.

[29] United Nations Development Programme, *East Timor United Nations Development Assistance Framework (2003–05)*, (Dili: UNDP, 2002), p. 7. The same report suggested that about 40 percent of the population spoke Indonesian. The 2004 census found that a much higher percentage of the population over six years old—that is, 38 percent—claimed knowledge of Portuguese, while 59 percent claimed knowledge of Indonesian. However, the question asked by the census-takers in this case was a very general one—"Can you speak, read, or write in the languages below?" There was no attempt to measure competence. Direcção Nacional de Estatistica, Table 2.4, Population in Private Households, Aged Six Years or Over, by Competence in Official Languages and Sex According to Age Groups, *2004 Census*, online at http://dne.mopf.gov.tl/census/tables/national/index.htm, accessed May 22, 2008.

[30] The census suggests that in the twenty-to-thirty-year-old age group, the group that would have most benefited from Indonesian schooling, 82 percent spoke, wrote, or read Indonesian, while 45 percent spoke, wrote, or read Portuguese.

[31] From my field notes. I happened to be in Dili when Pope John Paul II died in 2005, and I saw many signs and graffiti messages that praised his contribution to Timor's liberation struggle.

This issue caused a significant split between the political elite and the urban middle class. Bahasa Indonesia was named a "working language" for the interim. However, the government showed its commitment to Portuguese through the immediate implementation of policies to promote the language. The school curriculum was changed to Portuguese, starting from primary school, even though few teachers were available to teach in the language and children arrived at school without any basis in it. Civil servants were required to study Portuguese for several hours a week. The court system immediately switched to the use of Portuguese, also. In a context in which these various institutions were still undergoing the painful process of rebuilding, and in which public servants were getting used to new and unfamiliar roles, the additional burden of being required to learn and use a new language caused a considerable amount of discontent.

Members of the professional classes charged with implementing the policy interpreted the insistence that they acquire Portuguese not merely as an unnecessary extra burden, but also as a challenge to their cultural integrity and to their fitness to participate in the project of nation-building. Many individuals in this position became convinced that this policy had been designed deliberately to exclude them and empower the political elite at their expense.

The court system was a part of the state apparatus that was hard hit by the policy. The judiciary under Indonesian rule had been entirely staffed by Indonesians, and consequently, when the Indonesians departed, nobody remained who had experience of running trials. This was the one area in which UNTAET moved swiftly to promote Timorese to positions of power. Leaflets were distributed calling for individuals with legal training to present themselves to UNTAET. As a result, about forty individuals emerged with evidence that they possessed law degrees, all from Indonesian universities. After undergoing a brief training program in Dili, these individuals were appointed as judges, prosecutors, public defenders, and private lawyers, and set to work, with the benefit of assistance from international technical advisors.

The difficulties of the situation became readily apparent. None of the newly appointed personnel had any experience of legal work, and several of the recruits, interviewed in 2005, admitted that serious problems with the court system had ensued. Backlogs of cases were stacking up, and the government had taken its own decision to prioritize judicial quality as part of its drive to create an image of modern, clean, and effective governance. As Alkatiri commented in a speech to donors: "Without a Justice that is fast, clear, and without the shadow of suspicion, we can never create the conditions for being 'invaded' by potential investors."[32]

Consequently, after 2002, the government took the controversial actions of reversing the permanent status awarded to the judges and court personnel by UNTAET, putting them on probation and requiring them to pass a written evaluation. None of the judges, prosecutors, or defenders passed the test. As a result, they were stripped of their positions pending their successful completion of a two-and-a-half-year training course, to be run by international judges recruited from Portuguese-speaking countries around the world. This policy alienated the struggling court personnel.

One judge interviewed summed up the very real dilemma faced by the government as it attempted to revamp the new justice system:

---

[32] Mari Alkatiri, "Decision Time," speech to donors, Dili, April 6, 2006.

From my point of view, the justice system founded here initially under UNTAET —I myself say that it failed. Because we presided over a lot of cases and sent a lot of people to jail—why didn't they send us for training in advance? On the other hand, during the transitional period they were right to found a justice system here. We needed to have Timorese inside these institutions.[33]

However, the enthusiasm with which the government replaced "failed" local personnel with international personnel, the withdrawal of their status and benefits, and the government's insistence that so many members of the legal profession undergo a training program conducted in Portuguese alienated many of the individuals involved. The program came to be regarded as punitive in intent and led to suspicions that the government had a political agenda in mind. A lawyer and a judge complained:

Before I received a salary—but now it's a scholarship. I cannot support my family. The scholarship is less than the salary was … I did a five-year degree in Indonesia. Our families are not rich people. They supported us through hard work in the districts, or they borrowed money. How did they plan to pay it back? On the assumption that when we finished our schooling we would support them in turn, and be independent. But now life here is very expensive. This government doesn't understand the situation.[34]

In January, after the exam results, they cut all our government salaries. The failed students had to return their mobile phones, cars, motorbikes. We received a scholarship from the United Nations Development Programme of $200 a month … Some resigned. Already one public defender and two judges have resigned and got different jobs in different areas. It has made people very stressed. In the UNTAET time we were given consideration. Now we have "no capacity."[35]

A particular complaint centered on the use of the Portuguese language for training and for the judicial system. The lawyers did not speak Portuguese; they had received their legal training in Bahasa. Furthermore, the applicable law in Timor after 1999 continued to be Indonesian law, despite a challenge to this mandate by the president of the Court of Appeal, Claudio Ximenes, another former exile and member of the pro-Portuguese Timorese diaspora. Insistence on the use of Portuguese in training and in court was highly problematic and required the use of multiple translators, particularly since no Portuguese-Bahasa dictionary existed. Many lawyers and judges felt that the government was deliberately making their work harder, as a ploy to exclude them from participation in the business of state-building and government.

[This policy] only benefits some small groups that are able to speak Portuguese. Most people are not able to speak Portuguese. They speak Bahasa or Tetum. To

---

[33] Timorese judge (1), name withheld upon request, personal interview, Dili, May 2005.

[34] Timorese lawyer (1), name withheld upon request, personal interview, Dili, May 2005.

[35] Timorese judge (1), name withheld upon request, personal interview, Dili, May 2005.

talk about justice, at least you have to say something that people understand ... The government made this decision as a political strategy. For example, in our generation, we are more influenced by the Indonesian culture and education. In our father's generation, a small group of people spoke Portuguese, so the government facilitates those people in their work by speaking Portuguese ... I myself, basically, I am not against Portuguese—to have Portuguese skills is to have more skills in communication ... However, if I were the president I would choose to have a referendum on language so the people could decide for ourselves. So far our leaders decide by themselves, and choose Portuguese, so it means that again we are colonizing our people.[36]

This brewing discontent was compounded by a speech made by the prime minister, mentioned by several lawyers interviewed in 2005, in which he described those who had earned their qualifications through the Indonesian educational system as *"sarjana supermi"* (instant noodles) degree holders, thus labeling them as scholars whose qualifications were cheap, of poor quality, and quickly cooked up. This comment did little to promote good relations with the court system. Disgruntled lawyers commented:

They insulted us. They say we have no capacity, no experience, we need more training. Those who graduated from Indonesian schools are not qualified enough. We are beset with frustration and stress everyday. That is in the news. Since independence, we have been marginalized. They say we are not qualified because we graduated from Indonesian schools. The Indonesian system is not good compared to that of other countries. We are marginalized because of language. Because they don't want to recognize that we were colonized by the Indonesians.[37]

According to me, the government would like to trash the Indonesian image, especially in our generation. This is an obstacle that makes it difficult for us to participate in the new life, new culture, new systems. A lot of people here are now looking back again to the Indonesian times. They say that when we were governed by Indonesia, life was different. Because of that, the government tries to trash the image of Indonesia in this country. This is one way that the government wants to try to erase the experience of the Indonesian language here ... They don't want people to make comparisons between this government and the Indonesian government. So we lose the opportunity to work in our own country. The government tries to put pressure on us.[38]

Most of the lawyers and judges I interviewed in 2005 acknowledged that there were problems in the court system, but they had been so alienated by the government's proposals that they rejected all claims that the new evaluations and training were related to government concerns about quality. They believed that the new training regime had been deliberately designed and implemented to boost the

---

[36] Timorese lawyer (2), name withheld upon request, personal interview, Dili, May 2005.

[37] Timorese lawyer (3), name withheld upon request, personal interview, Dili, April 2005.

[38] Timorese lawyer (4), name withheld upon request, personal interview, Dili, May 2005.

Lusophone elite at the expense of the Indonesian-trained generation, for political purposes. They argued that the government's decision to import international judges from Portuguese-speaking countries around the world had exacerbated problems in the Timorese court system, producing new delays as international, Portuguese-speaking judges struggled to digest a body of law written only in Indonesian. Ordinary people became even more alienated from an already poorly accessible judicial system as they found they could not understand discussions of their own cases. Discontented judges, lawyers, and citizens were convinced these policies facilitated the dominance of the executive over a passive judiciary made up of foreigners who were only in Timor for the vast expatriate salaries they could earn. Some lawyers pointed to particular cases in which Timorese judges had made decisions against the government, and argued that the government's institution of the training program had been designed as a deliberate attack on the independence of Timor-Leste's judiciary, in response.

A particular target of fury, alongside the prime minister, was the president of the court of appeal, Claudio Ximenes, a Timorese who had trained in Portugal, worked there as a judge for many years, and was believed by many interviewees to hold a Portuguese passport. A number of interviewees made a particular point of remarking that Ximenes—the person responsible for implementing the regime that had stripped them of their salary and status—was employed not by the Timorese government, but by UNDP, and that he earned a very large international salary, even though he was Timorese. Ximenes was seen as the architect of a policy that awarded jobs and power to the Portuguese at the expense of the Timorese. The most charitable comment on this issue was made by one lawyer working at the Serious Crimes Unit:

> Our political leaders have been living outside, and are now coming to work in Timor-Leste. They don't know the situation here.[39]

Contending Authenticities: FRETILIN, the Clandestine Movement, and the Church

Unfortunately for FRETILIN, complaints that the government had grown alienated from the people were widespread in 2005. This was particularly true among members of the younger generation, veterans of the clandestine movement. FRETILIN was ultimately unsuccessful in consolidating its early dominance because the tropes of authenticity its leaders relied on conflicted directly—competed, even—with those of its most likely local constituency of activists and party-builders, the various organizations of the clandestine movement. A particular incident from my field research illustrates this. It occurred one afternoon in Dili, as I was driving to a meeting at the FRETILIN Central Committee. On the way, I asked Joaquim, my taxi-driver, if he supported FRETILIN.

> "I used to follow them," he replied, "but not any more."
> "Why not?"
> "Because they haven't worked well for the country."

---

[39] Timorese lawyer (5), name withheld upon request, personal interview, Dili, May 2005.

This was a common response from townspeople I spoke to in East Timor, even those, like Joaquim, who claimed to have been active in the clandestine movement. Before I could pursue the conversation further, I received a phone call from the FRETILIN office. The official I was due to meet was tied up in a meeting and wanted to delay our appointment by an hour. The taxi pulled up at our destination, and as I pondered how to fill in the extra time, Joaquim asked, "Would you like to visit the grave of a Timorese martyr?" "OK," I said.

He drove me to Santa Cruz Cemetery, and we went inside. Joaquim led me through the maze of ornate, flower-bedecked marble tombs to a small grave marked by a plain white cross, located on the far side of the cemetery. On the cross was the name Sebastiao Gomez and a few words showing that he had died in Motael on October 1991.

> "This the grave of Sebastiao Gomez, who was killed by the Indonesians at Motael Church," Joaquim said. "Do you know about this?"
> "Yes, I do."

The funeral of Sebastiao Gomez in 1991 was the occasion of the Santa Cruz Massacre.

> "I was here that day," Joaquim continued. "The Indonesian military were all around there. They started shooting, many people died."

We stood in silence for a few moments. Then,

> "Look at this grave," Joaquim said. "It's very small, very plain. This is why I don't like FRETILIN any more. This man was a martyr for the resistance, and they haven't even built him a decent grave."

The question of where the Timorese dead were to be buried—like the question regarding the portrayal of the Khmer Rouge and the DK era presented in Cambodian history books—was one that had important implications for the shared national narrative about the war, as well as implications for which figures would be recognized as having played lead roles in the conflict. As international donors awarded grants for the construction of a huge heroes' cemetery at the F–FDTL (FALINTIL–Forças de Defesa de Timor Leste, FALINTIL–Defense Force of East Timor) base in Metinaro, on the side of a mountain overlooking the sea, families of young people who had died in connection with the activities of the 1990s clandestine movement were left to bear funeral expenses alone. The question of who could be recognized as a "veteran" and who was not entitled to that epithet was a vexed and divisive one, in a nation of heroes, with important financial and status implications.

In 2002, Xanana Gusmão had appointed a commission to establish the definition of "veteran" and to register the names of all Timorese citizens who qualified for this status. This proved difficult. The number of commissions working on the issue proliferated as different kinds of veterans were identified and those who had been recognized made claims. One commission focused on those who had fought with the resistance between 1975 and 1979; another focused on FALINTIL (Forças Armadas da Libertação Nacional de Timor-Leste, Armed Forces of the National Liberation of East Timor) members. In 2004, a Commission for Resistance Cadres Affairs had to be established to deal with the claims for recognition from those who had participated in the clandestine movement. In 2005, the secretary-general of the Timorese Women's Organization complained that women were not represented on the commissions. Although the commissions reported in 2005, and they distributed some medals, contested claims remained a problem, and the government was criticized by its opponents in the 2007 election campaign for failing to act swiftly on the issue of identifying veterans and for failing to provide benefits to those who were identified unequivocally. It is unclear whether failures to act more effectively on these kinds of issues, which if handled well could have easily boosted the government's popularity, represented ineptness by the leadership, or the inherent thorniness of the issue, or a deliberate decision to play down the contribution either of FALINTIL or of the clandestine movement in achieving independence. Either way, these failures drew attention to a sense that the government was out of step with the public mood. This failure in turn was attributed to the fact that the government was dominated by former exiles.

The position of the returnees was, to a great extent, a product of history. FRETILIN's structure within East Timor had been destroyed under the Indonesians, and the departure of Xanana from the party had undermined the party's hold on the resistance movement as a whole. Jose Reis, the party's secretary-general, commented that after 1999, "the structure of FRETILIN was totally destroyed. We had the top structure, but the lower structure was totally destroyed."[40] The lower levels of the party had to be reconstructed in order to hold a party congress, and one thousand new grassroots members were inducted into the party between 1999 and 2001. This rapid expansion caused its own problems:

> It was not easy to get a consensus in the party. All of the top leaders of FRETILIN had been killed, almost 90 percent, as a result of the war. The survivors [who remained in the country] were only two—Mahunu and Xanana. And there were the other members outside the country … Also, some leaders declared that they were not FRETILIN members any more. Things became more difficult when Xanana declared he was no longer the FRETILIN leader. He was the top resistance fighter. So at the time it was difficult or impossible to achieve consensus between the leaders and the militants.[41]

Eventually, Reis reported, "The leadership of the party was able to convince the militants," by emphasizing the party's origins: the top leaders managed to convince, not only the militants of FRETILIN, but also the majority of the people of Timor, "to feel that this is a holy party, because it was the only party that could liberate the country from colonialism."[42]

The designation of FRETILIN as a "holy party" was effective in winning votes in 2001, but it was unhelpful in establishing substantive links that could keep a leadership in touch with public opinion even as it was working under intense pressure from international donors and elites struggling among themselves. The challenge of transforming the party into an organization that could mobilize support

---

[40] Jose Reis, FRETILIN secretary-general, personal interview, Dili, June 2005.

[41] Ibid.

[42] Ibid.

for the national government was great. Another central committee member, Hernani da Silva, commented:

> From 1980 to 1999, the relationship between people and party was more one of spirit: the party had initiated the resistance, but was not really well-structured ... [Now] we have organizations from the central to the hamlet level. There are different bodies at the district, subdistrict, and *suco* [village] level. We should communicate through official channels. Coordination should follow this functional line. Then the women's organizations and youth groups should be integrated. But right now we cannot operate fully. First, because of the capacity within the party. We have very limited human resources and financial resources ... We have no professional workers, no facilities. No means to organize our militants. We have no means to do that. We have a name, but functionally we are not operating.[43]

Perhaps as a result of the weaknesses described here, the growing discontent within the country was not fully recognized by FRETILIN until too late. Focused on glowing reports from international donors, and distracted from the business of party-building, FRETILIN's leaders became dangerously isolated. The mismatch between the ideological orientations of the returnees and the ideals and aspirations of those who had been nurtured at home during the resistance were not addressed, and perhaps not even registered.

These divisions were dramatically exposed, however, during a set of events in 2005 that brought the FRETILIN government into direct confrontation with an entity whose organizational structure effortlessly outmatched FRETILIN's and which maintained claims to an authenticity *par excellence:* namely, the Roman Catholic Church. Relations between FRETILIN and the Church had always been sour. In the early 1970s, the Church was viewed by the FRETILIN leadership as a tool supporting colonial domination and a source of "obscurantism" from which the people needed to be liberated. The Church was similarly suspicious of FRETILIN's radical Marxism. Over the course of the independence struggle, however, as FRETILIN was increasingly marginalized abroad, the Church became more and more central in Timor-Leste. Its ready organization of parishes and priests, its increasing Timorization, its use of Tetum liturgy, and its provision of places of refuge increased both the presence and the influence of the Church as an actor in Timorese politics and society.

The Church was a particular target of violence in 1999. The massacres of parishioners in Liquiçá and Suai presaged a lifting of the relative immunity awarded the Church during the period of the Indonesian occupation, and priests and nuns were killed alongside civilians. As a result, the heroic role of the Church has been recognized in the new constitution, alongside that of FALINTIL, the clandestine movement, and the diplomatic front.

After independence, the Church continued to be important, not just as a provider of spiritual sustenance, but also as an organizer of relief and development programs, in partnership with international agencies such as the Catholic Relief Service and CARITAS. Encouraged by the new bishop of Dili, Bishop Ricardo, the

---

[43] Hernani Coelho de Silva, FRETILIN central committee member, personal interview, Dili, June 2005.

Church became increasingly active in these kinds of programs. CARITAS Dili, for example, which was based at the Dili Cathedral and worked through the Dili Diocese, launched parish-based health and social service programs using committees of volunteers overseen by priests and catechists.

In 2005, a dispute emerged between the Church and the FRETILIN government that indicated the extent to which the two organizations could split the loyalties of the Timorese nation. The government was engaged in talks with international agencies regarding the establishment of a new educational curriculum. During these talks, the question of religious education was discussed, and the agencies raised the issue of the constitutional separation of church and state as a potential obstacle to the teaching of religion in schools. It was suggested that religious education should be made an optional part of the curriculum.

The Church reacted rapidly and strongly. The stakes quickly came to be framed in terms of national identity. Both FRETILIN and the Church claimed to represent the nation, FRETILIN by virtue of its role in liberating the Maubere people not only from Indonesian rule but from poverty and obscurantism, the Church through its claim to have suffered with the people through the years of warfare and its determination to protect them from the dangers of radical leftist ideology. Claims on both sides were exaggerated. FRETILIN in 2005 was far from the radical Marxist outfit the Church portrayed. And while the Church was by no means progressive in its thinking, it was not the regressive colonial institution FRETILIN caricatured. The Catholic Church represented an important resource for grassroots organization in a country where these were few. Its influence was demonstrated in the Church's response to the debate. For almost a month, the Church maintained demonstrations in Dili, organizing the transport of thousands of young people from the various districts, attiring them in official protest T-shirts, feeding and accommodating them in Dili, and, perhaps even more remarkably, ensuring that they did not get into trouble. Although large, prolonged, and noisy, the demonstrations did not become violent. Indeed, the demonstrators kept a statue of the Virgin Mary prominently displayed at the front of the crowd and spent much time singing hymns and Lionel Richie songs.[44] The demonstrations represented an impressive show of power, a display that was noted by Ramos-Horta, who subsequently ran for president without a party organization but with the backing of the Church.

The dispute with the Church dealt a blow to Alkatiri personally, from which he never really recovered. The demonstrations of April 2005 crystallized a public perception of Alkatiri as an outsider, an anachronism who did not really understand Timorese identity in the twenty-first century. The religious dimension of the conflict drew attention to another facet of this same issue: Alkatiri's own status as a Muslim in a nation of Christians. In conversations at the protest site, and on banners hoisted for the occasion, the demonstrators increasingly aimed their anger at Alkatiri personally. Banners read, "The People Don't Accept the Dictator Alkatiri," and "The People Don't Trust Alkatiri." One demonstrator, when asked why he had come to join in the protest, commented, "I'm here because Mari Alkatiri wants to trash our religion." Other demonstrators expressed concerns about corruption and "the people's suffering," another theme that figured on banners held by protestors. One read, "Many people work, but don't have money. Who is responsible for that? The

---

[44] Author's observations, Dili, April 2005.

Government!"[45] These complaints targeted Alkatiri more indirectly, but recognizably.

Increasingly, the outsider status of the prime minister and his closest associates at the top level of the national government came to represent the basic character of the institution, as many citizens concluded that the government's policies promoted hierarchy and exclusion. The prime minister and the other leading members of the FRETILIN delegation who had lived as exiles before coming to power were regarded as out of touch with East Timor's identity and aspirations as a result of having missed the formative experience of the Indonesian occupation.

This was a difficult challenge for the former exiles to respond to. In their own eyes, as founders of FRETILIN and as early pioneers who first helped forge a nationalist consciousness, they were the vanguard of the nationalist revolution. In the brief interlude of political openness between 1974 and 1975, they had worked tirelessly to spread this consciousness among the Timorese people. The efforts made by FRETILIN in the early 1970s to popularize the socialist nationalism of Portuguese Africa, however, had long since paled into insignificance, as far as most of the population was concerned, beside the brutal impact of the Indonesian occupation, and the very different sort of nationalism—conservative and anti-communist, with a strong emphasis upon religion—that so many citizens had imbibed from the Indonesian system.

This was an attitude that the delegation of former exiles failed to understand or appreciate. Xanana Gusmão, also, in an interview in 2002, commented that East Timorese culture in the early 1970s was more "authentic" than the culture promoted by the Indonesians. Concerning the language question, he stated:

> One of the aspects of the Portuguese presence here was that they didn't touch our traditional structures. They didn't touch our beliefs. In some way our people felt that, yes, there are Portuguese here, occupying our country, but in our houses we can be ourselves. Of course when the Indonesian troops came, it was brutally and abruptly different. It was a war. *Q. And Indonesians immediately tried to impose their own culture on East Timor?* A. Yes.[46]

The return of the FRETILIN exiles to Timor and their accession to power entailed that the two forms of nationalism confront one another directly. For those who had participated in the 1970s resistance movement, the Indonesianization of Timor was to be resisted. It represented oppression and deculturation and was consequently invalid as an expression of Timorese identity. By interpreting Indonesia's intervention in this manner, FRETILIN cadres shaped a narrative that resembled that promulgated by the border resistance fighters in Cambodia, who rejected the rebirth of the Khmer nation under Vietnamese tutelage as tainted and corrupt. The FRETILIN leadership desired to restore aspects of Portuguese culture that had been expunged by Indonesian occupation, and which they regarded as defining the Timorese identity as separate from that of Indonesia. At the same time, they sought to reject all that was backward and "obscurantist" in the Portuguese legacy itself. As a result, language was in; religion was out.

---

[45] Notes from field journal, Dili, April 15, 2005.

[46] Andre Vitchek, Interview with Xanana Gusmão, *ZNet Interviews,* April 12, 2002, online at http://www.zmag.org/content/Interviews/vltcheck_eastimor.cfm, accessed April 10, 2008.

Although the strategies of the FRETILIN government were viewed by many as simple ploys to empower a tiny elite at the expense of the majority, there was a broader philosophical issue at stake regarding Timor's path to modernity. Although discussion of this issue became entangled with a row over authenticity and origins, it was essentially a debate over the future. The FRETILIN government argued that Portuguese language and culture were part of Timorese history, and that restoration of Portuguese had "always" been FRETILIN policy, as had the establishment of a secular state. In returning to these policies, they argued, they were recapturing the authentic Timorese experience. This argument was intended to legitimize an agenda that would prise open a backward, church-dominated society, making it more receptive to progressive education delivered via Western aid and South-South solidarity. The generation of Timorese citizens who had grown up under the Indonesian occupation took a different line. For them, Timorese identity was intimately connected with defense of the territory, and it emerged from participation in the struggle on domestic soil. Taking this as a starting point, they concluded that the obvious path to the future must be guided by a recognition of gains that had been made in terms of education and modernization under the Indonesians, and this path forward had to be built upon the Indonesian legacy, along with the legacy of the resistance, using the Church as a source of social cohesion and political mobilization.

This was the strategy that Jose Ramos-Horta, guided by hindsight, appeared poised to adopt in 2006. In his inaugural speech as prime minister, Ramos-Horta claimed that the new government's "main focus" would be "the poor and forgotten in the rural areas," who would be served by economic revitalization projects that had a quick impact. In order for the government to reach the "poor and forgotten," it would have to pay greater attention to district-level public servants, the *liurai* (traditional leaders) and *chefes de suco* (village chiefs). At the same time, he remarked:

> The Timorese Catholic Church is the only continuous solid institution that has absorbed the fabric of Timorese ... This Government, then, invites the Catholic Church to assume a bigger role in education and in the human development of our people and in the fight against poverty.[47]

Ramos-Horta described the Timorese as "a people deeply spiritual, whose day-to-day lives are inspired and influenced by the spirits of the past and by supernatural beliefs that are fused with Christian beliefs." For this reason, "we cannot support or impose modern models of secularism or Europeanism."[48]

By 2006, the FRETILIN government was in crisis for two reasons. It had failed to convince the population that its gatekeeping prowess could benefit them. Although FRETILIN had generally pleased the international donors, its performance in negotiations concerning offshore oil and gas resources had pleased no one. Nationalists at home rejected the government's compromises, while the outcome of the negotiations did not award FRETILIN resources that could be spent,

[47] Jose Ramos-Horta, address delivered after he was sworn in as prime minister of the Democratic Republic of Timor-Leste, Dili, July 10, 2006, translated from the Portuguese by the Embassy of Timor-Leste in Australia, online at www.pcug.org.au/~wildwood/06jul10horta.html, accessed September 20, 2007.

[48] Ibid.

immediately, to alleviate the dire economic circumstances in Timorese villages. Meanwhile, international aid was largely absorbed at the center or left unspent.

At the same time, FRETILIN's claim to authenticity, sufficiently powerful to award it a majority of votes in the elections in 2001, had been ruined by divisive and burdensome cultural policies, the failure to recognize key groups of "heroes," and its spat with the Church. The local election results of 2005, and the presidential and parliamentary results of 2006, showed a wave of discontent sweeping through the country from the west, most evident in the enclave of Oecussi, which had suffered particularly from lack of government attention. Although FRETILIN retained its strong support in the eastern districts of Baucau, Lautem, and Viqueque, in the rest of the country its support collapsed. In the presidential elections, FRETILIN won only 28 percent of the vote in the first round. This was despite fielding a candidate— Francisco "Lu Olo" Guterres—with impeccable credentials as an ex-FALINTIL commander who had spent the whole of the resistance era in the mountains and whose opponent was the former exile Jose Ramos-Horta. But Ramos-Horta had long distanced himself from the FRETILIN delegation based in Portugal, choosing instead to cultivate close ties with Xanana. Despite his own Portuguese descent, he was viewed as maintaining a wider range of international ties, for example with Australia. Most importantly, he achieved an unassailable aura of authenticity by the strategy of campaigning on a platform of support for and from the Church. In the 2006 parliamentary elections, FRETILIN was again the largest single party, but, once again, the various opposition parties—most notably, Xanana's newly formed CNRT party, Xavier do Amaral's ASDT, and Fernando Lasama's PD (Partido Democratico, Democratic Party)—united against FRETILIN to form a coalition government that kept FRETILIN out of power. Its share of the vote fell from 57 percent in 2001 to only 29 percent in 2007, a vote share that was, again, largely confined to the eastern districts.

A comparison of FRETILIN with the Cambodian parties suggests that the mythology of authentic nationalism is a vexed affair in post-conflict settings. Those who expected to wield it effortlessly to enhance their own glory found it to be a more complex issue than they had expected. Candidates who had returned from elective exile, in particular—even those claiming the most glittering nationalist credentials— represented easy targets, in part because their belief in their own authenticity was belied, in the eyes of their potential constituents, by their absence, both during the war and in the post-war situation. Experience of suffering was a great unifier in the post-conflict context in both countries, as was the personal claim that one had seen the war through to the end with other survivors. This claim to solidarity with the poor, expressed above all by staying and fighting, had greater resonance than claims to knowledge of international—and unreliable—donor politics.

Second, and more importantly, those who had lived outside the country during wartime had great difficulty taking control of effective local organizations and, consequently, remained essentially absent from village politics, even in the post-conflict setting. The importance of this is illustrated by the success of the former exile Ramos-Horta, once he had hitched his 2007 election campaign to the Church. The organizational power of the Church, combined with Ramos-Horta's alliance with Xanana—the nationalist to end all nationalists—outweighed the claims to authenticity made even by so venerable a figure as Lu Olo, competing on the back of a divided and, in the western regions at least, disintegrating FRETILIN. The absence of high-profile FRETILIN leaders during the war made them easy targets for campaign jibes and protest banners, but their real problem was their continued lack of any real leverage at the local level into the peace, as ordinary Timorese found the vision of the heroic Maubere nation becoming stale and fragmented in the context of international intervention, the message that Timorese professionals showed a "lack of capacity," and the experience of economic collapse.

The two phenomena were swiftly linked by the Timorese people. The claim, expressed by more than one interviewee in Dili during the Church protests in April and May 2005, that "the government doesn't understand what the Church means to us, because they weren't here," summed up the public mood and reflected the general political ineptness of the FRETILIN government. Many of the government's mistakes stemmed from their failure to understand organizations such as the clandestine movement, to appreciate the mindset of the Indonesian-educated, Catholic youth, and to recognize the need to explain their policies in a manner that could mobilize support and attract constituencies.

Both FRETILIN and the Cambodian opposition parties were unable to construct a feasible vision to bridge the yawning gap between the promise and reality of the international intervention around which they oriented their politics. The inherent difficulty in articulating a trajectory for rapid modernization, in the face of failing economies, powerful donors, and a fragmented local polity, was compounded by weak local party organizations, which offered no new insights or corrective advice coming up from the grassroots. In attempting to act as mediators between the international and the local, both the neoliberal Rainsy and the economic nationalist Alkatiri ended up privileging the international, in a manner that made their organizations appear to represent out-of-touch, compromised, comprador elites. National actors were essentially challenged to wrest power from international actors, in the form of both material resources and independence of action, in a way that could be effectively portrayed as both representing a coherent and defensible account of authenticity, but which also offered some sense of a pathway to the future, within the limiting constraints of political action in an aid-dependent context. This was a challenge that Hun Sen dealt with adeptly and that Xanana Gusmão and Jose Ramos-Horta rapidly learned to handle. Mari Alkatiri, Norodom Ranariddh, and Sam Rainsy were less capable in meeting the challenge. The next, and final, chapter of this study examines the implications of this politics for the way in which ideas of political community emerged at the local level in post-intervention Cambodia and Timor-Leste.

CHAPTER VIII

EMPTY SHELLS: NATIONALISTS ADRIFT IN THE DEPENDENT PEACE

"When I put down my soldier's pack, I became an empty shell. Now I am nothing."
> Demobilized Soldier, Cambodia, 2000[1]

The discussion of tropes of legitimacy highlights the importance—even in the most dependent of communities—of domestic constituencies to the survival of governments. The key question is whether the dependent community that emerges from an act of international intervention meant to end a war offers ordinary people a meaningful framework within which to imagine their own citizenship and organize participation. Stripped of the heroism with which it was imbued in the war years, recast as backward, impoverished, and underdeveloped, incapable of making its own decisions, and reliant on the impatient charity of others, the post-conflict state can easily be perceived as a rather poor affair, even by a war-weary population eager for peace. The task of elites is to create not only a narrative that can elicit allegiance, but a web of practical connections that links the state to society, in a manner that can give form to claims of central representation, authority, and legitimacy, in the eyes of at least a section of the population.

This chapter discusses such political efforts and their outcomes in Cambodia and Timor from the perspective of people struggling to make their living in periurban and rural settings. Their perceptions of the government and its relationship to the population are derived from interview and survey data drawn from my own fieldwork in Cambodia from 1996 to 2003 and in Timor in 2005, and from the published research of others during a similar period. The discussion begins by laying out perceptions of the national government from the perspectives of different groups in Timor-Leste and Cambodia, and then goes on to discuss the relative importance of local and international horizons in the formulation of political and economic strategies. It concludes by reflecting on the implications of the experience of Timorese and Cambodian citizens for conceptions of legitimacy and strategies for political action in dependent communities.

---

[1] Quoted in Annette Marcher and Vong Sokheng, "An Empty Shell," *Phnom Penh Post*, November 10–23, 2000, online at http://www.phnompenhpost.com/, accessed July 12, 2007.

"HE'IN DE'IT" (JUST WAITING): THE DEMOCRATIC REPUBLIC OF TIMOR-LESTE, AS SEEN FROM LIQUIÇA AND LALEIA

Tibar is a *suco* (village) located in Liquiça District, just fifteen minutes' drive west from Dili. The main road from the coast cuts through the village, leading up to Ermera and the coffee plantations in the hills. It is a busy place, with a population of more than 2,500.[2] Bus services and *mikrolets* (minibus services) shuttling between Ermera and Dili pass through. Lower Tibar has a school and clinic. It also has coffee-processing facilities and warehouses which in 2005 at the time of this survey were being revitalized by the Co-operativa Café Timor (Timor Coffee Co-operative) after a period of disuse following the end of the Indonesian era. These businesses employ wage labor from Tibar. The village boasts a National Training Development Center, run by the Portuguese, offering training in carpentry, plumbing, and stonemasonry; a government abattoir; and a residential health center run by the Ryder Cheshire Foundation. Several households in Tibar include a member who is employed by these organizations, but more rely upon market gardening and animal husbandry, or earn a subsistence living by selling goods to traffic passing along the road. There are three or four kiosks, selling a range of groceries, and some palm wine vendors' stalls. In the lower half of Tibar, households produce woven wickets for sale. In the upper half, most houses along the road display bundles of firewood or larger cuts of wood for building, in the hope of attracting business from passing traffic. As villages in Timor go, this one is well-connected and close to the center of the economy. Its aspirations for upward mobility are attested to by the number of households with members working or studying in Dili. One household surveyed had family members living in Australia.

Compared with Liquiça town to the west and Dili to the east, Tibar escaped large-scale destruction in 1999, although it was threatened by the feared Besi Merah Putih (Red and White Iron) militia from Maubara—the same militia group responsible for the massacre in Liquiça Church in April of that year. In response to the threat, Tibar's *chefe de suco* (village chief) traveled up to the Remexio in the mountains to seek advice from FALINTIL (Forças Armadas da Libertação Nacional de Timor-Leste, Armed Forces of the National Liberation of East Timor) Commander Taur Matan Ruak. Taur Matan Ruak, villagers said, advised the *chefe* to pretend to cooperate with the militias—a strategy that was apparently pursued so effectively, the villagers recalled, that they were able to save themselves and hide 650 pro-independence supporters fleeing the militias in Dili at the same time. As compared to Dili and Liquiça, relatively few Tibar houses were burned down during the militia violence accompanying the Indonesian withdrawal in 1999.

Subsequently, Tibar's geographical accessibility put it in the swing of things as far as international assistance was concerned. In 1999, CARITAS Australia distributed food in the area, while families who fled to West Timor in 1999 were returned to Tibar by UNHCR (United Nations High Commissioner for Refugees) and given roofing materials to rebuild their homes. Under the Community Empowerment Scheme, a water project was initiated with the assistance of the International Committee of the Red Cross, which organized village labor (unpaid, the villagers noted) to pipe running water to a number of standpipes dotted around

---

[2] The 2004 Census counted 2,571 individuals in Tibar. Online at http://dne.mopf.gov.tl/census/tables/district/Liquica/population/tables/table4_3_1_3.htm, accessed November 4, 2008.

the village. The United Nations International Children's Emergency Fund issued every house a septic tank for sanitation. After independence, occasional rice distribution to needy villagers continued, organized from the District Administration with INGO support. CARE International (Cooperative for Assistance and Relief Everywhere) ran monthly clinics in the community center, distributing free food to parents of underweight children. CARE had also distributed seeds to villagers for their market gardens, although the villagers gave varying accounts of how successfully these grew. A Japanese NGO renovated the primary school.

Despite these efforts, life had gotten harder in economic terms since the Indonesian era. The cost of living had risen. In the Indonesian era, transport to Dili had been cheap, and so had schooling for children. Some villagers who were interviewed remarked that, unlike the dollar, the rupiah had value.[3] Electricity had been cheap in the Indonesian era, while UNTAET (the United Nations Transitional Administration in East Timor) had not bothered about collecting electricity bill payments at all. While interviewees appreciated the value of independence in terms of safety and freedom—"now it is better, you can walk around, you might not have a job, but at least no one will come and intimidate you"—they made it clear that independence had been disastrous for them economically.

Tibar's well-connected periurban status entailed that it was hit harder than many areas of the country by the political and economic transition. Unlike remote subsistence villages in the interior, Tibar was integrated into the national economy and had been relatively prosperous during the Indonesian period. Since the country achieved independence in 1999, jobs had been lost in the coffee industry. Previous profits from supplying the markets and restaurants of Dili with market garden produce had also disappeared when the Indonesians left. The Indonesians, villagers commented, ate the same food as the Timorese—indigenous vegetables that thrived in the climate and the soil, and which Timorese knew how to grow. But fellow Timorese had no money to buy local market produce, and UN staff members ate imported food that the villagers didn't know how to produce. Even if villagers had grown produce for which there was some demand, the skyrocketing price of fuel made the cost of transporting goods to market prohibitive.

Those who had shifted to collecting firewood to sell, or who had borrowed money to open roadside kiosks, were struggling. One problem was lack of imagination in entrepreneurship. As a local schoolteacher pointed out, "in this community, if someone tries to open a business, like a kiosk, then everyone else does the same ... everyone opens a kiosk. Then they all move to firewood. Then palmwine."[4] More important was a lack of customers:

> There's no chance for us to open a business because we would just be waiting for people from Dili to come and buy what we have. We don't have the money to buy and sell to each other. People open a kiosk, and sometimes if you really need something you'll buy it from the kiosk, but it's very expensive. You're covering the cost of their loan.[5]

---

[3] The United Nations Transitional Administration in East Timor, in consultation with the National Consultative Council of East Timor, adopted the US dollar as the unit of currency in Timor in place of the Indonesian rupiah on the advice of the International Monetary Fund in January 2000.

[4] Villager (1), personal interview, Tibar, East Timor, May 2005.

[5] Villager (2), personal interview, Tibar, East Timor, May 2005.

The state of the economy in Tibar reflected a wider condition in post-conflict Timor—that of extreme and debilitating economic and political fragmentation. Although the roads were good, transport was expensive, as was accommodation in Dili; markets had changed so rapidly as to appear impenetrable. One INGO worker noted that transport costs within Timor were more expensive than those for many overseas routes, so that Dili's purveyors imported rice from Vietnam, rather than from the eastern districts, just along the coast road, and Dili's markets sold frozen chickens from Brazil instead of from local farmers.[6] Villagers in Tibar in 2005 were able to gain access to limited resources from the international agencies in the village for collective purposes, but if they sought loans or grants for private business needs, they faced fees that they regarded as insurmountable. For these reasons, microcredit schemes intended to stimulate local businesses were regarded by villagers as the road to financial ruin:

It's been almost nine months since we dropped out of that scheme, because it was too expensive. They came to ask us if we'd like to borrow again, but we said no. We are not public servants who earn a salary. We survive by selling firewood. [The scheme is] too expensive. There are no customers, and the interest is really high.[7]

A lot of the community here try to borrow from microcredit, but it is not successful; everyone fails because there are no customers ... Also you have to put up assets as a guarantee. If the business fails, people will come and take your land; the government will come and take the land.[8]

Villagers interviewed in 2005 drew comparisons between the post-independence era and the Indonesian era, remarking upon the sense of isolation that had come with independence. In part this was economic isolation. Although decrying the violence of the Indonesian era, villagers gave the Indonesians credit for three things: provision of jobs and markets; low prices; and generosity, albeit selective, with respect to aid.

While Timor was occupied by Indonesia, the combination of aid and development projects and security measures, which gave rise to the ubiquitous and hated military checkpoints, had comprised the basis of a fairly dense web of state-society relations in Tibar. Investment in public facilities entailed the presence of Indonesian staff working in the villages and regular visits from Indonesian officials, described as occasions for singing, dancing, and feasting. Villagers who held official village positions during the Indonesian era reported close, if not necessarily friendly, relations. One former community council member recalled that the Indonesians paid council members a quarterly salary, in return for which council members held regular meetings to consult with community elders and made development plans for projects to be funded by the regime. A water system was established in Tibar by this means, along with a school and a community center. Several villagers recalled receiving material aid. The former council member, a schoolteacher, said:

---

[6] David Boyce, personal interview, Dili, East Timor, April 2005.

[7] Villager (3), personal interview, Tibar, East Timor, May 2005.

[8] Villager (4), personal interview, Tibar, East Timor, May 2005.

... then life was better. There was lots of support and aid from the national government. They used to bring animals—pigs and goats—and delivered them straight to the people. I prefer that system. But sometimes also they acted like dictators—they wanted to kill people.[9]

Equally, a number of villagers claimed that they had been excluded from receiving assistance during the Indonesian era. They claimed that building supplies and animals were distributed only to the families of council members via Indonesian networks marked by corruption, collusion, and nepotism, or KKN (*korupsi, kolusi, dan nepotisme*). Even so, although corrupt and abusive, the Indonesian occupation had prompted vibrant economic and organized political activity—both collaborative and oppositional—in Tibar. No matter whether they loved them or hated them, residents couldn't miss the fact that the Indonesians were indisputably there, in the village, organizing, assisting, and abusing the population. By contrast, "after the Indonesian time, when we entered independence, everything stopped."[10]

Although input from the center ceased with the end of the occupation, local political activity did not. Following the departure of the Indonesians, the community in Tibar, as in villages throughout Timor, rapidly organized politically, electing a four-man committee referred to as the *selcom* (council) for each *aldeia* (hamlet).[11] *Selcom* members were invariably veterans of the clandestine movement, and became responsible for organizing aid distribution in the emergency period and after, for conducting investigations and mediating conflicts such as boundary disputes, and for mobilizing the community to engage in public events such as clean-up days and elections. The rapid constitution of the *selcom* reflected the tradition of self-mobilization bred within the clandestine movement over the years of the Indonesian occupation.

The *selcom* committees were consulted by NGOs and used generally by the district authorities as a vehicle for passing on information, both upwards and downwards, and organizing the community to receive material aid such as rice and building supplies. However, the authority of these committees remained tenuous, for neither UNTAET nor the post-independence government perceived them as sufficiently legitimate to justify salaries, expense budgets, or facilities for the committee members until formal local elections had been held to reconfirm the status of those who had been chosen unofficially. These were scheduled for 2005: in Tibar, at the time of this research, the 2005 elections were expected but had been delayed.[12]

One *chefe aldeia* described his position:

I have no salary and am given no reimbursement for expenses either—this is a volunteer's job. The government doesn't really recognize this job. From the Indonesian time, we had a salary and a certificate. We have often complained to the government, saying that we are having a difficult time, but the government

[9] Villager (1), personal interview, Tibar, East Timor, May 2005.

[10] Villager (2), personal interview, Tibar, East Timor, May 2005.

[11] Following Portuguese practice, Timor's subnational administrative hierarchy contains four levels: *distritu* (districts); *sub-distritu* (subdistricts); *suco* (village); and *aldeia* (hamlet).

[12] It was finally held in September 2005, and the *chefe de suco* for Tibar lost his seat.

says we have to wait because this is a temporary job. We've just won independence, [they say], so you'll have to wait.[13]

The *chefe de suco* agreed with this assessment. He had also emerged from the clandestine movement in 1999 to take the job of *chefe* for Tibar. As *chefe*, he was responsible for administering more than five hundred households, in conditions of dislocation and hardship, with poor infrastructure and communications. He commented:

The position I hold now is difficult. This is a really new nation, and this is a volunteer job. It is a difficult life. There is no support from the government—nothing at all ... I am not against the government, but the truth is, if they don't support the job we're doing in the base, it's not going to work.[14]

The government's lack of support imposed significant constraints on what the *chefes* could, or would, do. Because fuel was so expensive in Timor in 2005, people traveled as little as possible. The *chefes* found that even their purportedly simple duties, such as making regular trips around the village to consult and inform people, were financially burdensome. Tibar's *chefe de suco* commented: "We're starting to think that we are the same as the rest of the community—we have a function but we have no support, so we prefer to do our private jobs."[15] Because of the expense, this leader rarely ventured further afield to consult with district or central government officials, although he claimed that he had made representations to the government, at the district and national levels, to try to elicit more funds for local administration, but had been unsuccessful. Some villagers were sympathetic to the predicament of the *chefes*, regarding them as hamstrung by the lack of resources—"Their children also study in school, so they have to focus on their own economy." Others regarded the *chefes'* inaction as a betrayal of their duty to the people. *Chefes* themselves said they were under pressure not to present too many demands to the government:

We cannot ask for too many things from the government because the government will say no. So we just wait. The government complains about the budget on the radio, saying there are limits on the money that can go to the *aldeias* ... This place was destroyed by a flash flood, and we requested the government to send aid to the community, but the government said no, we do not have enough money for this situation.[16]

Villagers' complaints about the *selcom* also referred to apparent partisanship in the distribution of aid. Some individuals claimed that the *selcom* favored their own families in this distribution and others claimed that they favored FRETILIN members, while still others asserted that the committees distributed aid fairly, according to need. Given that the *selcom* emerged from the clandestine movement, and that houses of the clandestine movement were targeted by militias in 1999, whereas other houses in Tibar were spared destruction, all three assertions may have

---

[13] Villager (5), personal interview, Tibar, East Timor, May 2005.

[14] *Chefe de suco*, personal interview, Tibar, East Timor, May 2005.

[15] Ibid.

[16] *Chefe aldeia* (1), personal interview, Tibar, East Timor, May 2005.

been true. However, this partisan distribution of aid was regarded, at least by those outside the favored circle, as a significant violation of community principles. Many of those who were dissatisfied articulated this violation as an extension of the practices of KKN employed by the Indonesians, while others felt the insult had been dealt by Timor's own government and so perceived themselves as politically marginalized, echoing the complaints of angry Dili lawyers who had lost their jobs for failure to pass the new qualifying exams.

Such critiques extended beyond the activities of the local authorities and were directed against the central government itself. Residents of Tibar were well aware of the level of international aid flowing into Timor, and they drew disparaging comparisons between the amounts of money announced by donors and the resources they saw arriving in their own village. Again, complaints focused on two points: first, the concern that the money had somehow disappeared and therefore had probably gone into the pockets of government officials, as it used to when the Indonesians held power; and, second, the claim that the residents of Tibar, as equally valid members of the heroic nation, were morally entitled to receive an equal share of the money.

> There have been a lot of offers of international aid from international donors. They came and promised there would be a lot of international support, and you people here will have access to that aid, to money and other support ... But it never came true, we had no help rebuilding our houses ... During our guerrilla fight, we as a community offered a lot of support to people—small things, but with big value. Now those people sit in government but don't think about us.[17]

> We do hear on the radio that other countries want to help Timor, but we don't know where the money goes ... We were the ones who worked hard to fight for independence. We pushed the Indonesians out—the unity of the population is the reason the Indonesians aren't here any more. But now the government doesn't care about us ... The Indonesian time was a very difficult time—we lost a lot of family members. Even I was taken out to be killed, but I escaped ... So the government should meet with us now. To give us information.[18]

> My husband did clandestine fighting against Indonesia. I tried to claim support from the government, but no one responds ... Our government used to promise to the community that if we fought for independence, everyone would have a house and a car, but then that never happened. The government has had the opportunity to get rich on the back of our suffering.[19]

Interviewees in Tibar claimed that the community had been closely involved in the clandestine movement and had provided support to FALINTIL units based in Ermera. They represented their former links with FALINTIL as close ones, and contrasted that situation with the absence of connections to Timor's post-

---

[17] Villager (6) personal interview, Tibar, East Timor, May 2005.

[18] Villager (7), personal interview, Tibar, East Timor, May 2005.

[19] Villager (8), personal interview, Tibar, East Timor, May 2005.

independence government. Their alienation from their own government formed a central theme in their discontent.

Local *chefes* who were interviewed also suspected government corruption—"the government should keep the sugar in their hands and not spill it; the reality in the government sector is that they are letting it slip through their fingers."[20] Alternately, they regarded the poverty of Tibar as a result of diversion of aid by central government actors to their own support bases, a comment that prefigured claims that government officials had favored the Firaku (easterners) at the expense of Kaladi districts, such as Liquiça:

> The people have heard that a lot of support and aid has come from the West, but some people haven't received aid. Only small numbers have received aid, because aid is always based in the government areas.[21]

Equally resented were failures of communication between the village and the central government. Local authorities claimed they were not allowed to petition the national government directly, but were required to direct their complaints via the state hierarchy, built of *suco*–subdistrict–district–central government. For villagers living as close to the center as Tibar, this was frustrating, since this line of communication did not appear to work. Villagers cited a range of issues—flooding and hunger, for example—concerning which they had made representations to the district or central government, but had received "no response," leaving them unsure whether their messages had gotten lost on the way or simply been ignored. One *chefe aldeia* who was interviewed estimated that "out of every five requests, they will perhaps choose one."[22] Villagers emphasized the frustration caused by this lack of response and complained that the higher levels of government had given them no good explanations concerning the processes for selecting and rejecting petitions and the reasons for the purported lack of funds. They regarded the government's failures as more evidence of its bad faith.

One *chefe* interviewed responded to these sorts of criticisms by suggesting that villagers' complaints reflected their failure to appreciate the substance of independence:

> The idea of independence—it means that to feel independent, if you want something done, you have to have knowledge of how to develop this thing, how to work by yourself, not wait for people to come and develop it for you.[23]

A similar point was made by a Timorese official working with the United Nations Development Programme on local development projects:

> People ask, when is the government coming to give things to us? ... I tell people, you have to understand that we voted for independence, not dependence—we have to use our own resources.[24]

---

[20] *Chefe aldeia* (1), Tibar, personal interview, Tibar, East Timor, May 2005.

[21] *Chefe aldeia* (2), Tibar, personal interview, Tibar, East Timor, May 2005.

[22] *Chefe aldeia* (3), Tibar, personal interview, Tibar, East Timor, May 2005.

[23] *Chefe aldeia* (4), Tibar, personal interview, Tibar East Timor, May 2005.

[24] Reinaldo Soares, UNDP, personal interview, Dili, East Timor, July 2005.

This association of "independence" with self-reliance had been a key component of nationalist ideology in Timor-Leste since the mid-1970s. Broadly associated with bottom-up, participatory development using local materials and resources, rather than reliance upon foreign investment and debt, its intent was to promote empowerment and autonomy. However, when transformed into a justification for tight spending policies under the Alkatiri government following independence, this approach made few allowances for a period of transition, or for providing support to citizens as villagers adjusted to the loss of particular sets of economic support strategies and the expense of investing in new ones. Like the government's strategy of requiring that certain professionals be conversant in Portuguese, tight spending policies justified by the rhetoric of self-reliance were simply imposed by the Alkatiri government, with the conviction that ends justified means, and that teething troubles would be short-lived. Both strategies assumed a cost-free return to a remembered village, to use James Scott's term;[25] however, the village remembered by the Timorese elite and the village remembered by Tibar residents were not the same.

The elites' remembered village was a community that operated as a self-contained subsistence unit with undisputed authority structures, capable of mobilizing labor and materials for small-scale public works that were legitimized by custom as operating to the mutual benefit of all—even if, in fact, they privileged certain needs and perspectives over others. This reality, if it ever existed, had long since vanished in places like Tibar, where residents had derived their advantage under the Indonesians from integration in a national economy, rather than from isolated self-sufficiency. For villagers in Tibar, subsistence-based moral economies[26] had long since ceased to apply; their livelihood strategies were oriented toward education and upward mobility. They aspired to jobs in public service for their children. Extra benefit from aid or development projects translated into more children at school for more years; large windfalls might cover the cost of a high school or university education in Dili. Integration into a wider economy than that of the village had generated an outward-looking and entitlement-oriented culture. Consequently the villagers resented messages extolling self-reliance, which were interpreted as an injunction to "stay in our place." These elite prescriptions were even more intensely resented in a context where villagers heard regular media reports describing the inflow of millions of dollars of aid. The result was a significant loss of government legitimacy.

Ultimately, villagers viewed Timor's central, district, and even local government as an obstacle to, rather than a vehicle for, prosperity. After only three years of independence, many of the villagers in Tibar questioned the need for national government involvement in their affairs, calling instead for direct relationships between the local and the international level in terms of provision of aid and support.

---

[25] James Scott, *Weapons of the Weak: Everyday Forms of Peasant Resistance* (New Haven, CT: Yale University Press, 1987).

[26] This term is used by James Scott to describe social attitudes to risk management and economic planning characteristic of subsistence societies. James Scott, *The Moral Economy of the Peasant: Rebellion and Subsistence in Southeast Asia* (New Haven, CT: Yale University Press, 1977).

> I would like to say that, in the future, if there is another opportunity to help here, please don't send it through the national level—come straight to the community.[27]

In such comments, the local and the international loom large, while the nation appears remote, self-serving, and characterized by exclusion and patronage. This picture of the Timorese government is perhaps an unfair one, but it is the picture that became widespread in Timor and was used by the Timorese Roman Catholic Church, as well as by sections of the elite who were opposed to the Alkatiri government. Accusations of corruption and patronage were at the core of the 2006 crisis, both as it played out in Dili and as it was portrayed by the watching Australian media, which were quick to label Timor-Leste as a "failed state." Hard evidence of seriously corrupt practices, however, has been rare in post-independence Timor.

Ultimately, the central government's failure in Tibar arose from an acute sense among villagers of its absence in their lives, an absence that contrasted with their memories of both the Indonesian regime and FALINTIL, which had been powerfully present locally, via the clandestine movement, during the war. Since Tibar was located so near the political and economic center of the Timorese nation during the Indonesian era, Tibar's residents felt as if their community had drifted to the margins since the war ended and was now overlooked by a government whose attention was focused elsewhere:

> Government people sit in their chairs in their offices and won't come to the village to see what is happening.[28]

> We suggest to government—please open your eyes. These demonstrators gathering in Dili ... please give young people more opportunity to work and develop their minds. I am too old, but they still need a job to do.[29]

> I would like to ask the government to change its attitude. It should see the people and look after the people.[30]

The active presence of INGOs did not plug this gap. Indeed, it exacerbated it, due to the weakness of local government in mediating relationships between villagers and INGO representatives. In Liquiça, the district administrator described the extent and nature of the INGO presence:

> There is a really long list of NGOs working here—CARE, SIDA [Swedish International Development Cooperation Agency], UNDP, Oxfam. There are a lot of international agencies working with the community. I have got a long list, but

---

[27] Villager (6), personal interview, Tibar, East Timor, May 2005. I encountered a similar attitude on the part of Cambodian interviewees in the mid-1990s, yet that attitude changed as the Cambodian government subsequently based its legitimacy in large part on its ability to intercede between donors and the poor.

[28] Villager (9), personal interview, Tibar, East Timor, May 2005.

[29] Villager (4), personal interview, Tibar, East Timor, May 2005.

[30] Villager (10), personal interview, Tibar, East Timor, May 2005.

I'm afraid I couldn't find it this morning. They are working in education and agriculture, infrastructure, capacity for general development, roads, irrigation, health.[31]

INGO staff members consulted with the district administration over their plans, and the district administration was charged with monitoring and facilitating their work. However, the capacity of the district administration to act as a strong bridge between international NGOs and communities, to organize community input into INGO schemes, was limited. Liquiça's district administration employed only one staff member with responsibility for tracking and monitoring all these projects. Consequently, the administration's input was largely confined to attendance at opening and closing ceremonies. Although technically in charge, the district administration, in fact, was subordinate, relying on the goodwill of INGOs to facilitate monitoring. The district director of one international NGO working in Liquiça commented: "In Liquiça, the district administration is very cooperative—they need our money so they have to be cooperative. Sometimes they confess, you manage our department here."[32]

The district's budget could only cover basic salaries, a condition that left it dependent on donor projects for any kind of activity in the *sucos*. The district administrator commented that even getting funds to pay for her travel to the various subdistricts could be difficult and that communicating information from the district to the *suco* level was a problem.[33]

The weakness of local authorities entailed that villagers experienced their relationships with international aid agencies as problematic and alienated. While residents of Tibar appreciated the facilities offered by the permanent presence of the Portuguese training center and the Ryder Cheshire Foundation, they felt, on the whole, that their interactions with organizations such as CARE and UNHCR were obstructed by barriers having to do with language and power, and the inadequacy of local leadership. They felt that international NGOs and UN agencies did not listen to the people, and assumed that they knew best. Thus, the people were given the role of passive recipients, rather than active collaborators, and aid was wasted through lack of communication:

The UN staff never came into the life of the community to see what the community needs ... They came here because of people's needs, but they just come and go, so how do they know what people need?[34]

In sum, in this region of Timor-Leste, common difficulties in mediating between international donors and local recipients were exacerbated by the top-down approach to state-building adopted by the UNTAET and the Alkatiri government, under the pressures created by Timor's aid dependence. The donor agencies' general caution in allocating budgets, their emphasis upon competition for international projects, rather than provision of discretionary local funds, and their failure to support local government fragmented the polity and the economy, leaving villagers

[31] District administrator, Liquiça District, personal interview, Liquica, June 2005.

[32] Bendito Freitas, Stromme Foundation, personal interview, Dili, April 2005.

[33] District administrator, Liquiça District, personal interview, Liquiça, June 2005.

[34] Villager (11), personal interview, Tibar, East Timor, May 2005.

impoverished, frustrated, and forgotten. As one villager commented, "It is not so much a lack of resources, but a lack of leadership."[35]

The idealistic ideology promoting self-reliant entrepreneurial action, based upon a vision of subsistence villages in the interior, ignored the reality, in Tibar as in many other parts of Timor, of the extent to which local politics and economics had been integrated with Indonesian networks during the occupation. Guided by this ideology, Timorese government officials and donors failed to help construct an effective system of local government to connect the villages to the center and failed to build upon unifying civil-society resources, such as the Church, the clandestine movement, and the Tetum language. These failures combined with the stultifying effects of economic collapse and inflation to give rise to a disastrous fragmentation of the post-conflict economy, society, and polity.

As many villagers commented, the population was left "just waiting" (*he'in de'it*) in confusion and growing outrage, as their perception of a unified nation of heroes, each deserving consideration from an obligated government, was dismissed and ignored. When their aspirations for independence were disappointed, villagers were quick to frame current difficulties in the context of their experience of Indonesian interregional discrimination and KKN. Under these circumstances, the emergence of political hostilities between fragmented populations alleging unfair treatment was a likely outcome, requiring only an initial spark of protest and the machinations of elite and external actors to fan the flames.

Sentiments strikingly similar to those outlined above were expressed by villagers interviewed in Laleia, in the eastern district of Manatuto. Laleia is a rice-growing area that stretches from the coast to the mountains, between the coastal town of Manatuto, located to the west, and Timor's second city of Baucau, located to the east. The town of Laleia, situated on the borders of the *suco*s of Haturalan and Lifau, is Xanana Gusmão's home town. Like Tibar, it is well-connected, as it is situated on the main coast highway between Dili and Baucau and served by the Dili–Baucau bus services, and it hosts the subdistrict headquarters. During the Indonesian occupation, the town of Laleia was the site of a thriving market that attracted traders from Baucau and Manatuto, as well as from the mountains. The market was burnt down during the 1999 conflicts, as was the school.

Like Tibar, Laleia was developed during the Indonesian occupation, and it benefited not only from the construction of roads and markets, but also from irrigation of the flood plain that flanks the Laleia River. Across the river from the old town, there is a large new town built to house transmigrants from Indonesia who farmed in the area prior to 1999. Laleia suffered more deeply than Tibar from the Indonesian terror. During the occupation, Laleia stood at the turnoff into the mountains for anyone traveling from the coastal strip between Dili and Baucau to FALINTIL's eastern base in the *suco* of Cairui. The town was a center of resistance activity; the *liurai* [traditional dynastic ruler] of Laleia, who has a house in the town, tells stories of entertaining Indonesian soldiers on his front veranda while members of his household passed supplies to FALINTIL guerrillas out of the back door.

Laleia's suffering in 1999 was also more extreme than Tibar's. A militia named Alfa Team, operating from Manatuto, was responsible for widespread destruction. The notorious Indonesian Battalion 745, based in Los Palos, retreated through Laleia following the vote, pausing to shell the area on September 21 and to burn buildings

---

[35] Villager (6) personal interview, Tibar, East Timor, May 2005.

and kill civilians on the way. The *suco*s of Lifau and Hatularan bore the brunt of the destruction and were almost razed; the interior *suco* of Cairui, home to FALINTIL in the mountains, was left alone.

Like Tibar, Laleia received emergency food aid and rebuilding materials from UNHCR after 1999. The Community Empowerment Project, which funded the water project in Tibar, brought US$40,000 into Laleia, which was used for road and bridge reconstruction, as well as to purchase chairs for the Lifau school and communally owned kitchen equipment that could be rented out to villagers in Hatularan. Part of this relief effort was organized through microcredit transactions, rather than through grants, although people who were awarded these loans faced the same problems as had the residents of Tibar; the district administration remarked that only eighteen out of ninety loans made in Manatuto District had been repaid. More recently, Laleia had attracted Japanese funding for two development projects via the United Nations Development Program's Recovery, Employment, and Stability Program for Ex-Combatants and Communities in Timor-Leste (RESPECT) programme. These were used to repair water systems damaged in 1999 and to rebuild the market. UNICEF and the World Bank had rehabilitated the primary schools, and the ministry of health had rebuilt the clinic. The local authorities were awaiting news, in 2005, of a US$150,000 project for renovating the irrigation systems in the rice fields, and a Japanese NGO had recently visited the region with the intention of setting up an irrigation project.

Like Tibar, Laleia had reestablished its administration on the basis of a local civil society inherited from the resistance era and before. The historic Portuguese church and the youth movement associated with the clandestine movement were each a focus of activity. The town of Laleia was home both to the traditional *liurai* and his family, and to a subdistrict, *suco*, and *aldeia* administrative structure that had emerged from the clandestine movement. In 2005, following local elections, the modern and traditional authority systems operated alongside one another with an obvious degree of unease and a certain amount of hostility, but without open conflict.

A striking difference between Laleia and Tibar was the presence, in Laleia, of a long-term development strategy. This strategy focused on the market, which had formed the basis of the town's prosperity in the past and which people anticipated could do so again. Rebuilding the market would attract traders from Dili and Baucau, bringing prosperity to the area and buyers for local produce. Local people regarded the future of rice farming as bright if funding could be found to repair the irrigation systems. Unlike the leaders of Tibar, caught between the collapse of the coffee industry and the recession in Dili, *chefes* in Laleia regarded economic problems as relatively temporary.

Laleia had benefited from closer engagement with its district administration, compared with the situation in Tibar, particularly with respect to aid projects. Closer relations between the district, subdistrict, and *suco* levels had produced a system in which officials were well-drilled in the details of different aid programs and their requirements, in contrast to conditions in Tibar, where the *chefes* reported distant or even hostile relations with the district administration. *Chefes* and group leaders in Laleia talked of the training and assistance they had received from the Manatuto district office in preparing proposals for international aid funding and in executing projects. The *chefe de suco* of Lifau in Laleia, who had held the position since 1972, through the Indonesian era to independence, and been reelected in 2005, reported holding regular monthly meetings in the *suco* to discuss development projects. In Tibar, by contrast, the *chefe* commented that such organizational meetings were held only when a project was due to start. In Laleia, the *chefes* had been instructed in the procedures of participatory development, and they talked in detail about inclusion and about consulting at least the men in the community in order to assess their needs. In Tibar, the *chefe de suco* commented, "We live with the community in the village, so we know what people need. We relay information from the village to the international staff, and we know what happens in community life."[36]

But despite differences in leadership style, officials in Laleia faced problems resembling those confronted by officials in Tibar: their budgets were too small to cover travel or to pay for hosting meetings, and they had been given no office in which to hold meetings and receive visitors. The *chefe de suco* of Lifau commented that he frequently paid out of his own pocket for refreshments for meetings and said, "I am embarrassed to receive guests in my house because of its poor condition."[37] In Laleia, a roof had been erected over an open area in the town center to serve as a meeting place, but the walls necessary to turn this structure into an office were lacking. Following his election in 2005, the *chefe* of Lifau had begun receiving a budget for expenses, but at US$50 a month it was, he said, insufficient.[38]

Interviews with personnel in the district office suggested that the close relations and strong communications enjoyed between Laleia and the district might not be representative of all subdistricts in Manatuto. The district administrator remarked that it was easier to conduct development activities in Manatuto itself and in places like Laleia than in the mountains: "Far from Manatuto, they don't know how to access the money, and they don't know how to submit proposals to the district level. Also it is hard for us to monitor projects that are far away."[39]

Despite the town's relative success, some residents of Laleia were concerned that their town was not receiving its fair share of available resources. One villager argued that Manatuto itself had received more aid than Laleia: in Laleia, two out of ten proposals for funding were accepted by the district level, whereas in Manatuto eight out of ten were accepted, he alleged. This, he said, was because the group of staff members in the Manatuto district administration that selected projects was dominated by individuals from Manatuto itself:

> When they have a debate to select proposals, from here in Laleia we have only one staff member there who participates. Manatuto subdistrict has a lot. It's a democratic country, so the majority will win.[40]

As in Tibar, there was a perception in Laleia that international aid was not trickling down evenly to communities across the country as it should, but was remaining pooled at the center:

---

[36] *Chefe de suco*, personal interview, Tibar, East Timor, April 2005.

[37] *Chefe de suco*, personal interview, Laleia, East Timor, July 2005.

[38] Ibid.

[39] District administrator, Manatuto, personal interview, Manatuto, East Timor, July 2005.

[40] Group leader, market rehabilitation project, Laleia, personal interview, Laleia, East Timor, July 2005.

Sometimes international donors send millions and millions of dollars to Timor, but the money stays in the center and doesn't arrive at the community level. They should go to the community so the community can feel the benefits. I cannot complain about the government because we are proud of our government, but you can see that our daily life is really miserable. The government needs to decentralize money [and divert it] to the community's life.[41]

One interviewee in Laleia commented that the problem was focused at the central level, rather than the district level, "The district administrator can't be corrupt because there is no money in the district. Money all stays at the central level."[42]

Also, as in Tibar, individuals in Laleia who had been involved in aid projects described their interaction with higher levels of government and with international aid agencies in a manner that emphasized their own sense of atomization. Despite the better and closer relations between the *suco* and district levels that typified this region, compared with Tibar, and the more energetic formulation of development plans within Laleia itself, there remained a sense that the community had been disempowered in its relationship with influential actors beyond its boundaries:

We can't say whether the district administrator has done a good job or not. He has power. It's his job to get international aid to come here. We have no right to say whether he has done a good job or not. We only receive what they offer.[43]

While the community had worked hard to form the requisite committees demanded by various international programs, this effort had not translated into a sense of control over development. Leaders of groups mobilized to submit proposals and implement projects for the RESPECT program commented that they were happy with the outcome of their projects and hoped to have an opportunity to participate in this kind of development project again. But these development initiatives did not leave structures behind them, and in this way they were less effective than the activities of the clandestine movement. Committees were formed when funding became available, and they dissolved when it ran out, with little sense that they would exert an ongoing impact on social organization. The "community" called into being by the programs demanding community participation was artificial; it did not represent local structures of power and authority, and it was clearly recognized as a construct dependent on criteria imposed from outside. One group leader, asked if his group continued to work on development initiatives, said that they were waiting to see whether there would be a new funding scheme, and, if so, if there would be new criteria for the kinds of groups that might take part: "It depends on the situation. To set up a new group, we have to base it on the idea proposed by the government."[44] This interviewee added that the villagers had been unable to help define the criteria for aid that flowed in: "We were given no chance to advise the top level of the UNDP programme. We are simple people in the village ... I don't know about the future."[45]

---

[41] Group leader, water project, Laleia, personal interview, Laleia, East Timor, July 2005.

[42] *Liurai*, personal interview, Laleia, East Timor, July 2005.

[43] Group leader, water project, Laleia, personal interview, Laleia, East Timor, July 2005.

[44] Ibid.

[45] Ibid.

In Laleia, success in submitting proposals to win international funding consequently widened participation in development strategizing at the local level, but did not significantly alter the people's perceptions that the relationships between the international, national, and local levels were marked by inequities in power. Interviewees in Laleia, like interviewees in Tibar, believed they were disadvantaged by selection processes in comparison to other subdistricts with better connections to the center. Applications for international funding submitted by persons in Laleia garnered more disappointments than successes, replicating the experience in the country overall, where 931 proposals for projects, worth a total of US$8,438,273, were submitted, but fewer than a quarter of these projects, worth a total of only $1,074852, were approved.[46] The local people in Laleia, as in Tibar, perceived that their role was to act as aid entrepreneurs, competing with others to attract the attention of international NGOs, striving to reorient local habits of collaboration to meet externally imposed criteria, and focusing upon upward accountability. Important factors in success were the leadership and energy of local level officials and their ability to cultivate relationships with powerful external actors in the district, in the central government, and in international NGOs.

This approach to development introduces considerable tensions with respect to nation-building. While the strategies are intended to promote local control, their strong focus on the local level as the site of development—as opposed to facilitating broader national or regional development initiatives—in fact encouraged political fragmentation, particularly since local persons had no opportunity to provide input in planning and thereby assert some control over the selection and designs of the projects that would be funded. This situation frustrated local citizens. Authorship of the various proposals encouraged short-lived alliances of groups at the local level in response to external conditions, but the effort did not cement these relations over the longer term, nor did it link these local committees into representative regional or national structures of decision making. The result was an increased, rather than reduced, sense of atomization.

In Timor-Leste, the speed with which the identities of Firaku and Kaladi were repoliticized in 2006 to overwhelm that of Maubere, a historic category encompassing all Timorese ethnic groups, reflects the sense of people within Tibar and Laleia—communities studied in 2005—of their own isolation from a distant, inaccessible, and poorly defined "national" administrative sphere. This sense of alienation, combined with intense competition for aid funds, produced considerable discontent. Given the depth of their need and extent of their efforts, interviewees in both districts were inclined to believe that government members at the central level were either pocketing substantial funds or channeling funds to their own home villages and supporters, rather than following approved criteria ... and of course, in some cases, they were. Even in Laleia, the hometown of the president of the republic, interviewees expressed concern regarding patronage within the district administration. In both places, the atomization of a previously powerful sense of national community was keenly felt, and villagers expressed concern that they were "forgotten."

[46] "The RESPECT Program in Timor-Leste," *Lao Hamutuk Bulletin* 5,5–6 (2004), online at http://www.laohamutuk.org/Bulletin/2004/Dec/bulletinv5n5.html, accessed August 7, 2007.

These concerns, voiced by villagers a year before the 2006 crisis, explain why organizational issues within the armed forces, and political machinations among the elite, caused a generalized crisis that resulted in the emergence of a highly politicized cleavage within the country as a whole. The extent of voters' dissatisfaction was expressed in elections in 2007, and FRETILIN's vote fell by 50 percent as compared to 2001. In Liquiça district, FRETILIN's vote in both the second-round presidential and the parliamentary elections in 2007 collapsed to 12 percent. In Manatuto, FRETILIN gained just 17 percent of the vote in the parliamentary elections and 19 percent in the second round of the presidential elections.[47]

"HIEN TVEU" (DARE TO DO): CAMBODIA, ON THE CAMPAIGN TRAIL

The Cambodian government's strategy since 1993 has been very different from that of the Timorese government. The Cambodian People's Party (CPP) had learned a salutary lesson in the dynamics of power through its experience of governing in the 1980s. During the 1980s, the Vietnamese had attempted to build a government from the top down, a government whose policies were strictly confined by ideology, and which faced, in consequence, extreme difficulties in forming attachments with communities and local chiefs. The extent of the death toll, of internal displacement, and of confusion in 1979 entailed that rebuilding a local authority structure was extremely difficult.

Unlike in Timor, in Cambodia there was no highly valued, self-motivated, and well-organized clandestine movement to step into the breach. What was in place—and was, to an extent coopted by the incoming regime—was a more-or-less organized system of Khmer Rouge cadres, including some who had been purged in the later years of the DK (Democratic Kapuchea) regime. Stephen Heder reports that the incoming government announced that it would practice "leniency vis-à-vis those who are honest and who understand and sincerely correct their wrongdoings"[48]—a provision that permitted the new government to rely on ex-Khmer Rouge from the Eastern Zone to administer the country. Heder suggests that former Khmer Rouge occupied about a fifth of the positions in the new Party Central Committee and leading state structures and were chiefs of seven of the eighteen provinces and municipalities. More former Khmer Rouge were coopted as village or commune chiefs under the new regime.[49]

Appointing new chiefs was one thing; getting them to do what they were told was another. During the 1980s, local authorities performed extremely poorly in

---

[47] Results taken from the Comissão Nacional de Eleições Timor-Leste website, online at http://www.cne.tl/, accessed September 18, 2007.

[48] Solidarity Front for the Salvation of the Kampuchean Nation, *Communique*, December 2, 1978, cited in Stephen Heder, "Hun Sen and Genocide Trials in Cambodia," in *Cambodia Emerges from the Past: Eight Essays*, ed. Judy Ledgerwood (De Kalb, IL: Northern Illinois University Southeast Asia Publications, 2002), p. 188.

[49] Ibid. The most powerful member of the incoming government, Chea Sim, was, according to Evan Gottesman, "valued by the Vietnamese for his ability to coopt Khmer Rouge defectors," and he built an extensive patronage network of former Eastern Zone cadres. Evan Gottesman, *Cambodia After the Khmer Rouge: Inside the Politics of Nation-Building* (New Haven, CT: Yale University Press, 2002), p. 47. Ben Kiernan sees the same situation slightly differently, suggesting that former Eastern Zone Khmer Rouge cadre, purged in 1977–78, were returned "in local elections and with popular acclaim." Ben Kiernan, *The Pol Pot Regime: Race, Power, and Genocide in Cambodia under the Khmer Rouge, 1975–79* (Chiang Mai: Silkworm, 1997), p. 455.

implementing central directives regarding conscription, rice procurement, and collectivization. Aware that these policies, imposed from above, were largely unenforceable, local authorities largely went their own way. They derived a healthy profit in bribes through their collusion with villagers seeking to dodge the draft, hide produce from state procurement drives, or avoid collective labor in favor of household cultivation. At the same time, when faced with pressure from above, they were capable of using violence to enforce compliance on the part of those who could not afford the payoff. This lack of cooperation on the part of local authorities, and the inability of the center to exert power over them, represented the key weakness in the functioning of the 1980s state.

In response to this situation, as described in Chapter 6, the CPP erected a new system of power drawing upon old forms.[50] The forms closely resembled traditional informal networks of patron-client relations, but they were reoriented to the needs of modern state consolidation and civil war, through their focus upon eliciting resources from the population via various shady economic deals and ubiquitous demands for bribes. These resources were then used to fund political power gambits; the large sums of money paid to defecting Khmer Rouge commanders in the mid-1990s to secure their loyalty are one example. This style of rule was legitimated—among those who directly benefited from it, at least—by a new ideology that promised, and extolled, protection against external threats, envisaged as the threat posed by returning opposition parties and by international actors that would seek to dominate the government. Broader legitimation was achieved by two means: through the plowing of resources elicited via this discretionary sphere into highly visible and overtly politicized development projects aimed at the rural poor; and through the creation and maintenance of an atmosphere that threatened violence and menace, intended to encourage conformity to the system on the part of nervous villagers. This was a system designed to remind villagers continuously that they (unlike their contemporaries in Tibar and Laleia) were far from forgotten.

For much of the 1990s, Cambodia remained on a war footing. Even in areas of the country from which the Khmer Rouge insurgency appeared distant, communes and villages still hosted the armed militias that had been mobilized for security purposes during the 1980s. Weapons were widespread, and insecurity in the countryside was complemented by instability within government. However, for those within the state apparatus, life was increasingly good. Privatization of land and expansion of businesses such as logging awarded village and commune chiefs significantly more opportunities to make money than they had enjoyed heretofore. Their loyalty to the regime increased accordingly, and the local authority structure became the linchpin of the CPP's strategy for maintaining power, which officials reinforced through a system of village surveillance, designed to regiment and intimidate villagers, even as new ideas of democracy, rights, and participation were being promoted by opposition political parties, newspapers, and nongovernmental organizations.

For villagers across much of rural Cambodia, life improved, but much more slowly. Although economic activity picked up following land privatization, significant aid flows were slow to reach rural areas. The stability and the relative political openness that followed the deployment of UNTAC (United Nations

---

[50] This point is made by Serge Thion, "The Pattern of Cambodian Politics," in *Watching Cambodia,* ed. Serge Thion (Bangkok: White Lotus, 1993), p. 135.

Transitional Authority in Cambodia) in the capital city spread only gradually across rural Cambodia over the course of the 1990s. Rural life was dominated by continued fear of local authorities, now acting on behalf not only of their own interests, but of the central government's also. Threats from shadowy insurgents and rogue military men hiding in the surrounding forest entailed that villagers were dependent upon the protection of village and commune chiefs, even while fearing the violence they were equally capable of inflicting. The Khmer proverb, "caught between the tiger and the crocodile," was frequently invoked to describe the position of villagers caught between threatening and corrupt local authorities and violent insurgents.

Those who dealt with local authorities were required either to pay a bribe or invoke a family or patronage connection. For individuals without either the cash to make payments, or the requisite connections, contact with the authorities was a hazardous business, best to be avoided in general. Human rights workers interviewed in 1996 gave examples to characterize the situation as follows:

> There was a very serious incident in one family. The daughter was raped by the local authorities, and [her family] just did not know where to go to make a complaint. They thought if they went to the district, or the commune, it would be useless, because all those guys are friends with each other.[51]

> Most Cambodian officials, they just use power for their own interests ... Because if you are a policeman, you have a gun, and because you have this, you can get anything that you need. That's the problem.[52]

However, conditions began to change in rural Cambodia at the end of the decade, following the reemergence of the CPP as the dominant party at the national level and the successful cooption by the CPP of the Khmer Rouge insurgency. Outside the towns, where the Sam Rainsy Party remained a player, the CPP was now the predominant force in Cambodian politics. At the same time, the CPP itself sought to rationalize its own local structures, bringing some of the more corrupt and abusive authorities to heel as a means of both increasing flows of income to the central level and promoting the party's own popularity among the voters. Several reforms were initiated, including a vigorous weapons collection process, which resulted in the collection and destruction of 200,000 light arms between 1997 and 2007,[53] and the demobilization of village and commune militias. These demilitarization initiatives were accompanied by a decentralization process, which has been marked by two major developments. The first was the election of commune councils in 2002, which were to replace the appointed chiefs that had been in place since the 1980s. The second was the expansion of a village-based participatory development program, called the Seila (Foundation Stone) program, that had been operating in the northwest provinces since the mid–1990s, and which was now implemented in all Cambodia's provinces.

---

[51] Human rights NGO activist, Kampot Province, personal interview, Kampot, March 1996.

[52] Public defender, Phnom Penh, personal interview, Phnom Penh, January 1996.

[53] Christina Wille, "Finding the Evidence: The Links between Weapons Collection Programmes, Gun Use, and Homicide in Cambodia," *African Security Review* 15,2 (2006), online at http://www.smallarmssurvey.org/files/portal/spotlight/country/asia_pdf/asia-cambodia-2006b.PDF, accessed February 23, 2007.

These activities, following close upon the end of the war and the stabilization of the national political situation, reduced levels of violence and political tension in rural villages. The reduction of the commune's security role and the increased role it was awarded in development—changes that coincided with the election of commune councils—altered, to an extent, the nature of the relationship between local authorities and villagers. One study carried out in 2005 suggested that the attitude of villagers toward government had shifted following the replacement of the commune chiefs appointed in the early 1980s by elected, multiparty commune councils in 2002. Joakim Öjendal and Kim Sedara suggest that the commune election marks a watershed in the history of rural Cambodia in the minds of rural people, and that it signifies a shift from top-down to bottom-up governance. In interviews, Öjendal and Kim found that commune chiefs appreciated this change, finding their new responsibilities easier than the thankless task of imposing unwanted directives on a reluctant population. Öjendal and Kim describe new terminology used to characterize the relationship between people and local authorities; the tiger and the crocodile no longer feature, but instead villagers evoke their close cooperation with their village chiefs with the phrase *pheap chea dai kou* (like a pair of clasped hands). Öjendal and Kim describe processes of consultation conducted via village meetings, which, although they do not include all villagers, are participatory in the sense that people are allowed to speak and the commune chief acknowledges the need to listen. While having a voice does not necessarily mean having a say, it is possible now for villagers to ask questions of local authorities without fearing for their lives.[54]

To an extent, this shift has been triggered by new requirements for commune councils, which are expected not only to compete for votes, but also to get involved in mobilizing villagers for development initiatives. The spread of local participatory exercises, as modeled by the Seila program, infused a content into commune activities that had not previously existed, producing a requirement that commune officials engage more directly and frequently with villagers, and giving them something to talk about.

Begun in the northwest provinces of Cambodia in 1996, and spreading to the whole of the country after 2000, the Seila program was unique in Cambodia at the time. The wide discretionary powers of these same provincial authorities, typical in the 1980s, had been severely constrained by the reorganization of the regime between 1989 and 1993; Seila represented one of a very few opportunities for provincial governors to make development decisions for their provinces. The program established provincial development committees chaired by provincial governors and comprising line ministry staff, who oversaw the distribution of a "provincial investment fund" to support capital investment projects proposed by communes. The program initially operated through elected Commune Development Councils established to facilitate it, and later via the elected commune councils that emerged in 2002, and its central focus was upon supporting provincial and commune planning and coordination mechanisms. After the 2002 local elections, a small commune fund was provided directly to communes via the Seila program to support local initiatives. Seila thus provided a budget that could be spent on delivering local goods to local people so long as the monies were expended in conformity with the bookkeeping standards and needs-assessment processes

---

[54] Joakim Öjendal and Kim Sedara, "*Korob, Kaud, Klach*: In Search of Agency in Rural Cambodia," *Journal of Southeast Asian Studies* 37,3 (2006): 507–26.

promulgated by the program. The Seila program invested US$78 million in the capital projects it generated between 1996 and 2001, and almost US$170 million between 2001 and 2005. Most of the capital investment was spent on small-scale infrastructure, such as repair of roads and bridges, which had been severely damaged, especially in the northeast provinces, by the war.[55]

This provision of budgets to the local level was successful in injecting a sense of purpose into an otherwise impoverished and aimless set of local government structures. One provincial governor, who had held his position since the 1980s, described the difference that the provision of a discretionary budget made to his position. He said that previously, "We just waited for orders from above," but after the establishment of the Seila program, officials could take control, plan for the future, and, in doing so, elicit support from the population.[56] Given the absence of rural development institutions, funding, or processes in rural Cambodia in the 1990s, the Seila program, with its detailed eleven-step process for identifying needs and funding and implementing projects, filled a yawning gap in the state–society relationship.

However, as with participatory development projects in Timor, there were limits to the sense of empowerment that this sort of initiative could bestow. The Seila program identified the reform of the state–society relationship, through the promotion of bottom-up practices of participatory decision making, transparency, and accountability, as one of its key concerns. A large number of evaluations and studies were generated by the program to try to establish whether a change in the culture of government had been produced.

Necessarily, given the large number of other changes ongoing at the same time, the evidence of results is highly equivocal. Although the Seila program gave provincial, commune, and village authorities a budget to discuss, and a set of forums within which to discuss it, it is unclear whether the customary hierarchy of relations between the various levels of government was significantly challenged. A 2001 study, investigating the impact of Seila on the involvement of villagers in local governance, found that villagers were aware of Seila activities in their own village, but unaware of activities at the commune level. While they were involved in competing for money, and spending it once it had flowed into their orbit, they were not involved in the decision-making process itself that selected among proposals or determined expenditure. This limited villagers' ability to demand accountability from their elected commune representatives.[57] More recent studies have suggested that villagers have become increasingly aware of the importance of the commune level, but not very aware of the mechanics of the planning process, in part due to the limited availability of information. The same study found that villagers were concerned about the technical standards of some projects that had been implemented; they claimed that officials and contractors collaborated to supply substandard materials in order to skim budgets.[58] In other words, Seila, like the RESPECT program in Timor, delivered tangible, popular, and useful benefits to

---

[55] Figures supplied by the Seila Secretariat, Phnom Penh.

[56] Ung Samy, Governor of Pursat Province, personal interview, Pursat, October 2004.

[57] Robin Biddulph, "Civil Society and Local Governance: Learning from the Seila Experience," Kuala Lumpur: UNOPS, July 2001.

[58] Robin Biddulph, *PAT [Permanent Advisory Team] Empowerment Study—Final Report,* (Phnom Penh: Permanent Advisory Team on the Seila Program, Partnership for Local Governance, 2003.)

villagers, in response to their own assessments of their needs. However, it was less successful in empowering villagers with respect to a wider, imagined sphere beyond the lived world of the village, kin, and patronage networks, and in encouraging face-to-face encounters between villagers and influential elites outside those usual networks. Such programs do not bring into being an "imagined community" at the national level. Rather, they magnify the local sphere of the village as the preeminent sphere within which villagers ought to frame their concerns.

Furthermore, with Seila, as with RESPECT, the fact that villagers' proposals were quite likely to be rejected tended to rob the villagers of confident anticipation, rather than award them with a feeling of power. In both these cases there is anecdotal evidence of villagers tiring of the work involved in producing proposals that may not lead to anything, particularly as time passes and the most urgent and obvious needs have been addressed. One study found that, over time, the circle of people consulted in local planning tended to contract back towards the same small politicized circle that had always been in control, in part because local chiefs found that mobilizing villagers to participate in plans that subsequently did not attract funding made them unpopular.[59]

While the Seila program and the institution of local elections have created more opportunities for interaction between villagers and local authorities, and have reduced the level of fear in the state–society relationship at this level, neither of these reforms has substantially expanded the horizon within which villagers feel empowered and represented. Villagers refer to a uniform *tnak loeu* (high class), which governs above the level of the commune council, a group of elites they prefer to avoid. Their reluctance to become embroiled in negotiations with these elites has been reinforced by the actions of the government itself. The expansion of decentralization reforms has been concomitant with a move on the part of the government to crack down on protest movements in the capital city. These had emerged from the mid-1990s, alongside growing opportunities for travel and the national discourse of democracy and national elections, promoted by UNTAC. The protests comprised noisy, public, and long-lasting demonstrations, in which protestors sometimes camped out for days or weeks in front of the national assembly building, complaining about a variety of issues, from wages in the garment industry to the price of fuel to land-grabbing in the provinces.

Though such protests were initially treated with circumspection, the government's tolerance for these kinds of demonstrations decreased markedly from 2002 on, again weakening the sense that citizens might have access to a national sphere of decision making. Brutality in the policing of protestors became increasingly common, and the municipal government in Phnom Penh showed a growing inclination to ban altogether the mildest of activities, even when organized by well-established and conservative human rights organizations. Thus, the citizenry's increasing ability to question local-level authorities in Cambodia accompanied a sharp decline in the short-lived ideal, promoted by UNTAC, of public questioning of national-level authorities. To this extent, decentralization, rather than boosting democratic control, has let the national government off the hook with regard to the

---

[59] See Caroline Rusten, Kim Sedara, Eng Netra, and Pak Kimchoeun, *The Challenges of Decentralisation Design in Cambodia* (Phnom Penh: Cambodia Development Resource Institute, 2004), p. 121.

big picture, diverting villagers' attention back to small-scale issues with limited potential for mobilizing more widespread political movements.

There is some evidence of increasing willingness, among Cambodian villages, to mobilize groups of dissenters to lobby village or commune officials over issues such as land and natural resource privatization.[60] Though this kind of resistance would have been unthinkable in the 1990s, when rural dissidents fled to Phnom Penh for protection from local authorities, the situation has, to an extent, reversed in the 2000s, as increasingly local protests are dealt with through the structures of commune governance. The overwhelming dominance of the CPP at the local level—it secured all but twenty-one commune chief positions in the 2002 local elections, and all but thirty in the 2007 local elections, out of a total of 1,621 such positions nationally—renders protest much more manageable, and prevents specific cases of discontent from linking with, and reinforcing, either the opposition-minded population in the cities, or the broader nationalist tropes that remain common in Cambodian opposition rhetoric regarding the likelihood of the government "selling the country to the Vietnamese." Indeed, the local level has become so manageable that commune councils have been made the linchpin of the government system, responsible for appointing village chiefs and electing members of the national senate. In 2008, the Cambodian government passed an organic law governing the organization of subnational governance, which is designed to devolve power from ministries at the national level to provincial and district administrations, and to institute councils at these levels. District and provincial councils will be elected by commune councilors.[61] These moves have further intensified the elevation of the local over the national in terms of public participation in developing strategies for development.

Whereas in Timor the elevation of the local occurred in a context in which the national level was largely viewed as absent or absconded by citizens, in Cambodia, politicians strongly promote nationalist discourses in villages. By far the most dominant of the contending narratives promoted is the version that is closely associated with the CPP and Prime Minister Hun Sen. In his many speeches, delivered in villages across the country, Hun Sen tells stories of national development and progress that give substance to the imagined community of the nation by linking the country's history and future to the activities of networks of key individuals. In these stories, he rarely invokes the institutional trappings of modern statehood: the administrative pyramid of government, with its system of formal appointments, or the formal education system, for example. Rather, he describes the actions of individuals embedded in webs of patronage relations, which, increasingly, converge upon the prime minister himself, in a crude facsimile of Sihanoukist cosmologies of power. Hun Sen's activities and his narratives—the personal presence of the prime minister in all areas of the country; his constant journeying from one village to the next; his description of the personal donations of equipment, infrastructure, and development funding, offered by himself and other prominent figures; his public assertions of his intention to protect loyalists and his boasts

---

[60] Centre for Advanced Study and World Bank, *Justice for the Poor? An Exploratory Study of Collective Grievance over Land and Local Governance in Cambodia* (Phnom Penh: World Bank, 1996).

[61] Royal Government of Cambodia, *Organic Law on Administration and Management of the Capital, Provinces, Districts and Khans,* 2008, Art. 13.

concerning the spectacular fall of rivals and challengers—all tell a story of an imagined community that operates through personal connections and personal power. This is a narrative that accurately reflects the power awarded the prime minister through his position at the apex of a complex network of resource-extraction activities, in which a percentage of profits is always passed upwards.

There are two aspects to this rhetorical national sphere. One is its vulnerability, particularly to traitors, terrorists, and spies, entailing the need for a strong government led by powerful, influential men. A second is its dependence. In Hun Sen's political rhetoric, dependence is a key issue, dealt with in strikingly different ways than in Western aid discourse. Whereas in aid discourse dependence is regarded as highly problematic, since it threatens to stultify the emergence of necessary entrepreneurial zeal in post-emergency populations, in Hun Sen's political rhetoric dependence is promoted as a natural state of affairs, the appropriate form of relations between leaders and followers. In this rhetoric, and in the practices of the Cambodian state, personal loyalty, solidarity, and mutual relations of obligation form the stuff of not only politics, but development economics. According to this narrative, the state–society relationship is based, not upon representation and downward accountability, but upon trust, loyalty, and reward. While this portrayal gives substance to the national sphere, which becomes increasingly associated with the figure of Hun Sen himself—a "strongman" who "dares to do [*hien tveu*]" and who protects and assists his loyal supporters accordingly—it is profoundly disempowering to ordinary people.

However, this narrative works because it accords closely with the experience of villagers, not only with respect to the Cambodian government, but also with respect to donors. In democratic exercises, as in participatory development, a strong emphasis on going through the motions in the hope of eliciting external support dominates thinking about participation in Cambodian villages. Consequently, in local-level election campaigns, as in local development, the importance of exhibiting loyalty to leaders and providing them with support, manifested through agreement and applause, is highly valued, while open dissent, even in extreme circumstances, represents a sure route to dispossession and marginalization.

This continual reemphasis on the connection between development and loyalty is particularly evident in the CPP's reliance on its development record in mobilizing support during elections. The CPP claims responsibility for the vast majority of visible development projects in Cambodian villages, either as a result of its management of international aid, or as a result of its own generosity. Development is mediated and, often, instigated by meritorious benefactors (*saboraschon*) who sponsor development projects as a means to make merit for themselves and to reward the loyalty of their clients.

While there are inherent difficulties in estimating the amount of money that goes into these kinds of projects, the visual impact of them is huge. The personal monogram of Prime Minister Hun Sen is inscribed in shining gold on the low roofs of hundreds of rural schools, while the CPP's *devada* (angel) logo swoops across temple murals across the country. The prime minister or other high-ranking party officials are invariably personally present to "inaugurate" these gifts, at ceremonies that offer another opportunity for the distribution of presents to villagers. These activities crescendo in the approach to elections. Hun Sen's diary for June 2003, covering the weeks leading up to the start of that year's national election campaign, indicates the scale of these activities. In the three-and-a-half weeks prior to the start of the campaign on June 26, Hun Sen attended twenty-seven engagements, more than one a day. Of these, twenty-one were inauguration or ground-breaking ceremonies for infrastructure developments. Of these, four were funded by donations from the Japanese government and one by private entrepreneurs, but the remaining sixteen were funded by either Hun Sen himself, by other high-ranking CPP officials, or by the CPP, through sources such as their Disaster Relief Fund.

The projects that were being celebrated included the construction or improvement of eight temples, one bridge, four roads, four schools, and one district office. At each ceremony, the prime minister offered more gifts. According to his cabinet's public record, that month Hun Sen promised to build fifty-eight school buildings, five bridges, and forty-three kilometers of road, and he gave away nearly US$170,000 in cash, more than 400 tonnes of rice, 130 tonnes of cement, and 320 sewing machines, as well as computers, printers, photocopiers, generators, televisions, and other electronic equipment.[62] Over the years, this kind of activity equates to the expenditure of millions of dollars, rivaling programs such as Seila in its impact on village infrastructure. Unlike negotiations sponsored by Seila, in this process the benefactor, Hun Sen, makes no attempt to elicit participation and input from villagers regarding their preferences or needs; the villagers' role is confined to applauding and expressing thanks and happiness. But as with the Seila program, the source of the gifts, their place in a wider horizon of politics and economics, and the decision over whether anything will be provided at all, comes from a *tnak loeu*, beyond the people's control.

These gifts are intimately connected to the CPP narrative of nationhood and power. The CPP claims authorship of Cambodian development, as it claims authorship of Cambodia's "rebirth." In speeches delivered across rural Cambodia, Hun Sen makes a point of reminiscing about skeins of acquaintance between himself and the commune he is addressing, starting from the war years and recalling visits in this or that year, scheduled for various purposes. His accounts of his travels across the country, his exploits, his dedicated opposition to the genocidal "Pol Potists," and his personal ascent from simple farm boy to prime minister have the effect of knitting together the nation across space and time; his own footsteps link the village to the nation. The rise of Hun Sen himself from poverty to power, and his efforts for the country along the way, link the personal autobiography of the prime minister to national history and associate his own patronage with the development and protection of the nation.

This rhetoric is highly effective in winning votes, but not necessarily because villagers regard it as particularly helpful to their own lives. Villagers, in fact, express in private a good deal of skepticism about the nature of the gifts they receive. Gifts are no substitute for livelihoods, whether these might be obtained through jobs, natural resources, or land, and for the rural poor in Cambodia, the means to earn a living are in increasingly short supply. *Saboraschon* development is funded by kickbacks from large investors, including logging companies and plantation owners. Their interests collide, in some rural communes, with well-established local strategies of self-reliance. Concessions that grant large tracts of land or forest to powerful entrepreneurs dispossess villagers of natural resources such as orchards and resin trees, a loss that arouses deep resentment from the dispossessed.

---

[62] The details of Hun Sen's program given here are taken from his website, "Cambodia New Vision," online at www.cnv.org.kh, accessed August 9, 2004.

However, the CPP has been highly effective in two ways. First, it has been successful in identifying itself with the protection and nurturing of the nation. By claiming to be the nation's only reliable guardian, the party leaves scant room for the emergence of formal state institutions that could facilitate the divorce of ideas of the nation from ideas of the party. Consequently, since 1997, voters generally, and rural voters in particular, have had few alternatives and have felt pressed to reelect the CPP as the only party that can control the country and get things done. Second, the CPP has put a premium upon loyalty, such that villagers are reluctant to be identified as dissenters and potentially excluded not only from future benefits, but from the protection of the local authorities. This prevents different rural constituencies of discontented groups from linking up in an organized or sustained manner to form a unified opposition movement that could challenge the government, and the opposition's failure to coalesce has reinforced the government's domination of conceptions of the nation. The fragmentation of the local level and the inescapability of the Cambodian People's Party within the local sphere and within the institutions of state renders democratic politics at the national level largely a question of going through the motions.

This pattern has persisted despite the election of multiparty commune councils, which were intended to pluralize the local sphere. Interviews conducted at the provincial and the commune level in Battambang, Kompong Cham, Kampot, and Takeo provinces during the 2003 election campaign suggested that the scale of the CPP's dominance of village life had changed very little since the 1980s. For example, in Veal Vong, an urban commune on the outskirts of Kompong Cham town, an NGO election observer commented:

> The commune chief is the head of the party—FUNCINPEC and SRP don't have any power. They only have a name. They are afraid of intimidation ...[63]

The SRP first deputy chief commented:

> Although we have elected commune councils, the district and the party still control everything. Among commune councilors, the opposition party members are still bypassed.[64]

He added, "All village chiefs still belong to the CPP, and they are very likely to cause conflict in local areas." Such conflicts, he argued, emerged from strategies of intimidation and threat used by village chiefs to pressure villagers into voting for the CPP. The problem stemmed from the fact that "people in the commune and village authorities are still affiliated to the party, and they work for the party, not for the government."[65] Interviews with village chiefs bore out this assertion. One village chief in the commune commented: "We work hard to explain to people about the political agenda of the CPP, but other parties have the right to express their political agenda as well." He added,

---

[63] Committee for Free and Fair Elections in Cambodia (COMFREL) provincial representative, Kompong Cham, personal interview, July 2003.

[64] SRP first deputy commune chief, Veal Vong, personal interview, Kompong Cham, July 2003.

[65] Ibid.

Now there are two sectors—one is state, and one is party. I work for both ... In some places, we do call people to vote for this or that party, but in my village we don't.[66]

The same village chief acknowledged the influence of the party on questions concerning development within his village. He explained that most development assistance came from the CPP, and that he reported to the CPP district office about the needs of his village, after consultation with five other CPP members in the village. He commented further that he knew who in his village belonged to which party, although he could not always be sure that everyone voted for the party to which he or she allegedly belonged.[67]

The various roles of this individual—as state official, representative of village development needs, party worker, and also, in this case, as the head of the *wat* committee in the village—were closely intertwined in his account, with the party playing the dominant role and only tenuously distinguished from the state. Other village chiefs who were interviewed drew clearer distinctions between party roles and state roles, claiming, for example, that they were only allowed to campaign for the CPP in the evenings and on the weekends. However, it is unlikely that this distinction was either evident or pertinent to voters.

In Battambang, concern as to difficulty of separating state from party extended to the personnel of the Commune Election Committee (CEC). Since village and commune chiefs were barred from membership of these committees, the committees were often staffed by local school teachers. An SRP member in Peam Ek commune in Battambang complained:

All CEC staff members are government employees, mainly schoolteachers. They are the clients of the government, so I don't trust them because after the election they will return to work in their daily routines and be directly controlled by CPP. Do you think that they are accountable for other parties besides CPP? The answer is clearly not.[68]

The committee members' inescapable ties to the party were regarded as their key electoral asset by CPP supporters and local officials. In Wat Tamim commune in Battambang province, CPP village chiefs commented, "People make their judgments based on the feasible outcome in their community."[69] Similarly, the CPP commune chief in Ta Khaen commune in Kampot province described his constituents as interested in "what they can see." He said,

People here are not educated, 70 percent can't read, children don't go to school. But they know which party they love. They can see which party comes to help them. Big people come, and the people see, and they vote as they see, [based on] who comes to solve their problems, build roads, build schools.[70]

---

[66] Village chief, Veal Vong commune, personal interview, Kompong Cham, July 2003.

[67] Ibid.

[68] SRP chief, Peam Ek, personal interview conducted by Kim Sedara, Battambang, July 2003

[69] Village chief, Wat Tamim, interview conducted by Kim Sedara, Battambang, July 2003.

[70] Commune chief, Ta Khaen, personal interview, Kampot, July 2003.

That the CPP was the only party that regularly delivered gifts to the electorate was a campaign message that was propagated widely by the party.

Given these conditions, it is not surprising that rural Cambodian voters face constant pressure to declare a CPP allegiance. In 2003, in three of the six communes studied, opposition supporters reported being asked, "If you vote for the SRP, where will you live?" by local officials whom they considered powerful enough to expropriate their land. A FUNCINPEC commune council member in Ta Khaen commune reported that he was constantly under pressure to switch to the CPP, in return for a favorable judgment in an undecided land dispute. SRP members in the same commune said that villagers were reluctant to travel outside the commune to attend SRP campaign rallies for fear of "receiving trouble" when they returned.[71] Although fear has decreased in Cambodian communes, and violence surrounding elections is markedly less than in the 1990s, the stigma of being identified as an opposition supporter is still routinely described as something villagers seek to avoid.

This pressure has been effective, even in situations where individuals face stark injustices. During interviews conducted in a relocated squatter village in 2001, individuals commented on the dilemma facing them. The residents had been forcibly removed from the area where they had previously lived—in a long-standing squatter settlement in the center of Phnom Penh—following a mysterious fire that razed most of the houses. The following morning, a bulldozer was sent by the municipality to clear away the rest of the houses. The prime minister stepped in, offering donated land outside the city on which the displaced residents could rebuild. This was an unattractive offer, for the proferred land was too far away for the recipients to commute from there to Phnom Penh to engage in their regular livelihoods, but there was no work to be had in the new area. At the same time, the gift was better than nothing. To receive it, would-be residents were required not only to refrain from protesting their initial expulsion from the squatter camp, but actively to court the local authorities through a range of bribes and through expressions of loyalty and gratitude. The gift was highly effective in stamping out a brief protest effort by the squatters, who tried to reoccupy the site where they had lived. One interviewee commented:

> I felt frightened that it would be too late for me to come here if I stayed over there too long. I rushed to come here, but even so I didn't get such a good place—it's not near the market. If I'd come early, I could have got a place near the market. Some families wanted to stay at the old place, but we were told that if we came too late, all the land would be shared out already, and we wouldn't get anything.[72]

Among interviewees, many complained that outsiders, who had not been residents of the former squatter area, had bribed local authorities in order to receive land to which they were not entitled. The representative of one family that had waited for a week in the rain to be allocated land described feelings of disempowerment in this situation: "We don't want to be thought of as rebellious. We are afraid that if we are thought of as rebellious, there'll be some problem."[73] Interviewees also described

---

[71] SRP member, personal interview, Kampot, July 2003.

[72] Resident, Samakki village (1), personal interview, July 2001.

[73] Resident, Samakki village (2), personal interview, July 2001.

how a visit to the site from Prime Minister Hun Sen was stage-managed so as to ensure appropriately grateful responses from the villagers:

> There's no one we can complain to. Even though one day Prime Minister Hun Sen came to speak, we were not given any right to complain. In the meeting, we just sat down, and we were told not to make any complaint ... The organizers of the meeting, and also the police, told the people here before Hun Sen arrived that if we have any problems, we shouldn't ask him about them, we should just sit quietly and not make any complaints.[74]

While this form of politics has been highly successful in stabilizing the rural political situation and ensuring the continued support of farming households for the CPP, it has been far less successful with respect to the relatively mobile landless, who have little to lose. Government policies designed to deal with, for example, squatters and garment workers—two large and relatively well-organized groups of rural-urban migrants—suggest the government's willingness to use violence to control unruly groups. Another large cohort of landless and potentially troublesome constituents is made up of the young people who reached adulthood after land distribution in 1989 and who have been unable to establish households and livelihoods due to the scarcity of newly available land. Though currently fragmented and poorly organized, this group is highly problematic for the CPP. In the cities, the large numbers of young and unemployed represent a new problem that will increase over coming years, given the youthfulness of the Cambodian population as a whole. A high prevalence of gang membership, drug abuse, and violent crime among the youth in Phnom Penh has been well documented. However, the response from this group to their marginalization reflects fragmentation and social alienation rather than organized political dissent.

The story of post-intervention politics in Cambodia's villages is a success story to the extent that the people's freedom from both want and fear is considerably more widespread than it was before: both violence and poverty have decreased. As in Timor, this evolution has not been accompanied by new relations of representation and accountability. Unlike Timor, Cambodians have been given a vehicle through which they can identify themselves as a member of a national political community; that vehicle is the Cambodian People's Party. The extent to which villagers are prepared to accept the CPP's claims and status as legitimate depends upon circumstance. For the landed, life is gradually improving, so rocking the boat appears foolish. For the landless, life is hard, but mounting an organized protest to influence the government and thereby improve the situation seems nearly impossible. Among these dispossessed citizens, reluctance to concede legitimacy to these arrangements is evidenced by growing signs of alienation, rather than overt protest, expressed through falling electoral participation, migration, and growing social ills such as gang membership and drug addiction, even as poverty apparently falls and the economy grows.

For both groups, the opportunities for political action have shrunk to avenues defined by interpersonal contacts. Above all, these comprise hierarchical channels of communication with local authorities and with patrons, but these are characterized by steep inequalities of power. Neither local democracy nor participatory

---

[74] Resident, Samakki village (3), personal interview, July 2001.

development mechanisms in Cambodia significantly increase the power of local villagers to influence the distribution of the external resources upon which they rely. Like Timorese local authorities, Cambodian commune officials seek to attract international aid both through compliance with various processes modeled upon Seila and through compliance with the patronage-oriented mechanisms adopted by the CPP. In neither case, however, does this translate into any kind of representation or control in decision making. The people's lack of influence over their potential government benefactors is replicated in the relationship of villages to external investors.

Once again, the result is an atomized form of development. Under these conditions, the local looms large as an island of mutual cooperation among familiar neighbors, but the national is difficult to imagine except in the guise of the *saboraschon*, who arrives in the village from time to time, offering gifts and menaces. This association of the national level with personalities at the top of a party-dominated state structure is familiar from the Sihanouk period, as is the strong promotion of the idea that any kind of dissent or deliberation at this level is inherently dangerous and likely to lead to renewed catastrophic warfare. The dynamics of post-conflict intervention have produced a situation in which this paternalistic, personality-centered structure can be reproduced, crowding out a secular concept of the nation as a community with structures for participation and deliberation, and conceptualized as a network that links the familiar local level to a sometimes generous, but also demanding, capricious, and unknowable, international sphere.

THE DISAPPEARING NATION: BETWEEN GLOBAL ASPIRATIONS AND LOCAL REALITIES

Under conditions of post-conflict aid dependence, the nation, in both Cambodia and Timor, was supplanted as a key sphere for political aspiration and orientation by the local and the international. In each case, the post-conflict community evolved so that local-level institutions came to be increasingly familiar and accountable, but lacking in power; at the same time, international actors came to be perceived as immediately engaged and powerful, but entirely beyond villagers' control. The national level—intermediate between the local and international—is imagined in a more complex manner. On the one hand, it is associated with long-standing aspirations for independence, sovereignty, and autonomy, and regarded as potentially representative of an historic identity—Khmer or Timorese—that is highly valued. At the same time, the slenderness of the threads connecting the local sphere to the national sphere, and the emptiness of the national level, its poor functioning, usurpation by particular parties or individuals, and its failure to take control of issues pertaining to development or justice, make the imagined community of the nation actually quite difficult to envisage.

From one perspective, the demise of nationalism might be something that is practically inevitable, given globalization, and normatively desirable, given the bloody history of the twentieth century. However, neither globalization nor post-conflict intervention entails the end of the state, the entity presiding over national territory. On the contrary, previous chapters have described the transformation of the state under conditions of globalization, and the ways in which the geographical and conceptual borders between the inside and the outside of the nation-state are policed by interventionary actors. Both these processes seek to preserve the links between people, state, and territory, even while political and economic power become freed from such constraints.

In the context of the contemporary global political economy, political organization in dependent communities such as Cambodia and Timor-Leste has transformed each country, although to differing extents. In both cases, the impact of aid dependence and international prescriptions for post-conflict reconstruction have led to a significant reduction in the discretionary sphere of national policy-makers, such that efforts to mobilize national participation, through, for example, elections, have perforce focused on procedures rather than substance. The power to make political decisions concerning substantive issues involved in resource distribution has been reallocated, with ambiguous results. On the one hand, more participation in decision making is offered to ordinary villagers; but, on the other hand, increased focus on the local level has the effect of confining individuals within smaller spheres of influence, giving them power over smaller resource bases. The stifling effect of the shrinking of the political sphere is even more forcefully felt because of the very presence of international agencies, their continued real control over the disbursement of aid funds to pay for villagers' development plans, and the contrasting example offered by the lifestyles of their wealthy, powerful, and internationally mobile staff members.

What does this reallocation of political power mean for the political aspirations and strategies of individuals? This study suggests that, for many, this reallocation of power has been experienced as profoundly disempowering. In Cambodia, where the radical nationalism of the past had brought such disaster, this kind of disempowerment was less actively resisted within civil society than in Timor, where it represented an intense disappointment. As one Timorese NGO activist commented:

> The current situation demonstrates that our nationalist spirit, which was very high during the resistance, has been eroded by the nation-building process because of lack of participation; and in the end, our sense of ownership of our state has been whittled away little by little. So the aid did not enforce our independence, but sometimes destroyed our hopes.[75]

Within Timor-Leste, individuals, such as NGO activists and other white-collar workers, who had expected the national government to seek them out for their contributions, felt particularly let down when they were integrated into resource-management and "capacity-building" networks over which they felt they had no control and within which they felt little valued. This was evident from the strikes and complaints faced by UNTAET. However, this same kind of discontent emerged in Timor-Leste after the UN ceased to be a factor. In Cambodia, similar individuals found it difficult to stake out terrain for independent political action, for they were caught between the soulless technical solutions prescribed by international agencies, on the one hand, and the exclusionary patronage politics of the CPP, on the other. One manifestation of the sense of alienation that this caused was an enthusiasm for

---

[75] Guteriano Nicolau S. Neves, "The Paradox of Aid in Timor-Leste," talk presented at the seminar on "Cooperação Internacional e a Construção do Estado no Timor-Leste," University of Brasilia, Brazil, July 25–28, 2006, online at http://www.laohamutuk.org/reports/06ParadoxOfAid.htm, accessed September 19, 2007.

emigration. The strenuous efforts to police would-be emigrants has reflected the continuing significance of state boundaries for both national elites and international policy-makers.

Countries such as Cambodia and Timor are largely immune from the realities of large-scale brain drain; their education systems are not sufficiently recognized in the outside world to qualify degree holders for work permits abroad, rendering visa barriers prohibitive. According to official economic estimates, a relatively small proportion of the population can afford to move. For professionals and public servants, dreams of escape revolve around opportunities for study and work overseas, whether permanently or for a short period. Aid donors are keen to assist nationals to gain international qualifications, however the beneficiaries are heavily policed in order to ascertain that the newly acquired qualifications and talents will be taken back "home" to develop the needy country rather than used to permit the holder empowered access to the international labor market. This is the source of a considerable degree of contention. One (unsuccessful) applicant for an AusAID scholarship to undertake masters-level study in Australia, interviewed in 2002, when asked where he saw himself in five years time, simply replied, "Overseas"—an answer that was in direct contradiction to the aims of the scholarship program but summed up the ambitions of many local aspirants.[76] East Timorese recipients of AusAID grants, interviewed in Australia in 2005, were subject to stringent restrictions on their movements while being supported by grant funds. One student, who had gained an MA in Australia and returned to Dili to work, spoke of the difficulties he faced in fitting back into Timor after four years away. "I just stay in my room and watch DVDs. I want to go and live in Sydney—get my PR [permanent residence]. My head is still full of Australia."[77] He said that he planned to try to get a job teaching in Australia, as he had heard there were teaching shortages there, as a means to get permanent residence, once he had served the required time back in Timor.

Similar problems hampered a Portuguese scholarship scheme that had provided funding for 314 East Timorese students to study in Portugal. The program was abandoned due to a high drop-out rate, yet a number of the students whose funds had been cut did not return to Timor. Lao Hamutuk noted in 2002 that only eight of the 314 students had returned to Timor; many others "no longer attend their courses but remain in Europe to work."[78] It is clear that these expatriate students took advantage of laws that awarded some Timorese rights to apply for Portuguese citizenship if they were residing in Portugal. These were rights that many Timorese took up in the early post–1999 period, but which subsequently became much more difficult to access. Faced with a potential influx of Timorese immigrants, the Portuguese embassy in Dili imposed more and more stringent restrictions on those seeking visas to travel to Lisbon, requiring deposits, references to show ongoing employment in Timor, and other guarantees, all meant to insure that these travelers would eventually return "home."

---

[76] Personal communication from the applicant, Phnom Penh, September 2001.

[77] Local employee at an international aid agency in Dili, personal communication, Dili, May 2005.

[78] Lao Hamutuk, "Portuguese Support in the Education Sector," *Lao Hamutuk Bulletin* 3,7 (2002), online at http://www.laohamutuk.org/Bulletin/2002/Oct/bulletinv3n7.html# Education, accessed August 7, 2007.

This kind of policing extended into the sphere of nongovernmental activism. In the 1990s, training NGO activists in international networking was an important aspect of international assistance to domestic NGOs in Cambodia. Yet Cambodian NGO activists going abroad for conferences in the 1990s were similarly heavily policed. One NGO leader interviewed said that embassies awarding visas would blacklist organizations if their employees absconded while abroad on training programs or attending workshops.[79] There was heavy pressure on NGOs to limit overseas travel to those persons most likely to return, or face penalties as a result. Nevertheless, although data is not available, anecdotal evidence of individuals who absconded while on overseas visits abounded in the NGO sector in Phnom Penh in the 1990s. The imposition of these kinds of controls on activists and students in post-conflict Timor and Cambodia reflected the widespread aspiration to leave the country—an aspiration that was fostered, rather than reduced, by the impact of international aid. Intervention and aid brought Cambodians and Timorese into close working relationships with individuals hailing from an empowered, glamorous, and wealthy global sphere. Contrasted against such luxury, the disempowerment, hardships, and poverty of life in the post-conflict nation became doubly apparent. The nostalgic comment of one former UNTAET staff member, made in a café on the beachfront at Areia Branca just outside Dili in 2005, summed up the sense of marginalization felt by local staff when the UN juggernaut moved on, leaving them behind:

> During UNTAET, this would have been packed with UN cars, parked all along here. We used to come to this place for our Friday afternoon meeting—the beach would have been crowded, everyone would have been here. Now they are all gone, and only I remain.[80]

The individual in question spent much time pursuing applications for study abroad.

These kinds of international ambitions were of course entertained only by the very few, those who had been privileged to interact with even more privileged international staff members. Other opportunities for legal migration from post-conflict states were rare. Middle-class mothers in Phnom Penh sought to marry their offspring to members of the diaspora; one such mother told me in 2008 that marriages of convenience to Australian citizens could be arranged for a fee of US$100,000. Some families arranged to have children adopted by extended-family members residing in Australia or Canada. For many other would-be migrants, however, the only opportunity to leave was through legal migration schemes that placed Khmer workers in factories in South Korea, Thailand, and Malaysia, or through illegal migration across the border to Thailand. For the rural poor, realistically, escaping the village involved joining the transnational underclass, a class whose political disempowerment is exacerbated by the repressive nature of internationally policed migration regimes; by the violence and abuse of underground people smugglers and traffickers; and by the "discipline" of the market as this manifests itself in sweatshops and construction sites across Asia.

Even so, a range of studies in recent years show that migration from Cambodia to Thailand from the northwest provinces is widespread, with a large majority of

---

[79] NGO activist, Khemera, personal interview, Phnom Penh, October 1995.

[80] Former UN local staff member, personal interview, Dili, June 2004.

households having members with migrant histories. Furthermore, the flow of people is increasing.[81] One study noted that the experience of migration encourages further migration. Although a majority of migrants reported receiving poor treatment in destination countries, by employers and by police, as returning migrants they found it difficult to "reintegrate" back into the village because of joblessness, low living standards, and debt, and therefore they often ended up migrating again.[82] Another study noted that while 77 percent of respondents said that they migrated to Thailand to work in order to generate income, almost a quarter said they migrated to broaden their experience and opportunities. These ambitions reflect not merely the economic hardship prevalent in Cambodia, but the grimness of social and political life in aid-dependent communities generally.[83] Many patriotic state builders certainly exist in post-conflict countries such as Cambodia and Timor-Leste, but they represent only one side of the story. For many individuals in post-conflict societies, their contribution is neither politically valued nor particularly well remunerated; and escaping this confinement becomes a key aspiration, further undermining the idea of the nation as something more than a nostalgic fantasy featuring a chimeric home.

Postwar international intervention, then, reverses the relationship between the international and the domestic arenas that had been accepted during wartime. In both Timor and Cambodia, the domestic realm was portrayed during the war as the heroic stage upon which good and evil forces fought battles over the soul of the People. In this scenario, international backers represented Machiavellian forces behind the scenes, but ultimately it was national armies and their leaders who were perceived as having made sacrifices to fulfill a national aspiration of freedom. The liberation of the homeland represented the ultimate hope. While these stories may have been poorly connected to reality, they offered a basis for imagining a national community that was lost after the transition to peace. Peace and intervention brought a new national myth to the fore, one in which domestic survivors of the war were transformed into a generalized group of backward and incapacitated victims, emerging from a mire of pointless violence in which their country had floundered while the rest of the world marched onwards. Following intervention, it was international political actors who claimed to be heroic, since they had sacrificed comfortable Western lifestyles in the interests of providing aid and expertise to the impoverished and traumatized Asian population, people who must make renewed sacrifices in their efforts to "catch up" with the rest of the world ... efforts which, somehow, never seem to pay off.[84]

This myth offers considerable resources to certain members of the elite, in particular those who return from elective exile, or those most closely associated with the intervenors. For other sections of the elite, it represents a challenge that can be dealt with by reference to self-interested tropes of "authenticity" and by the

[81] See for example, Analyzing Development Issues Team, *Labour Migration to Thailand and the Thai-Cambodian Border* (Phnom Penh: Cooperation Committee for Cambodia, 2003); International Labour Organisation, *Destination Thailand: A Cross-Border Labour Migration Survey in Banteay Meanchay Province, Cambodia* (Bangkok: International Labour Office, 2005).

[82] Analyzing Development Issues Team, *Labour Migration to Thailand and the Thai-Cambodian Border*, p. 11.

[83] International Labour Organisation, *Destination Thailand*, p. 36.

[84] Some international actors are, of course, also perceived as villainous, but either way they are seen as powerful and in some sense as forces that control the shape of local destinies. I am grateful to an anonymous reviewer for Cornell SEAP Publications for raising this point.

appropriation and incorporation of ideas about international progress into a new narrative of national destiny. For the middle class, it is a myth that strongly encourages flight and pursuit of Western passports, jobs, and qualifications. It is a myth, however, that offers little to the poor except the certainty that they will be marginalized. While democracy is mandated, democratic decision making is suspect because of the dysfunctionality of the population itself. While the efforts of the poor must be elicited in order to promote the process of their reform, this is accomplished within highly policed, atomized, and localized spheres of activity.

Aid dependence ushered in a period of tension in both countries under study here. In East Timor, although the resistance movement had been highly fragmented throughout the war years, all those who participated looked to a unifying and specifically national ideal of liberation. Although deferred, this ideal of a longed-for liberation imbued the nation as an imagined community with a sense of purpose in the minds of different groups of Timorese around the country. After independence, with liberation achieved, but under conditions of aid dependence, a new unifying ideal failed to emerge to take its place, in a context where liberation proved to be painful and impoverished. Neither development nor democracy has been sufficient to promote a new sense of national community. Democratic rituals, such as elections, although national, have been organized in a manner that is designed to demobilize, rather than mobilize, political constituencies. Civil society is internationally oriented, casualized, and fragmented rather than being specifically national in scope. In development, the nation suffers even more: development initiatives take the form of village-level planning or international investment. The state plays a merely facilitative role; the nation is barely consulted.

Conceptualized as an antidote to authoritarianism, and designed to promote "grassroots" perspectives and voices, this approach can, in fact, appear alienating to citizens in a post-conflict context. Attempts to merely "switch off" destructive nationalist tropes, while, at the same time, undermining sovereignty and atomizing individuals, reorienting them towards self-reliant, local-level entrepreneurial action in the interests of "development," are problematic. They leave important political orientations unresolved, demand an unrealistically rapid reconstruction of ideas about citizenship and community, and underestimate the extent to which people invest emotion and identity in wartime rhetoric. The problem is particularly acute in a context where the economic incentives associated with reorientation are minimal and uncertain.

Meanwhile, the poor must use the meager resources available to them to attempt to elicit desperately needed support in an environment in which the embrace of self-reliance would mean the abandonment of any aspiration beyond bare subsistence. In this context, associational life becomes oriented towards the capture of resources rather than involving community deliberation over the performance of social, political, and economic activities. Thus tension arises in situations when villagers spend significant amounts of time on "needs assessments" and other participatory exercises, intended to feed into donor decision making, only to find that their painstakingly crafted proposals have been unsuccessful. Doctrines advocating self-reliance, participation, and empowerment require that villagers expend considerably greater amounts of energy to secure essentially the same crumbs of assistance. In Timor-Leste, particularly, these post-conflict rewards contrast rather unfavorably with Indonesian development assistance, which came in the form of gifts of animals and jobs in public works programs. The "welfarist" approach is criticized by Timor's current donors on the grounds that it breeds dependency rather than entrepreneurial spirit. However, in a high-cost economy, where the main productive industries have collapsed entirely, entrepreneurial spirit can easily start to seem a waste of energy, particularly when it is imposed by donors and ends in disappointment.

Similarly, the democratic process transforms into an acquisitive exercise, as citizens vote to support the likeliest channel for aid. The comment of a voter interviewed by Reuters in Timor-Leste in June 2007 could easily have been uttered by a Cambodian voter at any time in the preceding fifteen years:

> We will go and cast our ballots because we are stupid people and will ask the victors to then repair our huts and provide us with more food.[85]

Cambodian voters regularly complain in private about the quality of the gifts they receive from leaders, and the endless injunctions, by politicians, to *"cham s'aek"*— wait until tomorrow.[86]

The inadequacy of political imaginings gave rise to a powerful sense of alienation, particularly evident in urban centers. These urban areas swelled rapidly during the 1990s in Cambodia as a result of rural-to-urban migration; however, a lack of jobs and housing for these new arrivals, as well as for a new generation coming of age, prompted a powerful sense of dislocation and disenfranchisement. A population emerged that belonged nowhere, lodged in overcrowded conditions with more-or-less accommodating relatives, possessing neither economic resources nor a political voice. This situation exacerbated tensions within families, and between generations, producing, in particular, concerns about the behavior of the young. Research has documented high levels of gang membership, drug use, and violence among youth in Phnom Penh.[87] Meanwhile, rates of voter turnout declined from over 90 percent in the 1998 national election to 75 percent in the 2008 national election. In commune elections, turnout declined from 87 percent in 2002 to 66 percent in 2007. In Phnom Penh, turnout in the 2007 commune elections fell below 60 percent.[88]

In Timor-Leste, similar phenomena are evident and rapidly became tied up with the politicization of regional cleavages. The sense of fragmentation prevalent in the country has been demonstrated by a number of related developments: the tense

---

[85] "East Timor Elections," Reuters Television, Lequidoe, Liquiça, and Dili, East Timor, June 26, 2007, 05:46:17.

[86] This phrase was regularly used by villagers in conversations concerning the election campaigns in 1998 and 2003. Attitudes towards gifts are explored in more detail in Caroline Hughes, "The Politics of Gifts: Tradition and Regimentation in Contemporary Cambodia," *Journal of Southeast Asian Studies* 37 (2006): 469–89.

[87] See for example, Gender and Development (GAD), *Paupers and Princelings: Youth Attitudes Towards Gangs, Violence, Rape, Drugs and Theft*, (Phnom Penh : GAD, 2003); see also data from the United Nations Office of Drugs and Crime Asia and Pacific Amphetamine-Type Stimulants Information Centre website, which notes increase in the use of methamphetamines, or *yama*, between 2003 and 2006, and particular concentration of drug use among the young, with 55 percent of users aged between 18 and 25 and a further 20 percent aged between 10 and 17 years, http://www.apaic.org/TRENDS/cambodianew.html#dc, accessed 4 November 2008.

[88] Figures taken from the National Election Committee website, online at http://www.necelect.org.kh/English/elecResults.htm, accessed September 18, 2007; also from Committee for Free and Fair Elections in Cambodia (COMFREL), *Final Assessment and Report on the 2007 Commune Council Elections*, (Phnom Penh: COMFREL, 1997), online at http://www.comfrel.org/images/others/1188360503COMFREL%20CCE%20Report%20Final%20without%20Pictures.pdf, accessed November 5, 2008, p. 63.

relations between former FALINTIL members, former members of the clandestine movement, and the government; the rise of "security groups" of discontented youth; and the promulgation and exploitation of the labels "Firaku" and "Kaladi," which acquired a new significance in 2006 through being used to criticize the process of state–building itself. Timor's highly mobilized society, which functioned effectively in keeping the nationalist dream alive through the worst years of the Indonesian occupation, has become a liability in an aid-dependent era during which neither economic hope nor political accommodation have been offered.[89]

The domestic perceptions of citizenship, community, and nation that emerge from these relations of power are rather empty ones. As was true for the solder quoted at the start of this chapter, who regarded himself as transformed by demobilization into an "empty shell," many citizens have experienced a profound loss of purpose attendant upon the shift from national mobilization in support of warfare to demobilization and integration into global structures of economic development. Clearly, for most people, peace on almost any terms is preferable to war. Yet the sense of impotence felt by those whose lives have been altered by postwar political reorganization is strong, and for some groups, particularly for those trapped in poverty, the disappointment may be significant enough to encourage them to take up arms again. The readiness of unemployed youth to join gangs, the reluctance of demobilized soldiers to "go home," and the disorientation of villagers who feel disempowered by their distance from national and international spheres in which their opportunities and conditions of life are predetermined, all point to the failure of procedural democracy and participatory development to award a sense of control to individuals in post-conflict societies. In the suburbs of Phnom Penh and Dili, and the towns and villages of the Cambodian and Timorese countryside, individuals who survived bloody conflicts have been stripped of the sense of citizenship in an imagined, autonomous community. They now face a choice between two grim options: entrapment in a shrinking, dependent, but familiar local sphere, or flight, on unfavorable terms, into a fragmented and threatening global economy.

---

[89] See James Scambary, Hippolito Da Gama, and Joao Barreto, *A Survey of Gangs and Youth Groups in Dili, Timor-Leste* (Dili: AusAID, 2006).

Bibliography

Abrahamsen, Rita. *Disciplining Democracy, Development Discourse and Good Governance in Africa.* London: Zed, 2000.

Adams, Brad. "Demobilization's House of Mirrors." *Phnom Penh Post,* November 23 to December 6, 2001. Online at www.phnompenhpost.com., accessed September 20, 2007.

Aglionby, John. "Bungled UN Aid Operation Slows East Timor's Recovery." *The Guardian,* August 30, 2000, posted online at http://www.etan.org/et2000c/august/27-31/30bungl.htm., accessed September 20, 2007.

"Agreements on a Comprehensive Political Settlement to the Conflict in Cambodia." Paris, October 23, 1991. Online at http://documents-dds-ny.un.org/doc/UNDOC/GEN/N91/361/63/img/N9136163.pdf?OpenElement, accessed September 13, 2008.

Akashi, Yasushi. "To Build a New Country, the Task of the UN Transitional Authority in Cambodia." *Harvard International Review* 3 (1992): 34–35, 68–69.

Alkatiri, Mari. Address at a forum hosted by Marion Hobbs in association with Asia 2000 Foundation, Institute of Policy Studies, Centre for Strategic Studies and New Zealand Institute for International Affairs. Wellington, August 18, 2003. Online at http://www.primeministerandcabinet.gov.tp/speeches.htm, accessed September 20, 2007.

— Remarks from opening session of Timor-Leste Development Partners Meeting. Dili, May 18, 2004. Online at http://www.primeministerandcabinet.gov.tp/speeches.htm, accessed September 20, 2007.

— Speech delivered at Extractive Industries' Transparency Initiative Conference. London, March 17, 2005. Online at http://www.laohamutuk.org/Oil/Transp/05PMtoEITI-UK.htm., accessed September 20, 2007.

— "Decision Time." Speech delivered at the opening session of the Timor-Leste Development Partners Meeting. Dili, April 4, 2006. Online at http://www.primeministerandcabinet.gov.tp/speeches.htm, accessed September 20, 2007.

Alonso, Alvaro, and Ruairí Brugha. "Rehabilitating the Health System after Conflict in East Timor: A Shift from NGO to Government Leadership." *Health Policy and Planning* 21,3 (2006): 206–16.

Amnesty International. *Cambodia: Human Rights Concerns, July to December 1992.* London: Amnesty International, February 1993.

Analyzing Development Issues Team. *Labour Migration to Thailand and the Thai-Cambodian Border*. Phnom Penh: Cooperation Committee for Cambodia, 2003.

Anderson, Benedict. *Imagined Communities: Reflections on the Origin and Spread of Nationalism*. London: Verso, 1991.

— "Imagining East Timor." *Arena Magazine* 4 (April–May 1993).

Ang, Bunhaeng, and Martin Stuart Fox. *The Murderous Revolution: Bunhaeng Ang's Life with Deuch in Pol Pot's Kampuchea*. Bangkok: Orchid Press, 1998.

Annan, Kofi. "Report of the Secretary General to the Security Council on the Protection of Civilians in Armed Conflict." UN Doc. S/1999/957. September 8, 1999.

— "We the Peoples, the Role of the United Nations in the 21st Century." United Nations Secretary General's Millennium Report. New York, NY: United Nations, 2000. Online at http://www.un.org/millennium/sg/report/full.htm, accessed September 20, 2007.

Archibugi, Daniele. "Immanuel Kant, Cosmopolitan Law and Peace." *European Journal of International Relations* 1 (1995): 429–56.

Ashley, Richard K. "Living on Border Lines: Man, Poststructuralism, and War," in James Der Derian and Michael J. Shapiro, *International/Intertextual Relations: Postmodern Readings of World Politics*. New York, NY: Lexington, 1989, pp. 259–321.

Ayers, Alison. "Demystifying Democratisation: The Global Constitution of (Neo)liberal Polities in Africa." *Third World Quarterly* 27,2 (2006): 321–38.

Ballard, Brett. *Reintegration Programmes for Refugees in South East Asia: Lessons Learned from UNHCR's Experience*. Geneva: UNHCR, 2002.

Bannon, Ian, and Paul Collier, eds. *Natural Resources and Violent Conflict: Options and Actions*. Washington, DC: World Bank, 2003.

Barber, Jason, and Ker Munthit. "Hun Sen Talks Tough to the West." *Phnom Penh Post*, December 15–28, 1995, p. 3.

— "'Puppet' Ranariddh Lashes Coalition." *Phnom Penh Post*, April 5–18, 1996, p. 10.

Bayart, Jean-Francois. *The State in Africa, the Politics of the Belly*. Harlow: Longman, 1993.

Beauvais, Joel. "Benevolent Despotism: A Critique of UN State-Building in East Timor." *New York University Journal of International Law and Politics* 33 (2000–01): 1101–78.

Becker, Elizabeth. "Low Cost and Sweatshop Free." *New York Times*, May 12, 2005. Online at http://topics.nytimes.com/top/reference/timestopics/people/b/elizabeth_becker/index.html?offset=20&s=newest, accessed January 10, 2007.

Berger, Mark. "From State-Building to Nation-Building: The Geo-Politics of Development, the Nation–State System and the Changing Global Order." *Third World Quarterly* 27,1 (2006): 5–25.

Bickerton, Christopher J., Philip Cunliffe, and Alexander Gourevitch. *Politics without Sovereignty: A Critique of Contemporary International Relations*. London: UCL Press, 2007.

Biddulph, Robin. *Civil Society and Local Governance: Learning from Seila Experience*. Kuala Lumpur: UNOPS, July 2001.

— *PAT Empowerment Study — Final Report*. Phnom Penh: DFID/SIDA, November 9, 2003.

Bit Seanglim. *The Warrior Heritage: A Psychological Perspective on Cambodian Trauma*. El Cerrito: Bit Seanglim, 1991.

Booth, Anne. "Africa in Asia? The Development Challenges Facing Eastern Indonesia and East Timor." *Oxford Development Studies* 32,1 (2004): 19–35.

Bou Saroeun. "Cambodia's Soldiers Start New Lives as Civilians." *Phnom Penh Post*, October 26–November 8, 2001. Online at www.phnompenhpost.com, accessed September 20, 2007.

Boutros-Ghali, Boutros. "An Agenda for Peace, Preventive Diplomacy, Peacemaking and Peace-keeping." Report of the Security General to the Security Council. UN document A/47/277-S/24111. June 17, 1992. Online at http://www.un.org/Docs/SG/agpeace.html, accessed September 20, 2008.

— "Supplement to an Agenda for Peace, Position Paper of the Secretary General on the Occasion of the Fiftieth Anniversary of the United Nations." UN document A/50/60-S/1995/1. January 3, 1995. Reprinted in Boutros Boutros-Ghali. *An Agenda for Peace 1995*, second edition. New York, NY: United Nations, 1995.

— "An Agenda for Peace: One Year Later." *Orbis* 37 (1993): 323–32.

Boyce, James. "The International Financial Institutions: Post Conflict Reconstruction and Peacebuilding Capacities." Paper prepared for a high-level panel at the threats, challenges, and change seminar entitled "Strengthening the UN's Capacity on Civilian Crisis Management." Copenhagen, June 8–9, 2004. Online at http://www.cic.nyu.edu/archive/conflict/Boyce%20-%20IFIs%20&%20peacebuilding%20-%20June%202004.pdf, accessed September 20, 2007.

Brereton, Helen, and Sok Chan Chorvy. *Gender Analysis of Cambodia's Pilot Demobilization Project and Gender Mainstreaming Recommendations for the Full Demobilization Project*. Phnom Penh: World Bank, 2001.

Brown, Frederick Z., and David G. Timberman, eds. *Cambodia and the International Community: The Quest for Peace, Development and Democracy*. New York, NY: Asia Society, 1998.

Brown, MacAlister, and Joséph Zasloff. *Cambodia Confounds the Peacemakers*. Ithaca, NY: Cornell University Press, 1998.

Burki, Shahid, and Guillermo Perry. "Beyond the Washington Consensus: Institutions Matter." Washington, DC: World Bank, 1998. Online at http://www-wds.worldbank.org/external/default/WDSContentServer/WDSP/IB/1998/11/17/000178830_98111703552694/Rendered/PDF/multi_page.pdf accessed September 20, 2007.

Cabral, Estevao, and Julie Wark. "Timor-Leste: Behind the Demonisation of Mari Alkatiri," unpublished manuscript, on file with the author.

"Cambodia Says Anti-Corruption Law Delayed by Foreigners." *ABC Radio Australia.* January 3, 2007. Online at http://www.abc.net.au/ra/news/stories/s1820635.htm, accessed September 20, 2007.

Cambodian Rehabilitation and Development Board of the Cambodian Development Council. *Cambodia Aid Effectiveness Report 2007.* Phnom Penh: Royal Government of Cambodia, 2007.

Carnahan, Michael, William Durch, and Scott Gilmore. *Economic Impact of Peacekeeping.* Final Report. New York, NY: United Nations Department of Peacekeeping Operations, 2006. Online at http://www.un.org/Depts/dpko/lessons/, accessed September 19, 2007.

Carrington, Kerry, Stephen Sherlock, and Nathan Hancock. *The East Timorese Asylum Seekers: Legal Issues and Policy Implications Ten Years On.* Current Issues Brief no. 17 2002-3. Canberra: Department of the Parliamentary Library, 2003.

Centre for Advanced Study and World Bank. *Justice for the Poor? An Exploratory Study of Collective Grievance over Land and Local Governance in Cambodia.* Phnom Penh: World Bank, 1996.

Centre for Strategic and International Studies and Association of the United States Army. "Post-Conflict Reconstruction: A Task Framework." Washington, DC, May 2002. Online at http://www.csis.org/images/stories/pcr/framework.pdf., accessed September 20, 2007.

Cerny, Philip. "Globalisation and the Changing Logic of Collective Action." *International Organisation* 49,4 (1995): 595–625.

Chabal, Patrick, and Jean-Pascal Daloz. *Africa Works: Disorder as Political Instrument.* Oxford: James Currey, 1999.

Chan Sophal and So Sovannarith. "Cambodian Labour Migration to Thailand, a Preliminary Assessment." Working Paper 11. Phnom Penh: Cambodia Development Resource Institute, 1999.

Chan Vuthy and Sok Hach. "Cambodia's Garment Industry Post-ATC—Human Development Impact Assessment." Phnom Penh: Economic Institute of Cambodia, 2007. Online at http://www.eicambodia.org/UNDP/download/UNDP_Cambodia_Garment_Post_ATC_table_content.pdf, accessed February 17, 2007.

Chanda, Nayan. "Easy Scapegoat, People Blame the UN for All Their Woes." *Far Eastern Economic Review,* October 22, 1992, p. 18.

Chandler, David. *The Tragedy of Cambodian History, Politics, War and Revolution Since 1945.* New Haven, CT: Yale University Press, 1991.

— "The Burden of Cambodia's Past." In Frederick Z. Brown and David G. Timberman, eds., *Cambodia and the International Community: The Quest for Peace, Development and Democracy.* New York, NY: Asia Society, 1998, pp. 33–47.

Chang Pao-min. "Kampuchean Conflict: The Continuing Stalemate." *Asian Survey* 27 (1987): 748–64.

Chesterman, Simon. "Peacekeeping in Transition: Self-Determination, Statebuilding and the UN." *International Peacekeeping* 9,1 (2002): 45–76.

— *You the People: The United Nations, Transitional Administration, and State-Building.* Oxford: Oxford University Press, 2004.

Chimni, B. S. "The Geopolitics of Refugee Studies: the View from the South." *Journal of Refugee Studies* 11,4 (1998): 350–74.

Chopra, Jarat. "The UN's Kingdom of East Timor." *Survival* 42,3 (2000): 27–39.

— "Building State Failure in East Timor." *Development and Change* 33,5 (2002): 979–1000.

Christopher, Warren. "America's Leadership, America's Opportunity." *Foreign Policy* 98 (1995): 6–27.

Clifford, James. *Routes, Travel and Translation in the Late Twentieth Century.* Cambridge, MA: Harvard University Press, 1997.

Cock, Andrew Robert. "The Interaction between a Ruling Elite and an Externally Promoted Policy Reform Agenda: The Case of Forestry under the Second Kingdom of Cambodia, 1993–2003." PhD dissertation, La Trobe University, 2007.

Coelho da Silva, Hernani. "Four Years of Governance in Timor-Leste: An Overview." Paper presented to the conference entitled *Beyond the Crisis in Timor Leste.* Canberra, June 9, 2006. Online at http://devnet.anu.edu.au/Timor-Leste_Beyond%20the%20Crisis_Seminar_Home.php, accessed September 20, 2007.

Collier, Paul, V. L. Elliot, Havard Hegre, Anke Hoeffler, Marta Reynal-Querol, and Nicholas Sambanis. *Breaking the Conflict Trap: Civil War and Development Policy.* World Bank Policy Research Report. Washington, DC, and Oxford: World Bank and Oxford University Press, 2003.

Commission for Reception, Truth and Reconciliation in East Timor. *Chega! The Report of the Commission for Reception, Truth and Reconciliation in East Timor (CAVR).* Dili: CAVR, 2005. Online at http://www.etan.org/news/2006/cavr.htm, accessed September 10, 2007.

Commission on Global Governance. *Our Global Neighbourhood.* Oxford: Oxford University Press, 1995. Online at http://www-old.itcilo.org/actrav/actrav-english/telearn/global/ilo/globe/gove.htm, accessed May 10, 2008.

Commission on Human Security. *Human Security Now*. New York, NY: Commission on Human Security, 2003.

Commission on Post-Conflict Reconstruction. *Play To Win*, final report. Washington, DC: Centre for Strategic and International Studies and Association of the United States Army, 2003.

Committee for Free and Fair Elections in Cambodia (COMFREL). *Final Assessment and Report on 2007 Commune Elections*. Phnom Penh: COMFREL, 2007. Online http://www.comfrel.org/images/others/1188360503COMFREL%20CCE%20Report%20Final%20without%20Pictures.pdf, accessed November 5, 2008.

Cornish, Flora, Karl Peltzer, and Malcolm MacLachlan. "Returning Strangers: The Children of Malawian Refugees Come 'Home'." *Journal of Refugee Studies* 12,3 (1999): 264–83.

Council for the Development of Cambodia. *The Cambodia Aid Effectiveness Report 2007*. Phnom Penh: CDC, 2007. Online at http://www.cdc-crdb.gov.kh/cdc/aid_management/AER-Report-2007-FINAL.pdf, accessed September 19, 2007.

Cox, Robert. "Social Forces, States and World Orders" in *Approaches to World Order*, ed. Robert W. Cox and Timothy Sinclair. Cambridge: Cambridge University Press, 1996, pp. 85–123.

— "Critical Political Economy" in *International Political Economy: Understanding Global Disorder*, ed. Bjorn Hettne. London: Zed, 1995, pp. 31–45.

Crampton, Thomas. "Ex-Rebel's Vision for East Timor." *International Herald Tribune*, November 1, 2001. Online at http://www.iht.com/articles/2001/11/01/t5_0.php., accessed September 20, 2007.

Crisp, Jeff, and Andrew Mayne. *Review of the Cambodia Repatriation Operation*. UNHCR Evaluation Report. Geneva: UNHCR, 1993.

Crispin, Shawn. "Cambodia's Coming Energy Bonanza." *Asia Times Online*, January 25, 2007. Online at http://www.atimes.com/atimes/Southeast_Asia/IA26Ae01.html, accessed February 9, 2007.

Cristalis, Irena. *Bitter Dawn, East Timor, a People's Story*. London: Zed, 2002.

Curtis, Grant. *Cambodia Reborn? The Transition to Democracy and Development*. Washington, DC: Brookings Institute, 1998.

Del Mundo, Fernando. "Cambodia: The Killing Fields Revisited." *Refugees* 112 (1998). Online at http://www.unhcr.org/publ/PUBL/3b81031e4.html, accessed September 20, 2007.

Democratic Republic of East Timor Government. *Constitution of the Democratic Republic of Timor Leste*. Dili: Assembleia Constituinte, 2002.

Democratic Republic of Timor-Leste Government in consultation with Development Partners. "Poverty Reduction Strategy Paper—National Development Plan, Road Map for Implementation of National Development Plan, Overview of Sector Investment Programs—Strategies and Priorities for the Medium Term." Washington, DC: International Monetary Fund, 2005. Online at http://www.imf.org/external/pubs/ft/scr/2005/cr05247.pdf., accessed September 20, 2007.

Diamond, Larry. "Rethinking Civil Society: Toward Democratic Consolidation." *Journal of Democracy* 5,3 (1995): 4–14.

DiPalma, Giuseppe. *To Craft Democracies, An Essay on Democratic Transitions.* Berkeley, CA: University of California Press, 1990.

Dolan, Chris, Judith Large, and Naoki Obi. "Evaluation of the UNHCR's Repatriation and Reintegration Programme in East Timor, 1999–2003." Geneva: UNHCR Evaluation and Policy Analysis Unit, 2004.

Donnan, Shawn. "Complications Follow the Painful Birth of Timor." *Financial Times,* December 4, 2003. Online at http://www.etan.org/et2003/december/01-6/04compl.htm, accessed September 19, 2007.

Doyle, Michael. "Liberalism and World Politics." *American Political Science Review* 80 (1986): 1151–63.

— *UN Peacekeeping in Cambodia: UNTAC's Civil Mandate.* Boulder: Lynne Rienner, 1995.

Duffield, Mark. *Global Governance and the New Wars, the Merging of Development and Security.* London: Zed, 2001.

Dunn, James. *East Timor, A Rough Passage to Independence.* Double Bay: Longueville, 2003.

East Timor Observatory. "Transition: Halfway to Independence." November 6, 2000. Online at http://members.tip.net.au/~wildwood/NovTrans.htm, accessed September 20, 2007.

— "East Timor Defence Force: The Price of Security." May 17, 2001. Online at http://www/pcug.org.au/~wildwood/01maydefence.htm., accessed September 20, 2007.

Edwards, Penny. "Imaging the Other in Cambodian Nationalist Discourse Before and During the UNTAC Period" in *Propaganda, Politics and Violence in Cambodia: Democratic Transition under United Nations Peacekeeping,* ed. Stephen Heder and Judy Ledgerwood. London: M. E. Sharpe, 1996, pp. 50–72.

— *Cambodge, the Cultivation of a Nation, 1860–1945.* Honolulu, HI: University of Hawai'i Press, 2007.

Ellis, Stephen. *The Mask of Anarchy: The Destruction of Liberia and the Religious Dimension of an African Civil War.* London: Hurst, 1999.

Ethical Trading Action Group. "Lessons from Corporate Social Responsibility Initiatives in the Apparel and Textile Industries." Submission to National Roundtables on Corporate Responsibility. Toronto, Canada, Sept 12, 2006. Online at http://en.maquilasolidarity.org/sites/maquilasolidarity.org/files/ETAGsubmission0906.pdf, accessed September 12, 2007.

Falby, Patrick. "Fraud Found in Demobilization Process." *Phnom Penh Post*, October 25–November 7, 2002. Online at www.phnompenhpost.com, accessed September 20, 2007.

Fatton, Robert. *Predatory Rule, State and Civil Society in Africa.* Boulder, CO: Lynne Rienner, 1992.

Fernandes, Kenneth. "A Summary of 2006 Evictions in Cambodia." *Cambodian Eviction Monitor* 1 (2006): 7. Online at http://www.cohre.org/store/attachments/Eviction%20Monitor%20Jan-Dec%202006.pdf, accessed September 2, 2008.

Filipetto, Lisa. "Joint Development Partner Statement on Public Administration Reform." Ninth Meeting of the Government-Donor Coordination Committee (GDCC). Phnom Penh, February 12, 2007. Online at http://www.cdc-crdb.gov.kh/cdc/gdcc/ninth/ninth_australia.htm, accessed March 2, 2007.

Foo, Lora Jo, and Nikki Fortunato Bas. "Free Trade's Looming Threat to the World's Garment Workers." Sweatshop Watch Working Paper. October 30, 2003. Online at http://www.sweatshopwatch.org/media/pdf/SWtradepaper.pdf, accessed December 4, 2007.

Fox, Fiona. "The Politicisation of Humanitarian Aid." A paper presented at the seminar on Politics and Humanitarian Aid: Debates, Dilemmas and Dissensions, Commonwealth Institute, London, February 1, 2001.

French, Lindsey. "From Politics to Economics at the Thai-Cambodian Border: Plus Ca Change ..." *International Journal of Politics, Culture and Society* 15,3 (2002): 417–70.

Friends International, *The Nature and Scope of the Foreign Child Beggar Issue (especially related to Cambodian Child Beggars) in Bangkok.* Phnom Penh: Friends International, 2006.

Frieson, Kate. "The Political Nature of Democratic Kampuchea." *Pacific Affairs* 61,3 (1998): 405–29.

Fukuyama, Francis. *State Building, Governance, and World Order in the Twenty-first Century.* New York, NY: Profile, 2005.

Fullbrook, David. "China's Growing Influence in Cambodia." *Asia Times Online,* October 6, 2006. Online at http://www.atimes.com/atimes/Southeast_Asia/HJ06Ae01.html, accessed February 9, 2007.

Gallie, W. B. "Essentially Contested Concepts." *Proceedings of the Aristotelian Society,* 56 (1956): 167–98.

Galtung, Johan. "Twenty-Five Years of Peace Research: Ten Challenges and Some Responses." *Journal of Peace Research* 22,2 (1985): 141–58.

Garment Sector Monitoring Project. Eighth Synthesis Report on the Working Conditions Situation in Cambodia's Garment Sector. February 2004. Online at http://www.betterfactories.org/content/documents/1/8th%20Synthesis%20Report%20-%20English.pdf, accessed December 1, 2006.

Gender and Development (GAD), *Paupers and Princelings: Youth Attitudes towards Gangs, Violence, Rape, Drugs, and Theft.* Phnom Penh: GAD, 2003.

Gentile, Carmen. "Analysis: Cambodia Oil, Blessing or Curse?" UPI, December 20, 2006. Online at: http://www.cambodia.org/blogs/editorials/2006/12/analysis-cambodia-oil-blessing-or-curse.html, accessed February 5, 2007.

Gills, Barry, and Joel Rocamora. "Low Intensity Democracy." *Third World Quarterly* 13,3 (1997): 501–23.

Global Commission on International Migration. *Migration in an Interconnected World, New Directions for Action.* Geneva: Global Commission on International Migration, 2005.

Godfrey, Martin, et al. "Technical Assistance and Capacity Development in an Aid-Dependent Economy: The Experience of Cambodia." *World Development* 30,3 (2002): 355–73.

Gottesman, Evan. *Cambodia After the Khmer Rouge: Inside the Politics of Nation Building.* New Haven, CT: Yale University Press, 2002.

Government-Donor Partnership Working Group, Sub-Working Group no. 3. "Practices and Lessons Learned in the Management of Development Cooperation: Case Studies in Cambodia," a report. Phnom Penh, January 2004. Online at http://www.cdc-crdb.gov.kh/cdc/aid_management/practices-lessons-learned.pdf, accessed September 20, 2007.

Group of Experts for Cambodia. Report Pursuant to General Assembly Resolution 52/135. New York, NY: United Nations, 1999. Online at http://www1.umn.edu/humanrts/cambodia-1999.html, accessed September 18, 2007.

Grupu Estudu Maubere (Maubere Students Group). "A People's State Against a Capitalist State," a discussion paper. Dili, May 23, 2006. Posted on Back Door Newsletter on East Timor. Online at http:///www.pcug.org.au/~wildwood/06may23gem.html., accessed September 20, 2007.

Gunn, Geoffrey. "The Five-Hundred-Year Timorese *Funu*," in *Bitter Flowers, Sweet Flowers: East Timor, Indonesia, and the World Community*, ed. Richard Tanter, Mark Selden, and Stephen R. Shalom. Sydney: Pluto, 2001, pp. 3–14.

Gusmão, Xanana. "Autobiography," in Xanana Gusmao, *To Resist is to Win!*, ed. Sarah Niner. Richmond, VA: Aurora Books, 2000, pp. 3–70

— "A History that Beats in the Maubere Soul," in Xanana Gusmão, *To Resist is to Win!*, ed. Sarah Niner. Richmond, VA: Aurora Books, 2000, pp. 85–126.

Guteriano, Nicolau S. Neves. "The Paradox of Aid in Timor-Leste." Presented at the seminar on "Cooperação Internacional e a Construção do Estado no Timor-Leste." Brasilia, July 25–28, 2006. Online at http://www.laohamutuk.org/reports/06ParadoxOfAid.htm, accessed September 20, 2007.

Habib, Naila. "The Search for Home." *Journal of Refugee Studies* 9,1 (1996): 96–102.

Hardt, Michael, and Antonio Negri. *Empire.* Cambridge, MA: Harvard University Press, 2000.

Harvey, Paul, and Jeremy Lind. *Dependency and Humanitarian Relief: A Critical Analysis.* London: Overseas Development Institute, 2005.

Heder, Steve. "Hun Sen and Genocide Trials in Cambodia," in *Cambodia Emerges from the Past: Eight Essays,* ed. Judy Ledgerwood. DeKalb, IL: Northern Illinois University South East Asia Publications, 2002, pp. 76–219.

Heininger, Janet. *Peacekeeping in Transition, United Nations in Cambodia.* Washington, DC: Brookings Institute, 1994.

Hendrickson, Dylan. "Cambodia's Security Sector Reforms: Limits of a Downsizing Strategy." *Conflict, Security, Development* 1,1 (2001): 67–82.

Hewson, Martin, and Timothy Sinclair. "The Emergence of Global Governance Theory," in *Approaches to Global Governance Theory,* ed. M. Hewson and T. Sinclair. New York, NY: State University of New York Press, 1999.

High Level Panel on Threats, Challenges and Change. *A More Secure World—Our Shared Responsibility.* New York, NY: United Nations, 2004.

Hippler, Jochen. "Violent Conflicts, Conflict Prevention and Nation Building—Terminology and Political Concepts," in *Nation-Building: A Key Concept for Peaceful Conflict Transformation?*, ed. J. Hippler. London: Pluto, 2005, pp. 3–14.

Hoffman, Stanley. "The Crisis of Liberal Internationalism." *Foreign Policy* 98 (1995): 159–77.

Hohe, Tanja. "Totem Polls: Indigenous Concepts and 'Free and Fair' Elections in East Timor." *International Peacekeeping* 9,4 (2002): 69–88.

Hood, Ludovic. "Security Sector Reform in East Timor, 1999–2004." *International Peacekeeping* 13,1 (2006): 60–71.

Hubbard, Michael. "Cambodia: A Country Case Study," a report produced for the OECD-DAC task force on donor practices. Edgbaston: University of Birmingham, 2002. Online at http://www.idd.bham.ac.uk/research/Projects/oecd/country_reports/TFDP_Cambodia_6%20Dec.pdf., accessed September 20, 2007.

Hughes, Caroline. *The Political Economy of Cambodia's Transition, 1991–2001.* London: RoutledgeCurzon, 2003.

— "The Politics of Gifts: Tradition and Regimentation in Contemporary Cambodia." *Journal of South East Asian Studies* 37 (2006): 469–89.

"Hun Sen: 'Live and Die with the People,'" *Phnom Penh Post* 21 April 21–May 3, 1996, online at http://www.phnompenhpost.com/index.php/1996050319154/National-news/Hun-Sen-Live-and-die-with-the-people.html, accessed September 20, 2008.

International Commission on Intervention and State Sovereignty. *The Responsibility to Protect.* Ottawa: International Development Research Centre, 2001.

International Labour Organisation. *Destination Thailand, a Cross-Border Labour Migration Survey in Banteay Meanchay Province, Cambodia.* Bangkok: International Labour Organisation, 2005.

International Republican Institute. "Survey of Cambodian Public Opinion," a PowerPoint presentation. January 27–February 26, 2008. Online at http://www.iri.org/asia/cambodia/2008%20May%2027%20Survey%20of%20Cambodian%20Public%20Opinion,%20January%2027-February%2026,%202008.pdf, accessed September 16, 2008.

Irvin, George. *Rebuilding Cambodia's Economy: UNTAC and Beyond.* Working Paper Series no. 149. The Hague, Netherlands: Institute of Social Studies, 1993.

Joliffe, Jill. *East Timor: Nationalism and Colonialism.* St Lucia: University of Queensland Press, 1978.

Jones, Sydney. *Resolving Timor Leste's Crisis.* International Crisis Group Asia Report no. 120. Brussels, October 10, 2006. Online at http://www.crisisgroup.org/library/documents/asia/timor/120_resolving_timor_lestes_crisis.pdf., accessed May 21, 2008.

Kaldor, Mary. *New and Old Wars: Organised Violence in a Global Era.* Cambridge: Polity, 2001.

— *Global Civil Society, an Answer to War.* Cambridge: Polity, 2003.

Kaplan, Robert. "The Coming Anarchy: How Scarcity, Crime, Overpopulation, Tribalism and Disease are Rapidly Destroying the Social Fabric of Our Planet." *The Atlantic Monthly,* February 1994. Online at http://www.theatlantic.com/, accessed September 17, 2007.

Karl, Terry Lynn. "The Hybrid Regimes of Central America." *Journal of Democracy* 6,3 (1995): 72–86.

Keck, Margaret, and Kathryn Sikkink. *Activists Beyond Borders: Advocacy Networks in International Politics.* Ithaca, NY: Cornell University Press, 1998.

Keen, David. "A Rational Kind of Madness." *Oxford Development Studies,* 25,1 (1997): 67–75.

Ker Munthit. "New Text Gives Cambodians Glimpse of Khmer Rouge Period." *International Herald Tribune,* June 18, 2007. Online at http://www.iht.com/articles/2007/06/18/news/cambo.php?page=2, accessed September 20, 2007.

Khmer Buddhist Research Centre. "The Vietnamization of Cambodia: An Irreversible Act? (on the Basis of Information Collected in Cambodia)," in *Buddhism and the Future of Cambodia.* Rithisen: Khmer Buddhist Research Centre, n.d.

Kiernan, Ben. *The Pol Pot Regime: Race, Power, and Genocide in Cambodia under the Khmer Rouge, 1975–1979.* Chiang Mai: Silkworm, 1997.

Kohen, Arnold S. "The Catholic Church and the Independence of Timor," in *Bitter Flowers, Sweet Flowers: East Timor, Indonesia, and the World Community,* ed. Richard Tanter, Mark Selden, and Stephen R. Shalom. Sydney: Pluto Press Australia, 2001, pp. 43–53.

Krasner, Stephen. *Sovereignty, Organised Hypocrisy.* Princeton, NJ: Princeton University Press, 1999.

Lake, Anthony. "From Containment to Enlargement." Lecture at the John Hopkins University School of Advanced International Studies, Washington, DC, October 23, 1993. Reprinted in *U.S. Policy Information and Text* 97 (1993): 6–12.

Lao Hamutuk. "The Provision of School Furniture: Assessing One Component of the World Bank's Emergency School Readiness Project." *Lao Hamutuk Bulletin* 2,5 (2001): 12–15.

— "Portuguese Support in the Education Sector," *Lao Hamutuk Bulletin* 3,7 (2002): 4–5.

— "The RESPECT Program in Timor-Leste," *Lao Hamutuk Bulletin* 5,5–6 (2004): 1–8.

— "An Overview of FALINTIL's Transformation to F-FDTL and Its Implications." *Lao Hamutuk Bulletin* 6,1–2 (2005): 1–6.

Lebillon, Philippe. *Geopolitics of Resource Wars, Resource Dependence, Governance and Violence.* London: Frank Cass, 2005.

Ledgerwood, Judy. "UN Peacekeeping Missions: The Lessons from Cambodia." *Asia Pacific Issues,* 11 (1994).

— "Patterns of CPP Repression and Violence During the UNTAC Period," in *Propaganda, Politics and Violence in Cambodia: Democratic Transition under United Nations Peacekeeping,* ed. Steve Heder and Judy Ledgerwood. London: M. E. Sharpe, 1996, pp. 114–33.

Legge, Michelle, and Thor Savoeun. *Nine Years On: Displaced People in Cambodia.* Phnom Penh: Ockenden International, 2004.

Lloyd Parry, Richard. "The Shark Cage." In Nicolaus Mills and Kira Brunner, eds. *The New Killing Fields: Massacre and the Politics of Intervention.* New York, NY: Basic Books, 2003, pp. 185–206.

Marcher, Anette, and Vong Sokheng. "The Day after Demob: Old Soldiers Find Themselves Left High and Dry," *Phnom Penh Post,* November 10–23, 2000. Online at www.phnompenhpost.com, accessed September 20, 2007.

Marcus, George. "Ethnography In/Of the World System: The Emergence of Multi-Sited Ethnography," *Annual Review of Anthropology* 24 (1995): 95–117.

Martin, Marie. *Cambodia: A Shattered Society,* trans. Mark W. McLeod. Berkeley, CA: University of California Press, 1994.

McCarthy, James. *Falintil Reinsertion Assistance Program Final Evaluation Report.* Dili: International Organisation of Migration, 2002.

McDowell, Christopher, and Marita Eastmond. "Transitions, State-Building and the 'Residual' Refugee Problem: The East Timor and Cambodian Repatriation Experience." *Australian Journal of Human Rights* 2 (2002): 7–30, online at http://www.austlii.edu.au/au/journals/AJHR/2002/, accessed September 18, 2007.

McLeod, George. "Cambodia Finds Oil and Changing Fortune." *Bangkok Post.* December 17, 2006. Online at http://www.indocan.com/pressreleases.html, accessed September 18, 2007.

Metzl, Jamie Frederic. "The Many Faces of UNTAC: A Review Article." *Contemporary South East Asia* 17,1 (1995): 85–96.

Millet, Fabien Curto, and Rathin Rathinasabapathy. "East Timor: The Building of a Nation, an Interview with Sergio Vieira de Mello." *Europa Magazine,* November 2001. Online at http://users.ox.ac.uk/~ball1024/ SergioVDM_interview.pdf, accessed September 18, 2007.

Mills, Nicolaus, and Kira Brunner, eds. *The New Killing Fields: Massacre and the Politics of Intervention.* New York, NY: Basic Books, 2003.

Mkandawire, Thandika. "Crisis Management and the Making of 'Choiceless Democracies,'" in *State, Conflict, and Democracy in Africa,* ed. Richard Joséph. Boulder, CO: Lynne Rienner, 1999, pp. 119–36.

Morris, Kelly. "Comment." *Guardian Online.* July 10, 2000. Online at http://www.laohamutuk.org/reports/news02.html, accessed September 20, 2007.

Mouffe, Chantal. "Preface: Democratic Politics Today," in *Dimensions of Radical Democracy: Pluralism, Citizenship, Community,* ed. C. Mouffe. London: Verso, 1992.

— "Democracy, Power and 'the Political,'" in *Democracy and Difference: Contesting the Boundaries of the Political,* ed. Seyla Benhabib. New Haven, CT: Princeton University Press, 1996, pp. 245–56.

— *The Democratic Paradox.* London: Verso, 2000.

Nandy, Ashis. "State," in *The Development Dictionary: A Guide to Knowledge as Power,* ed. Wolfgang Sachs. London: Zed, 1992, pp. 265–6.

National Election Committee, website, online at http://www.necelect.org.kh/ English/elecResults.htm, accessed September 18, 2007.

Neher, Clark D. "Asian-Style Democracy." *Asian Survey* 34,11 (1994): 949–61

Nevins, Joseph. *A Not-So-Distant Horror, Mass Violence in East Timor.* Ithaca, NY: Cornell University Press, 2005.

Newman, Edward. "The 'New Wars' Debate: a Historical Perspective is Needed." *Security Dialogue* 35,2 (2004): 173–89.

Nye, Robert, and John D. Donahue, eds., *Governance in a Globalizing World.* Washington, DC: Brookings Institute, 2000.

O'Brien, Robert, Anne Marie Goetz, Jan Aart Scholte, and Marc Williams. *Contesting Global Governance: Multilateral Economic Institutions and Global Social Movements.* Cambridge: Cambridge University Press, 2000.

O'Donnell, Guillermo, and Philippe Schmitter. *Transitions from Authoritarian Rule: Prospects for Democracy, Tentative Conclusions about Uncertain Democracies,* vol. 4. Baltimore, MD: Johns Hopkins University Press, 1986.

Olsen, Gorm Rye. "Europe and the Promotion of Democracy in Post Cold War Africa: How Serious Is Europe and for What Reason?" *African Affairs* 97,388 (1998): 343–67.

Orr, Robert. "The United States as Nation-Builder: Facing the Challenge of Post-Conflict Reconstruction," in *Winning the Peace,* ed. Robert Orr. Washington, DC: CSIS, 2004.

Owen, Taylor, and Ben Kiernan. "Bombs Over Cambodia." *The Walrus,* October 2006. Online at http://www.yale.edu/cgp/Walrus_CambodiaBombing_OCT06.pdf., accessed September 20, 2007.

Pape, Eric. "On the River with Rainsy in Search for Votes." *Phnom Penh Post,* May 22–June 4, 1998, p. 14.

Petrin, Sarah. *Refugee Return and State Reconstruction: A Comparative Analysis.* New Issues in Refugee Research Working Paper no. 66. Oxford: Refugee Studies Centre, 2002.

Pin Sisovann. "A Delicate History." *Cambodia Daily Weekend,* March 23–24, 2002, online at http://www.camnet.com.kh/cambodia.daily/selected_features/textbook.htm, accessed October 21, 2008.

Pinto, Constancio. "The Student Movement and the Independence Struggle in East Timor: An Interview," in *Bitter Flowers, Sweet Flowers, East Timor, Indonesia and the World Community,* ed. Richard Tanter, Mark Selden, and Stephen R. Shalmom. Sydney: Pluto, 2001, pp. 31–42.

Postlethwaite, Susan. "Oil Spigot Set to Flow in 2011." *Phnom Penh Post,* September 7–20, 2007. Online at www.phnompenhpost.com, accessed September 20, 2007.

Power, Samantha. *Chasing the Flame: Sergio Vieira de Mello and the Fight to Save the World.* London: Allen Lane, 2008.

Prum Sam Ol, Peng Chiew Meng, and Elizabeth Uphoff Cato. *Starting Over: The Reintegration Experience of Returnees, Internally Displaced and Demobilized Soldiers in Cambodia.* Cambodian Veterans Assistance Program Executive Secretariat Background Report. Phnom Penh: Cambodian Veterans Assistance Program, 1996.

Przeworski, Adam. "Minimalist Conceptions of Democracy: A Defense," in *Democracy's Value,* ed. Ian Shapiro and Casiano Hacker-Cordon. Cambridge: Cambridge University Press, 1999, pp. 23–55.

Pugh, Michael. "The Political Economy of Peacebuilding: A Critical Theory Perspective." *International Journal of Peace Studies* 10,2 (2005): 23–42.

Rainsy, Sam. Responses to callers, 2003 election campaign radio call-in show. FM 102, Phnom Penh, July 12, 2003. Recorded by FM 102, transcribed by Rithy Duong, translated by Caroline Hughes.

Ramos-Horta, José. *Funu—The Unfinished Saga of East Timor.* Trenton, NJ: Red Sea Press, 1987.

—   "East Timor is Worthy of Your Help," an opinion piece. *International Herald Tribune,* June 14, 2001.

— "East Timor: The Challenges of Independence," a special lecture. Asian Studies Centre, St. Anthony's College, Oxford, June 10, 2002. Recorded and transcribed by Caroline Hughes.

— Speech to the United Nations Security Council. New York, NY, May 5, 2006. Online at http://www.pm.gov.tp/speech5may.htm, accessed September 20, 2007.

— Address delivered at swearing-in ceremony as prime minister of the Democratic Republic of Timor-Leste. Dili, July 10, 2006. Translated from Portuguese by the Embassy of Timor-Leste in Australia. Online at www.pcug.org.au/~wildwood/06jul10horta.html., accessed September 20, 2007.

Rees, Edward. *Under Pressure: Falintil-Forças de Defesa de Timor Leste, Three Decades of Defence Force Development in Timor-Leste: 1975–2004*. Working Paper no. 139. Geneva: Geneva Centre for the Democratic Control of Armed Forces, 2004.

República Democrática de Timor-Leste Government in Consultation with Development Partners. "Poverty Reduction Strategy Paper—National Development Plan, Road Map for Implementation of National Development Plan, Overview of Sector Investment Programs—Strategies and Priorities for the Medium Term." Washington, DC: International Monetary Fund, 2005. Online at http://www.imf.org/external/pubs/ft/scr/2005/cr05247.pdf, accessed September 19, 2007.

Rhodes, R. A. W. *Understanding Governance: Policy Networks, Governance, Reflexivity and Accountability*. Maidenhead: Open University Press, 1997.

Richmond, Oliver. *The Transformation of Peace*. Basingstoke: Palgrave, 2005.

Robinson, Geoffrey. "If You Leave Us Here, We Will Die," in *The New Killing Fields: Massacre and the Politics of Intervention*, ed. Nicolaus Mills and Kira Brunner. New York, NY: Basic Books, 2003, pp. 159–84.

Rodan, Garry, Kevin Hewison, and Richard Robison. "Theorising Markets in South East Asia: Power and Contestation," in *The Political Economy of South-East Asia, Markets, Power and Contestation*, third edition, ed. G. Rodan, K. Hewison, and R. Robison. Oxford: Oxford University Press, 2006, pp. 1–38.

Rodan, Garry, and Kanishka Jayasuriya. "More Participation, Less Contestation: New Trajectories for Political Participation in South East Asia," *Democratization*, 14,5 (2007): 767–72.

Royal Government of Cambodia. *Constitution of the Kingdom of Cambodia*. Phnom Penh: Royal Government of Cambodia, 1993.

— *National Strategic Development Plan, 2006–2010*. Phnom Penh: Royal Government of Cambodia, 2006.

Royal Government of Cambodia, Ministry of Foreign Affairs and International Cooperation. *Background on the July 1997 Crisis: Prince Ranariddh's Strategy of Provocation*. White Paper. Phnom Penh, July 9, 1997.

Ruggie, John Gerard. "Territoriality and Beyond: Problematizing Modernity in International Relations." *International Organization* 47 (Winter 1993): 139–74.

Rusten, Caroline, Kim Sedara, Eng Netra, and Pak Kimchoeun. *The Challenges of Decentralisation Design in Cambodia.* Phnom Penh: Cambodia Development Resource Institute, 2004.

Sachs, Jeffrey, and Andrew Warner. "The Curse of Natural Resources." *European Economic Review* (2001): 827–38.

Scambary, James, Hippolito Da Gama, and Joao Barreto. *A Survey of Gangs and Youth Groups in Dili, Timor-Leste.* Dili: AusAID, 2006.

Scheiner, Charles. "The Case for Saving Sunrise," a submission to the government of Timor Leste. Dili, July 28, 2004. Online at http://www.laohamutuk.org/Oil/Sunrise/04sunrise.html.

Scott, James. *Weapons of the Weak, Everyday Forms of Peasant Resistance.* New Haven, CT: Yale University Press, 1987.

— *The Moral Economy of the Peasant: Rebellion and Subsistence in Southeast Asia.* New Haven, CT: Yale University Press, 1977.

Shawcross, William. *Sideshow: Kissinger, Nixon and the Destruction of Cambodia.* New York, NY: Simon and Schuster, 1979.

Shoesmith, Dennis. "Timor-Leste: Divided Leadership in a Semi-Presidential System." *Asian Survey* 43,2 (2003): 231–52.

Smith, Anthony. *The Ethnic Revival.* Cambridge: Cambridge University Press, 1981.

Smith, Michael G., and Maureen Dee. *Peacekeeping in East Timor, the Path to Independence.* International Peace Academy Occasional Paper Series. Boulder, CO: Lynne Rienner, 2003.

Smith, Steve. "US Democracy Promotion: Critical Questions," *American Democracy Promotion, Impulses, Strategies and Impacts,* ed. Michael Cox, G. John Ikenberry, and Takashi Inoguchi. Oxford: Oxford University Press, 2000, pp. 63–83.

Son Soubert. "The Historical Dimensions of the Present Conflict in Cambodia." *Buddhism and the Future of Cambodia.* Rithisen, Khmer Buddhist Research Centre, n.d.

Soum Sekomar. *Acts of Invasion by the Yuon against Cambodia.* Paris: Pruy Nokor, 1997.

Stepputat, Finn. "Repatriation and the Politics of Space: The Case of the Mayan Diaspora and Return Movement." *Journal of Refugee Studies* 7,2/3 (1994): 175–85.

Stern, David S. "State Sovereignty: The Politics of Identity and the Place of the Political," in *Perspectives on Third World Sovereignty, the Postmodern Paradox,* ed. Mark Denham and Mark Owen Lombardi. London: Macmillan, 1996.

Strohmeyer, Hansjoerg. "Building a New Judiciary for East Timor: Challenges of a Fledgeling Nation." *Criminal Law Forum* 11 (2000): 259–85.

Suhrke, Astrid. "Peacekeepers as Nation-Builders, Dilemmas of the UN in East Timor." *International Peacekeeping* 8,4 (2001): 1–20.

Tanter, Richard, Mark Selden, and Stephen R. Shalmom, eds., *Bitter Flowers, Sweet Flowers: East Timor, Indonesia and the World Community.* Sydney: Pluto, 2001.

Tanter, Richard, Desmond Bell, and Gerry Van Klinken. *Masters of Terror: Indonesia's Military and Violence in East Timor*. Oxford: Rowman and Littlefield, 2006.

Tarrow, Sydney. *The New Transnational Activism*. Cambridge: Cambridge University Press, 2005.

Taylor, Charles. "The Dynamics of Democratic Exclusion." *Journal of Democracy* 9,4 (1998): 143–56.

Taylor, John. *East Timor, the Price of Freedom*. London: Zed, 1999.

Thet Sambath and Nick Engstrom. "On the Road Again: Deported from Thailand, the Headstrong March Right Back." *The Cambodia Daily*, October 23–24, 2003. Online edition, http://www.cambodiadaily.com/, accessed September 20, 2007.

Thion, Serge. "The Pattern of Cambodian Politics," in *Watching Cambodia*, ed. S. Thion. Bangkok: White Lotus, 1993, pp. 119–35.

Timor Sea Office. "Fact Sheets—Summary." Dili: Timor Sea Office, 2003–04. Online at http://www.timorseaoffice.gov.tp/summary.htm

Traub, James. "Inventing East Timor." *Foreign Affairs*, 79,4 (2000): 74–89.

Traube, Elizabeth. "Mambai Perspectives on Colonization and Decolonization," in *East Timor at the Crossroads: The Forging of a Nation*, ed. Peter Carey and G. Carter Bentley. London: Cassell, 1995.

Trowbridge, Erin. "Back Road Reckoning," in *The New Killing Fields: Massacre and the Politics of Intervention*, ed. Nicolaus Mills and Kira Brunner. New York, NY: Basic Books, 2003, pp. 207–25.

Tulloch, Jim, Fadia Saadah, Rui Maria de Araujo, Rui Paulo de Jesus, Sergio Lobo, Isabel Hemming, Jane Nassim, and Ian Morris. *Initial Steps in Rebuilding the Health Service in East Timor*. Washington, DC: National Academies Press, 2003.

United Nations. "Recent Violence, Rise in Armed Groups Threaten Success in Timor-Leste, Peacekeeping Under-Secretary-General Tells Security Council." Press Release SC/7683. New York, NY, March 10, 2003. Online at http://www.un.org/News/Press/ docs/2003/sc7683.doc.htm, accessed September 19, 2007.

— *Report of the Special Representative of the Secretary-General on the Situation of Human Rights in Cambodia*. UN Doc. E/CN.4/1998/95.20 February 1998. Online at http://daccessdds.un.org/doc/UNDOC/GEN/G98/105/80/PDF/G981058 0.pdf?OpenElement, accessed September 23, 2008.

— *The United Nations and Cambodia, 1991–1995*. New York, NY: United Nations, 1995.

— Website of the Peacebuilding Commission. Online at http://www.un.org/peace/peacebuilding/, accessed August 22, 2006.

United Nations Development Programme. *East Timor United Nations Development Assistance Framework (2003–05)*. Dili: UNDP, 2002.

United Nations General Assembly. "An Agenda for Peace." General Assembly
    Resolution. UN document A/RES/47/120, September 20, 1993. Reprinted in
    Boutros Boutros-Ghali. *An Agenda for Peace 1995,* second edition. New York,
    NY: United Nations, 1995.

United Nations High Commission for Refugees. *State of the World's Refugees, 1995: In
    Search of Solutions.* Oxford: Oxford University Press, 1995.

— *The Problem of Access to Land and Ownership in Repatriation Operations.* Geneva:
    UNHCR Inspection and Evaluation Service, 1998.

— *State of the World's Refugees, 2000: Fifty Years of Humanitarian Action.* Oxford:
    Oxford University Press, 2000.

— *The State of the World's Refugees 2006: Human Displacement in the New Millennium.*
    Oxford: Oxford University Press, 2006.

United Nations Independent Special Commission of Inquiry for East Timor, a report.
    Geneva: UN, October 2, 2006.

United Nations Transitional Authority in Cambodia Human Rights Component.
    Final Report. Phnom Penh: UNTAC Human Rights Component 1993.

United Nations Transitional Authority in Cambodia Information/Education
    Division. "Report on Public Perceptions of the UN in the City of Phnom
    Penh." Analysis Report, September 18, 1992. Reprinted in *Between Hope and
    Insecurity: The Social Consequences of the Peace Process in Cambodia,* ed. Peter
    Utting. Geneva: United Nations Research Institute for Social Development,
    1994. Online at
    http://www.unrisd.org/unrisd/website/document.nsf/462fc27bd1fce0088
    0256b4a0060d2af/0989f68532e21da580256b6500558beb/$FILE/beet.pdf,
    accessed September 24, 2008. p. 102.

Vieira de Mello, Sergio. Statement. Lisbon Donors' Meeting on East Timor, June 22–
    23, 2000. Online at
    http://siteresources.worldbank.org/INTTIMORLESTE/Resources/Opening
    +Sergio.pdf, accessed May 22, 2008.

Vitchek, Andre. "Interview with Xanana Gusmao." *ZNet Interviews,* April 12, 2002.
    Online at
    http://www.zmag.org/content/Interviews/vltcheck_eastimor.cfm,
    accessed April 10, 2008.

Walsh, Richard. *Timor Leste Public Financial Management Report.* Les Arcs-sur-Argens:
    Linpico, 2007. Online at http://ec.europa.eu/europeaid/what/economic-
    support/public-finance/documents/timor_leste_en.pdf, accessed April 10,
    2008.

Warner, Daniel. "Voluntary Repatriation and the Meaning of Return to Home: A
    Critique of Liberal Mathematics." *Journal of Refugee Studies* 7,2/3 (1994): 160–
    74.

Wasson, Erik, and Yun Samean. "Villagers Vow to Fight Land Sale in Ratanakiri."
    Cambodia Daily, January 23, 2007: 1–2.

Whitworth, Sandra. *Men, Militarism, and Peacekeeping, a Gendered Analysis.* Boulder, CO: Lynne Rienner, 2007.

Wille, Christina. "Finding the Evidence: The Links Between Weapons Collection Programmes, Gun Use and Homicide in Cambodia." *African Security Review,* 15,2 (2006). Online at http://www.smallarmssurvey.org/files/portal/spotlight/country/asia_pdf/asia-cambodia-2006b.PDF, accessed February 23, 2007.

Wolfensohn, James. "Foreword," in *Post-Conflict Reconstruction: The Role of the World Bank.* Washingon, DC: World Bank, 1998.

Working Group on Weapons Reduction. *NGO Report on the 2001 Demobilization Programme: Observations and Recommendations.* Phnom Penh: Working Group on Weapons Reduction, 2002.

World Bank. *Country Assistance Strategy for the Democratic Republic of Timor-Leste for the Period FY06–FY08.* Dili: World Bank, 2006.

— *Doing Business Project.* Online at http://www.doingbusiness.org/map/, accessed September 18, 2007.

— *Post-Conflict Reconstruction: The Role of the World Bank.* Washington, DC: World Bank, 1998.

— *The Role of the World Bank in Conflict and Development: An Evolving Agenda.* Washington, DC: World Bank, 2002.

— *Timor Leste Education: The Way Forward.* Dili: World Bank, 2003.

— *World Development Indicators.* Online at http://siteresources.worldbank.org/DATASTATISTICS/Resources/table6_11.pdf, accessed September 19, 2007.

— *World Development Report 1997: the State in a Changing World.* Washington DC: World Bank, 1997.

World Bank and Asian Development Bank. "*Economic and Social Development Brief: Healing the Nation,*" Dili: World Bank and ADB, 2007, available online at http://www.adb.org/Documents/Books/ESDB-Timor-Leste/ESDB-Timor-Leste.pdf, accessed April 10, 2008.

Zakaria, Fareed. "The Rise of Illiberal Democracy." *Foreign Affairs* 96,6 (1997): 22–43.

INDEX

SOUTHEAST ASIA PROGRAM PUBLICATIONS
Cornell University

Studies on Southeast Asia

Number 48 *Dependent Communities: Aid and Politics in Cambodia and East Timor,* Caroline Hughes. 2009. ISBN 978-0-87727-748-4 (pb.)

Number 47 *A Man Like Him: Portrait of the Burmese Journalist, Journal Kyaw U Chit Maung,* Journal Kyaw Ma Ma Lay, trans. Ma Thanegi, 2008. ISBN 978-0-87727-747-7 (pb.)

Number 46 *At the Edge of the Forest: Essays on Cambodia, History, and Narrative in Honor of David Chandler,* ed. Anne Ruth Hansen and Judy Ledgerwood. 2008. ISBN 978-0-87727-746-0 (pb.)

Number 45 *Conflict, Violence, and Displacement in Indonesia,* ed. Eva-Lotta E. Hedman. 2008. ISBN 978-0-87727-745-3 (pb.)

Number 44 *Friends and Exiles: A Memoir of the Nutmeg Isles and the Indonesian Nationalist Movement,* Des Alwi, ed. Barbara S. Harvey. 2008. ISBN 978-0-877277-44-6 (pb.)

Number 43 *Early Southeast Asia: Selected Essays,* O. W. Wolters, ed. Craig J. Reynolds. 2008. 255 pp. ISBN 978-0-877277-43-9 (pb.)

Number 42 *Thailand: The Politics of Despotic Paternalism* (revised edition), Thak Chaloemtiarana. 2007. 284 pp. ISBN 0-8772-7742-7 (pb.)

Number 41 *Views of Seventeenth-Century Vietnam: Christoforo Borri on Cochinchina and Samuel Baron on Tonkin,* ed. Olga Dror and K. W. Taylor. 2006. 290 pp. ISBN 0-8772-7741-9 (pb.)

Number 40 *Laskar Jihad: Islam, Militancy, and the Quest for Identity in Post-New Order Indonesia,* Noorhaidi Hasan. 2006. 266 pp. ISBN 0-877277-40-0 (pb.)

Number 39 *The Indonesian Supreme Court: A Study of Institutional Collapse,* Sebastiaan Pompe. 2005. 494 pp. ISBN 0-877277-38-9 (pb.)

Number 38 *Spirited Politics: Religion and Public Life in Contemporary Southeast Asia,* ed. Andrew C. Willford and Kenneth M. George. 2005. 210 pp. ISBN 0-87727-737-0.

Number 37 *Sumatran Sultanate and Colonial State: Jambi and the Rise of Dutch Imperialism, 1830-1907,* Elsbeth Locher-Scholten, trans. Beverley Jackson. 2004. 332 pp. ISBN 0-87727-736-2.

Number 36 *Southeast Asia over Three Generations: Essays Presented to Benedict R. O'G. Anderson,* ed. James T. Siegel and Audrey R. Kahin. 2003. 398 pp. ISBN 0-87727-735-4.

Number 35 *Nationalism and Revolution in Indonesia,* George McTurnan Kahin, intro. Benedict R. O'G. Anderson (reprinted from 1952 edition, Cornell University Press, with permission). 2003. 530 pp. ISBN 0-87727-734-6.

Number 34 *Golddiggers, Farmers, and Traders in the "Chinese Districts" of West Kalimantan, Indonesia,* Mary Somers Heidhues. 2003. 316 pp. ISBN 0-87727-733-8.

Number 33   *Opusculum de Sectis apud Sinenses et Tunkinenses (A Small Treatise on the Sects among the Chinese and Tonkinese): A Study of Religion in China and North Vietnam in the Eighteenth Century*, Father Adriano de St. Thecla, trans. Olga Dror, with Mariya Berezovska. 2002. 363 pp. ISBN 0-87727-732-X.

Number 32   *Fear and Sanctuary: Burmese Refugees in Thailand*, Hazel J. Lang. 2002. 204 pp. ISBN 0-87727-731-1.

Number 31   *Modern Dreams: An Inquiry into Power, Cultural Production, and the Cityscape in Contemporary Urban Penang, Malaysia*, Beng-Lan Goh. 2002. 225 pp. ISBN 0-87727-730-3.

Number 30   *Violence and the State in Suharto's Indonesia*, ed. Benedict R. O'G. Anderson. 2001. Second printing, 2002. 247 pp. ISBN 0-87727-729-X.

Number 29   *Studies in Southeast Asian Art: Essays in Honor of Stanley J. O'Connor*, ed. Nora A. Taylor. 2000. 243 pp. Illustrations. ISBN 0-87727-728-1.

Number 28   *The Hadrami Awakening: Community and Identity in the Netherlands East Indies, 1900-1942*, Natalie Mobini-Kesheh. 1999. 174 pp. ISBN 0-87727-727-3.

Number 27   *Tales from Djakarta: Caricatures of Circumstances and their Human Beings*, Pramoedya Ananta Toer. 1999. 145 pp. ISBN 0-87727-726-5.

Number 26   *History, Culture, and Region in Southeast Asian Perspectives*, rev. ed., O. W. Wolters. 1999. Second printing, 2004. 275 pp. ISBN 0-87727-725-7.

Number 25   *Figures of Criminality in Indonesia, the Philippines, and Colonial Vietnam*, ed. Vicente L. Rafael. 1999. 259 pp. ISBN 0-87727-724-9.

Number 24   *Paths to Conflagration: Fifty Years of Diplomacy and Warfare in Laos, Thailand, and Vietnam, 1778-1828*, Mayoury Ngaosyvathn and Pheuiphanh Ngaosyvathn. 1998. 268 pp. ISBN 0-87727-723-0.

Number 23   *Nguyễn Cochinchina: Southern Vietnam in the Seventeenth and Eighteenth Centuries*, Li Tana. 1998. Second printing, 2002. 194 pp. ISBN 0-87727-722-2.

Number 22   *Young Heroes: The Indonesian Family in Politics*, Saya S. Shiraishi. 1997. 183 pp. ISBN 0-87727-721-4.

Number 21   *Interpreting Development: Capitalism, Democracy, and the Middle Class in Thailand*, John Girling. 1996. 95 pp. ISBN 0-87727-720-6.

Number 20   *Making Indonesia*, ed. Daniel S. Lev, Ruth McVey. 1996. 201 pp. ISBN 0-87727-719-2.

Number 19   *Essays into Vietnamese Pasts*, ed. K. W. Taylor, John K. Whitmore. 1995. 288 pp. ISBN 0-87727-718-4.

Number 18   *In the Land of Lady White Blood: Southern Thailand and the Meaning of History*, Lorraine M. Gesick. 1995. 106 pp. ISBN 0-87727-717-6.

Number 17   *The Vernacular Press and the Emergence of Modern Indonesian Consciousness*, Ahmat Adam. 1995. 220 pp. ISBN 0-87727-716-8.

Number 16   *The Nan Chronicle*, trans., ed. David K. Wyatt. 1994. 158 pp. ISBN 0-87727-715-X.

Number 15   *Selective Judicial Competence: The Cirebon-Priangan Legal Administration, 1680–1792*, Mason C. Hoadley. 1994. 185 pp. ISBN 0-87727-714-1.

Number 14   *Sjahrir: Politics and Exile in Indonesia*, Rudolf Mrázek. 1994. 536 pp. ISBN 0-87727-713-3.

Number 13   *Fair Land Sarawak: Some Recollections of an Expatriate Officer,* Alastair Morrison. 1993. 196 pp. ISBN 0-87727-712-5.

Number 12   *Fields from the Sea: Chinese Junk Trade with Siam during the Late Eighteenth and Early Nineteenth Centuries,* Jennifer Cushman. 1993. 206 pp. ISBN 0-87727-711-7.

Number 11   *Money, Markets, and Trade in Early Southeast Asia: The Development of Indigenous Monetary Systems to AD 1400,* Robert S. Wicks. 1992. 2nd printing 1996. 354 pp., 78 tables, illus., maps. ISBN 0-87727-710-9.

Number 10   *Tai Ahoms and the Stars: Three Ritual Texts to Ward Off Danger,* trans., ed. B. J. Terwiel, Ranoo Wichasin. 1992. 170 pp. ISBN 0-87727-709-5.

Number 9   *Southeast Asian Capitalists,* ed. Ruth McVey. 1992. 2nd printing 1993. 220 pp. ISBN 0-87727-708-7.

Number 8   *The Politics of Colonial Exploitation: Java, the Dutch, and the Cultivation System,* Cornelis Fasseur, ed. R. E. Elson, trans. R. E. Elson, Ary Kraal. 1992. 2nd printing 1994. 266 pp. ISBN 0-87727-707-9.

Number 7   *A Malay Frontier: Unity and Duality in a Sumatran Kingdom,* Jane Drakard. 1990. 2nd printing 2003. 215 pp. ISBN 0-87727-706-0.

Number 6   *Trends in Khmer Art,* Jean Boisselier, ed. Natasha Eilenberg, trans. Natasha Eilenberg, Melvin Elliott. 1989. 124 pp., 24 plates. ISBN 0-87727-705-2.

Number 5   *Southeast Asian Ephemeris: Solar and Planetary Positions, A.D. 638–2000,* J. C. Eade. 1989. 175 pp. ISBN 0-87727-704-4.

Number 3   *Thai Radical Discourse: The Real Face of Thai Feudalism Today,* Craig J. Reynolds. 1987. 2nd printing 1994. 186 pp. ISBN 0-87727-702-8.

Number 1   *The Symbolism of the Stupa,* Adrian Snodgrass. 1985. Revised with index, 1988. 3rd printing 1998. 469 pp. ISBN 0-87727-700-1.

SEAP Series

Number 23   *Possessed by the Spirits: Mediumship in Contemporary Vietnamese Communities.* 2006. 186 pp. ISBN 0-877271-41-0 (pb).

Number 22   *The Industry of Marrying Europeans,* Vũ Trọng Phụng, trans. Thúy Tranviet. 2006. 66 pp. ISBN 0-877271-40-2 (pb).

Number 21   *Securing a Place: Small-Scale Artisans in Modern Indonesia,* Elizabeth Morrell. 2005. 220 pp. ISBN 0-877271-39-9.

Number 20   *Southern Vietnam under the Reign of Minh Mạng (1820-1841): Central Policies and Local Response,* Choi Byung Wook. 2004. 226pp. ISBN 0-0-877271-40-2.

Number 19   *Gender, Household, State: Đổi Mới in Việt Nam,* ed. Jayne Werner and Danièle Bélanger. 2002. 151 pp. ISBN 0-87727-137-2.

Number 18   *Culture and Power in Traditional Siamese Government,* Neil A. Englehart. 2001. 130 pp. ISBN 0-87727-135-6.

Number 17   *Gangsters, Democracy, and the State,* ed. Carl A. Trocki. 1998. Second printing, 2002. 94 pp. ISBN 0-87727-134-8.

Number 16   *Cutting across the Lands: An Annotated Bibliography on Natural Resource Management and Community Development in Indonesia, the Philippines, and Malaysia,* ed. Eveline Ferretti. 1997. 329 pp. ISBN 0-87727-133-X.

Number 15 *The Revolution Falters: The Left in Philippine Politics after 1986*, ed. Patricio N. Abinales. 1996. Second printing, 2002. 182 pp. ISBN 0-87727-132-1.

Number 14 *Being Kammu: My Village, My Life*, Damrong Tayanin. 1994. 138 pp., 22 tables, illus., maps. ISBN 0-87727-130-5.

Number 13 *The American War in Vietnam*, ed. Jayne Werner, David Hunt. 1993. 132 pp. ISBN 0-87727-131-3.

Number 12 *The Voice of Young Burma*, Aye Kyaw. 1993. 92 pp. ISBN 0-87727-129-1.

Number 11 *The Political Legacy of Aung San*, ed. Josef Silverstein. Revised edition 1993. 169 pp. ISBN 0-87727-128-3.

Number 10 *Studies on Vietnamese Language and Literature: A Preliminary Bibliography*, Nguyen Dinh Tham. 1992. 227 pp. ISBN 0-87727-127-5.

Number 8   *From PKI to the Comintern, 1924–1941: The Apprenticeship of the Malayan Communist Party*, Cheah Boon Kheng. 1992. 147 pp. ISBN 0-87727-125-9.

Number 7   *Intellectual Property and US Relations with Indonesia, Malaysia, Singapore, and Thailand*, Elisabeth Uphoff. 1991. 67 pp. ISBN 0-87727-124-0.

Number 6   *The Rise and Fall of the Communist Party of Burma (CPB)*, Bertil Lintner. 1990. 124 pp. 26 illus., 14 maps. ISBN 0-87727-123-2.

Number 5   *Japanese Relations with Vietnam: 1951–1987*, Masaya Shiraishi. 1990. 174 pp. ISBN 0-87727-122-4.

Number 3   *Postwar Vietnam: Dilemmas in Socialist Development*, ed. Christine White, David Marr. 1988. 2nd printing 1993. 260 pp. ISBN 0-87727-120-8.

Number 2   *The Dobama Movement in Burma (1930–1938)*, Khin Yi. 1988. 160 pp. ISBN 0-87727-118-6.

Cornell Modern Indonesia Project Publications

Number 75 *A Tour of Duty: Changing Patterns of Military Politics in Indonesia in the 1990s*. Douglas Kammen and Siddharth Chandra. 1999. 99 pp. ISBN 0-87763-049-6.

Number 74 *The Roots of Acehnese Rebellion 1989–1992*, Tim Kell. 1995. 103 pp. ISBN 0-87763-040-2.

Number 73 *"White Book" on the 1992 General Election in Indonesia*, trans. Dwight King. 1994. 72 pp. ISBN 0-87763-039-9.

Number 72 *Popular Indonesian Literature of the Qur'an*, Howard M. Federspiel. 1994. 170 pp. ISBN 0-87763-038-0.

Number 71 *A Javanese Memoir of Sumatra, 1945–1946: Love and Hatred in the Liberation War*, Takao Fusayama. 1993. 150 pp. ISBN 0-87763-037-2.

Number 70 *East Kalimantan: The Decline of a Commercial Aristocracy*, Burhan Magenda. 1991. 120 pp. ISBN 0-87763-036-4.

Number 69 *The Road to Madiun: The Indonesian Communist Uprising of 1948*, Elizabeth Ann Swift. 1989. 120 pp. ISBN 0-87763-035-6.

Number 68 *Intellectuals and Nationalism in Indonesia: A Study of the Following Recruited by Sutan Sjahrir in Occupation Jakarta*, J. D. Legge. 1988. 159 pp. ISBN 0-87763-034-8.

Translation Series

Volume 4   *Approaching Suharto's Indonesia from the Margins,* ed. Takashi Shiraishi. 1994. 153 pp. ISBN 0-87727-403-7.

Volume 3   *The Japanese in Colonial Southeast Asia,* ed. Saya Shiraishi, Takashi Shiraishi. 1993. 172 pp. ISBN 0-87727-402-9.

Volume 2   *Indochina in the 1940s and 1950s,* ed. Takashi Shiraishi, Motoo Furuta. 1992. 196 pp. ISBN 0-87727-401-0.

Volume 1   *Reading Southeast Asia,* ed. Takashi Shiraishi. 1990. 188 pp.

ISBN 0-87727-400-2.

The Many Ways of Being Muslim: Fiction by Muslim Filipinos, ed. Coeli Barry. Copublished with Anvil Publishing, Inc., the Philippines. 2008. ISBN 978-08772-760-50 (pb.)

Language Texts

INDONESIAN

Beginning Indonesian through Self-Instruction, John U. Wolff, Dédé Oetomo, Daniel Fietkiewicz. 3rd revised edition 1992. Vol. 1. 115 pp. ISBN 0-87727-529-7. Vol. 2. 434 pp. ISBN 0-87727-530-0. Vol. 3. 473 pp. ISBN 0-87727-531-9.

Indonesian Readings, John U. Wolff. 1978. 4th printing 1992. 480 pp. ISBN 0-87727-517-3

Indonesian Conversations, John U. Wolff. 1978. 3rd printing 1991. 297 pp. ISBN 0-87727-516-5

Formal Indonesian, John U. Wolff. 2nd revised edition 1986. 446 pp. ISBN 0-87727-515-7

TAGALOG

Pilipino through Self-Instruction, John U. Wolff, Maria Theresa C. Centeno, Der-Hwa V. Rau. 1991. Vol. 1. 342 pp. ISBN 0-87727—525-4. Vol. 2., revised 2005, 378 pp. ISBN 0-87727-526-2. Vol 3., revised 2005, 431 pp. ISBN 0-87727-527-0. Vol. 4. 306 pp. ISBN 0-87727-528-9.

THAI

A. U. A. Language Center Thai Course, J. Marvin Brown. Originally published by the American University Alumni Association Language Center, 1974. Reissued by Cornell Southeast Asia Program, 1991, 1992. Book 1. 267 pp. ISBN 0-87727-506-8. Book 2. 288 pp. ISBN 0-87727-507-6. Book 3. 247 pp. ISBN 0-87727-508-4.

A. U. A. Language Center Thai Course, Reading and Writing Text (mostly reading), 1979. Reissued 1997. 164 pp. ISBN 0-87727-511-4.

A. U. A. Language Center Thai Course, Reading and Writing Workbook (mostly writing), 1979. Reissued 1997. 99 pp. ISBN 0-87727-512-2.

KHMER

Cambodian System of Writing and Beginning Reader, Franklin E. Huffman. Originally published by Yale University Press, 1970. Reissued by Cornell Southeast Asia Program, 4th printing 2002. 365 pp. ISBN 0-300-01314-0.

Modern Spoken Cambodian, Franklin E. Huffman, assist. Charan Promchan, Chhom-Rak Thong Lambert. Originally published by Yale University Press, 1970. Reissued by Cornell Southeast Asia Program, 3rd printing 1991. 451 pp. ISBN 0-300-01316-7.

Intermediate Cambodian Reader, ed. Franklin E. Huffman, assist. Im Proum. Originally published by Yale University Press, 1972. Reissued by Cornell Southeast Asia Program, 1988. 499 pp. ISBN 0-300-01552-6.

Cambodian Literary Reader and Glossary, Franklin E. Huffman, Im Proum. Originally published by Yale University Press, 1977. Reissued by Cornell Southeast Asia Program, 1988. 494 pp. ISBN 0-300-02069-4.

HMONG

White Hmong-English Dictionary, Ernest E. Heimbach. 1969. 8th printing, 2002. 523 pp. ISBN 0-87727-075-9.

VIETNAMESE

Intermediate Spoken Vietnamese, Franklin E. Huffman, Tran Trong Hai. 1980. 3rd printing 1994. ISBN 0-87727-500-9.

* * *

Southeast Asian Studies: Reorientations. Craig J. Reynolds and Ruth McVey. Frank H. Golay Lectures 2 & 3. 70 pp. ISBN 0-87727-301-4.

Javanese Literature in Surakarta Manuscripts, Nancy K. Florida. Vol. 1, *Introduction and Manuscripts of the Karaton Surakarta*. 1993. 410 pp. Frontispiece, illustrations. Hard cover, ISBN 0-87727-602-1, Paperback, ISBN 0-87727-603-X. Vol. 2, *Manuscripts of the Mangkunagaran Palace*. 2000. 576 pp. Frontispiece, illustrations. Paperback, ISBN 0-87727-604-8.

Sbek Thom: Khmer Shadow Theater. Pech Tum Kravel, trans. Sos Kem, ed. Thavro Phim, Sos Kem, Martin Hatch. 1996. 363 pp., 153 photographs. ISBN 0-87727-620-X.

In the Mirror: Literature and Politics in Siam in the American Era, ed. Benedict R. O'G. Anderson, trans. Benedict R. O'G. Anderson, Ruchira Mendiones. 1985. 2nd printing 1991. 303 pp. Paperback. ISBN 974-210-380-1.

To order, please contact:
Mail:
Cornell University Press Services
750 Cascadilla Street
PO Box 6525
Ithaca, NY 14851 USA

E-mail: orderbook@cupserv.org

Phone/Fax, Monday–Friday, 8 am – 5 pm (Eastern US):
Phone: 607 277 2211 or 800 666 2211 (US, Canada)
Fax: 607 277 6292 or 800 688 2877 (US, Canada)

Order through our online bookstore at:
www.einaudi.cornell.edu/southeastasia/publications/